PLANET ON PURPOSE

YOUR GUIDE TO GENUINE PROSPERITY,
AUTHENTIC LEADERSHIP AND A BETTER WORLD

Brandon Peele

BALBOA.
PRESS
A DIVISION OF HAY HOUSE

Balboa Press books may be ordered through booksellers or by contacting:

Balboa Press
A Division of Hay House
1663 Liberty Drive
Bloomington, IN 47403
www.balboapress.com
1 (877) 407-4847

Print information available on the last page.

ISBN: 978-1-5043-9247-1 (sc)
ISBN: 978-1-5043-9248-8 (e)

Balboa Press rev. date: 03/19/2018

CONTENTS

Part Four
Answering the Call

ACKNOWLEDGEMENTS

In some regard, this book was a five-year journey, in another regard it was a 40-year journey, the result of my life experiences and the enormous contributions of my family, friends and teachers. I was not alone for any of this book and would never have started it, much less finished it, were it not for the hundreds of people who contributed to my journey and this book.

You

Thank you, dear reader, brother, sister, comrade in the Global Purpose Movement. I have been loving and courting you since the beginning. It is your purpose journey, fulfillment, self-expression and purpose-driven leadership that inspired me to write this book. Thank you for your bravery and your struggle to live a fulfilled, high-impact, high-reward life of purpose. My hope is that you find this book useful, that it empowers you on your purpose journey. I would also like to make a request. Please contact me via the ensouled.life site and share your thoughts on any misstatements, omissions or crimes of wrong-headedness or long-windedness. There will be a second edition and I want to ensure it includes your invaluable contributions.

Family

I thank my mother Nancy Martin, my father Robert Peele, and my stepfather Dennis Martin for their love, emotional support, encouragement, financial loans, and sage advice. Without them, I would not have been able to make the investment of time and money required to follow my purpose and write this book. Thank you for the adventurous, loving and abundant upbringing you provided Carson and me. Thank you for all the books, memorable adventures and the great schools your hard work afforded us. Your 20-year child-rearing effort to develop my mind, body, soul and spirit gave me the foundation to ask big questions, and the last twenty years of your guidance and mentorship has allowed me to follow my heart and continually take risks. I love you. Thank you for believing in me.

Thank you for ensuring that Carson and I spent the majority of our childhood playing outside, making art or reading. These were rich gardens for my young soul to develop, imagine and create. As such, my journey to soul and purpose is very much a fond remembrance. Further, your desire that Carson and I become well-rounded men is the prime desire of my life; this book is my attempt to pay it forward by empowering a whole, soulful and well-rounded human presence on Earth.

I thank my Uncle Mark and Aunt Amy for being the nucleus of my West Coast family, for providing me with refuge, fun and great times, as I fell in and out of love, as I searched for myself and began my purpose journey. Thank you for your generosity, warmth and companionship.

I thank my fiancée, Stephanie Staidle. Thank you for your love, insight, fearlessness and timely coaching. Thank you for your stand for me and us. You've helped me see so much of what is possible in my life and the world, and by extension, this book. Thank you, love.

Community

I thank the founders of ManKind Project, Bill Kauth, Ron Herring and Rich Tosi, for creating such a rich training - the New Warrior Training Adventure - and the worldwide community of MKP men on purpose. The consistent and intense shadow work and healing I've had the privilege to do over the last decade in MKP circles and New Warrior Training Adventure Weekends has been essential to me and to this book. Without this work and the repeated shadow piercings - reaching through my shadow to heal and stand in firm in my purpose -, I would have nothing to offer here. Thank you. Thank you to all the great men with whom I've sat in circle, with whom I've staffed NWTA weekends, who facilitate this work and inspire me with the depth of their courage and vulnerability, especially Chris Kyle, Gary Arnstein, Dave Klaus, Jonathan Ainscow, Leo O'Brien, Jeremy Stayton, Michael Keeth, Andrew Sokolsky, Danny Wilhite, David Callen, Mickey Kay, Eric Thomas, Alex Lindblad, Jed Waldman, Matt Winters, Brian Edgar, Paul Battaglia, John Maher, Jeffrey Brown, Frederick Marx, Ron Cotterel and Ray Arata. Special thanks to Boysen Hodgson and Matt Kelly for your stand to get this book and much needed work out into the world. Special thanks to Bill Kauth for your generosity with your time and empowering me to understand the contours of ensouled community.

I thank the San Francisco Landmark community for inspiring me, training me, standing for me, empowering me to lead, giving me the power to make my life a match for the contours of my soul, and change the world with the sacred power of word. Special thanks to Patty Ruiz, Xav Dubois, Sherron Hogg, Rachel Dubois, Alan Maravilla, Jeffrey Chin, Piper Davies, Jae Yee and Jessica Yee-Campbell.

I thank all the leaders of the Global Purpose Movement for their leadership and courage, and for their entrepreneurial savvy, scholarship, mentorship and dedication to the cause, especially Cynthia Hendricks, Jon Darrall-Rew, Dustin DiPerna, Emanuel Kuntzelman, Carly Visk, Andrea Dennis, Sam Clayton, Rikk Hansen,

Audrey Seymour, Beth Scanzani, Tim Kelley, Jonathan Gustin, Marcy Morrison, Susan Mashkes, Susan Lucci, Laura Larriva Page and Dustin Timmons.

I thank all the people who have taken the Purpose Challenge and the Global Purpose Expedition, especially those of you who have stepped up to lead this work for the world - Jon Darrall-Rew, Spencer Honeyman, Michael Stern, Kara Hess, Oscar Medina, Vanessa Benlolo, Jean Yzer, Elena Iorga and Izabella Sepulveda.

I thank my comrades in the "Political Economy Book Club" - Matt Stillman, Gabrielle Blocher and Pawel Rzeczkowski. It was from of our rich scholarship and countless discussions that many of the ideas in Part Four originated.

I want to thank my two friends, Purpose Guides Institute colleagues, former roommates and mentors, Praveen Mantena and Susan Mashkes. Your intellect, passion and transformative wisdom have deeply influenced me. You've helped me face uncomfortable truths (latent sexism, racism, fear, tyranny, mistrust), transform myself, see what is missing in my thinking and ways of being, and have thus meaningfully evolved this book.

Book Team

I thank the editorial team of Susan Lucci, Susan Mashkes, Cris Espinosa, Mandy Viscai, Jennifer Nowak and Emily Steffen for their diligence in ensuring this book was ready for print. You gave more than was asked, invested your heart and intellect in this endeavor and continually stood for a bigger and better version of this book. Thank you!

A special thanks to Susan Mashkes. Susan, I love you! Your generosity, intellect and formidable pedigree and experience as a Psychotherapist, Interfaith Minister, Purpose Guide™ and human potential historian were invaluable in the development of this book.

I thank Tim Kelley (True Purpose® Institute, Founder), Jonathan Gustin (Purpose Guides Institute, Founder) and Bill Plotkin (Animas Valley Institute, Founder). It was a privilege to consult with each of you on this book, as you are the source of the three leading purpose/soul guiding schools in the West. Your combined scholarship and experience in the realm of soul discovery is unparalleled.

Tim, thank you for your generous time and attention. Thank you for demanding that I write the book I said I was going to write, a purposeful path forward for our whole species, and not yet another treatise against modernity.

Jonathan, thank you for being my Purpose Guide™, and giving me access to my soul and the power to live it. Thank you for taking my calls, answering my request to be trained and creating the Purpose Guides Institute. Thank you for making the enormous physical, emotional and financial sacrifices that were needed to bring PGI to life. Thank you for training me and the other folks in the cohort. Thank you for assembling an unprecedented team of Guest Faculty (Bill Plotkin, Tim Kelley,

Joanna Macy, Terry Patten, Sera Beak and Steve McIntosh). Lastly, thank you for your scholarship that informs so much of my understanding of soul and purpose.

Bill, thank you for beating the underworld drum so loudly and consistently through your books. Thank you for the depth of your underworld excavations and scholarship, for illuminating what is now necessary for humanity to create, as you so beautifully say, "artisans of cultural renaissance".

I thank all my friends and colleagues who invested their time and intellect into making this book the best it can be. Thank you, Grant Hunter, Nathan Greene, Sona Chilingaryan, Scott Hartman, Josh Coccellato, Kevin Gianni, Sharon Reinbott, Katya Kolesnikova, Stephan Martin, Sean Feit-Oakes, Brian Edgar, Dave Klaus, Nick Polizzi, Nancy Martin, Sam Clayton, Gleb Tsipursky, Jonathan Gustin, Dennis Martin, Suzy Karasik, Robito Chadwin, Mark Tognotti and Stephanie Staidle.

I thank all of you who financially invested in the crowdfunding campaign to bring this book to market. Special thanks to Jonathan Gustin, Pat Sandone, Nancy Martin, Bob Peele, Nathan Ansell and Terry Lynch.

A special thanks to Kevin and Annmarie Gianni for the studio time to record the audio book. Thanks to Julia Casillas for recording the intro/outro. Thanks to Dave Cavnar for his sound editing. Thanks to the ManKind Project for producing this audio book project. Thanks to Jared Brick for his help with the crowdfunding campaign.

Other Significant Influences

To Srikumar Rao, you set me on the path of self-inquiry in your groundbreaking course, Creativity and Personal Mastery. Without the CPM crowbar smashing to bits my materialist, individualist and objectivist worldview, I would never have been able to dive headfirst into the deep end of physics, philosophy, spirit, mystery and soul.

To Chris Kyle, you believed in me as a teacher and Guide when there was no reason to. Your mentorship in purpose course facilitation, and your embodiment as a loving, healed and whole man, inspire and serve me and all the men of the ManKind Project.

I'd be remiss if I did not honor the multiple giants on whose shoulders I stand, from whose work I have benefitted. These giants have helped me develop my mind, my body, my soul and my spirit.

- Mind - Richard Tarnas, Brian Swimme, Ken Wilber, Plotinus, Carl Sagan, Michael Murphy, Lana and Lilly Wachowski, Baruch Spinoza, Georg Wilhelm Friedrich Hegel, Chris Martenson, Charles Eisenstein, Jared Diamond, Howard Zinn
- Body - Herschel Walker, Pete Guinosso, Lucid Dawn

- Soul - (in addition to those I've already mentioned) Michael Meade, Thomas Moore, James Hillman, Carl Jung, Clarissa Pinkola Estes
- Spirit - David Scoma, Sri Nisargadatta, Stephen Mitchell, Jed McKenna, Richard Rose, Herman Melville, Shankara, *The Upanishads*, *The Bhagavad Gita*, *The Gnostic Gospels*, the *Tao Te Ching*

Source

Last and most, I thank you, Mystery. This book is of, by, for and through you. Thank you for the privilege of bringing forth this book.

FOREWORD BY TIM KELLEY

Why another book about purpose? There are so many! Why read this one?

The answer is simple: this is the most comprehensive book about higher purpose ever written. I'm really happy that so many speakers, authors and consultants are motivated to write and speak about purpose. It is the megatrend of our time, and their efforts are educating the public about purpose in a way that has never happened in human history. The increasing collective understanding and pursuit of purpose are transforming people's personal lives, as well as the face of business, in ways that seemed too much to hope for a few short years ago. As a growing body of research shows, following your purpose leads to better health, greater happiness, fulfilling work, longer life, satisfying relationships, and even more money.

But all the noise about purpose makes it harder and harder to pick out the few gems that are worthy of your time. Most books on the subject are either about someone's personal story of finding his or her own purpose, or inspiring examples of other people or organizations that are living theirs. As I observed in the introduction to my book, *True Purpose*, the usual text may include a short, simple exercise that might get you a vague purpose statement, but usually nothing sophisticated.

This book is entirely different. Brandon has surveyed the entire landscape of purpose methodologies, including work by thought leaders like Bill Plotkin, James Hillman, Joanna Macy, Michael Meade, and Clarissa Pinkola Estes, as well as research by institutions like Harvard, Stanford, Cornell, NYU and UCLA. He incorporates the best practices from the different schools of thought about purpose into a singular journey that you will take to find and manifest your purpose. But he doesn't stop there: this book also includes a thorough evaluation of how purpose touches the different aspects of human society, including business, science, history and politics. Brandon looks at it through both the lens of our current society and the impact of our general lack of collective purpose, as well as painting a vision of the world that we can create together, using our individual and collective purposes as guides.

This collective vision is the key: when you embark on the path of purpose, whatever your personal motive, you are becoming part of a global movement, a participant in the greatest project of our time. The goal of this project is to remake human society in a new image, one that creates meaning and fulfillment for all people.

Your individual desires are a critical component in our collective vision: what kind of world would you like to create? To live in? Think of our planet and our culture as an art project, a vast mural, and yourself as one of millions of artists working together to create it. Only you can paint your section of the mural, and your purpose is your paintbrush.

More than any other generation, Millennials (those born after 1980) are called to purpose at a young age. Many actively seek their purpose in their very first job, or languish in their parents' basement, suffering from a lack of purpose and direction. At the same time, the Baby Boomers and Generation X are reaching the age when a need for greater purpose and fulfillment traditionally sets in. This has created a perfect storm, an unprecedented need for meaning. And this need for meaning is both personal and collective, though the first step in the search for greater fulfillment is the quest for your individual higher purpose.

Brandon has compiled the very best thinking and techniques for finding your purpose in this book. I am keenly aware of the low odds that any of my readers will do the exercises I assign them in my book; Brandon has solved that problem by coupling his book with an online program.

Brandon will also guide you in the manifestation of your purpose. This is far more important than you might realize: manifesting your purpose is far more difficult than finding it. I learned this the hard way, when I realized that most of the clients I had worked with had gone back to the way they were before finding their purpose. Brandon wisely says that finding your purpose is 10% of the effort; manifesting it is 90%.

Of course, it is in the manifestation of your purpose that the joy resides. Taking action on your purpose puts a wind in your sails that is hard to describe, if you've never experienced it. Most people know this state of flow and alignment only in fleeting moments. When you are being actively guided by your purpose, this state becomes something you can create whenever you choose.

If you are a leader, you have an obligation to those you lead that extends beyond your personal need for meaning. Those who follow you will be far better off if you use your purpose to guide them. And if you really want to make a difference, find the higher purpose of your organization! As so many business thought leaders have observed, companies that follow a higher purpose vastly outperform those that don't.

Whatever your motive, you have found yourself on the path of purpose, with the perfect guidebook in your hand. Turn the page and take the next step!

Tim Kelley

Author of True Purpose and founder of the True Purpose® Institute

INTRODUCTION

"You've got mail from the Utah State Police," said my Dad to me on the phone.

(silence)

"When are you going to stop breaking the law?" he continued.

By this point, at age 26, I had arrest records in California, Louisiana, Indiana, Illinois and Wisconsin, and it would only be another couple months before I would spend a night in the care of the NYPD.

"I don't know. I've had some bad luck."

"Yeah, I thought this was a phase. This is a trend, Brandon."

I could feel my Dad's judgment and disappointment. My parents gave me every advantage growing up - great schools, abundant nature, books, sports and, most importantly, their love, support and encouragement. And in my twenties, despite having what I thought I wanted - a cool job and an active social life - I felt empty inside. Something was missing. I knew there was more to my life than partner track at a professional services firm. I knew there was more to my life than suburban comfort. I knew there was adventure and magic in the world. I knew there was a great work inside of me, but I had no clarity or guidance as to how to even begin searching for it. Regrettably, and like so many, I ignored the call to discover my purpose.

I continued to spend my days in cubes, my nights and weekends escaping my days, and my foggy mornings driving to work with a growing sense of despair. Underneath it all was a deep yearning that I could not name, what I now know to be the call to live a life of purpose, impact and adventure.

> Purpose is that feeling that you are a part of something bigger than yourself, that you are needed, that you have something better ahead to work for. Purpose is what creates true happiness.
> -Mark Zuckerberg (Zuckerberg, 2017)

As far as I knew, a life purpose didn't exist. I grew up in the Chicago suburbs in the 80's and 90's, surrounded by well-meaning adults, but without any conversation about a life's purpose. Although 97% of Americans believe that living a life of purpose is important (Rainey, 2014), somehow, we did nothing to legitimately explore the question. In absence of the purpose conversation, we did what was expected to gain acceptance, status and money.

My culture took little boys with big hearts and wild eyes and shamed them for their emotions, creativity and bodies, shamed them for just being boys. The result was that we believed we were defective girls who just couldn't sit still in class. We believed our society and the media, when they told us that unless we were "great" by a physical, social, sexual and economic standard, and almost always through dominating others, we could not have love or acceptance. In absence of genuine elders and the purpose conversation, we felt like we had to initiate ourselves with whatever we could get our hands on - reckless dares, military careers, Tough Mudders, heroic amounts of drugs and alcohol, or check out and dissociate with weed and video games.

My culture took little girls with big hearts and wild eyes and shamed them for their emotions and bodies. We made them believe that they were defective supermodels who had to repress, starve, mutilate and diminish themselves for love and acceptance. We created a culture of harassment and oppression in which to become women. We made women believe that unless they became men or unless a man rescued them and took them back to the suburbs to reproduce, that they too were worthless.

As I approached marrying age, I joined my generation's walk down the aisle, a march of ticking biological clocks, uncultivated purposes, untreated neuroses and false bravado. We moved up in our companies, got married and moved to the suburbs. I saw the people I love surrender the wildness of their souls, for a safe and predictable existence inside narrow economic and gender roles. I witnessed the common mistake of believing the sacred role of parenting to be the entirety of a life's purpose.

I saw noble warriors ground down in the service of a culture and economy that wasted their potential on insufferable client dinners and PowerPoint presentations. I saw authentic feminine power buckle and warp as it "leaned in" to glass ceilings, 50-hour work weeks, 15 hours of commuting and the unending demands of motherhood. I saw sexless disconnected marriages. I saw the implicit social contract to watch reality TV and spectator sports, and buy temporary happiness in the form of consumer products and household goods, as attempts to patch over the very real need for a life of deeper meaning.

> "When our parents graduated, that sense of purpose reliably came from your job, your church, your community, but today, technology and automation are eliminating many jobs, membership in a lot of communities has been declining and a lot of people are feeling disconnected and depressed and are trying to fill a void in their lives."
>
> -Mark Zuckerberg (Zuckerberg, 2017)

As I looked out at my own future, I saw my own sexless marriage and anxiety-driven 50-hour work week. I saw myself enduring another 15 hours of traffic in the blurry shuffle between travel soccer, music lessons, math tutors and the boxes of home, office, gym, restaurants and boutiques. I saw myself grinding it out for four decades to acquire a modest pile of chips, earmarked for vacations, retirements and college funds. I saw myself continuously devise new ways to ignore what poet Mary Oliver terms, my "one wild and precious life", through golf, remodels, home-brewing, fantasy football and the Food Network. I saw myself already pining for that one day when this insane bargain would end in a white-shoed shuffle between tee times, doctor's appointments, condo board meetings, funerals and early-bird dinners. I saw a hunched over version of myself wondering "is this all there is?"

And yet this was normal. Like crabs in a crab pot, each time we tried to escape and do something different, we'd pull each other back down. We'd ridicule each other. We told each other that this was just the way life is, and that the best you can hope for is to accept the deal and die with the hope that you improved matters for your kids.

During my twenties, I found that I could no longer toe the line. I boiled with anger inside of my 80-hour investment banker work weeks, mundane gossip at fundraisers, and the suburban future that it led to. I felt betrayed by the American Dream. It seemed boring, oppressive, unimaginative and a huge waste of everyone's time and potential.

So, I pulled the ripcord. I began emulating those who had opted out of the bargain - rebels like Axl Rose, Bill Hicks and Hunter S. Thompson. Inspired by these men and iconic breakout movies like *Fight Club* and *American Beauty*, I washed off the stink of corporate life each weekend and blasted myself into oblivion with a reckless and expanding portfolio of escapes. So, I found myself in the hospital and jail a lot.

I spent a decade seeking to placate what Senior Jungian Analyst, Clarissa Pinkola Estes PhD, calls the *hambre de alma*, the hunger of the soul, (Estes, 1992, p. 6) through every available means - traveling to legendary parties such as Carnival (Brazil), Mardi Gras (New Orleans) and the Full Moon Party (Thailand), playing rugby, riding bulls, jumping out of airplanes and curling up inside liquor bottles, coke straws and executive assistants. And don't get me wrong, it was fun, at least initially. But, the highs never lasted. By Monday morning, I was back to square one - miserable, isolated, uninitiated, unrooted, insecure and unable to touch anything real.

Between these spirited binges, and without any access to my emotions aside from anger, I proclaimed to all who would listen that I was going to break the cycle. The prospect of becoming a pot-bellied, cube-farmed, sports-loving, lawnmower-pushing Dad made me want to blow my brains out. I was not going to die in a condo board meeting without a passport, when there were thousands of adventures that called to me. I was not signing up for a life where I had to ply my wife with liquor and jewelry for sex. I was not going be that guy who traded his ambitions and lust for adventure for a "honey-do" list. I could not bear the prospect of raising my kids to think that this was what a man looked like, yet I was unaware of any viable alternative.

I know the pain of contributing my talents to what feels like a purposeless economy, while so much of the world suffers. I know what it is to believe a real life of adventure, impact and authentic prosperity is always just around the corner, after the next promotion, or the kids going to college, or retirement. I know the suburban hell Henry David Thoreau forecasted in _Walden_:

> The mass of men lead lives of quiet desperation. What is called resignation is confirmed desperation. From the desperate city, you go into the desperate country... A stereotyped but unconscious despair is concealed even under what are called the games and amusements of mankind. (Thoreau, 1854, p. 8)

Thankfully, I had a course correction during my MBA program at Columbia Business School. I was radically ejected from the path to suburbia and my equally unimaginative attempts to escape it. I took Srikumar Rao's course, _Creativity and Personal Mastery_, where I began to discover the finer stuff of the human experience; the contours of an authentic purpose-driven life, what it meant to create a career that made the world a better place, and to reconnect with the desire to live the only life I could - my own.

After graduate school, I spent the next several years on an intense journey into the question of my own existence. I sought truth in Indian ashrams and San Francisco's rich transformational offerings: meditation retreats, psychotherapy, psychotropics, philosophy meetups, Burning Man, powerful personal development programs, men's circles, and finally, purpose discovery work at age 34.

I was guided by Jonathan Gustin, now the Founder of the Purpose Guides Institute. Through our work together, I began to unpack the meaning I had made about my life and the limitations on my life that this meaning had imposed. I was led through numerous purpose discovery methods and had life altering breakthroughs, revealing the heretofore hidden aspects of my life's purpose. For the first time since childhood, I felt what it meant to truly like myself. Actually, I fell in love with myself. I felt excitement. I was free and empowered to create a life that was the full expression of my soul.

In the three months after my work with Jonathan, I left my sexy Silicon Valley start-up job, started a purpose-driven venture that served customers all over the world, and was covered by major media outlets like USA Today, Fox News and TechCrunch. I also ended an unfulfilling relationship, created a vibrant community of friends and recreated my family relationships with strong boundaries, empathy and compassion. Over the next few years, I began guiding others on their path of purpose discovery. I also saw my body change from a bloated 255 lbs. to a lean 225 lbs., and my romantic relationships transform from dysfunctional and resentful, to rich and emergent partnerships based in open communication, respect and love. In a very real sense, I was reborn from my purpose discovery journey, but not as a result of teeth-gnashing, white-knuckling will. I made these choices easily, with the clarity that comes from a deep connection to purpose.

> "Your beliefs become your thoughts. Your thoughts become your words. Your words become your actions. Your actions become your habits. Your habits become your values. Your values become your destiny."
>
> -Mahatma Gandhi

As a Certified Purpose Guide™, I've had the pleasure of working with people as young as fifteen and as old as ninety-two. I've worked with Dads, Moms, retirees, doctors, nurses, atheists, Catholic Priests, Dalai Lama Fellows, scientists, CEOs, artists, inner-city youth, athletes, technology entrepreneurs and executives from Fortune 500 companies like Google, Apple, Morgan Stanley and Johnson & Johnson. I've delivered online purpose programs to thousands of people from over 50 countries. I have seen the power of purpose and have witnessed its amazing, scientifically-validated benefits transcend class, race, gender, sexuality, ability and creed. As you are starting to discover, I live, eat and drink purpose. I am a total convert, an unashamed lover of the power of purpose.

On my journey, I also discovered that purpose is essential to leadership, that without it there is only reactive, marginally effective management, and the implicit agreement to win at someone else's game, to fulfill on another person's idea of success. I experienced that my purpose grants me access to create my own game and lets me share a bold vision for the world, inspire others to discover, lead, serve and creatively contribute with their unique purpose.

As such, it is my honor, duty and privilege to be of service and make this powerful purpose discovery education available to you, to empower you to live the life you were meant to live, a life you love, and awaken your purpose-driven leadership, your Shambhala Leadership.

The Shambhala Leader is a new type of leader, an answer to the 12th century Tibetan prophecy of the Shambhala Warrior, one that was given to Joanna Macy by Choegyal Rinpoche to share in the West (Awakin.org, 6/1/2017). This prophecy states that there will come a time when barbarian powers will use weapons of unimaginable destruction to seize control of humanity for personal gain. A new warrior class will rise with the powers of insight (inner purpose and outer wisdom) and compassion, penetrating into the heart of barbarism and transforming that which no longer serves humanity (limiting beliefs and the inefficient political, economic and cultural structures for meeting our needs).

The prophecy of the Shambhala Warrior calls for a return of the sacred masculine and divine feminine, an integrated and embodied warrior that fights to protect, serve, connect, integrate, unify, evolve and inspire.

To fulfill on this prophecy, we need a new class of leaders who are 1. Purpose-awakened, 2. Embodied, 3. Heart-opened and 4. World-wizened, aka the Shambhala Leader. It is up to us to now awaken our purpose, step into our Shambhala Leadership, lovingly embrace humanity as it is, inspire a new future, dismantle our weapons of mass destruction and manufactured consent, and create a planet that works for all beings.

It is my absolute certainty that finding and living your purpose will align and electrify your whole life, as it has done for me and the millions of our purpose awakening brothers and sisters on this planet (you'll meet them in "Chapter 1: Purpose, the New Normal?"). In recognition of this power, it is with great honor and reverence that I play my part to make this work widely available.

A Purposeful Life is Our Birthright

I realize I am incredibly privileged to have been raised with abundant resources, even if poor in purpose. I am lucky to call suburbia my childhood home. I am lucky I didn't have to fight for my life in the inner city, desert or jungle. Instead of spending my first 25 years playing sports and chasing women, I could have spent them surviving political strife and economic hardship, or as a sex slave, or as a refugee escaping war, or working tirelessly for decades just to get my kids into a position to have middle class problems and existential crises.

Although purpose is every human's birthright, it is often considered a luxury of the rich; as for those without means, it is of far greater importance to secure adequate food, shelter and safety than to fret about a life of purpose. As mythologist, Michael Meade describes in *The Genius Myth* (Meade, 2016), in the absence of elders, in the absence of the purposeful initiation of our youth, we live inside two fogs. The rich experience the "white fog" of meaninglessness, of being numbed out, of compromise, of having sold out, seeing little in the way of truth or genuine value in the world or their experience of life. The poor are in the "red fog", in a world of survival, violence, injustice, poverty, disease, death and destruction, waking each day in fear, grief and/ or rage. Regardless of which fog clouded your upbringing, regardless of the impacts of the fog, the fog source is the same: disconnection from purpose at the individual, cultural, economic and political levels.

And yet, rich or poor, the life purpose question always calls us into service. It brings us into the world, into our local and global issues of inequality, oppression, war, poverty, corruption, suffering, pollution and disease. Purpose stretches us into action, offering our gifts and creating a world that works for everyone. Every single person I've guided recognizes their purpose as one that makes an enormous contribution to the lives of others.

Thus, if we want to rapidly improve the human and ecological condition, we cannot allow this powerful education to be a plaything of the navel-gazing wealthy. We can easily make it widely available - it can live in our homes, our schools, our jobs and churches. And it must, or this cycle will continue and our youth will perpetually find themselves inside either the white or the red fog. As Michael Meade elucidates:

> A society is playing with fire each time it rejects the innate nobility of its youth. For youth not only carry within them the dream of the future, they also tend to act out the imbalances and injustices of society as well as the deep grievances of their communities. Injustices that are not faced inside a culture will eventually be lived out on its streets as a kind of fate. (Meade, 2016, p. 197)

As Meade reveals, the red and white fogs are bound together in a shared destiny. Those trapped in a white fog find salvation in creating a world that allows each of us trapped in the red fog to realize the nobility of our souls, recognize our purpose, make our highest contribution and be justly rewarded, economically, politically and socially.

> Good role models are important at all levels of society... but a living dream brings forth the true nobility of the soul. What remains trapped in the opportunity gaps, in the divides caused by racism and bigotry, in the midst of failing institutions as well as in the shadows of dilapidated buildings is the long-deferred dream of freedom that can only grow when offered to everyone. Those who would deny any young person the opportunity to learn and find a purpose in life have already lost their own dream... (Meade, 2016, p. 197)

If every human is empowered to awaken to their life's purpose, and to tap into the deep wealth of all their networks and talents, it will merely take years instead of decades to create a world that works for everyone. And purpose doesn't just benefit humans alive today: it is also a gift to the future of our species and all living beings.

Before you dive head first into your purpose and this book, I'd like to offer you three arguments that point to purpose being the most interesting conversation on the planet right now.

Reason #1 to read this book:

Your purpose is a highly effective and efficient path to creating an exciting life, a legendary career and a better world.

This book will connect you to your life's purpose and empower you to passionately create a purpose-driven career. I recognize that this is a bold claim and all too often an abused promise by authors and agents of personal transformation. This book is different, in that it attempts to be the most scientifically informed book on the subject to date, and it includes instructions to access a proven online low-cost purpose discovery course (with a 95% effectiveness rate). As you'll discover in Chapters 4, 5, 6 and 7, research from leading institutions such as Harvard and Stanford, suggests that your life's purpose will add up to seven years to your life, quintuple your productivity, quadruple your engagement at work, increase your fulfillment at work by 62%, increase the likelihood of you being a leader by 50%, and increase your experience of abundance by 47% and love by 31%, and increase your attraction.

In Part One of this book, you will explore what purpose is, what it feels like to discover it, and the overwhelming evidence in favor of putting your purpose to work in your career. You will discover what George Bernard Shaw meant when he said:

> This is the true joy in life, the being used for a purpose recognized by yourself as a mighty one; the being a force of nature instead of a feverish, selfish little clod of ailments and grievances, complaining that the world will not devote itself to making you happy. I am of the opinion that my life belongs to the whole community, and as long as I live it is my privilege to do for it whatever I can. I want to be thoroughly used up when I die, for the harder I work, the more I live. I rejoice in life for its own sake. Life is no brief candle to me; it is a sort of splendid torch which I have got hold of for the moment, and want to make it burn as brightly as possible before handing it on to future generations. (Shaw, 1903)

As Shaw knew well, purpose is critical to a successful and fulfilling career. The reason for this is the relationship that purpose has to *flow* (being immersed in a personally meaningful task with short feedback loops and moderate difficulty). A 2013 McKinsey & Co. report established that when executives are in flow, they are 500% more productive (Cranston, Keller, 2013). Imagine getting a whole week's worth of work done in a day? This powerful upgrade fuels extraordinary leaders, entrepreneurs and enterprises the world over.

Purpose is what drives numerous visionaries, like Eileen Fisher (Eileen Fisher

Clothing), Elon Musk (Tesla), Oprah Winfrey (OWN), John Mackey (Whole Foods) and Seane Corn (Off the Mat), to change millions of human lives and create billions of dollars of wealth. They continue to create massive change in their industries and yet, these visionaries are but the tip of the iceberg, a few of the more notable members of the Global Purpose Movement.

Companies and customers all over the world are using this power to lead, succeed and create a world that works for everyone. Companies that lead with purpose, such as Johnson & Johnson and Canon, on average outperform the stock market 15-to-1 (Collins, Porras, 1994), and have a growth rate that is triple that of their peers (McCleod, 2012). These companies leverage the 55% of global customers who choose products that have a higher purpose, all else being equal (Nielsen, 2014).

Part Two of this book invites you into your purpose, your inner uprising, with the Global Purpose Expedition. When you go online to register for the Global Purpose Expedition, you will join a global community of purpose awakening leaders and move through numerous highly effective purpose discovery exercises, empowering you to create a life, community and career that express your purpose. As mentioned, 95% of people who completed the Global Purpose Expedition (and its predecessor, the Purpose Challenge) reported a deeper connection to their life's purpose, and recommended it to their friends and family. They have reported outstanding results including, but not limited to, new purpose-aligned careers, homes and relationships, healing dysfunctional family wounds, losing weight and overcoming addictions. The exercises will give you new insights into your life's purpose, as well as the fuel to lead and accelerate your career. They will provide you with tools to overcome resistance to living your purpose and empowering you to take consistent action as you move your purpose out into the world. In Part Two, you will explore a roadmap to create a career that expresses your purpose and awakens your Shambhala Leadership.

Reason #2 to read this book:

This is happening.

By virtue of having picked this book up, you are part of a global awakening of people who are finding and living their life's purpose to create a purposeful life and stepping into their Shambhala Leadership to create a planet on purpose. When you step forward with your purpose, you will actively participate in an unprecedented evolutionary advance in human history, one that I believe has a greater capacity to accelerate human flourishing than that of the Enlightenment.

Edelman, a leading global communications strategy firm, has declared that "purpose is the new paradigm" in our global economy. Edelman's 2017 Trust Survey revealed that 87% of global consumers believe businesses should put at least as much emphasis on social interests as business ones (Edelman, 2017). In the last five decades, we've transformed our economy, realizing numerous efficiencies, such as manufacturing operations (1970's), capitalization structure (1980's), organizational development (1990's) and information technology (2000's). The fifth transformation, in the decade in which we now find ourselves (2010's), is that of the inner game, connecting the purpose inside of every business person with the purposes of the world's customers, investors, partners and employees.

In the next chapter, "Purpose, The New Normal?", you will explore this cultural and economic movement. You will feel that this is indeed happening. So, the questions are: What will be your response to this movement? Will you let this emerging best practice pass you by and experience another five years of the same relationships, the same jobs, personal dynamics and health, while the rest of the world comes alive with their Shambhala Leadership? Or will you awaken your life's purpose and live a high-impact life, on fire with the best body, career and relationships you can imagine?

Reason #3 to read this book:

Purpose is now an existential necessity.

Never before in human history has so much depended on so little. By reading this book, by going online to complete the Global Purpose Expedition, and expanding the scope of your purpose in Part Three, you will step into your Shambhala Leadership.

Purpose is not only your ticket to an extraordinary life, a legendary career and freedom from a life of purpose substitutes - chemicals, overwork, mindless media and consumerism - but freedom to make a huge impact and change the world.

The accessibility of powerful purpose discovery education could not have come at a better time. The cost of our species being disconnected from its purpose is that we have consumed ourselves into an environmental, cultural and economic catastrophe. We have driven ourselves to the brink of collapse with unprecedented levels of environmental toxicity, war, poverty, disease, species extinction, social and moral decay, and political corruption.

As you'll discover in "Chapter 17: Humanity's Midlife Crisis", numerous reports from many of the world's leading risk experts at the United Nations (United Nations, 2014), the United States Department of Defense (GAO, 2014), insurance company Swiss Re's (Swiss Re, 2017), investment management firm PIMCO (PIMCO, 2016) and investment management firm GMO (GMO, 2016), warn that our current carbon-dependent consumer economy of purpose-substitutes is not just bad business, but existentially suicidal. Unless we stop ravaging our planet to consume and fill the purpose-sized hole in our lives, our species will face a precipitous decline in quality of life and numbers. Jared Diamond PhD warned in his book, *Collapse* (Diamond, 2006), that, if this die-off is anything like previous collapses, it could be as large as 80% of humanity, or almost 6 billion human lives. Your purpose, when combined with the efforts of others living their purpose, sources identity internally, eliminating the need to fill a purpose-sized hole. Purpose may indeed be what is needed to save humanity.

It can be argued that it is this purpose-sized hole in the heart of Western Civilization that drove demand for purpose-substitutes, as well as the models and consequences for doing so, e.g. colonization, slavery and imperialism. In absence of a connection to our purpose and values, we were ripe for distraction. Unscrupulous merchants plundered the planet in pursuit of stimulants (tea, sugar, tobacco, cocoa), fashion (silk, gold, silver, gems) and the cheap means of production to procur and produce them (slaves, coal, oil). As Yuval Noah Harari PhD concluded at the end of his landmark history of the human species, *Sapiens*, now more than at any time in our history, humanity needs to connect with its own purpose to survive:

> ...despite the astonishing things that humans are capable of doing, we remain unsure of our goals and we seem to be as discontented as ever... We have... very little idea what to do with all that power. Worse still, humans seem to be more irresponsible than ever. Self-made gods... we are accountable to no one... wreaking havoc on... the surrounding ecosystem, seeking little more than our own comfort and amusement, yet never finding satisfaction. Is there anything more dangerous than dissatisfied and irresponsible gods who don't know what they want? (Harari, 2015, pp. 415-416)

In a sense, my book is a continuation of Dr. Harari's foundational conversation about how we got here and what we're supposed to do. Purpose is not only your access to the life you want, but may be our species' solution to soulfully, sustainably, creatively and abundantly writing the next chapter of our story.

Purpose for America, Purpose for the World

Your purpose is also the connective tissue that heals our deeply wounded society. Purpose is fundamentally transpartisan. It is a human issue, one that deepens and expresses our conservative values, as it radically increases freedom, empowerment, impact, economic abundance and self-reliance, and one that deepens and expresses our progressive values, as it liberates us from the tyranny of choices of what to do with our lives, careers and volunteer efforts. It sources our identity internally, clearing the path for organic, soulful action. Purpose is an equalizer that frees us from narrow identities of politics, religion, gender, sexuality, race and culture, connecting us more deeply to each other and fostering a spirit of acceptance, contribution, diversity, self-expression, generosity, commonwealth and compassion. When your purpose awakens in you, you will find yourself remarkably less dependent on others (more self-reliant - conservative) and also more giving towards others (more compassionate - liberal), and yet freed from either of these partisan identities, as your identity is now primarily that of your life's purpose.

As a result of connecting and leading with your life's purpose, you will also have access to a deeper patriotism: not a nostalgic return to simpler times, but a patriotism to life itself - to human flourishing and ecological resilience. Purpose-driven politics honors the goodness and virtue in all points of view, preserves their diverse contributions and works collaboratively with all concerned parties towards emergent, creative win-win-win solutions that elevate the whole.

Thus, purpose isn't just a self-help movement. It isn't just a best practice for life, documented by volumes of research, up there with eight hours of sleep, exercise, meditation and a balanced diet. It is now an existential necessity, one that empowers us individually, and heals us collectively, providing the connective tissue to evolve our species culturally, politically, economically and ecologically.

Know this upfront: I want your purpose.

The first reason I wrote this book is because I want your purpose. Not like a trade with the devil, but I want your life's purpose to live out loud. It is my purpose to be useful to you, to awaken each individual human to their purpose and thus awaken the whole of humanity into a far more purposeful and generative expression. As such, I am fully committed to you living with joy and purpose in every part of your life. Because of my commitment to you, together we will hunt down and transform your limiting beliefs. Together, we will tenderize, sauté and digest them, so that all that remains of you is your bigness, your Shambhala Leadership.

This is a lifelong process, but it begins here, right now, with your purpose discovery journey. I want to know and love you in your fullness and to see your purpose unleashed upon a world that begs for it, that aches for it.

The second reason I wrote this book is because the connection between one's life purpose and one's leadership and impact is not well understood. My intention is to synthesize and deliver a broad and digestible understanding of these subjects and how they relate to each other.

In Part Two, you will explore how purpose and leadership evolve together, but here's a brief summary:

1. Purpose evolves from:
   a. Having no purpose
   b. To having a declared purpose (for ego, wealth, power and tribe)
   c. To a higher purpose (for others/service)
   d. To unitive purpose (for the whole of existence)
2. Correspondingly, leadership evolves from:

a. Egocentric leadership. Archetype: mafia boss.
b. To reactive / sociocentric leadership (for ego, wealth, power and tribe). Archetype: manager, white collar professional.
c. To creative leadership (from one's higher purpose, in service). Archetype: social entrepreneur.
d. To Shambhala Leadership (for the whole of existence) Archetypes: industry leader, enlightened statesperson, humanitarian, cultural artisan.

It doesn't matter where you find yourself in the purpose/leadership progression. Wherever you are at is great. However, there are tools you can use to move yourself further along in this progression, yielding more power, freedom, fulfillment, impact and reward. As mentioned, at this moment in human history, you are being called to uplevel your purpose and leadership.

Parts Three and Four of this book empower you to embody your purpose, step into Shambhala Leadership and create a world that works for us all. As you move through these sections, you will find your purpose discovery and leadership journey firmly inside human history, inside the unfolding evolution of our Cosmos, inside a modern context, connecting your purpose to the call from future generations. You will connect with the triple purpose of the human species:

1. HUMAN: To create a world that allows every human to discover their purpose and work as an expression of their purpose
2. EARTH: To claim our role as ecosystem steward, to guide the Earth community towards biodiversity and resilience
3. COSMOS: To further express the purpose of the Cosmos and realize greater goodness, truth and beauty

From this place, you will be empowered to step into your Shambhala Leadership, becoming fully responsible for all that is, was, and will be in the Cosmos.

Of course, you don't have to do this. You can stop before Part Three. Simply finding your higher purpose and choosing to live it, in your health, love life, family, career and community is a huge gift to yourself and our species.

If you want to step into Shambhala Leadership, however, you must become world-wizened by continually expanding your worldview. You must locate yourself in the tension between your understanding of the world as it is and the call from future generations. When your worldview includes an awareness of the world as it is, and an understanding the purpose of the Cosmos, the Earth and humanity, your purpose becomes the fullest expression of what your soul wants you to do AND also what the world needs you to do. By continually expanding your worldview, you will live the fullness of your unique life's purpose, lead with it and play a crucial and historical role in the survival and flourishing of the human species.

The third reason I wrote this book, is that I believe that humanity can only be saved by accelerating the already underway Global Purpose Movement. More purpose-ignorant economic, social, and technology policies will only create more of the same purpose-ignorant problems, only at greater scale. If we continue to fix software problems (psychology - *hambre de alma*, our purpose-sized holes) with the hope of purpose-ignorant hardware solutions (policy, politicians, consumer goods, media, chemicals) we will only get more of the same symptoms - more inequality, disempowerment, depression, cultural decay, disease, addiction, deforestation, ecocide, corruption, pollution and exploitation, and accelerate the already occurring genocide upon future generations.

However, when we fix a software problem with a software upgrade, we have the right tool for the job and have addressed the core issue. Your higher purpose is your software license to create a personal narrative for your life, to cause purposeful outcomes in every area of your life. Your embodied purpose is your license to create a new world, with all of reality's 52 cards face up. Multiply this effect, by your 7.5 billion sisters and brothers, and we have a brand new Earth, an entirely new definition of what it means to be a human being, what it means to be a part of a species, planet and Cosmos on purpose.

We get the politicians we deserve. The rise of fascist demagogues like Trump, Putin, Farage, Erdoğan, Duterte, Assad and Kim Jong Un are not accidents. Their rise to power is the result of the prevailing culture, the psychological and spiritual development of humanity. If we want different politicians, we have to be different. We must be the leaders we want. We cannot wait for heroes.

Like many of my colleagues, I believe this is an "all hands on deck" moment for our species. We must purposefully ignite the mass of humanity to crave and create structural, political and economic reform - not just new policies on top of our broken structure, but a new understanding of what it means to be human and govern ourselves accordingly. We need surgery, not pills. And now with purpose discovery education making its way into the mainstream, we have an unprecedented opportunity to respond with a mass movement of purpose-driven leadership, economic empowerment and political reform all over the world.

> *"Although attempting to bring about World Peace through the internal transformation of individuals is difficult, it is the only way."*
> *-H.H. Dalai Lama*

"The most important freedom is to be who you really are. There can't be any large-scale revolution until there is a personal revolution, on the individual level. It's got to happen on the inside first."

-Jim Morrison

"Our psyche is set up in accord with the structure of the universe, and what happens in the macrocosm likewise happens in the infinitesimal and most subjective reaches of the psyche."

-Carl Jung

We are not merely standing in front of a burning planet with a purpose hose, however. This can also be fun! In a sense, this crisis and opportunity allows us to be kids again. As my friend and colleague Sam Clayton, muses, we are indeed superheroes: "We actually get to save the world!" We can embrace the excitement of being the first generation in human history that actually *can* save the world.

Heretofore, most of our crises have only been local. With all of human existence now deeply interconnected and dependent on the entire system working, just as we did as children with capes jumping off couches, we get to save the world by living our purposes out loud. And we must do this. Evolutionary theologian, Michael Dowd, believes this moment in our history reveals more than just chaos, but a sacred opportunity:

> When we look to the looming issues facing us: overpopulation, species extinction, global warming, the growing gap between the rich and poor - many people feel overwhelmed. When I look at these things, through sacred deep-time eyes, I get excited. Because if we didn't have problems at this scale - problems that are undeniably and indisputably in need of our attention - we'd keep pushing off the changes that we need to make for another several hundred years. (Martin, 2010, p. 118)

We must see the opportunity in this chaos and find the excitement to create and lead, despite all that is being destroyed around us. Humanity's darkest hour and most fertile capacity for purposeful regeneration seem to have arisen simultaneously. We are the ones we have been waiting for. Help isn't coming. We can actually solve our very real adult concerns by employing the grandeur of our visions from childhood, awakening, embodying and leading with our life's purpose. We are doing more than weaving our idealism and the chaotic world together, but weaving ourselves back into the world to reveal new expressions of our individual and collective purpose.

It is on the ground of uncertainty and in the face of the unknown that the inner story of our souls becomes most pertinent and important. The soul requires an outer drama so that it can reveal its full imagination for life and its inner myth... When the story of the world becomes less clear, it is the unfolding of the inner life of the soul that might provide the best way to proceed. (Meade, 2010, p. 5)

Fully embodying, expressing and evolving your purpose is a lifelong love affair between the macro and micro. The key to humanity's survival and flourishing and YOUR awakening, success and fulfillment is one and the same. It is inside you and it is also co-arising out in the world. *You have a purpose.* Your purpose, when revealed in its fullness, will empower you to achieve the life you want, a life of vitality, self-expression, prosperity, meaningful impact, and connection, AND put you on the court as a Shambhala Leader creating a world that works for everyone. But first, you have to fight for it, to break free from your fear, skepticism and self-doubt. You must triumph over the limiting beliefs you have about yourself AND the world. And this fight will take everything you've got.

You are worth fighting for and I am with you in this fight.

I am proud to be a loving warrior at your side, fighting for the bigness of your soul's revelation and expression in the world. I realize that "warrior" is not a common or politically correct word to use these days, because most of humanity identifies the experience of war with a moral sense of wrongness and needless suffering. Of course, I do not mean war in that way. I don't mean we are people who take up arms and willfully inflict harm on others.

Rather, we are called to awaken in the Shambhala Warrior tradition. Let us awaken to our unique life's purpose and join together as Shambhala Leaders, committing to human flourishing on this planet - a broad, rapid, and deeply contextual purpose awakening.

I invite you into this fight.

My task is to be with you in the trenches as we trumpet the battle cry that unites every fight for peace, abundance, justice, creativity and sustainability - the one unified front of truth over ignorance, of radical self-expression over repressed conformity, of a diverse unity over the illusion of separation, of love over fear, of thriving over decline. Together we will answer the call from the future with the cry: "WE ARE COMING!" and create a world that includes the human species over one that does not, one of purpose over almost certain death.

However, this is not a kumbaya purpose drum circle. This is a dangerous mission and I'm going to spend the next few pages trying to get rid of you. It is my duty to prepare you for the journey by alerting you to three hazards on this path.

Hazard #1: A life of purpose is not for the meek, nor is this book for those who desire to merely intellectually satisfy themselves with an understanding of purpose.

You will need to be fully present, as if each word written here is the price of admission to your future, which indeed may be the case. However, the way most folks read is from the neck up. To find and live your purpose, you cannot rely on your brain alone. You will actually need to experience purpose. You will need your heart, intuition, resolve, breath and physical strength to endure the discomfort of your purpose discovery and embodiment. No purpose can be figured out with your brain, nor slapped onto a full, busy life of comfort and distraction.

To discover and live from your purpose, you will have to make sacrifices and devote time, resources and energy to the journey, e.g., with a Guide or a program like the Global Purpose Expedition. You must bravely go into the darkness, and be someone who makes themselves uncomfortable. This is powerful work, but it is work that you absolutely can do. Fifteen-year-olds and ninety-two-year-olds from all over the world have done this work, and you are no different.

Further, without putting the well-being of everything you currently value on the line, you will make this book itself just another purpose-substitute, just another use of time, energy and resources, nothing more than intellectual masturbation, an entertaining endeavor that ultimately changes nothing.

Now, you might be thinking that your life is just fine as it is. Great! I want you to consider moving from a good life and stepping into a legendary life. What would it be like if you had twice as much fun, impact, sex and wealth? What would it be like to tap into your deepest truth and awaken the beast of your Shambhala Leadership? Now is the opportunity to get clear on what you can gain from a life of purpose, or rather, what it is costing you personally to be disconnected from your purpose. In what ways are your body, lifestyle, relationships and career not optimal? What chips are you currently leaving on the table? Are you ok driving your Ferrari as if it is a wheel-barrow? Or are you going to open the throttle and feel your power in 5th and 6th gear?

Please also read this book critically with a pen in hand, marking it up with questions, concerns, points of agreement and dissonance. Challenge me. Wrestle with the material in a manner worthy of what is at stake. Unless you are willing to take every word in this book personally and actually work with a Guide or do the Global Purpose Expedition, consider giving this book to a friend who is hungry and ready to create a big life of impact, fulfillment, abundance, vitality and love.

Hazard #2: It takes a village to find and live a purpose.

If you want to find and live your life's purpose alone, by yourself, you will fail. Purpose is not something you can figure out by exposing your brain to the right words. It's not something that occurs in a vacuum, in isolation or on an island. This work has to be engaged with directly, and experienced in your relationships and in your community. Purpose awakening requires two types of interactions with others:

1. Personal accountability and support from a community of other folks in a program or with a trained Guide.
2. Sharing your life and purpose with the people that know you best, and receive reflection as to how your purpose is already expressed in the world and in your relationships.

Further, Parts Three and Four will be of no use to you unless you complete the Global Purpose Expedition online or work with a trained Guide. Parts Three and Four require that your identity is primarily sourced in your purpose, not in any pre-purpose religious, gender, cultural, economic or partisan identities.

Hazard #3: Purpose may not be what you need right now.

I stand for you to get everything you came here to do and be in this life, right now. Your purpose journey will be the most rewarding and most difficult work of your life. However, if your life is in shambles economically, psychologically or biologically, please attend to these matters first. Your economic security, and physical and psychological health are much more important than you finding your life's purpose.

If there is an acute crisis in your life, the time and energy spent on your purpose journey will not serve you.

If you are in an abusive relationship with a person or substance, please get clean. If you live in a place that is unsafe, unstable or otherwise dysfunctional, please move to a place you can properly call a sanctuary, where you are loved or, at minimum, well-received and nurtured. If you are unemployed, please just get a job, any job that will pay your bills and save you the agony of wondering where the next rent check will come from. If you work more than 45 hours a week, you must stop it. You will need all your spare energy for the purpose journey and time to marinate in the work, so please find work that allows you the freedom to leave your work at work. If you have a serious physical or psychological condition that is not being treated, please get help immediately.

Note: I am not a mental health or medical professional, and am not claiming to diagnose or treat you for any medical or psychological illness. If you continue with this book, and do the exercises, you assume full responsibility for your physical and psychological health, for your actions, impacts and outcomes, and agree not to hold me liable, or to hold liable anyone I cite in this book or with whom I work.

To sum up, please continue if you are (1) economically, physically and psychologically stable in your life; (2) willing to take full responsibility for your actions; (3) willing to explore your purpose in community; and (4) willing to question everything you encounter in this book from this moment forward.

Still here, I see. Great! I have failed to get rid of you. Thank you for your courage and grit. Even though you might not yet fully understand what you are signing up for, you are standing for the life you are meant to live. You stand for your own greatness, and are now about to burn away everything that is not your destiny, your Shambhala Leadership. From this place, I'm happy to enter into partnership with you on your purpose journey.

A Note on Terminology

Although this book is written for a modern, working professional, it will be useful to you regardless of how you identify culturally, professionally or spiritually. My desire is that you see that the continued cultivation of your life's purpose is a good idea, one worthy of your sustained attention, whether you hold purpose as an emerging scientifically-informed best practice, a personal religious expression OR both. As "purpose" is a term used differently in scientific and religious communities, I think it's important to acknowledge how these two communities treat the subject.

Folks who lean more to the religious side of the spectrum tend to view purpose as the extent to which they conform to God's will or the sacred texts of their particular tradition, and express divinity in their thoughts, speech and actions, e.g., "What would Jesus do?" Whereas, atheists and scientists tend to view purpose according to the scientific definition: as the extent to which you believe there is such a thing as meaning and purpose, how connected you are to it, and believe that your actions can express it (Crumbaugh & Maholick, 1964). Both perspectives, and all perspectives in between, are welcome here.

I also use many technical purpose guiding terms in this book, e.g., ego and soul, that also have a historical, spiritual and/or psychological heritage, but I use them in a fashion that is not wholly expressive of their institutional use. Like Tim Kelley, I use the term *soul* to refer to that part of you that knows your purpose (Kelley, 2009, p. 12). I use the term *ego* to describe that part of you that cares about looking good, staying safe, being comfortable. If the word *soul* does not resonate with you, feel free to sub it out for "highest self", "intuition", "deepest truth" or "authentic self".

Further, purpose work is not about destroying ego. As Bill Plotkin, PhD, and Author of *Wild Mind* states,

Ego possesses the heart, hands, senses, imagination, and intelligence to manifest, but doesn't know what's worth manifesting; it yearns to know the deeply authentic purpose of the Soul. Soul possesses the song that's worth singing, the dance that wants to be danced, but it has no way to manifest this in the world; the Soul yearns to be made real by the Ego. Ego is long on know-how and short on know-why; the opposite is true of the Soul.

(Plotkin, 2013, p. 25)

As Clarissa Pinkola Estes PhD, Senior Jungian Analyst, former Executive Director of the C.G. Jung Institute, Denver, explains in her book, *Women Who Run With the Wolves,* the human journey is about integrating ego with soul.

...ego and the soul vie to control the life force. In early life, the ego, with its appetites, often leads; it is always cooking something up that smells really good...

... sometimes in our twenties, sometimes in our thirties, but most often in our forties... we begin to let the soul lead. The power shifts away from brickabrack and frick-frack to soulfulness. And though the soul does not assume the lead by killing off the ego, the ego is demoted and given a different assignment in the psyche, which is essentially to submit to the concerns of the soul.

(Estes, 1992, p. 270)

For more detail on the manner in which I use these terms, please explore "Appendix A: A Note on the Use of Spiritual and Psychological Language".

I will define one more term right now, however, as I use it heavily. This is the phrase "best practices." Now, I don't mean best practices in the sense of what I, Brandon, think a best practice is *in my opinion.*

I use this term to reflect the current consensus and most recent research of our scientific community, e.g. it is a best practice to get a good night's rest, or drink 8 glasses of water each day. I use this term to describe the techniques and methods that, through experience and research, have proven to lead to a desired result. Because I want the best outcomes for all parties, I am committed to using the very best tools available, aka best practices. I am committed to using all knowledge, education, policy, methodology and technology at the disposal of our species to create a world that works for everyone and inspires us. And so, when I use this term, please know I make every effort to be sourced in the scientific consensus.

A Note to You

As a reminder, and like all non-fiction, this book is a work in progress, with a second edition planned. As such, anything you feel is erroneous, missing or wrong-headed, please let me know via the ensouled.life website. Thank you in advance, and enjoy your journey.

Anonymity

Throughout this book I describe conversations I've had with friends and clients. I've changed the names to protect the anonymity of these individuals.

PART ONE

Purpose Revealed

CHAPTER 1

Purpose, the New Normal?

"After the sale of our company, I'll have the time to reflect and do something important," said Matt, a technology entrepreneur and long-time friend.

"Why wait, brother? Someday might not never come."

"I know, but my kids are my top priority."

As I am prone to do with the people I love, I didn't hold back. "I get that, and YOU are doing a terrible disservice to them grinding away at something that doesn't bring you alive. You think they don't notice that their Dad isn't lit up? You think they don't see the dread in your face when you walk out the door? You think they don't see you zone out to sports, eat and drink too much?"

"Yeah, you're right. They do. I just don't see how to do it differently."

"Show them what it looks like to live life mightily. Do you want them to grow up thinking that it's ok to play small, to dread their career, to drink and zone out every night? It's not ok! Stop showing them that it is. Don't let them grow up thinking that their main male role model chose a small life of resignation, vice and compromise. It's not an either/or conversation. You can have both financial security and a purpose-driven career."

"I just don't see how it's possible to make a living doing good in the world. I've got to keep growing my business. If I take my eye off the road for a second, I could lose it all."

Matt is not an anomaly. Like most folks who have a family and mortgage to look after, he is heads down on creating a solid economic foundation to make life better for his family. Yet Matt feels trapped. He wants to live a true, honest and self-expressed life and build a career that makes the world better for his children and grandchildren. However, he faces what feels like a sea of risk and potential harm to those he loves when he considers the prospect. So, he marches forth with what he knows.

With his song still in his heart, Matt keeps his eyes on the road, while trying not to notice the burning world in his side mirrors, the flashing indicators signaling the impending failure of critical biological, social, political and economic systems upon which the life and livelihood of his family rely. He ignores genocide, racial injustice, starvation in Africa, the rise of demagogues, the objectification of women and the slow-motion collapse of democracy, our ecosystems and the American Dream. He ignores the pounding call to do something about it, to contribute his purpose-driven leadership. He also ignores the persistent white fog questions that afflict the comfortable: "Is this all there is? Is this what I came here for? Am I to just sit here and do nothing as the world burns? Am I to watch as my children's future is sold off to the lowest bidder by politicians?" And there is nothing wrong with this. Matt is not a bad guy, he's just a guy who wants to do his life differently, but doesn't yet see an alternative route.

Matt is not well-connected to his purpose, and obviously not in action expressing it. If your job isn't your fullest self-expression, odds are that you are experiencing something similar and may be part of the 87% of humanity that contributes economically, but is not engaged at work (Gallup, 2014). You may be experiencing some of the many personal costs of being disconnected from your purpose. Your personal dashboard might have blinking lights on it, indicators of illness, chemical addiction, overwork, depression, consumerism, media addiction, lethargy, or an unfulfilling love life.

In addition, you may also be present to the effects of *humanity* being disconnected from its purpose. If you open any newspaper on any given day, you are certain to discover that we live on a planet with rampant political corruption, a political media circus, disease, war, corruption, environmental pollution, injustice, social unrest and cultural decay.

Yet, despite this background radiation of purposelessness, the possibility of a purpose-awakened life and abundant livelihood is well within your reach and within the confines of this book. With 87% of humanity disengaged at work, it is fair to say that 13% of humans (949 million or almost one billion people) are indeed purpose aware or awakening and are purposefully engaged in the world and their careers. One billion people is a lot of people, but are they the emerging edge of the new normal?

Is Purpose the New Normal?

What does it take to say that purpose is the new normal? Not much, actually. In fact, it is possible that we may already have a critical mass of purpose-awakened/ing souls in humanity.

In the last 50 years, we've developed powerful new ways to understand how people, markets and society change, and how every meaningful evolution in the human condition starts small, and eventually reaches a tipping point. A tipping point occurs when 13.5% of a population starts doing something new, like using the internet, smartphones, social media, etc., and then the rest of the world recognizes that it is a good idea and joins in. Why 13.5%? That is the threshold, articulated in *Diffusion of Innovations* (Rogers, 1962) and popularized by Malcolm Gladwell's

The Tipping Point. The tipping point is the moment when a particular cultural, technological or economic phenomenon rapidly increases its velocity of adoption. At this point, behavior shifts from a slow rate of adoption (from change agent to change agent), increases speed (from change agents to influencers) and eventually to a rapid growth rate (from influencers to the mainstream).

With respect to purpose as a movement or trend, it isn't a hard fact yet, because we are not totally certain whether the people identified in the Gallup study actually know their purpose or were living it at work. However, numerous studies suggest that 13% is likely the low-end estimate of the size of the Global Purpose Movement. Evidence from numerous populations, such as US consumers, workers, CEOs, Millennials and Baby Boomers, suggests that purpose is fast becoming the new normal:

- **20%** of global CEOs know their purpose (Craig, Snook, 2014).
- **28%** of the United States workforce is purpose-driven (LinkedIn/ Imperative, 2016).
- **35%** of adults (80 million) in the United States are Cultural Creatives, people whose careers and lifestyles extend outside of themselves to benefit purposeful goals (sustainability, personal growth, diversity, peace, equality), up 175% from 1995 (Ray, 2010).
- **55%** of global consumers will pay more for a product that has a higher purpose (Nielsen, 2014).
- **73%** of global consumers would switch brands if that brand had a higher purpose (Edelman, 2012)
- **78%** of global citizens are more likely to buy from businesses who sign up to meet the UN's Global Goals for Sustainable Development (PwC, 2015)
- **87%** of global consumers believe businesses should put at least as much emphasis on social interests as business ones (Edelman, 2017).
- **91%** of American corporate employees believe that it is the top responsibility of a company to positively impact society (Deloitte, 2013).
- **94%** of American Millennials want a job that makes a positive impact on society and the environment (Millennial Impact Report, 2014).
- **97%** of Americans believe that having a sense of purpose is important (Rainey, 2014).

It is clear that by many measures, purpose is becoming the new normal and is moving into the cultural mainstream in a number of important ways. The American media, long a stronghold of purpose substitutes, is now replete with notable figures taking a stand for their purpose and values, inspiring millions of Americans to march forward into purpose-aligned action. The most outspoken purpose-driven celebrities include Ashley Judd, Kareem Abdul-Jabbar, Rosario Dawson, Robert

Redford, Angelina Jolie, Harrison Ford, Beyoncé, Brad Pitt, Katy Perry, Edward Norton, Sarah Silverman, Tim Robbins, George Clooney, Julia Roberts, Leonardo DiCaprio, Susan Sarandon, Jimmy Kimmel, Meryl Streep, Michael Jordan and Julianne Moore.

Teen heartthrob Justin Bieber even put out an album, *Purpose* (Def Jam Records, 2015) devoted to his fall from grace and restoration of dignity, via the power of purpose. Bieber joins Lady Gaga, Jack Johnson, Tracy Chapman, Dixie Chicks, Beyoncé, Nahko, Pink, Common, Christina Aguilera, Bruce Springsteen, Michael Franti, Katy Perry and many others, who have taken on the difficult task of purposefully raising consciousness through mainstream music. Katy Perry declared that 2017 is the year that "purposeful pop" will raise the collective consciousness of the mainstream (Johnston, 2/14/17).

Of equal if not greater merit, is the explosion of research, methodologies and nonfiction on the subject of purpose, e.g., Thomas Moore's *Care of the Soul* (1994), James Hillman's *The Soul's Code* (1996), Bill Plotkin's *Soulcraft* (2003), Tim Kelley's *True Purpose* (2009), Richard Leider's *The Power of Purpose* (2010), Michael Meade's *Fate and Destiny* (2010), Rod Stryker's *The Four Desires* (2011), and Aaron Hurst's *The Purpose Economy* (2016).

We are already seeing 9 million American Baby Boomers who have begun their second purpose-driven careers, with another 31 million of them actively searching for and creating their next purposeful career (Encore.org, 6/10/2014). Therefore, purpose is not an odd Millennial curiosity or the mid-life crisis of Gen X or the Boomer's new luxury item. It's not just a curious phenomenon for sociologists to study and marketers to leverage, but is perhaps already the new normal for what it means to be a human being.

As indicated in the studies above, purpose is moving into the global workplace with accelerating velocity. Connecting with one's life purpose or feeling connected to a company's purpose is now the #1 factor in determining workplace satisfaction, making purpose more than twice as important as the #2 factor, the strength of the company's leadership (Happiness Research Institute, 2016).

Yet, purpose may also be the "old normal", a more accurate expression of who we are and always have been as a species. Perhaps this billion-strong inner uprising is merely a group of people who are remembering, and the journey to soul is a timeless journey for us to more fully become who we are and step into a big life of impact, abundance, vitality, love and connection. We see evidence of the call to live truthfully throughout numerous fields and traditions:

> In Gnostic Christianity from Jesus: "If you bring forth what is within you, what you have will save you. If you do not have that within you, what you do not have within you will kill you." (Miller, 1992, p. 316)

In mainstream Christianity: "Walk in the ways of thine heart." (Ecclesiastes 11:9, KJV)

In history: "The destiny of man is his own soul." (Herodotus)

In Buddhism: "Work for a goal; do not continue in purposeless actions, cultivate your own talents." (Atisa)

In Hinduism: "It is better to strive in one's own dharma than to succeed in the dharma of another. Nothing is ever lost in following one's own dharma, but competition in another's dharma breeds fear and insecurity." (Bhagavad Gita)

In Sufism: "Everyone has been made for some particular work and the desire for that work has been put into every heart." (Rumi)

In the theater: "To thine own self be true." (Shakespeare)

In art: "Make your work be in keeping with your purpose." (Leonardo da Vinci)

In literature: "Every man is the son of his own works." (Cervantes)

In psychology: "Musicians must make music, artists must paint, poets must write if they are ultimately to be at peace with themselves. What human beings can be, they must be." (Abraham Maslow)

In mythology: "Follow your bliss." (Joseph Campbell)

So, I invite you to explore the very real possibility that purpose is more than the new normal, but a deep and sacred remembering, an ancient truth obscured by the screens, frenzy and market forces of modern life. For more on the deep history of who we are and have always been, please explore "Appendix B: The History of Purpose."

Regardless of how ancient or sacred this movement is, what we now know is that there is an inner uprising of people, perhaps one billion or more people, who have chosen to heed the wisdom of the ages. A growing number of us have chosen to live our lives engaged and on purpose, living longer, happier, healthier, more connected, abundant lives of impact. The question that remains is this: "Will you resist this awakening or embrace it?"

If you decide to embrace this new normal, here is what you can expect as you move through this book and on your purpose journey:

1. **PURPOSE SMARTS.** A broad knowledge of what purpose is, an understanding of its measurable benefits. (Part One)

2. **CLARITY ABOUT YOUR PURPOSE AND LEADERSHIP.** A deeper understanding of your purpose and what you must do to live it fully, lead with it and build a career to express it. (Part Two and taking part in the Global Purpose Expedition online or working with a trained Guide)

3. **WISDOM.** Knowledge of your place in human history and the unfolding purpose of the Cosmos, what that means for you - your relationships, career and health and for our species - and how to uplevel your higher purpose to unitive purpose. (Part Three)

4. **CONFIDENCE AND POWER TO CREATE A WORLD THAT WORKS.** A roadmap for creating a planet on purpose - politically, economically, ecologically and culturally. You now get to save the world, creatively expressing your purpose on an ever-larger scale. Start looking for a cape! (Part Four)

I recognize that these are bold promises, but they are ones that I make and deliver on time after time with my clients and the people I guide in my global online programs. I promise that you too, will know and be excited to live your purpose, and to play the biggest possible game you can with your life.

CHAPTER 2

What is Purpose?

"I can get you anything you want."

"Thanks, man." I said to my new party acquaintance, Evan. "Like what?"

It was the year 2000. I was 23, drunk and sitting in the backseat of a car, in between parties in Santa Monica, CA. Over the music, Evan turned to me from the front seat, "Weed, ecstasy, coke, acid, H. You name it."

"What's H?" I said excitedly. I knew H was heroin. Coke, ecstasy and LSD were old hat. Finally, I was going to get to do heroin, and experience a drug that I'd been told was like a 30-minute orgasm.

"Heroin," he said. "But be careful with it."

"Dude, I can handle anything. Get me some."

"Alright, take down my number."

The next day, as my roommates and I pieced together the evening over pizza, beer and watching football, I remembered that electrifying conversation in the car. I dug through the debris in my pockets, feeling around through my cigarettes, lighter and coke baggies to find a wad of cocktail napkins with phone numbers. I finally found the buried treasure - Evan's number.

I shot off a cryptic text that partiers carefully belabor, "Hey man, I really want to take that HEROIC journey we discussed. Hit me up - Brandon."

Luckily, as with so many close calls with danger in my twenties, Evan never called or texted back. Maybe he was all talk. Maybe I wrote the number down wrong. Maybe it was divine intervention.

Later that day I found myself in between games of volleyball in Manhattan Beach. As I took drags off my cigarette and looked out at the ocean, a deep sense of alarm arose. What the f....... Did I really try to buy heroin today? I had spent the last ten years of my life as a clean cut, scholar athlete from the Midwest, who had a good job, nice car and a pretty girlfriend. Why was I trying to destroy it?

In this moment, I knew something massive was missing, something beyond what I was conditioned to want, something entirely different from sex, partying, success and adventure. How could I have this supposedly great life and still want to torch it? How could heroin even be on my list of possible options? Why wasn't I thinking about something more acceptable like grad school or marriage? Why was I looking for the eject button?

I didn't yet know the name of what I really wanted. I wanted initiation, I wanted a calling, I wanted to do something that mattered. Yet "soul" and "purpose" weren't in my vernacular. They simply weren't part of my inherited cultural software. I didn't know where to begin, who to ask, or what language to use to create my question. My friends weren't looking for it, or at least they didn't talk about it. My parents didn't talk about it. I had no trusted, soul-initiated elders who said, "Follow me on this path." or "Look here." So, I took another drag off my cigarette, sighed, and did all I knew how to do. I started thinking about happy hour.

Looking back on the hundreds of poor decisions and excesses that punctuated my twenties, and the dozen or so that landed me in hospitals and jails, what was driving them all was an ache, a hunger for purpose, my *hambre de alma*, an unremitting desire to break free from the white fog of my default world and initiate myself into the realm of the real, my own soul.

My promise to you is that your path isn't so foggy, so ignorant, dangerous and solitary. My promise to you is that your path will be well lit by science and our species' wisest beings. My promise to you is that our whole species will soon live in a world that knows what purpose is, how it can be cultivated, lived, and led with to form the basis of a rich, fulfilling life of impact, joy, creativity and service. This chapter will empower you with a deep knowledge of what a life purpose is, so that your journey is much more efficient, better-informed and less perilous than mine.

Over the next several pages, we'll explore The Four Levels of Purpose (No Purpose, Declared Purpose, Higher Purpose, Unitive Purpose), and within the third level - Higher Purpose - we'll explore a high-definition understanding of your higher purpose via The Purpose Tree (the ten aspects of your higher purpose).

So, what exactly is purpose?

There are many models that you can use to explain, dissect and illuminate your purpose. They range from simple bumper sticker mottos - "Go big or go home", or "Don't worry, be happy," or "Do unto others as you would have them do unto do", or "Follow your bliss" - to academic and esoteric musings, e.g., the whole fields of philosophy, psychology, mysticism and theology. Broadly, these purpose frameworks and mantras are all valid and can be organized into a single evolutionary model of purpose, one that allows you to find which level of purpose you are operating with and provides you with a path to up-level your life with a deeper connection to purpose if you so choose.

The Stages of Purpose

		Primary Concerns	Life Philosophy	Socioeconomic Roles	Tools for Growth
STAGE FOUR	Unitive purpose	Holism, Generativity, Evolution, Compassion	"I am all that was, is and will be. I am fully responsible for the human and ecological condition."	Industry Leaders, Humanitarians, Cultural Artisans	Integrity, Embodiment, Context, Mentors, Spiritual Practice
STAGE THREE	Higher / Soul purpose	Authentic Self-expression, Service, Impact	"I must creatively express my soul's purpose. I seek to purposefully live, lead, thrive and enjoy life."	Purpose-driven Leaders, Change Agents, and Innovators	Purpose Discovery Programs
STAGE TWO	Declared purpose	Esteem, Achievement	"I make my circumstances and can be anything I want. I must work hard to be the smartest, richest, best or most altruistic in order to be valued or loved."	Leaders, Professionals, Entrepreneurs	Personal Development Programs
STAGE ONE	No explicit purpose	Pleasure, Belonging, Safety	"My circumstances are my reality. I do not believe I can have any life I want, so I go to work and enjoy the weekends."	Employees / Consumers	

Stage 1: No purpose

This stage is where you have no known purpose, or are ignoring the calls to live purposefully. You might content yourself with life's simple pleasures and just sort of float from one experience to another, chasing pleasure, avoiding pain, and dealing with life's circumstances as they arise, regarding them as beyond your control. It's perfectly fine to be in this stage. Many people are content to live their entire lives without an explicit relationship to their life's purpose or the power to create a bigger life of impact, abundance, connection and fulfillment.

More often than not, however, this stage is temporary. I learned the hard way that living without purpose creates problems, like a pattern of unfulfilling relationships and jobs, depression, ER visits, addiction, arrests and other health concerns. However, this is a vital stage, as it presents the largest opportunity for growth. This is the fertile soil from which the desire for a life's purpose grows.

Many leadership and personal development programs, life coaches and career counselors offer a taste of purpose, by having you declare and create a purpose based on your desires and values. In doing so, you will find yourself breaching stage two.

Stage 2: Declared purpose

This stage is where you simply declare you have a purpose, really any purpose. You say you want to be skinny, or be a Marine, or be wealthy, or build an app, or have a hot husband, or buy a boat, or be number one in your industry, or live according to the Ten Commandments, or build casinos and put your name on them, or make sure your kids can go to the college of their choice, or even declare that you want to find your higher purpose, your soul's purpose. It's perfectly fine to have a declared purpose, but know this is a purpose that comes from your ego, and is rooted in the concerns, social values and cultural mores of your upbringing. It is not rooted in the deeper identity of your soul.

A declared purpose exists inside a game created by someone else, generally a composite of the games outlined by the morality of the market, your religion, your parents' and culture's narratives, e.g., America's wealthy/skinny/youth gospel or the rebel/artist/Apple coda of "Think Different". And this is perfectly fine. Many people live full, joyful, creative, connected and abundant lives within a simple declared purpose, like "Be the Best" and the "Golden Rule". They can live with integrity, be kind, contribute to the best of their abilities and do what they can to help those they love.

However, even the Golden Rule and the rebel are someone else's purpose.

For example, when I was in business school and began doing personal development work, I declared a purpose to create a conscious media company. Before business school, I worked in digital media, so I thought this would be a good way to use my skills and experience towards an end that improved matters for the species. So, I took actions consistent with that purpose, found business partners, did two internships in television production, and wrote a business plan.

On this path of declared purpose, I also bit off a number of low-hanging spiritual and personal development fruits: I stopped drinking, stopped eating meat, started meditating and doing more spiritual, personal and leadership development programs. But not because my soul demanded it. I forced myself to do these things because they were consistent with my declared purpose. To be a conscious media executive, I thought I needed to do conscious things. So, I bought mala beads, did cleanses, practiced yoga, did ecstatic/Five Rhythms dancing, went to the Green Festival, pared down my possessions, chanted "Hare Krishna" with my hairy hippy girlfriend, ate spirulina smoothies, kale and tofu, read spiritual books and basically did everything I thought a conscious person should do. All this was just another attempt on behalf of my ego. And I looked ridiculous. I was a 6'2" frat guy, banker bro from the Midwest, sitting in his Om t-shirt, drinking kombucha and reading Marx.

After about a year with this declared purpose, I was offered a job in renewable energy. I took it, because I needed the money and also, because it seemed like just as good of a purpose to create a more sustainable energy economy as to deliver people transformational media experiences. At this level of purpose, opportunism is still a driving force. A declared purpose does not come with access to immutable soul knowledge, or the grit required to be unstoppable. I got stopped in my declared conscious media purpose as soon as someone else said they would give me regular paychecks to make the world a better place. Thus, one declared purpose is on equal intellectual footing as any other declared purpose, really. You make them up.

This type of purpose comes with a low level of certainty, as your ego really did just choose it. Your ego just said, "Yup, that sounds like a good purpose. I'll make it my own." A declared purpose doesn't provide you with the clarity and bone-rattling certainty that helps you answer the BIG questions, like "Who should I marry?", or "What problem am I uniquely designed to solve for humanity?" or "What career should I pursue?", or "Should I spend $100k on graduate school?", or "Who should be my mentor?"

Of course, you can always attempt to answer these in accordance with your declared purpose, e.g., "What would Jesus do?" A declared purpose is more rewarding and feels more aligned than having no purpose, but there is always that tiny, irrepressible sense of fraudulence, illusion and uncertainty, that personal knowledge that you are making all this up and justifying your decisions with whatever anecdote, quote or sacred text that supports it. The doubt that comes with this level of purpose prevents you from playing full out and taking the big creative and leadership risks.

To truly answer the BIG questions with bone-rattling certainty, to unlock the boundless creativity of your soul, and unleash the unstoppable determination and dogged persistence required to keep taking action when the world says no to you,

you need a higher purpose. Your access to a higher purpose is to work with a Guide or do a purpose discovery program.

Stage 3: Higher purpose

This stage is available to you after doing purpose discovery work, wherein all ten aspects of your soul's purpose are revealed to you as true and sourced internally. Access to your higher purpose also includes a process wherein you get to understand the source of your resistance to living your purpose, the disempowering narratives and limiting beliefs that keep you from taking purpose aligned action. So, in addition to having the clarity, confidence and certainty of your higher purpose, you also have the power to be unstoppable in living and leading with your purpose. By unstoppable, I mean you won't hear "no" as a reason to stop. You won't get stopped by your reasons/ internal resistance. "No" will simply mean, "try it another way." A bad mood will simply mean that it is time to create a new enlivening context and act. Your higher purpose grants you the grit and tools required to overcome the obstacles in your way. More on this in "Chapter 8: Your Path to Purpose".

To step into your higher purpose, you'll need a high-resolution view of it, something more rooted and granular than a declared purpose. To fully explore the contours of your higher purpose, I offer The Purpose Tree, a navigational metaphor to unearth and connect all ten aspects of your higher purpose.

[The Purpose Tree is a revised, re-visioned and augmented version of the Purpose Octagon™ created by the Founder of the Purpose Guides Institute, Jonathan Gustin. Jonathan was the first to offer a broad synthesis of eight aspects of soul and purpose (vision, values, core powers, essence, giveaway, task, message, delivery system) based on the work of Tim Kelley, Bill Plotkin and his other influences. After being trained by him, I added a few other elements I believe are necessary to root purpose in the inescapable context of existence (worldview), to descend purpose into the body (flow) and emotions (call) and create an overarching life narrative (story) - and a navigational metaphor (tree) to relate and express them. If you are a history buff, coach, therapist, spiritual leader, change agent or human potential junkie, you might enjoy exploring humanity's long history with soul and the genesis of the Purpose Tree in "Appendix B: The History of Purpose".]

We will now consider the Purpose Tree in detail before moving on to Stage 4: Unitive Purpose.

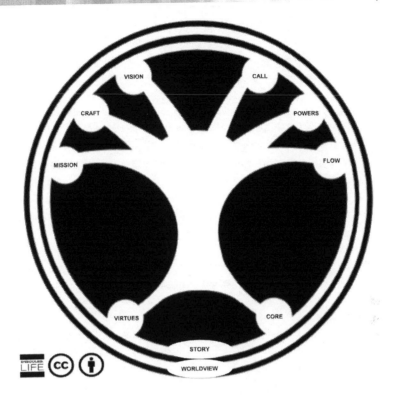

The 10 Aspects of Your Purpose:

- **The Call** - what most breaks your heart in the world, calling you to act
- **Vision** - your picture of the world perfected, pulling you into action
- **Powers** - your innate gifts, strengths and talents
- **Craft** - your highest contribution, your unique way of transforming others and achieving mastery
- **Mission** - your declaration to impact a group or dynamic in particular way and by when
- **Flow** - your most exhilarating, embodied activities resulting in loss of self-consciousness
- **Virtues** - your most cherished ideals and principles, what you are here to express and perfect, the ways of acting you want your life to be known for
- **Core** - your naturally radiating qualities
- **Story** - the central themes and lessons you have learned in life
- **Worldview** - your understanding of how reality works and the manner in which your identity is located within it

Dynamics:

- The Purpose Tree contains a vertical tension along the trunk, creating an upward pull of increasing energy and movement from above by The Call/Vision and generated from below by your Core/Virtues.
- The Purpose Tree also contains a creative vs. receptive horizontal tension. On the left are the more creative and ascendant aspects of purpose. On the right are the more receptive and inscendent aspects, what Thomas Berry refers to as "inscendence" a going within and fractally inhabiting of one's life from a place of soul. (Berry, p. 211, 1988).

The foundation of your purpose is the tree's root structure, containing the immovable, ever-present, unseen elements of your purpose, your deepest sense of identity as an individual (core and virtues). As the tree ventures upwards and the branches venture outwards, you increasingly express the bold, active, and declarative parts of your purpose, how you answer the call, craft your vision and focus your actions towards a desired impact. These are the unique ways your purpose interacts with, contributes to, enjoys and is rewarded by the world. All of these sit within your narrative of life (story) and your understanding of how the world works.

Now that you have general framework for your higher purpose, let's explore each aspect in greater detail, beginning with the call, craft, story and core. Although all aspects of your purpose are important, interrelated and contain lifetimes of growth, impact and evolution, I regard the below four as the four most powerful, as unlocking them will make the biggest difference in your experience of life and in your career, representing about 80% of the clarity most people need to live a BIG life. They answer your deepest and most foundational questions:

1. Who am I? (core)
2. How did I get here? Am I worthy of a big life? (story)
3. What most deeply moves me? What problem am I meant to solve? Who am I meant to serve? (the call)
4. What should I do? Which career allows me to make my highest contribution? Who are my masters, mentors and teachers? (craft)

The other six aspects round out the complete picture of who you are, establishing a deep soul-Cosmos/inner-outer coherence, empowering you to embody the world's soul as your own and moving you into Stage Four: Unitive Purpose. Now, let's explore your call, craft, story and core.

The Call

The call is what pulls you into your quest for purpose, meaning, evolution, adventure, mystery and service. It is the exciting possibility of being used by something larger than yourself to make a difference. It pulls you out of the norm, out of your concern for yourself, your safety, comfort and security. It calls you to evolve, to explore and become something you've never been, to achieve something you would never imagine being able to do.

> ...all work is a vocation, a calling from a place that is the source of meaning and identity, the roots of which lie beyond human intention and interpretation.
>
> -Thomas Moore (Moore, 1992, p. 181)

The call comes from two directions. First, you are tuned in to it through your deepest pain, a childhood wound that focuses your listening, that alerts you to similar wounding in the world. In this regard, each time you hear the call, it both excites you and breaks your heart. The call is a reminder of some form of abuse, abandonment, neglect, rejection or oppression that occurred in early childhood, and from which most if not all of your powers were born. This sacred wound forced you to generate yourself newly, develop tactics and strategies for coping with the wound. These ultimately became your powers - your strengths, gifts, abilities and talents. Each time you hear the call and answer it, you contribute your powers as medicine to simultaneously serve your people and heal your broken heart.

Secondly, the call doesn't occur in a vacuum. You are called into action by others. These are the people you are meant to serve, who have called you to step up, break free from your old ways of being and conception of self and step into your purpose, leadership and service.

The call is the emotional pull that has you craft a vision for a world that is free from your deepest pain. It impels you to master your craft and achieve mission after mission. The call empowers you to tell your story with authenticity and passion, such that every person you meet truly gets who you are and what your life is about.

Story

Your story gives you incredible self-authoring power over your life. It is the empowering way you tell the tale of all that you have overcome, what breaks your heart, the lessons you have learned, the powers you possess, your vision for the world and the person you have become as a result. At the heart of every human's story is their *upavita*, a Hindu word that refers to a golden thread woven through life. This thread is a theme, a story line that connects all the challenges you have overcome, lessons you have learned and the victories you have achieved. Connecting with your *upavita* does two beautiful things.

First it heals. It pulls your life into coherence, putting your whole life into the perspective of evolution and service. There are no longer incidents regarded as failures, only initiations that broke you open to become stronger and more resilient. In this sense, your story is your access to healing and knowing yourself as worthy of your vision, call and mission. Your story heals you and empowers you to see new opportunities to serve, empower and lead with your purpose.

Second, at the end of every good story is a moral, a message, the eternal truth or lesson that you have realized and learned in a variety of ways throughout your life; it is the one truth you feel most called to convey and propagate. It is what you want every person left with when they interact with you. You want them present to your story and truth, such that it empowers them to reach more fullness and wholeness as a human being. Your story feeds, sustains and supports your mission and craft.

Your story meets, connects and expresses your worldview. It is bound by what you understand about the world and brings it down to earth, empowering you to see and convey the totality of your purpose in the context of your largest sense of identity and the history of the species and Cosmos.

For example, consider my friend Jon. Jon is a Chinese Medicine doctor who was struggling in his career. He couldn't get excited about his clients' healing or the role he played in it, and as a result, his business was suffering. Even though Chinese Medicine is his craft, he was failing. He started driving for Uber and was contemplating a career change after spending 20 years studying with masters and developing his craft. It wasn't until he engaged head on with the story of his career that he could grow his business and do more good in the world.

Over the course of a few months and many conversations, he found his *upavita* and his story expanded beyond the technical performance of his practice (healing people efficiently and in a minimally invasive manner), to having spent 20 years empowering his clients to live big and bold lives of purpose, while disrupting the allopathic industrial illness industry. By cultivating his story to include the vital connection between his own challenges, spiritual journey and embodiment, as well as our global health epidemics and the power of purpose (ref. "Chapter 4: The Science of Purpose - Health"), he saw that what he was actually doing was empowering himself and his patients to be healthy, so that they could live their life's purpose, and make their highest contribution to change the world. With this pivotal recrafting of his story, from a tactical orientation to a historical and global one, he found new excitement for his career and was able to share this passion. Inside of this empowering story, he grew his practice, expanded his office, hired staff and created a network of other referral practitioners who are committed to the purposeful expression of their clients.

Core

Your core is a personal awareness of who you are without doing anything. It includes the essential, most specific and eternal aspects of your identity. It is comprised of your most essential qualities, who you are when you are abiding and resting. It is the effortless radiance of you. Your core is the feeling and sense of being you, the quality of coming from your heart, being fully at home, comfortable in your skin.

It is who you are when fear, judgment, limiting beliefs and self-consciousness simply have fallen out of view. Your core is the unmistakable, irreducible you-ness of you. It is a quality or set of qualities that have always been and always will be at your core. For example, the core of Socrates could be considered truth; the core of Christ could be considered compassion; the core of the Buddha could be considered awareness; the core of Churchill could be considered fortitude; and the core of Gandhi could be considered non-violence.

Your core is the same; it is immutable, true and complete from the day you were conceived until the day you die. As you progress on your purpose journey, you remove barriers, limiting beliefs and stories that prevent your core from radiating. In doing so, you reveal the deeper contours of your being and are empowered to make choices that allow you to more fully express who you are in every context, making your core more central in your life and eventually more obvious to others.

I describe my own core as joy, play and love. When faced with a difficult decision, I often ask myself, "What do I have to let go of to allow my core to radiate most brightly?" "What will bring a greater experience of joy, play and love?" "Which of these choices brings me more ease and allows me to simply be myself?" Often times what I find is that the freedom to be my core is a direct result of completing an outstanding task, restoring integrity or healing a fractured relationship. So, the core is not only abiding and receptive, but may also spark an action. These acts give me freedom to be playful, experience joy and create a world where love is more fully expressed.

Craft

> The more deeply our work stirs imagination and corresponds to images that lie there at the bedrock of identity and fate, the more it will have soul... work is central to the soul's *opus*. We are crafting ourselves - individuating...
> -Thomas Moore (Moore, 1992, p. 185)

Your craft is the unique way you add value in the world. Your craft is your soul-level unique transformative process, your genius, the specific way that you transform something or add value to someone, an organization, a dynamic or a situation. It is the result of learning and embodying the accumulated wisdom of the masters in your field and then innovating on top of them. Often it is the result of using many of your powers in a unique way to make your highest contribution to others. Dedication to craft is what produces Newton's calculus, Melville's *Moby Dick*, Shakespeare's

Sonnets, Tesla's electric car, Apple's iPhone and Rudolf Steiner's Waldorf School and permaculture method. As Thomas Moore, author of *Care of the Soul*, articulates...

> We may get to a point where our external labors and the *opus* of the soul are one and the same, inseparable. The satisfactions of our work will be deep and long lasting, undone neither by failures nor by flashes of success.
>
> -Thomas Moore (Moore, 1992, p. 199)

It is what indigenous cultures refer to as your giveaway or your gift to your tribe, the unique way you contribute to your people and future generations. It is highly specific, what Tim Kelley refers to as your *blessing* (Kelley, 2009). An apt analogy of Tim's for blessing is the washing machine. A washing machine takes dry dirty clothes and uniquely transforms them into wet clean clothes. It doesn't dry them, fold them or put them away. It doesn't grow the cotton, weave it, cut it, stitch it or retail it. It only does what it does. Your craft includes a deep knowledge of who you are meant to serve (often revealed by the call), the condition you find them in and the state in which you leave them.

For example, my craft is to awaken Shambhala Leaders, to empower people to change the world and lead with their life's purpose. Per the washing machine analogy, I take people without a strong connection to their higher purpose and turn them into purpose-aware, open-hearted, world-wizened and embodied industry leaders.

Shambhala Leadership expresses my vision and offers a new understanding for what it means to be a human at the individual and collective level. It includes all of my powers and missions, the processes for purpose discovery and embodiment, leadership, and awakening purpose at the collective levels of relationship, family, community, city-state, sovereign, species, planet and Cosmos. My craft commands me to learn from the greats in the fields of purpose (Tim Kelley, Bill Plotkin, Jonathan Gustin, Michael Meade), leadership (Warren Bennis, Dave Logan, Robert Kegan, Peter Senge, Bob Anderson & William Adams), political economy (Thomas Jefferson, Rianne Eisler, Joseph Stiglitz, Herman Daly, Charles Eisenstein, Paul Hawken), ecology (Joanna Macy, David Abrams, Rachel Carson) and culture (Marshall Mcluhan, Bill Kauth, Jean Baudrillard).

Awareness of your craft will reveal your masters as well, who you are meant to learn from and study with. Once revealed, you'll read their books, take their courses and start to formulate the specifics of your particular transformative process.

> Similar stories are told of Bach walking many miles to hear great music and spending late nights copying the works of composers he admired.
>
> -Thomas Moore (Moore, 1992, p. 188)

Your craft could take decades to come to full fruition. It literally could be something that only reaches its fullness late in your life. And even well after your craft reaches fullness, it is likely to open several lifetimes of questions and further refinements, something for others to fulfill on after you pass them the torch. It is also possible that your craft may only be appreciated many decades after your death like Van Gogh's *Bedroom in Arles* or Melville's *Moby Dick*. I realize that this might not be a very enlivening context, however, it is a very real possibility that your craft includes lifetimes of mastery and missions. That said, there will always be ways you can contribute your craft now, as it is to others, even if it has yet to fully mature.

Now it is not a requirement to immediately have your job be the explicit and only means of delivering your craft. Oftentimes, this takes a few years to affect a career shift towards your craft, especially if you have large financial obligations like college funds and mortgage payments. Or you may elect to keep your current job and just amplify opportunities to express your craft within it. For example, a person with a job in software sales may have a craft that is to empower people to see a new future for themselves. Her job is software sales, wherein she deeply connects with her clients and empowers them to more fully realize their purpose and create a new future through becoming a customer. Now she also does other things associated with her job, such as making forecasts and creating slide decks. And she may also deliver her craft outside of her job, e.g., as a parent, partner, friend or Little League coach.

With these four aspects of your purpose present, you can now answer the big life questions: "Who am I?" (core), "What am I doing here?" (call), "Am I worthy?" (story) and "What is my highest contribution?" (craft). These four aspects empower you to claim your place in the world.

> The soul... needs an articulate worldview, a carefully worked out
> scheme of values, and a sense of relatedness to the whole. It need
> a myth of immortality and an attitude toward death.
> -Thomas Moore (Moore, 1992, p. 204)

However, as I mentioned, this is only about 80% of the way to full-throttle purpose awakening. To move into the fullness of your purpose you'll need the ability to answer these other questions:

1. What does success look like? (vision)
2. What should I do right now? (mission)
3. What are my most valuable abilities? (powers)
4. How am I connected to and identified with the broadest possible understanding of reality? What is my place here? (worldview)
5. What brings me most alive and in the moment? (flow)
6. What are my most aligned ways of acting? (virtues)

Now let's explore these remaining aspects of The Purpose Tree.

Vision

Your vision is your picture of the world perfected. It is what all of existence would look like assuming you were a fully matured, highly evolved, benevolent dictator, one who could instantly reshape and bring fullness to humanity's expression on this planet. Your world vision answers your most sacred and deeply personal questions, such as: What world would fully and finally answer my call? What world would have my deepest pain rendered impossible and obsolete? Other questions your vision may satisfy are:

- What if every child's powers and craft were cherished and cultivated from day one and matured into a novel world-changing expression of what is possible, empowering us all to experience life more fully?
- What if the effect of our global political economy actually increased collective prosperity and strengthened biodiversity on the planet?
- What if self-doubt could be instantly erased?
- What if abundance fully and finally replaced lack?
- What if humanity discovered its species purpose?

Whatever your vision is, it is your stake in the ground, the flag you plant in your future, answering your deepest longing, what you declare is pulling you forward in your life and career. It is what gives your leadership its velocity and clarity, and allows others to craft their own vision and join you on a mission. An example of a beautifully articulated world vision is the pledge of the Pachamama Alliance, "a world that works for everyone: an environmentally sustainable, spiritually fulfilling, socially just human presence on this planet..."

Virtues

Your virtues are the lasting principles, ethics, ideals and standards by which you want your whole life to be known. They form the basis for your perfected and perfecting humanness, and guide you as you bring forth your vision. They form your ethical constraints, giving you the clarity to know which actions you will take and which actions you will not take. They empower your sacred "no", enable you to stand firm, exercise restraint, and hold out for a more purpose-aligned choice. They are the standards towards which you strive in all matters, the guidelines by which you craft your intentions, thoughts, speech and actions.

It is not possible to care for the soul while violating or disregarding one's own moral sensibility.

-Thomas Moore (Moore, 1992, p. 187)

For example, my virtues are integrity, wonder, courage and compassion. They empower me in making big decisions. Some of them are more natural descriptors of how I act, my perfected virtues (wonder and courage), and others are more aspirational, representing my growth edge of what I'm here to learn, embody and express, my perfecting virtues (compassion, integrity).

During a breakdown, I can break through it by stepping more fully into my virtues. Before I can do this, I need to really understand what happened.

1. First, I have to acknowledge what is so, what is the data of the situation, e.g., a partnership was not created.
2. Second, I have to distinguish the judgments, reasons, stories and meaning I'm making up about it, e.g., "It wasn't the right time", "I wasn't prepared enough", "I won't be successful".
3. Third, I get present to the emotions I'm experiencing as a result of what I'm making up about it, e.g., sadness, shame, anger.
4. Now that I've fully brought myself into the present, having expressed the data and distinguished the judgments and emotions, I can act from my virtues. To step back into powerful action, I take a look at which of my virtues needs to be expressed here.

Often it is all of them. Can I bring more wonder to the fore by exploring what was missing in the partnership? What specific actions were ineffective? I can also add greater integrity to the situation by addressing what was missing in the partnership proposal, and put forth a new structure to ensure that the concern is addressed. I can exercise compassion for myself by acknowledging that I work really hard, that my intentions were noble and that I took many purpose-aligned actions that simply didn't bear fruit. I can also be courageous, and re-open the discussion with the partner, despite their lack of interest, and inquire into any other ways I can be of service and meet a real need of theirs.

Mission

For your purpose to reach its full potential, you need the capacity to focus your efforts. Your mission is a focused and public declaration, combining your powers and craft, empowering you to live your virtues and dwell in your core as you actively manifest your vision. Your mission is specific. Your mission is designed to affect a particular community or dynamic in a particular way and over a certain amount of time.

In this way, missions are a unique aspect of your purpose, because you can complete them. They are unlike your roots (virtues and core), which can only expand and deepen. Your current mission will be complete at some point, and then you'll have an opportunity to go within, tell a new story, craft a new mission, and play an even bigger game with your life.

For example, Gandhi's vision was an independent state of India, and his mission was to peacefully liberate India from British rule as soon as possible. After he accomplished that, he needed a new mission to fulfill on his vision. And so, his soul revealed the mission of unifying India, to create a lasting peace between Hindus and Muslims. (Sadly, he was less successful with this mission.)

As perhaps a less august example, my current mission is to empower two million people to discover their life's purpose by 2020. Once I'm complete with that, I'll go within to see what there is to do; I'm already feeling the subtle pingings of what my future missions could be, e.g., awakening world leaders to their life's purpose, building an international team to evolve humanity's purpose, empowering governments to realize their purpose and create tangible pockets of collective purpose, building a quantified-self application that empowers people to bring their purpose more deeply into their career, relationships and community, building the "deep purpose state" (networks and marketplaces for connecting purpose-awakened people projects, partnership, jobs and dating), building a team to empower each country, industry and sector through an understanding of their collective purpose. These are all worthy endeavors, but I can only do one at time, so I choose the one in front of me: to powerfully deliver purpose discovery education to two million people.

Powers

Your powers consist of your full-level abilities, gifts, talents and strengths. These are the actions you perform that make a big difference for you and others. Distinct from your flow (see below), your powers include activities that greatly contribute to others, and express your unique place, form and function in the world. Your powers put you in gear and engage you, bringing you into the fullness of your soul's identity. People often know you for these actions.

> Power incubates within the soul and then makes its influential
> move into life as the expression of soul… the soul loves power…
> the soul is a gun, full of potential power and effect.
> -Thomas Moore (Moore, 1992, p. 129, 134, 135)

For example, my powers include public speaking, leadership, facilitation (group processes, e.g., men's work), writing, purpose guiding and teaching. When I'm doing these things, I make a huge difference for others. I love performing these tasks. Regardless of who the audience is or what the topic is, just put me on a stage or tell me to coach someone and I light up internally, something new gets created and I powerfully contribute to others.

Flow

Your flow activities are the most vital ways you enjoy and celebrate being alive in a human body. They make you feel alive, resulting in the feeling of being unified with the moment, as if the entire Cosmos conspired to make you and put you in this moment, to do this thing. They bring you alive, delight your senses and give you moments of transcendence, where your self-consciousness subsides and pure awareness arises. For example, I enjoy hundreds of activities that bring me into the present, e.g. when I sing karaoke, go on adventures to explore holy sites, play practical jokes, read philosophy, rock out to loud 80's music and 90's hip-hop, sip a good Islay scotch, write, eat ice cream sandwiches, play with children, play with pocket knives, snowboard, eat reubens or burritos, play rugby, see national parks like Yosemite and the Grand Canyon, make love, scuba dive, watch mafia and science fiction movies, follow politics, go to Burning Man, exercise my body, watch my fiancée sleep and enjoy outdoor concerts.

Of all of these, the ones that bring me most alive, deeply into flow, are 1. physical exercise, 2. reading great works, 3. singing karaoke, 4. being affectionate and intimate, and 5. exploring our species' holy sites. While these five bring me immense pleasure and feed my soul, I cannot make big life decisions based solely on some aggregate awareness of my passions/flow activities. That would be impossible. They are not a basis for making decisions about my career, where I live or my choice for a life partner. My flow activities don't give me access to my growth trajectory or clarity on my mentors. I certainly wouldn't marry someone simply because she also liked karaoke or she wanted to visit holy sites. Big life choices must be rooted in a more complete awareness of all the parts of your purpose.

Worldview

Of course, trees do not stand alone. Trees are often in a *stand*, embedded in the interconnected context of the forest; they are the home to thousands of species of insects and mammals, and thus serve a critical role in the forest ecology. As your core and virtues are your most unique and specific identity, your worldview is your broadest identity. It is your awareness of how reality works and how your identity is sourced by it. Your worldview is your understanding of and connection to the basic facts of existence, as well as your family, ancestors, the contributions of human civilization and the biosphere. Regardless of the scope of your story and mission, your purpose is rooted in, calls for and contributes to the health of the whole evolutionary ecosystem of humanity and the Earth.

...an ensouled body takes its life from the world's body..
-Thomas Moore (Moore, 1992, p. 172)

Most importantly, how you hear the call, create your vision, declare your mission, write your story and show up in the world depends on your worldview - what you know about the world and the story you use to express it. To continually hear the deeper call, your task is to adopt an ever-broader context and scope for your soul's purpose. This means being really curious about how the world works and how we got here, as the foundation upon which you contribute your powers and craft.

We live in a time in which context has never been more important. Indeed, there is a growing awareness of how important context is to the outcomes of our endeavors, to our health as humans and to humanity. Between 1900 and 2000, the use of the word "context" in the English language expanded by a factor of 20 times (Google Book Search, 6/13/2017). With the advent of context harnessing and worldview expanding tools like Wikipedia and social media, having an expansive worldview has become a core value of our species, as all of our main institutions, practices and ideologies (Christianity, Islam, capitalism, globalization, industrialization, internet, resource imperialism), have a global origin, scope, purpose and/or scale.

Yet few of us explicitly engage in the act of questioning and expanding our worldview so we can listen for a deeper call. This is why worldview is critical. From one view, an action can be seen as optimal, and from another, suboptimal. For example, a pregnant mother's decision to smoke a cigarette: from the perspective of the joy of smoking, she optimally chooses to smoke a cigarette to aid her enjoyment; from a larger perspective, knowing both the pleasure of smoking and the effects of smoking on a developing fetus, this action can be seen as clearly suboptimal.

As you move along your purpose journey, you'll discover that you can play an active role in expanding and developing the worldview that governs the expression and evolution of your purpose. As your worldview grows larger, your purpose is less constrained, the call gets louder and you become more powerful, free and self-expressed. In addition to doing purpose discovery work and removing your old meaning filters, you can also expand your worldview by understanding the consensus opinion of experts and the recent research in a number of important fields such as psychology, philosophy, religion, economics, ecology, politics, history and culture.

Your worldview is like the map upon which you live your mission. If your map is tiny and rigid, your mission will only extend to the end of your driveway. In this case, the extent to which you can live your purpose will also be tiny (and also continually challenged by others with larger maps, and thus with more power and freedom, for they see more of the territory, best practices and the impacts of your actions than you do). But if your map includes a more expansive and evolutionary understanding of the entire human, ecological and Cosmic territory, then your call will also be planetary or Cosmos-sized and your missions will be limited only by your imagination. If you want to play a big game with your purpose, you also have to develop a big and expanded worldview.

Once you have cultivated a high-definition understanding of your soul's purpose and have access to all ten aspects, you will feel yourself bursting, wanting to move your purpose, live and embody it, and lead others. Your soul naturally rises to meet and improve the world. As this bubbles up, you will find yourself pulled into the next level of purpose. To move more deeply into Stage Three, please explore these tools for developing your higher purpose: purpose guiding, shamanic journeys, medicine ceremonies and vision fasts.

Stage 4: Unitive Purpose

This is the stage wherein your higher purpose descends and integrates into your tissues as a way of being, and also goes global in the form of leadership. In this stage, you begin to function as, of, by and for the whole Cosmos and experience Unitive Purpose. To move into and through the Unitive Stage you have three key tasks:

1. **Mentorship** - where you seek out mentorship, books and programs from masters germane to your craft and mission.
2. **Integrate and Embody** - a multiple-year process of aligning and upgrading, every key area of your life to express your purpose, such that you move effortlessly and seamlessly between contexts and circumstances fully rooted, embodied and integrated.
3. **Purpose-aligned Action** - with your mentors and masters at your side, and an explicit relationship to your expanding worldview, you now are called to act, express and lead with your purpose.

Mentorship

As every soul, craft and vision is unique, every soul's need for mentors is unique. In the discovery process, your soul will reveal to you your masters and mentors. You will read their books, take their programs, and when you feel the call, you will work directly with one or more of them. For example, when I became clear that purpose guiding was essential to my craft, I identified the leading voices in the field (Bill Plotkin, Jonathan Gustin, Tim Kelley, Rod Stryker, Michael Meade), read their books and began my training and certification with Jonathan Gustin at the Purpose Guides Institute.

Integrate and Embody

Your access to embodying your purpose and your ever-expanding worldview, is through your integrity, becoming a leader who is the walking embodiment of purpose, taking consistent action, learning and reconciling all areas of your life (health, career, romance, family, community, finances, spirituality) with your purpose. Once you are through the purpose discovery process, you'll see the necessary alignment changes you need to make in these key life areas such that your day-to-day life is the perfect container and support system for your soul's purpose. You'll likely take on leadership programs, as well as spiritual, contemplative, somatic and integrative practices such as yoga, cross-training and martial arts to descend this new soul identity into your tissues. As you move through Part Two, you will explore integrity and leadership as the keys to the integration/unitive phase of your purpose journey.

Purpose-aligned Action

The discovery process is only the beginning of your purpose journey. Your access to staying connected to your soul is active - crafting and completing missions / your Purpose Projects. In the active expressions of your purpose, you will learn more by a factor of ten about your soul's purpose than in the initial discovery phase. You will see how your purpose must rise to meet the world as it is, how it needs to evolve and expand to make an even greater impact, and how you will need to grow, develop and expand to contain and support the expansion of your purposeful impact in the world. As you move through Parts Three and Four of this book you will discover these new horizons of impact.

Now that you understand the evolution and progression of your relationship to purpose, you need only declare what kind of purpose you want. Simply state that you wish to have no purpose (Stage 1) and just experience life as it comes. That's perfectly fine. Or you can declare a purpose right now (Stage 2). Just pick a person you admire or an outcome deemed desirable by others, declare yourself to be that person's disciple or in service of that desired outcome. That's also perfectly fine. Or you can reveal your higher purpose (Stage 3), by doing the work in Part Two and moving through the world with a deep understanding of who you are and what you came to do. This is also perfectly fine. Or you can declare that you will lead humanity in fulfilling its purpose (Stage 4), by unleashing your purpose, embodying it, meaningfully evolving your worldview beginning with Part Three, by choosing your masters and mentors, and playing a big game that elevates the whole human and ecological condition, beginning in Part Four.

Before you go any further, I request you take a moment to reflect: Which type of purpose feels most aligned with who you really are inside?

How to talk about your purpose

If you choose to have no purpose, it's easy to talk about purpose. Just say purpose is not for you and look for friends and colleagues who share your view. If you choose a declared purpose, just tell people what you are up to, do your best to justify it. Choose high-achieving friends and colleagues that share your view and are in-action living their declared purpose.

However, if you choose to awaken to your higher or unitive purpose, your task is to craft an authentic experience of life, requiring your purpose to be out front as the guiding principle by which you craft your relationships, career, family, and community. I have found that it can be difficult to express your purpose, especially when you have ten distinct parts of it. To succinctly express your purpose, it is helpful to distill your purpose into a powerful statement that expresses who you are, what you are doing and why you are doing it. To do this, a mission statement is quite useful. Mission statements allow you to boldly and succinctly tell people what you are up to in your big soulful life.

Your mission statement connects a few key aspects of your higher or unitive purpose. It is a concise reminder of who you are (core and virtues), what you care about (call and vision) and how you do it (powers and craft). After you've done your purpose work, you can craft your mission statement by following this formula: "As a (*core or virtues*) person/man/woman/citizen, I offer my (*craft*) for (*certain people or species*) in service of (*the call or vision*)."

Here's how I created my mission statement: First, I looked at the ten aspects of my purpose. As of the Spring of 2017, these are:

Vision: 7.5 billion humans awakened to their individual soul's purpose and connected to the tri-fold collective purpose of (1) Humanity - awakening every human to their purpose; (2) Earth - as Earth's apex ecosystem steward, cooperating politically, economically, culturally and ecologically in service of a just, sustainable, abundant, joyful and peaceful human presence on Earth; and (3) the Cosmos - embracing and leading the continued evolution of the Cosmos.

Virtues: Courage, compassion, integrity and wonder.

Powers: Purpose guiding, teaching, writing, speaking, leadership.

Core: Joy, play, love.

Craft: Shambhala Leadership.

Mission: Make purpose discovery education available to two million people before 2020.

Story: I know the pain of spending a quarter-century living someone else's life (declared/default purpose), and I exist to create a culture and political economy such that every human knows and is known for their purpose, and they are well-compensated as they make their highest contribution to the world. I have learned over and over that I am all that is, was and will be, that I am fully responsible for the human and ecological condition. My work in the world is my way of expressing this truth.

Flow: Physical exercise, reading great works, spiritual tourism, karaoke, physical affection.

Worldview: The worldview that informs this call and my mission is a global, integral, Cosmic and evolutionary perspective (which we will explore in greater detail in Part Three). Recent developments in physics confirm the existence of a unified reality, one also pointed to by numerous spiritual and religious traditions. Currently, however, our society, government and economy is structured upon a worldview of separation and individualism. A report from the United Nations' International Panel on Climate Change, based on over 9,200 peer reviewed studies (UN, 2014) confirms that this worldview of separation and individualism, as expressed through ecological overharvesting, mining and cultural consumerism, is accelerating the collapse of complex human civilization. My context includes the knowledge that our planet's governments and leaders are aware of these dynamics, but have been ineffective in addressing them.

Public and private institutions have been ineffective or resistant to making the changes needed to ensure the survival of the human species and the achievement of a just, sustainable and peaceful human presence on Earth. A cultural purpose movement is required to manifest this political, economic and ecological shift, to expedite the formation of new purposeful institutions, and ensure the survival of the human species.

The Call: The loudest call I hear is from the future, those who have yet to be born. I also hear the call of the living, the cry for a meaningful life, to be engaged making our highest contribution. I am called to transform culture through the broad and rapid distribution of purpose discovery and leadership development education.

When I combine my virtues, craft and vision, my mission statement becomes:

"As a man of integrity, compassion and courage, I empower people to awaken their Shambhala Leadership in service of a world that works for all beings."

Taken as a whole, your mission statement will become your battle cry, your "larger than you" identity, your place in the world, the unique vector in space-time that your soul inhabits, the one sentence that integrates and expresses your robust purpose. This statement is a guidewire for powerful decision-making in your career, love life, health, family, and community.

Now that you understand what purpose is, and the territory of your purpose exploration and continued evolution, let's dive into how it actually works in your life.

CHAPTER 3

How Does Purpose Work?

"The biggest difference purpose work made in my life is that I became clear that I had to do more than just sell. I wanted to have more impact, entrepreneurial freedom and creativity," said Allan, a startup founder and former client. I was catching up with him three years after our work together.

"Awesome, so how is your life different? What shifted?", I inquired.

He responded, "In 2015, I launched my company, built a great team, raised a significant round of financing, got married and had a child. As CEO, I now have the freedom to create, to make high-impact decisions. Our team has a shared sense of purpose to do right by each other and each others' families, and strike the balance between family values and our commitment to our team's success."

"Wow, no kidding!!! That's fantastic, Allan!"

As I learned later in that call, this was driven by his newfound comfort in sharing himself more freely with his colleagues and partners and inspiring them to join him on his mission. He is a testament to living life out loud, not just as an entrepreneur, but also as a husband and father.

You might be wondering how knowing your higher purpose will impact your life on a day-to-day basis. My colleague and mentor, Chris Kyle, and I developed a 3-part model for expressing how purpose works. (Chris is the co-creator of the Man on Purpose Course, The Conscious Men Summit and The Power of Purpose Summit, as well as a co-leader of the Mankind Project's New Warrior Training Adventure and the Founder of Launch Academy.) Chris and I believe your higher purpose delivers you three powerful functions:

1. Your higher purpose **reveals** the deeper truth of who you are and the talents you naturally possess;

2. Your higher purpose is the **guiding compass** for your life - a decision-making tool that empowers you to set firm boundaries, make purpose-aligned choices and lead; and

3. Your higher purpose **aligns** all aspects of your life (career, romance, health, family, community, spirituality, finances) and allows you to embody your purpose in all you do.

When taken together, your higher purpose becomes the most powerful decision-making tool you have, one that lets you step into greater fullness through purpose aligned-action. However, there is a lot of confusion as to how this actually works, as purpose is often used interchangeably with other terms like happiness and meaning.

What is the difference between purpose, happiness and meaning?

Though these terms bear some similarities and share some causative threads, in practice, they are distinct.

Meaning. Meaning is a fundamental human capacity, as fundamental as breathing, eating and sleeping. By fundamental, I mean there is no human who doesn't make meaning. As a fish swims in the inescapable context of water, humans swim in the escapable context of making meaning. By being a human, you constantly seek and attribute meaning to words, situations, gestures, actions, objects and meaning created by other people. As you cannot just decide to stop breathing or eating and expect to live, you cannot escape making meaning of the world, but you can be more conscious about the meaning you create, and from where this meaning is sourced.

For example, a very commonly cited meaning that people choose in their life is the meaning of romantic love, family and children. However romantic love, family and children are not all there is in life, nor do they represent the totality of one's life purpose. Romantic love, family and children are only expressions of, or vehicles through which, one lives a life purpose. Because we fall in and out of love, because family members grow old and die, because children grow up and out, we are not without our life's purpose when they choose to leave us. But rather, we are forced by the cycles of life to create and explore new sources of meaning. You can choose the meaning you give to the world and your circumstances. You can take on other people's meaning, refuse it, create your own, and/or discover your internal meaning, aka purpose. You can choose an empowering interpretation or a disempowering interpretation of events. This is entirely your choice as a meaning creator.

Happiness. Happiness, on the other hand, is an emotional and psychological experience, described as ranging from contentment to ecstatic joy. This phenomenon is also marked by a biochemical process in your brain, involving various neurotransmitters (dopamine, serotonin and oxytocin). Happiness occurs regardless of whether or not you know your purpose. What makes you happy makes you happy, whether that's founding an orphanage, watching TV, planting a garden, meditating or drinking a beer. However, as we explored above, as you have control over your narrative and your worldview, you also have a strong measure of control over what makes you happy.

An important distinction here is that, regardless of your worldview or narrative, if you pursue your own happiness as its own end, you will face the ugly end of the law of diminishing returns, wherein each successive happiness experience you pursue is less and less rewarding, or what psychologists call "hedonic normalization". Hedonic normalization means that increasing volumes of chemicals, purchases or experiences are required to register the same experience of happiness.

Over the course of your life, you have experienced a number of low hanging pleasure fruits, like sugar, alcohol, new clothes, gossip and new sexual partners. You likely witnessed the happiness effects wear off as quickly as they came on. Perhaps you became curious or motivated to find new sources of pleasure. Frequently folks turn to their passions or hobbies or decide to climb the tree of knowledge (to understand the universe and experience mental happiness). However, even a life devoted to hobbies, passions and knowledge will, without an explicit purpose in mind, also encounter the law of diminishing returns - hedonic normalization. Eventually we are called to descend our roots into the Earth for a deeper contentment, a sense of permanence and place. We are called to source our identity and experience of life internally, from soul. This shift from the happiness of pleasure, passion, hobbies and knowledge to the contentment of soul is what this book is designed to expedite.

Purpose. Purpose is a unique type of meaning. It is personal and organic. It is an awareness of who you are. Its results often include developing a narrative for your life and an empowering action plan to express this awareness. Provided you hold your purpose lightly as something continually growing and evolving within you, and that you have taken on evolving your worldview, your purpose is a type of meaning that you get to cultivate and co-author.

Moreover, purpose has nothing to do with the frequency of the experience of happiness, although the types of joy you can experience do vary depending on your connection to your life's purpose. Of the two primary types of happiness - lasting fulfillment and fleeting gratification - folks who have a strong connection to their life's purpose tend to gravitate towards fulfilling endeavors (building, learning, experimenting, creating, serving, connecting), endeavors that produce increasing psychological returns. Folks who have a weak connection to purpose tend to gravitate towards gratifying endeavors (chemicals, screens, consumerism), endeavors that produce decreasing psychological returns. One isn't necessarily better than the other, but the purpose-driven/fulfillment schema is correlated with better overall health, higher levels of leadership, income and wealth, and more exciting and loving relationships, as you'll discover in the next few chapters.

Oftentimes, the importance of connecting with your soul's purpose is sudden, such as during or after a war, a serious illness, the loss of a job, the dissolution of a marriage, or death of a loved one. At this point, the pursuit of surface-level pleasures, passions, and hobbies ends and the quest for soul purpose begins, heightening the desire for truth about yourself and world. In these "purpose crises", a deep hunger is formed for a soul-initiation, a moment in time when everything that is not the soul, that is not truth, that is not your unique reason for being falls out of focus or burns away, igniting the desire for communion with your soul and its message: your life's purpose.

Purpose also gives you greater capacity for discipline, and a reason to endure discomfort. You now have a reason to develop yourself, to pick programs, masters and mentors to bring your purpose into a greater expression. Your path to purpose is a mature acceptance of the fact that to become a soul-initiated adult, to live a life on fire and full of purpose, things might get uncomfortable on occasion, and that to keep moving through the story of your life, you must befriend and overcome your fear of change and avoidance of pain. In making hard, purpose-aligned choices, you enter the crucible: you become an adult, the type of person that can endure discomfort in the near term. As Viktor Frankl so beautifully illuminated in *Man's Search for Meaning*,

> In some ways suffering ceases to be suffering at the moment it finds a meaning, such as the meaning of a sacrifice. (Frankl, 1946, p. 113)

Through this discomfort lies all growth, the eternal source of your grit, resilience, energy and the confidence that makes hardship in the name of your life's purpose endurable. From the perspective of your story, you can see all the mistakes and failures of your past as teachings. You can hold all of your experiences with great reverence as comprising the fundamental conditions that created and refined your unique powers.

> "There are two types of pain. The pain of discipline and the pain of regret. Choose."
>
> -Anonymous

When you are connected to your purpose, you have a BIG powerful vision for your life, one that puts you in the driver's seat of your life, internally sources your identity, and to an increasing extent, also identifies you with the world, as your purpose is not inert, it puts you in action to answer the call. This soul-level identity is also the only identity that truly qualifies and empowers you to lead (see "Chapter 12: Shambhala Leadership"). Regardless of your current station, regardless of public opinion or your fortune, your purpose gives you the power to make new decisions and act.

As a result of this freedom to act, to make decisions that express your purpose, your success and fame will still be nice and enjoyable, but will be held much more lightly, as mere chapters in the long book of your life. Success and fame will come and go, but your purpose remains.

Now that you have clarity as to how purpose actually works in your life, let's explore all the amazing scientifically-validated results of choosing a life of purpose.

CHAPTER 4

The Science of Purpose - Health

"I quit smoking," said my Aunt Katie.

"What?! Congratulations! That's amazing. How did you do it?"

My Aunt Katie was one of my first clients. For 40 years, my Aunt Katie smoked Marlboro Light 100's, but smoking wasn't on her mind when we began our work together. She was in the middle of two terrible losses, the death of her mother (my grandmother) and the death her life partner, Fred. She was looking to find the firm ground beneath her, to connect with what was true about her, to create a life she loved amidst her loss, grief and the chaos of life without two of the people who had meant the most to her. By the end of our work together, she found a new sense of wholeness and self-love and was able to throw herself more fully into her artistic and culinary pursuits. Then, nine months after our work had completed, she called me to tell me about this new and unexpected development.

"I just realized how stupid it is. I don't need it. So, I just stopped cold turkey. It's been hard, but I can do it, because I know it's not me."

"Wow, I'm so proud of you, Aunt Katie."

"I've spent tens of thousands of dollars on this stupid thing and I've got nothing to show for it. It's stupid, so I'm done."

My Aunt Katie realized that there was no longer a purpose-sized hole inside of her, so she didn't need to fill it with anything, not with mindless addictions or anything else that didn't serve her fullest expression. She could just be fully and finally herself, and end her 40-year love affair with Philip Morris.

Katie is not an anomaly. When the electric current of purpose takes hold, people generally start making better decisions. They often quickly exit a host of dysfunctional habits, patterns, relationships and jobs in order to more fully express their life's purpose. Recent research has validated these amazing results. In the last 35 years, research from leading institutions such as Harvard, Stanford, Cornell, and UCLA has increased our understanding as to why purpose is the key to a long healthy life. As you'll discover in the research presented in following chapters, purpose now joins many commonly accepted best practices for life, such as a good night's rest, a balanced diet, and an active lifestyle.

The concept of a life's purpose may seem a little New Agey or in the domain of religion, mystics and philosophers, but it is now no longer an article of faith or something that people do when they get bored with fantasy football and flash sales. It's is now a measurable and achievable best practice. In 1964, two psychologists, James Crumbaugh and Leonard Maholick, were inspired by Victor Frankl's book, *Man's Search for Meaning*, and developed the 20-question Purpose in Life (PIL) test. The PIL test quantifies the extent to which A. one believes that life has a purpose, B. one can uphold a personal value system and C. has the motivation to achieve future goals and overcome future challenges (Crumbaugh, Maholick, 1963, pp. 43-48). Since then, researchers have been able to link purpose with:

- A long life
- A healthy heart
- A sound mind
- Feeling content
- Loving and high-attraction relationships
- Higher levels of income and wealth
- Leadership
- A more equal, kind, generous, curious and tolerant society
- A more sustainable, just and abundant economy

Is Purpose Religious?

No, not necessarily. The PIL test doesn't distinguish the source of the purpose and meaning in your life (ref. A, above). It makes no explicit distinction between a purpose sourced in religion or a purpose sourced internally. However, in 2012, researchers at the University of Gdansk, Poland discovered that purpose in life and religious beliefs are independently occurring phenomena, with many people who believe in God not connected to their own unique purpose and vice versa (Blazek, Besta, 2012). Further, it should be noted that around the same time that we started studying purpose (1960's), many folks in modern societies began to find it difficult to fully outsource the meaning of their lives to religion. As individualism and liberalism spread from mere intellectual developments into mainstream culture during the 1960's, for many people it became clear that institutional religions:

1. Did not offer relatable and practical ethical guidance, as many religious texts condoned slavery, sexism, patriarchy, genocide, murder and rape (vs. the emerging cultural value of equality expressed by the Women's Suffrage, Civil Rights and Sexuality Rights Movements), and

2. Did not empower people to realize their full potential due to institutional religion's role in restricting creativity, freedom, sexuality and soul (vs. the emerging 60's, Rock 'n' Roll, "hippie" culture that celebrated their diverse expression), and

3. Did not offer a cosmologically accurate interpretation of observable reality (e.g., Book of Genesis vs. science, carbon-dating, evolution, Big History and comparative religious studies).

Thus, purpose research seems to have co-arisen with the cultural shifts of the 1960s (accelerating the long diminishing cultural influence of institutional religions that began during the Enlightenment).

However, personal purpose may actually be the glue that unites the values of reason and faith, of individualism and collectivism, of selfishness and service. As you'll discover in the next four chapters, regardless of your political, religious or ethical views, finding your personal purpose is at once a supremely selfish endeavor - creating a healthy body, an abundant career and rewarding relationships - AND it is also a supremely *selfless* endeavor: orienting our lives in service of others, towards something larger than ourselves. As you will explore in "Chapter 7: The Science of Purpose - A Better World", and Part Four, the combined effects of humanity living on purpose could be the missing piece in solving the lion's share of our social, economic, political and environmental problems, and filling in the cultural and ethical gap left in the slow retreat of institutional religion from power.

Let's begin our exploration of the Science of Purpose with the first of the selfish reasons: your health.

Purpose Creates a Long Life of Vitality

Purpose creates both healthier cell structures and the motivation to make great diet and exercise choices. Although research has given us scientific language to prove these benefits, finding your purpose has long been advocated by philosophers (like Socrates and Plato), psychologists (like Frankl and Maslow), mystic poets (like Rumi and Whitman) and religious figures (like Jesus and Krishna). These luminaries believed deeply in the body-mind-soul-spirit connection, the deep connection between consciousness and form, and knew that by changing our being and thinking to align with our deepest truth and our purpose in life, we can change our bodies, our lives and our world. Luckily, we no longer have to take them at their word.

In a longitudinal study on Purpose in Life (PIL) and longevity, Dr. Patrick Hill of Carleton University and Dr. Nicholas Turiano of University of Rochester Medical Center (Hill, Turiano, 2014) discovered that "finding a direction for life and setting overarching goals for what you want to achieve can help you actually live longer, regardless of when you find your purpose."

Drs. Turiano and Hill reviewed results across age groups, and also concluded that the sooner we find purpose, the healthier we will be and the longer we will live. It appears that purpose does more than give you a reason to live, it gives you the means and physiology by which to live it. It seems as though purpose provides an internal navigation that keeps us on a healthy path, potentially empowering us to make healthy choices in our diet and lifestyle. Numerous studies confirm Hill's findings. The now famous Ohsaki study suggests that purpose can **extend your life by up to seven years!** (Sone, Nayaka, 2008). A strong connection to your life's purpose reduces your mortality rate by 23% (Hill, Turiano, 2014), your chance of having a stroke by 50% (Boyle, 2016), and of dying from a stroke - reduction in stroke mortality rate by 72% (Koizumi, 2008).

How does your purpose do all those things? Your purpose provides the internal motivation and clarity needed to make and sustain life-enhancing changes in your lifestyle, including:

1. Self-care

Connecting to your purpose gives you the energy for self-care and a renewed reverence for your body. It empowers you to nurture your body and mind with a healthy diet and regular exercise. Research from the University of Texas, Austin has shown that folks who know their purpose exercise more (Holohan, Suzuki, 2008). Your self-care ensures that you are best equipped to give away your powers toward the ends that most fulfill you and your life's purpose.

> "I have one life and one chance to make it count for something...
> I do whatever I can, wherever I am, whenever I can, for as long as
> I can with whatever I have to try to make a difference."
> -President Jimmy Carter

Further, purpose has a positive correlation with preventative health, as a recent study by Dr. Eric Kim at the Harvard School of Public Health illuminates (Kim, Strecher, Ryff, 2015). Dr. Kim and his colleagues were interested in the mechanics behind why people who know their purpose live longer, healthier lives. They discovered that compared to people with the lowest purpose scores, people with the highest purpose scores were 121% more likely to obtain flu shots, 228% more likely to obtain cholesterol tests and 133% more likely to obtain colonoscopies.

Moreover, women with high purpose scores were 330% more likely to obtain a mammogram and 210% more likely to receive a pap smear, while men with such scores were 386% more likely to receive a prostate exam. It appears, then, that when purpose is present, there is a concern for the life and well-being of the purpose itself which, of course, needs your sound mind and body, to be expressed.

2. Decreased appetite for vice and time for distraction

Despite the numerous passionate artists who took their relationship to drugs and alcohol to the limit and beyond, a life of purpose leaves little time or appetite for excessive vice or other self-destructive behaviors. This is not to say you do not or cannot bring yourself to enjoy a glass of wine or a cigar, but that your desire for habitual vices diminishes. When your purpose takes root, over time there arises a diminished desire for an excessive or indulgent lifestyle, a diminished desire to erode the biological foundation of a purposeful life with overeating, narcotics, smoking and excessive drinking, and a diminished desire to distract ourselves from our lack of purpose with consumerism, or sitting on the couch playing video games, or watching sports, reality TV or Netflix-binging the day away. Once that purpose-sized hole is filled with purpose, there simply isn't room for much else.

When you know your life's purpose, your primary source of pleasure is its expression in your career, relationships, family and community, as well as your own growth and development towards greater wholeness and impact in the world. Living your purpose and improving the human and ecological condition becomes your video game. Achieving optimum health is just one of the ways you get to play the game. Purpose can be an all-consuming endeavor, as many become fully engaged by it seeking to align every aspect of life, including leisure time, in the service of that purpose.

The Physiology of Purpose

It is likely that purpose changes your physiology. An aspect of your purpose, your story, is an empowering background narrative that can reduce stress and anxiety in times of discord, providing you with a sense of alignment, balance and peace even when things aren't going your way. This is important because the psychological experience of stress is accompanied by the increased levels of cortisol, norepinephrine and adrenaline in your body. According to Vivian Diller, PhD, when these three are present, they affect the body in the following ways (Diller, 2013). They:

1. Accelerate your heart rate
2. Inhibit your digestion
3. Constrict your blood vessels
4. Decrease your hearing and vision
5. Impair your cognitive function

6. Increase your blood pressure
7. Increase your blood sugar levels
8. Harden your arteries
9. Increase your fat storage
10. Lower your levels growth hormone
11. Increase your chances of osteoporosis
12. Disrupt your sleep
13. Decrease your muscle and collagen
14. Weaken your immune system

Further, research has shown that people who know their purpose sleep better. Harvard's Dr. Eric Kim discovered that for every point increase on a 6-point purpose scale, people have a 16% reduction in sleep disturbances (Kim, Hershner, Strecher, 2015). Of course, getting a good night's rest feels good, but more importantly researchers at the Division of Sleep Medicine at Harvard Medical School have concluded that poor quality sleep is linked with obesity, diabetes, heart disease, early mortality, hypertension, depression, anxiety and stress (Harvard Division of Sleep Medicine website, 6/27/2017). So, if purpose increases the quality of your sleep, it may also prevent a whole host of life threatening conditions.

It's possible that purpose improves the function of every biological life process. Research at UCLA and UNC from Drs. Frederickson and Grewen has linked the feelings of eudaimonia, which is a Greek term to reflect the well-being and optimism (*eu*) associated with purpose and virtues (*daimon*), with stronger cell structures and healthier genes, suggesting that "the human genome may be more sensitive to qualitative variations in well-being than are our conscious affective experiences." (Frederickson, Grewen, et al, 2013) Research at the University of Wisconsin from Drs. Ryff and Heller, has revealed a potential link between purpose in life and cell structures, by finding that purpose in life is correlated with lower levels of cortisol, which is the hormone that destroys cell tissue and ages us. Further they found that those who are connected to their purpose are more likely to have a strong heart, a healthy nervous system and immune system. (Ryff, Heller, et al, 2016)

So, the more relevant question may be: *What part of your body doesn't purpose improve?*

The Psychology of Purpose

Purpose has also been linked with how you think and feel. A study by Drs. Windsor, Curtis and Luscsz at Flinders University of Australia, confirm that people who know their purpose have better brain processing speed, more accurate memory and lower levels of disability and depression (Windsor, Curtis, et al, 2015). Purpose has been linked with a 42% increase in the experience of well-being and joy (Metlife,

2010). Purpose has also been demonstrated to be an effective strategy to combat depression in adults (Phillips, 1980) and teens (Telzer, Funglini, et al, 2014).

For many people struggling with depression, finding purpose may be a lifesaver. With the explosion in suicide rates in wealthy countries like the United States, purpose could play a huge role in restoring dignity and hope and, indeed, save the lives of those who have been marginalized by society or feel excluded from the American Dream. Purpose may even be an effective complementary means of rehabilitating our veterans, who return from the horrors of war with a skillset that is not designed for civilian life and many work environments.

The suicide rate of middle-aged (35-65) Americans has increased 30% between 1999-2010 (CDC.gov, 6/29/17), with US veterans committing suicide at an alarming rate of 22 per day (Department of Veteran Affairs, 6/29/17), twice the average of that of the rest of the country. It can be said that we have a suicide epidemic.

Purpose could play a vital role in restoring dignity and a lust for life for these groups who battle daily with the choice to end it all. Of course, purpose discovery and embodiment work is no substitute for treatments for acute psychopathologies, nor other social and economic programs that serve these groups, but it could prove to be a powerful ally in helping people establish a deeper identity than their injuries, feelings or circumstances may point to, create a life of vitality, abundance and love, and resurrect a sense of personal dignity and hope.

But how does purpose actually change a person's inner state?

Purpose is a Best Practice for Mental Health

Your purpose makes you smarter. Drs. Lewis, Turiano, Payne and Hill discovered that people who know their purpose in life have higher scores for memory, executive functioning and overall cognition (Lewis, Turiano, et al, 2016). As such, it is not surprising that being connected to your life's purpose, doubles the likelihood of learning something new each day (Gallup Healthways Global Well-Being Index, 2013). Since you are more engaged with your life (versus just trying to get through it to reach the evening/weekend/retirement), your mind is more active and your brain actually becomes healthier, creating new neural pathways, as demonstrated by the connection between discovering purpose and a decrease in the onset of Alzheimer's disease (Boyle, Wilson et al, 2012).

I believe the reason for this boon in mental health is that to discover and embody one's purpose, the path typically includes sustained reflection and psychological deconstruction. In the 1990's and leveraging earlier work of Roberto Assagioli in psychosynthesis from the early 1900's and Carl Jung's work on archetypes from the 1920's, the purpose discovery process was gifted a powerful tool by the field of psychology, what is now commonly called "parts work". Parts work is a set of techniques that allows you to clear the space for your purpose discovery and empowers you to create an integrated ego/personality structure around your life's purpose. The Voice-Dialogue Method (Stone, 1993) and the Internal Family Systems Model (Schwartz, 2001) contributed to the field of purpose discovery by providing a system for understanding the multiple aspects of your ego, and empowering you to move beyond them and into the deeper truth of your soul and its message - your life's purpose. You'll explore this in greater detail in "Chapter 8: Your Path to Purpose.

This discovery process guides you through your major fears and traumas from your past, every judgment you made about yourself and the world as a result. This work empowers you to create a cohesive concept of self, a whole and complete understanding and loving embrace of all of your parts. You fall in love with who you are and how you became yourself.

To move beyond purpose as a concept in your mind to a lived experience, you will need to understand the root cause of your limiting beliefs, the beliefs that keep you from discovering and taking action towards living your life's purpose. In Part Two of this book, you are encouraged to stop reading and start finding your purpose by working with a trained Guide or doing a purpose discovery program, such as the Global Purpose Expedition. When you do, you will examine the primary parts of your personal psychology, your Inner Critic, Skeptic, Image Consultant, Wounded Child, and Risk Manager (ref. the Voice-Dialogue-influenced methodology from Tim Kelley's *True Purpose,* 2009).

Once these parts of your ego are understood, you can reframe them, thank them and integrate them into your new whole and purposeful self. This results in greater acceptance and love of your entire life as it was and is now. Upon integration, for example, my clients report no longer regretting the past, nor fearing the future. Instead, they increasingly step into a full and unrelenting acceptance and love for what is: life, purpose and what must be done about it.

When you find your purpose, you can move through the world in a more mindful way, both literally and figuratively. Your healed and whole mind will be alive with possibilities and curiosity. You will constantly seek new ways to understand your life's purpose. You will begin to align every aspect of your life with your purpose and create new ways of expressing your life's purpose. You will begin crafting a life where you are in control, powerful, generative and in action.

In doing this, you will see that every part of your life sits within the broader narrative of your life's purpose.

With purpose, your identity no longer is sourced externally. Your experience is no longer driven by your circumstances, but by who you know yourself to be. In a sense, your purpose becomes your personal religion, a life narrative that includes and transcends every area of your life, and all events in it. Your "lows" aren't so low because they now represent only minor struggles. Your "lows" become empowering lessons in the grand narrative, the epic myth of your life of purpose. These setbacks don't kill you, they make you stronger, purifying you, edifying you for the next challenge, imploring you to call on new strengths, new capacities, new strategies to create the life and world you want.

But this doesn't mean you flatten out your life. Purpose is not numbing; rather, it's an energizing, catalytic force. With purpose, your highs also feel higher, as they vindicate the grand narrative of your life, and become a shared joy with those whom your purpose serves. When you have these moments of achievement, blessing or validation, you take in not only the joy of the successful act, but also the joy of the entire story - your life of purpose and all you have overcome to get to where you are.

CHAPTER 5

The Science of Purpose - Career

"All we need is beer and pussy."

When I was 23, my best friend Tim told me my new life's purpose. It was a warm summer night in Yosemite National Park and the euphoria of LSD turned our eyes to towering redwoods against the night sky. As we shared about our post-college work experiences, we realized we were both deeply disillusioned by what being a "grown- up" in America actually meant. The sheen was wearing off on my career in investment banking and Tim's in software sales for a San Francisco startup. We took this opportunity to revisit our predictable future as suburban dads in sexless marriages and spending five decades doing jobs that meant nothing. As we wandered the moonlit Yosemite Valley floor, we looked at our lives with new eyes.

After a long silence, Tim yelled, "I've got it!"

"Got what?" I yelled back.

"Come here! I've got it!"

"What, T-man?!" as I affectionately called him.

I closed the 10 yards between us on the trail and faced him.

"Look at me," he said.

"All we need..." He paused to shake his head and take in for himself the wisdom he was about to impart. He grabbed my shoulders, looked me square in the eyes and continued, "...all we need is beer and pussy."

After a few moments of silence, the profundity of this revelation hit me too, "Oh my God, you're right!" I paused. "It's so simple."

We looked at each other as if the seas had parted, as if every grown-up notion we'd ever heard of was false, as if college, working, family, the American Dream, the wealth gospel and everything else we had been fed by society, the media and our parents was a lie. How could there be anything else? Why would I do anything unless it included beer or sex?

Tim's conviction grew as he continued, "We don't need fucking jobs and shit. We don't need girlfriends, wives or mortgages. Fuck that shit!"

"Yeah! Fuck that shit!"

We ecstatically ripped off our shirts and started howling. Eureka! Purpose! Halleluiah! We had found a glimmer of hope, an "out", the truth that we could just pull the ripcord and eject from the drudgery of our professions, the spoken lies of the American Dream and unspoken malaise of suburban culture. Maybe we could move to an island and tend bar. Maybe be a tour guide for spring breakers. The options to just drink beer and chase girls were limitless.

In the way 16-year-olds can say "I love you" and mean it without understanding really what it means, in this moment I felt I had a purpose, and it was to break free from Midwestern conformity, from TPS reports (from the movie, *Office Space*) from long commutes and soulless work. In this moment, we elevated a juvenile utterance to a worldview, a battle cry, a mantra that gave me a more hopeful future than the one I was groomed for. In retrospect, it doesn't say much about the American Dream, if such a ridiculous, childish, acid-induced quip could best it in a flash. So, I spent my twenties spending my paychecks on alcohol, women, drugs, travel and extreme sports.

In 2001, after a few years of this "beer and pussy" purpose, multiple arrests and several drinks into a Saturday, I found myself face to face with the hollowness of my life and this stupid purpose. Sitting in Sharkeez, an open-air bar in Hermosa Beach, CA, I got present to the sad fact that I was a clown. I sat with the fact that my work meant nothing to me, that I contributed nothing to society, but was a parasite, extracting paychecks for partying. I saw that the purpose I had chosen was to consume to excess, shock people, make them laugh and if I wasn't blacked out, find something perverted to do with women after the bar closed. I viewed each hookup as a challenge to best myself, to perform increasingly inventive sex acts for the stories I could tell the next day.

I felt bereft of intrinsic value and substance, worthless unless I performed. I felt had to keep conning my employers to keep the checks coming and performing the outrageous physical and sexual stunts to be of value to my friends. This belief stayed with me throughout graduate school and set me up for a beautiful existential crisis thereafter.

It wasn't until actual soul-level purpose struck, in my early thirties, that I was able to finally love myself again and see myself as economically valuable and talented. I saw that I did actually have a role to play in the world and had formidable gifts to contribute in leadership, public speaking, writing and partnership development. Once I connected with my soul's purpose, a new energy infected me, illuminating the thousands of opportunities to joyfully and creatively self-express, to learn, to bring my full presence into each moment in my life and work, to make a contribution to others, while earning a healthy living. This expansion in self-love and potency had me leave behind my lucrative start-up job and jump head first into my own start-up, EVR1, and purposefully serve customers on four continents.

Likewise, when you step across the threshold of your life's purpose and bring it to your work, your life's purpose will become rocket fuel for your career. Now you might not have the same default purpose or coping mechanisms I had, but odds are you have some portfolio of limiting beliefs about your worth and career, and likely a few addictions (e.g., sugar, alcohol, tobacco) and behaviors (e.g., shopping, Netflix, gaming) to cope with them. In this chapter, we'll explore what happens when your identity is sourced in your purpose and you show up to work with it. We'll review the impacts your purpose can have on financial performance, leadership, engagement, sales, marketing, human resources, vision and entrepreneurial flexibility.

1. Purpose is the key to higher income and wealth.

Recent research suggests that people who know their purpose have higher levels of income and wealth, as well as income and wealth growth rates (Hill, Turiano, et al, 2016). Moreover, employees' connection to their purpose is correlated with a 47% increase in their experience of abundance (Metlife, 2010). Not only is there more income and wealth accumulation with a connection to your purpose, but the feelings of lack or want are simply not there, as the source of abundance and worth is less a function of praise, income and wealth, but rather a function of making your highest purposeful contribution.

Purpose is perhaps the most underrated growth driver in our global economy. Ask any orthodox economist what drives growth, and they'll say it's competitive advantage gained through monopoly power, the cultivation of intellectual property, access to cheap resources or a friendly relationship with legislators. However, there is something substantially more sustainable, interesting and ethical also occurring. Jim Stengel, the former CMO of Procter & Gamble, and an independent consulting group did a 10-year study of over 50,000 brands around the world and discovered that "those who center their business on improving people's lives have a **growth rate triple** that of their competitors, and they outperform the market by a huge margin" (McLeod, 2012).

In *Built to Last*, Jim Collins and Jerry Porras, presented a 70-year study illuminating how organizations driven by purpose and values outperform the market by 15-to-1, and outperform their industry peers by 6-to-1 (Collins, Porras, 1994). Numerous financial institutions have taken notice and have developed investment hypotheses to buy and hold these companies. The Parnassus Endeavor fund, for example, invests in companies that have company cultures designed to unlock the purposeful contributions of their teams such that they are regarded as great place to work. In doing so, this fund regularly beats the S&P 500. As of July 7, 2017, Parnassus Endeavor boasted a 25% annual return, beating the S&P annual return by over 7% (US News, 7/7/2017). Recently, Swiss Re, long a leader in sustainable and social investing, decided to move its entire $130 billion investment portfolio to track ethical indices, into instruments of companies with a higher purpose (Reuters, 7/6/17).

Further, 91% of executives in Deloitte's 2013 Core Beliefs and Culture Survey believe there is a strong positive correlation between purpose and financial performance (Deloitte, 2014). If you are a CEO, the purpose question holds even greater weight, as you have a fiduciary responsibility to serve your shareholders. By unlocking your purpose, that of each of your employees and that of the whole company, you will embark on one of the most effective paths to increased income and wealth. I believe the primary reason for this, is that people who are on fire with their purpose are more likely to be creatively engaged at work and also rise to higher-paying leadership positions.

2. Purpose is the key to a legendary career of leadership, impact and fulfillment.

In the comprehensive "Global Purpose Workforce Index" research report, purpose is illuminated as a driving force in distinguishing high performing careers from low performing careers. Folks who find their purpose are 50% more likely to be a leader, 47% more likely to promote their company, and boast a 64% higher level of fulfillment (LinkedIn/Imperative, 2016). Who wouldn't want that level of engagement for themselves and their team?

After all, can somebody who does not have a big vision for themselves and their career really inspire someone else? As Liz Maw, President of Net Impact, a membership organization of purpose-driven business people declares, "Emerging leaders are looking for one thing above all else in a career: purpose."

When you know your life's purpose, you are a visionary, you are creative and you are fulfilled by your career. You see all that you do is a function of your aligned, purposeful life. This means you give your all to each interaction and project, aware that how you do anything is how you do everything: engaged and on purpose.

3. Purpose is the key to high engagement and performance.

Your purpose empowers you to bring your full self into the moment, creatively solving problems and inspiring those around you with the full force of your being. Indeed, research has proven that knowing your purpose quadruples your likelihood of being engaged at work and doubles the likelihood of learning something new each day (Gallup/Healthways, 2013). This matters because companies with highly engaged workforces outperform their peers in earnings per share by 147% (Gallup, 2012).

Further, inspired employees are 225% more productive than employees who are merely satisfied (Mankins, Garton, 2017). Another powerful study from McKinsey

& Co., a management consulting firm, discovered that when executives are in flow (immersed in a personally meaningful task, with short feedback loops and moderate difficulty) they are 500% more productive than when they are not in flow (Cranston, Keller, 2013). Imagine going to work on Monday and getting as much done as you would otherwise do in a whole week?

The reason for this could be that when purpose is present, you bring more of your attention, creativity, skills and intelligence to the matter. Harvard University's Howard Gardner discovered in his groundbreaking work on multiple intelligences, that intelligence is only a factor in career success when the person is connected to a greater purpose (Gardner, 2007). Otherwise, intelligence is not a factor in being more effective and creative at work. The expanded contribution, engagement and performance that result from the connection to your life's purpose will set you apart from the field.

4. Purpose drives sales.

As Lisa Earle McLeod, author of *Selling with Noble Purpose*, has discovered, purpose is a key driver of the highest performing salespeople. For these individuals, the sales process becomes a natural expression of their life's purpose. McLeod made some interesting findings:

> "Six years ago, I was part of a consulting team that was asked by a major biotech firm to conduct a six-month long double-blind study of its sales force. The goal was to determine what behaviors separated the top salespeople from the average ones. The study revealed something no one expected: the top performers all had a far more pronounced sense of purpose than their more average counterparts. The salespeople who sold with noble purpose, who truly wanted to make a difference to customers, consistently outsold the salespeople who focused on sales goals and money." (McLeod, 2012)

5. Purpose attracts new customers.

Moreover, purpose is net attractor for customers. A 2010 Cone Communications study discovered that purpose is a key factor in consumer spending, as 93% of Millennials and 92% of mothers said they would switch brands if the company was involved in a good cause and the price was the same (Cone, 2010).

Brands that embody a higher purpose, like Eileen Fisher, Patagonia, Method, Whole Foods and Tesla, become net brand attractors, simply because they know who they are and are not afraid to share it. Purpose creates loyal fans versus temporary customers. For example, Patagonia actively discourages their customers from buying new products, via their lifetime return policy and lifetime design principles highlighted in their *Better Than New* ad campaign as well as the half-hour documentary/advertisement, *Worn Wear,* highlighting their customers' long-term (decades) use of Patagonia products. Only a company that puts its purpose first, would encourage people not to repeatedly buy their products, and this has proven to be marketing magic. Customers see and feel this authenticity and become life-long loyal customers and brand advocates, telling their friends about the movie and the brand's principles.

Further, purpose is net attractor not just for new customers, but for new customers who are willing to pay more, as a Burson-Marsteller study showed that 80% of consumers prefer to pay more for products and services that are responsibly produced (Burson-Marsteller, 2011). This preference is echoed in the 2014 Nielsen Research report that found that 55% of customers will pay more for a product that has a higher purpose, a 10% increase since 2011 (Nielsen, 2014).

6. Purpose is crucial in attracting and retaining talent.

Increasingly, people want to work for purposeful people and companies. To hire effectively in today's marketplace, companies need to lead with their purpose, as the future of the workforce, the Millennials, now demand it. 60% of Millennials have chosen their employer because they can express their purpose at work (Unlocking Millennial Talent, 2015). Moreover, purpose-driven employees have a 20% longer tenure (LinkedIn/Imperative, 2016), which represents a significant reduction in recruitment, training and development costs.

To attract and retain the best talent, companies need to nurture, evolve and embody the overarching corporate purpose, and train and develop their leadership to awaken their own life's purpose at work so that they can effectively recruit, retain, lead and inspire their teams.

Recent research from Denmark (Happiness Research Institute, 2016), has found that the number one factor in workplace satisfaction is the connection between the purpose of the company and the purpose of the employees. This factor is more than twice as important as the next most important factor, the efficacy of the company's leadership.

As we have explored, knowing your purpose allows work to be a fulfilling place of connection, growth, creativity and self-expression, as purpose-driven people are 64% more likely to be fulfilled and are 47% more likely to be a promoter of their employer (LinkedIn / Imperative, 2016).

Further, when you know yourself and are sitting in the center of your purpose, you are empowered to set healthy boundaries everywhere in your life. Your purpose is not only expressed in your career, but also in your self-care, your family and community relationships, and even your need for leisure and down-time. Your career is purposeful self-expression, not a thing you do in order to survive and enjoy your hobbies.

As such, your career exists within your purpose, not the other way around. Your purpose empowers you to give all you can within the limits you set, and not an ounce more, because what is important is the purpose of your whole life, not just your career. Knowing this, you set boundaries in your career, live a full life and thus avoid burnout, resentment and disengagement. The result is that you arrive each day to work on purpose, well-rested, well-fed, healthy, creative and energized.

7. Purpose clarifies career and strategic focus.

Your purpose empowers you to choose work, business models, outcomes, processes, projects, and partners that are aligned with your life's purpose. This in turn liberates you from the tyranny of approaching business from an opportunistic SWOT perspective (Strengths, Weaknesses, Opportunities, and Threats). Instead of boiling the ocean, asking what career you should have or what business should you be in, it becomes an organic process of exploring which business allows you to make your highest contribution, to achieve the greatest expression and impact. Indeed, global CEOs favor this approach and regard purpose as one of the top three things (along with ethics and values) on which to focus their attention (IBM, 2012).

With purpose, your business becomes an organic outgrowth of your soul. You no longer begin your work day with the questions: "How do I make money?", or "What do I need to do to get through the day?", but instead ask "How can I live in greater alignment with my life's purpose to create and serve my customers?" Take, for example, Whole Foods' "Higher Purpose Statement":

> "With great courage, integrity and love – we embrace our responsibility to co-create a world where each of us, our communities and our planet can flourish. All the while, celebrating the sheer love and joy of food." (WholeFoods.com, 7/5/2017)

And Eileen Fisher's "VISION2020":

> "Our vision is for an industry where human rights and sustainability are not the effect of a particular initiative, but the cause of a business well run. Where social and environmental injustices are not unfortunate outcomes, but reasons to do things differently." (EileenFisher.com/vision-2020/, 7/5/2017)

Fundamentally, the purpose of a company's founders is the company's vision and mission. If the founders do not know themselves, if they haven't had a rigorous purpose discovery experience (3+ months) that illuminates why they are here on Earth, it is highly likely that their vision and mission statement will be uninspiring, e.g., McDonald's 2013 mission:

> "McDonald's brand mission is to be our customer's' favorite place and way to eat and drink... Our worldwide operations are aligned around a global strategy called the Plan to Win, which centers on an exceptional customer experience - People, Products, Place, Price and Promotion." (corporate.mcdonalds.com, 2013)

The result of the founders not being connected to their individual life purpose is a company mission that is, at best, a guess, something supported by research and "big data" / market trends, not a battle cry from the heart. The goal of a business without purpose is singular: it is reduced to enriching the equity holders, often at considerable cost to its employees, customers, partners and the environment.

Without purpose, business people only have access to questions like:

- "How do we raise money?"
- "How do we get market share?"
- "How do we increase our stock price?"

Those operating from their purpose do consider such questions, but only after these primary questions:

- "Why do we exist?"
- "What is the net benefit we create for humanity and the environment that justifies the use of resources and the human potential required to achieve this proposed benefit?"
- "How can we listen to the evolving inner purpose of our team members and the evolving outer purpose of our species and planet to create a purposeful and profitable enterprise that joins the two?"

And these are the questions that empower businesses to thrive, evolve and make a huge net positive impact in the world.

8. Purpose drives entrepreneurial flexibility and powerful pivots.

When you are living your purpose, you are committed to your purpose, and are thus not as attached to specific outcomes, existing products, structures, messaging, or ways of doing things. Your purpose both anchors you in your deepest commitment and affords you the freedom and flexibility to achieve your vision a number of ways. In a recent Harvard Business Review study with Ernst & Young, *The Business Case for Purpose*, 84% of global executives believe that having a strong company purpose is necessary to transform a company (Harvard Business Review/Ernst & Young, 2015).

With purpose, you are empowered to make purpose-driven decisions, as opposed to acting from fear or by past-based attachments. From this place, you have the ability to shift strategies quickly in service of your purpose, and within the ethical constraints of your values (generally in a just and sustainable manner), thereby achieving a net positive impact in the lives of your customers, shareholders, partners, employees, communities and planet.

Without being anchored in purpose, strategy/pivot decisions are only opportunistic, relying on the shifting realities of the marketplace and what are perceived to be the core competencies of the company. When grounded in purpose, decisions are anchored in the deeper awareness of why a company exists and the impact they are out to cause.

For these reasons, purpose is a strategic advantage in your career and company. More importantly, choosing to move forward in your career without a connection to your purpose or to the company's purpose is a recipe for reduced income, wealth, market values, job satisfaction, impact and job security. Given all the lives and livelihoods that depend on your engagement, contribution, leadership - those of your family, team members, customers, investors and partners - the question is, "it is consistent with who you are and how much you love your people, to have a career that isn't an expression of your purpose?"

CHAPTER 6

The Science of Purpose - Love

"I think I love my wife. I'm not sure, though," said my friend, John.

He was stuck in a marriage he didn't feel like he could change or leave, so for years he stayed with his wife, experiencing increasing discord as well as, you guessed it, very infrequent sex and a household family dynamic that fluctuated between overt hostility and quiet resentment. John was experiencing a purposeless marriage. He and his wife didn't not know their purpose, so they had no foundation upon which to build a marital purpose. And they took to warring with each other in a zero-sum power struggle.

Without purpose, it is possible to still use the word "love," but if folks haven't done the work to first know and fall in love with themselves (a result of purpose discovery work), can they really love someone else?

When you craft a life of purpose and know who you are and what you want, your intimate relationships become interdependent partnerships, where you join together in the adventure of love, each coming from a place of individual wholeness, strength and self-awareness. From wholeness, you are better able to support each other in living your respective purposes in the world and allowing the natural flow of love between you and your partner. Research supports this: knowing your life's purpose yields a 31% increase in the experience of feeling loved (Metlife, 2010).

With purpose, you can love much more fully because you have cleared out many of the limiting beliefs that prevent you from giving and receiving love. All the stuff that "isn't you" (like parental judgments, and social narratives around fitness, beauty, age, education, race, religion, status) no longer clouds your judgment in mate selection or self-expression. You become free to love fully as you are, from a place of wholeness and self-love. You are complete and without apology for yourself. And from this place, you can enter fully into a romantic adventure, with your purpose, as well as an awareness of your quirks, wounds, imperfections, needs and desires. Although a connection to your purpose is by no means a prerequisite to fall in love or to feel love, it is a prerequisite of authentic partnership, which I define as:

Authentic Partnership (n): a union of two biologically mature, psychologically whole and purpose-aware adults, who choose a romantic partnership not out of need, but because they desire a romantic adventure, one that both serves their unique soul's purpose and thrusts the couple upon new frontiers to experience and develop their relationship purpose.

But exactly how does your purpose create the conditions for authentic partnership? Your purpose is the foundation of authentic partnership because it awakens what I call The Four Pillars of Authentic Partnership: 1. Self-Love, 2. Self-Sufficiency, 3. Attraction, and 4. Boundaries & Boldness.

1. Self-Love

Because you have done the work to examine your faults, traumas and fears, you accept and love yourself fully, knowing that your relationship to your purpose is your primary love relationship. Your partner, his/her needs and purpose are valued, but are secondary to your relationship to your own purpose. On this journey of finding your purpose, you develop a deep appreciation for your faults, strengths, powers, ethics, character and accumulated wisdom. And from this place you experience a deep love of self. From this place, you even find yourself sexy. You see yourself as your own beloved, and are thus deeply rooted in your center. You are full of love, regardless of your relationship status.

2. Self-Sufficiency

Your purpose is a license to feel complete, worthy, and happy to be by yourself. Purpose empowers you to feel content alone, yet excited and hopeful for whatever the future holds for your love life, in or out of relationships. Your purpose imbues you with faith that all be well, provided you keep taking purpose-aligned action, stepping into greater integrity with your purpose and pulling the thread that leads to your next stage of growth. This faith is a sense of being whole and perfect as you are right now, and yet your fullness is always expanding, as you grow and evolve in ever greater wholeness.

This rootedness is visible to the outside world. Rather than broadcasting what you think you should be or seeking out who society or your friends think you should date, purpose sends a powerful signal, a narrowcast (versus broadcast), a powerful dating signal that stands apart from other signals. Purpose narrowcasts the message: "I know myself, I know what I want, and I know what I don't want. I'm creating a huge purposeful life for myself and taking a stand for a better world. I'm not everybody's cup of tea, but I might be your cup. Although I love being alone with myself, I stand for a bigger expression of myself through romantic partnership. Because I love myself, warts and all, I can love and accept you, warts and all."

As psychotherapist and Zen practitioner, David Richo PhD, illuminated in his breakthrough relationship book *How to Be an Adult in Relationships,* psychologically mature adults are sourced internally, meeting the majority of their emotional needs themselves or outside of their romantic relationship. Purpose work illuminates the sources of life's triggers and places your identity and sense of worth firmly inside you, not dependent on circumstances or the behavior of others. Moreover, with your purpose at your core, you are on fire in all parts of your life, creating, serving and connecting with others. You are living a big life and your love relationship simply is not your primary focus.

Your relationship is still important, but you haven't fallen under the common delusion that it completes you or is the point of all human life. Your partner isn't a White Knight or Damsel in the Bell Tower. With purpose, you are complete regardless of your relationship status, and you engage romantically only if it increases your and your partner's ability to live your respective purposes.

And when this happens, it is a great gift to each other. With purpose, you don't need to lean on your partner as your emotional pharmacy, expect them to make it all better, or for them to be your source of meaning or self-worth. Rather, you two engage with each other powerfully from a place of want (versus need), as dynamic companions and lovers.

3. Attraction

Imagine for a moment that you are single, at a party, and you're introduced to two attractive people, who appear to you as potential romantic partners. However, before you actually meet them, you learn from a friend that each is single, went to a good college, earns a good living, and is physically healthy and good natured. But there is a difference: one of them knows their purpose.

Which one of these do you think will be more present with you? Which one do you think is more excited about their life? Which one do you think will be more interesting to talk to and have more aliveness in their life? Which one do you think has a better idea of what they want in a relationship? Which one do you think has more internal resources for dealing with adversity and being present in a relationship? Which one do you is going to be more creative and unrestrained in the bedroom?

Even if you've never picked up this book or knew anything about purpose, you're likely to develop a deeper connection with, and attraction to, the one who is alive with their soul's purpose. And there is good reason for that. Purpose aligns and expresses who you are. You are showing up fully, present and ready for adventure, not as a set of reactions that vary depending on your circumstances.

Research from Florida State University and Southern Utah University confirms that people who have a sense of meaning and purpose are regarded as more attractive - "more likeable, better potential friends, and more desirable conversation partners" (Stillman, Lambert, et al, 2010). Moreover, they discovered that for people with physical attractiveness considered average or low, a sense of purpose made them more attractive.

The result of being turned on by your life's purpose, the result of feeling whole and full of self-love, and perfectly content being alone, is an undeniable hotness, a powerful attraction. A gravitas has emerged. There is a solidity to you, a root system that lets everyone know you are in your center and can handle whatever life throws at you. In this place, you are on point and magnetic. You share your full self, vulnerably and without fear. You engage in activities and contexts that bring you alive, that allow you to express your life's purpose. The result is that you are naturally yourself. Other people see this and want to help you, be with you, be on your team, help you live out loud and bed you down.

4.   Boundaries & Boldness

From your foundation of living on purpose, you are able to set firm boundaries, not only in your career but also in your romantic partnerships. You are empowered to live according to your own virtues and ethics, to care for your own needs, to make requests to get your own needs met, and to love fully without fear of abandonment (as you are perfectly content alone) and without resentment. Your boundaries are firm, as your purpose empowers you to walk away from any relationship that doesn't serve you. The power of purpose, also affords you the capacity to make unreasonable requests, to speak your fantasies and ask for partnership in satisfying your deepest desires.

Full of self-love, self-reliance, and strong boundaries, you radiate wholeness and attract others, especially those who are similarly inclined and developed in their purpose. However, this purpose-driven love schema isn't a sanitized merger of developmental equals. Rather it is a surrender to the mysteries of the heart, soul, flesh and loins. It is moving through the world from a place of strength and wholeness, which also includes all the desires of the flesh, the hunger for new experiences, and a surrender to the unknown future and unfolding soul of the romantic union. In Chapter 21, you'll explore structures that deepen and expand such highly-functioning, emergent and purposeful relationships.

CHAPTER 7

The Science of Purpose - A Better World

"He's a retard," I said to a former lover, triggered by a newspaper article I was reading on a notable libertarian venture capitalist.

"What?! Please don't say that word," she exclaimed.

"Say what? 'Retarded'? This guy is the textbook definition of a retard," I said angrily.

"I agree with your point, but that word diminishes people with actual intellectual challenges."

And in that moment, I got what she meant. I could no longer use that word. It did not reflect my values, my purpose or my vision for a more evolved world. I've met many people with intellectual challenges, and have experienced their gifts and contributions. However, I grew up using that word. A lot. I was raised in a deeply segregated community and used that word, as well as other slurs that mocked people's bodies, economic class, race, religion, sexuality and gender. I grew up shaming all sorts of people and behaviors. It's just what we did. Of course, I knew it wasn't mature or politically correct to say any of these words, but I never connected this language with my purpose - I hadn't realized that in using words like this I was out of alignment and integrity with my life's purpose.

In that moment, calling this man a 'retard' wasn't just offensive to others, but saying it was personally out of integrity. In fact, it was the opposite of my purpose, and the imperative I have to love and accept humanity in all the ways it is, and is not. Using this word only diminished others based on circumstances out of their control, and doing so actually made no sense. Calling him a 'retard' didn't illuminate his immature worldview and the folly of his actions, but rather this act equated his poorly cultivated worldview and actions with the attributes of someone who hadn't made any errors.

In that moment, my purpose landed for me as something that went well beyond my career, health and relationships. It was now infecting my language, my values, my cultural attitudes and politics. My purpose compels me to speak and act in a way that is consistent with it, in a manner that has integrity. Once integrity and purpose are combined, the entire world begins to look like fair play for living purpose, wherein one moves through the world as the embodiment of purpose and seeing oneself as a change agent for living one's purpose and values everywhere.

As you will discover, your purpose cannot and will not stop at the door of your body, your bedroom, or your office. It is very much active, connecting your soul to your communities, and eventually to our whole species and planet. In this chapter, we'll explore the research that suggests that knowing your life's purpose does indeed create a better world; it creates a kinder, more diverse, tolerant, curious, generous and efficient society, a more creative and emergent culture, as well as a more generative, just and sustainable economy.

Below we'll explore seven key ways that purpose creates: (1) Economic Efficiency, (2) A Culture of Tolerance and Equality, (3) A Culture of Learning, (4) A Stronger Democracy, (5) A Culture of Giving, (6) A More Sustainable Economy, and (7) A More Abundant Economy. After which I will make the argument that purpose is what is missing in all our world-changing efforts.

1. An Economy of Efficiency and Performance

The benefits of living your purpose flow out into the greater community. As you explored in "Chapter 4: The Science of Purpose - Health", your purpose empowers you to be physically healthier, strengthening your mind, body, cell structures and extending your life by up to seven years. That's not only great news for you, but also positively impacts the whole society and strengthens our global economy. It shifts where you spend your time and health care dollars, from caring for your illnesses in the hospital to conditioning your beautiful body, and using it to physically explore our wondrous world through all sorts of activities, e.g., travel, art, making love, adventure and exercise. With healthier bodies and higher levels of income and wealth that purpose makes available, we have the capability to enjoy an abundance of purposeful leisure activities, many of which involve a commercial transaction.

Indeed, as a society, we suffer when we don't actively and purposefully care for our bodies. For example, in the United States, the CDC estimates that up to 40% of deaths are preventable, caused by lifestyle choices concerning diet, exercise, alcohol, drugs and tobacco (CDC, 2014). A diminished physiology and a robust medical services habit is the result of the accumulated consequences of engaging in purpose substitutes. As the Dean of University of California's School of Public Health, Steve Shortell, states,

> Fifty percent of the determinants of health are due to our behaviors; 20 percent to environmental factors; 20 percent to genetics; and only 10 percent to having access to medical care. Yet... we spend 96 percent of health expenditures on medical

services and only 4 percent on preventing disease and promoting health. (Shortell, 2010)

When you are alive with your purpose, you are a better steward of your physiology, as well as your overall well-being, and this reduces your need for medical care.

During my teens and twenties, I was constantly in the hospital for all sorts of reasons - bad skin, broken bones, allergies, cuts, sprains. In my last year of business school, at age 28, I was pushing 255 lbs., drinking heavily, chewing tobacco and ingesting any drug I could get my hands on. Although I began to make changes to course correct this pattern shortly thereafter, what if I hadn't? Can you imagine what another ten years of that life would have done to my body?

Since beginning my purpose journey, and via the contemporaneous and otherwise inexplicable desire for leafy vegetables and yoga, my body gradually transformed from a beefy 255 lb. rugby player, to a lean 225 lb. yogi. I haven't (knock on wood) been to see a doctor except for check-ups in the last five years.

As we explored in "Chapter 4: The Science of Purpose - Health", US adults over the age of 50 with the highest purpose scores, had 32% fewer doctor visits and spent 61% fewer overnights in the hospital per year, when compared to those with the lowest purpose scores (Kim, Strecher, 2014). Imagine reducing humanity's use of medical services by 32-61%? How much more time and energy would be used for creativity, service, economic contribution and leisure? How many fewer sick days would be taken? How much more productive would our whole economy be if we all weren't doing the bare minimum between weekends, but were all engaged in purpose-driven careers?

When we embody purpose at the collective level, we create a more efficient, energetic, connected and creative culture, and we decrease our orientation towards being ill, distracted, narcotized, sedentary, disconnected, detached, and docile.

2. A Culture of Tolerance and Equality

As your purpose becomes your primary love relationship, source of identity and governing narrative of your life, it liberates you from holding onto old beliefs and cultural ways of being that are not aligned with your purpose. Having worked with and taught thousands of people from over 50 different countries to help them discover their life's purpose, I have yet to encounter a purpose that is hateful. I have yet to encounter one purpose that is about harming others. Simply put, when soul gets involved, it creates generative outcomes like creativity, peace, empowerment, compassion, tolerance and understanding. The purpose discovery process includes rooting out beliefs that are dissonant with one's life purpose, and heals the personal wounds that fuel these dissonant beliefs.

When we do this sacred purpose work, without exception the result is that we work towards more unity, more empowerment, more acceptance, more diversity, and more justice in the world. Recent research from Harvard, Cornell and Carleton University positively correlated purpose with racial tolerance (Burrow, Stanley et al, 2014). What they found is that when people are connected to their purpose, they are less threatened by others who are different. Further, they naturally gravitate towards neighborhoods, endeavors and organizations that explicitly foster diversity. Purpose discovery education is thus a powerful tool for humanity to continue expanding its freedom and power over our racist, sexist, homophobic, and ageist history.

The result of each of us finding our purpose, is that we accelerate the already underway shift in humanity towards tolerance. In doing so, we take responsibility for humanity's beliefs and shift our personal and collective source of meaning from external (other people and organizations determining my experience) to internal (only my purpose and my relationships determine my experience).

3. A Culture of Learning

As we've explored, knowing your purpose doubles the likelihood of learning something new each day and quadruples your likelihood of being engaged at work (Gallup/Healthways, 2013). However, this amazing benefit is not just a privilege for adults, it has also been shown to increase the appetite of our youth for learning, impelling our children to discover the world fueled by their emerging and evolving purpose. When children are only briefly connected to their purpose their grades improve, yielding a 0.2 GPA increase on a four-point scale (Yeager, Henderson, et al, 2014). As William Damon, PhD, the author of *Path to Purpose* and Director of the Stanford Center on Adolescence, has discovered in his research:

> Purpose is the pre-eminent long-term motivator of learning and achievement. Any school that fails to encourage purpose among its students, risks becoming irrelevant for the choices those students will make in their lives. Schools that encourage purpose will see their students become energized, diligent and resilient in the face of challenges and obstacles (Parker, 2015).

Even more pronounced are the effects of purpose discovery education on college students. Bill Johnson of the University of North Carolina, Greensboro has been offering purpose discovery courses to his students since 2008. He has seen the graduates of his four *Life Design Catalyst Program* courses boast graduation rates that are 6-9% higher than those of the broader university population. (Johnson, 2017)

For parents who struggle with the academic engagement and performance of their children, and who know their children are capable of so much more, often what is missing is the child's connection to purpose. When parents ignite their own purpose, they model what full engagement looks like, they become a stand for the revelation of their children's purpose, and they employ a host of unique parenting practices that reveal their children's deepest desires and ignite purpose-driven learning. (More on creating a purposeful family in Chapter 21.)

4. A Stronger Democracy

An informed citizenry is a prerequisite to any democracy, so the better informed we are and the more engaged we are in the political process, the stronger our democracy. As we explored, your purpose moves out into action and exploration of the world. It doubles the chance of you learning something new, expanding your awareness of the world, and quadrupling your engagement in life. As worldview is an explicitly cultivated aspect of purpose, by cultivating and expanding it, we have a better map of reality and make more informed political decisions. The more we as a society awaken to our unique purpose, the more we learn and engage in all matters, the more informed we are, and the more optimal our political outcomes.

Moreover, when we are not yet awakened to the internal source of meaning, our life's purpose, we can vote only along existing belief systems (historic, nationalist, religious, racial, political, cultural, etc.). When we find our life's purpose, we achieve this freedom from external meaning and identity and can choose which politicians, policies and programs deliver the best outcomes for humanity and the environment. Purpose gives us this freedom - to choose and vote soberly, devoid of any historical precedent, or political, cultural, gender, sexual, religious or national identities.

5. A Culture of Giving

When your life becomes about serving something bigger than your own desires, needs and fears, others benefit. Purpose, by its very definition, is transpersonal, a call to improve the world on behalf of someone, something or some idea that is outside of and larger than you. As such, purpose has been proven to increase participation in philanthropic and volunteering activities by 50% (Gallup/Healthways, 2013). By awakening your purpose, your focus moves from self to other and eventually to the world, collectively igniting a cultural shift towards making a contribution to others, towards helping those who are less fortunate, towards being the cause of positive change in the world.

6. A More Sustainable Economy

Purpose discovery creates an appetite for new ways to contribute economically. As we are no longer concerned with acquiring money and goods for their own sake, or out of survival fear or social approval, and we are no longer caught in the "more-is-better" and "prosperity gospel" cultural narratives, we now are concerned with living in alignment with our purpose. When purpose puts you into action in your career to create a better world in accordance with your world vision, you create a more purposeful career AND you partner with, buy from and invest in more purposeful companies. Collectively, when everyone finds their purpose, we create a more purposeful economy.

Purpose combined with the power of the information/internet revolution is radically remaking corporations' presence, image and participation in humanity. Since the advent of the internet in 90's and explosive rise in social media usage, we can connect in real-time like never before. We have the capacity and the language to communicate causes and events globally within minutes. This has given us unprecedented access to how the sausage actually gets made, how companies really operate. Companies can no longer hide their illegal and immoral activities. Recent history is replete with thousands of cases of unfair labor and environmentally destructive business practices (e.g., Nike's 1996 subsistence-wage labor scandal and BP's 2010 Deep Water Horizon) and governmental abuses (e.g., the Snowden/Wikileaks revelations of illegal US military and intelligence activities). Armed with this new knowledge, consumers are banding together to act in the best interests of themselves and the planet, through boycotts, protests, divestment and shareholder activism, e.g., Black Lives Matter, Stand with Standing Rock/Dakota Access Pipeline, Occupy.

This is no longer just a phenomenon on liberal college campuses, in coffee shops, yoga studios and health food stores: this is a growing trend in the marketplace as a whole. The impact of purposeful people and businesses on the economy is profound, as consumers are purposefully voting with their dollars like never before. A market for purpose-driven goods has emerged, creating billions of dollars of wealth for companies living and profiting purposefully, and eroding billions of dollars of wealth from companies choosing to ignore the call.

This market demographic has been called by many names, such as conscious consumers, LOHAS (Lifestyles of Health and Sustainability) and Cultural Creatives. I prefer the term Cultural Creatives, as it is the name backed by the most data and research (a 10-year values study as presented by Paul Ray PhD and Sherry Ruth Anderson in their 2000 book, *Cultural Creatives)*. These are folks who explicitly seek to live their unique values of personal growth and development, diversity, equality, peace and sustainability whether they are creating their careers, their communities, their marriages, their consumer loyalties or their governments. Numerous notable purpose-driven enterprises have risen to express their purpose, live their values and meet the needs of these people, including Swiss Re, Parnassus Endeavor Fund, ClifBar, Patagonia, Whole Foods and Seventh Generation. As Paul Ray notes, this is a growing segment of the US population:

In the 1995 national study of Cultural Creatives they were 23.6% of US adults, 44 million of them. By 1999 they had increased to 26%, or 50 million adults. By 2008, they had increased to 35% or 80 million adults. (Ray, 2010)

7. A More Abundant Economy

Moreover, these purposeful companies are able to grow their market share and charge premium prices. As we explored in Chapter 5, Nielsen found that 55% of customers are willing to pay more for a product that serves a higher purpose, representing an 11% increase over 2011 (Nielsen, 2014). As such, offering purposeful products is a strategic economic advantage, allowing for the generation and retention of customers, empowering profitable companies, happier, more engaged teams and higher-paying jobs.

The widespread cultural desire for personal and corporate purpose has already caught the attention and interest of the corporate world, driving strategy and strongly influencing decision-making. It is little surprise, then, that in 2014 the words "purpose," "mission" and "change the world" were mentioned 3,243 times on earnings calls, at investor meetings, and in industry conferences - a 40% increase over 2009 (Deloitte, 2015).

Moreover, academia, typically a lagging indicator of social and cultural change, reflects this transition from a growth-obsessed purposeless economy to a purpose-driven economy. In 2008 there were over 350 professors from over 35 countries teaching social entrepreneurship, with 30+ national and international competitions, 800 different articles and 200 cases used in social entrepreneurship courses (Brock, Kim, 2011). Social entrepreneurship has now gone mainstream, as top-tier conservative late-movers in graduate business education like Harvard, Wharton and even that neoliberal stronghold, the University of Chicago, all now offer MBA degree programs in Social Enterprise or Social Entrepreneurship.

Given the evident benefits of living a life of purpose and the profitability to be realized by conducting purposeful business, the influence of purpose is likely to only expand in our economy. As global communications strategy firm Edelman noted, "Purpose is the new paradigm." (Edelman, 2017)

Purpose is what is missing in creating a better world.

It is time to declare war on purpose-agnostic civic participation and decontextualized inner work. It's is time for purpose.

Now you might be asking, why is purpose so important to creating a better world? Why can't we just keep meditating or praying or going to therapy or doing personal development work or paying taxes or giving to charity or voting to create a better world? There is a time and place for everything. However, none of these is sufficient alone, nor in aggregate, to actually make a dent in solving our world's problems. If they were, with our species' enormous talents, tools and power, we would have already fixed climate change, inequality, poverty, disease and war. It's time for some straight talk.

Let's start with voting, paying your taxes and giving to charity.

Giving to charities and voting feels good, and for some paying taxes even feels good. These efforts are life-affirming, but for many, the acts of voting, paying taxes and giving to charity are the boxes they check to tell themselves that they are a good person, and subconsciously, this gives them the permission to continue being selfish elsewhere in their life or staying ignorant or inactive around the systemic sources of suffering and dysfunction. This is what social psychologists, Anna Merritt, Daniel Effron and Benoit Monin call "moral self-licensing".

> Past good deeds can liberate individuals to engage in behaviors that are immoral, unethical, or otherwise problematic, behaviors that they would otherwise avoid for fear of feeling or appearing immoral. (Merritt, Effron et al, 2010).

Charity, voting and paying taxes give us the pretense of contribution without actually changing anything, and in most cases, edifying the status quo and powering the very institutions that create the suffering. Charities, specifically, address the symptoms of a failed state, and thus their very existence ought to be questioned. Charities perform the function for the giver of releasing steam, of temporarily purging one's moral guilt for the suffering in the world, giving one a sense of having made a difference, when actually nothing is permanently impacted by their gift. What is actually happening is that the state has failed to structure the political economy such that private and public institutions can provide adequate social services and create economic opportunities for its people. Charities make the cost of that failure less disastrous, public and politically expensive, and forestall necessary political reform. Charity is the soft-porn of change, when what is actually needed is a deep, radical and unrelenting political revolution led by purpose-driven leaders.

Like sports, religion and consumerism, charity, taxes and voting give us a sense of belonging, duty and connection to something greater than ourselves, without actually changing the core dysfunction of the system. This is not to suggest we should not vote, pay taxes or give to charity. We should do anything that expresses our unique purpose. However, human potential is almost unlimited and the impact we can make in our careers, families, communities and governments when we are lit up with purpose greatly exceeds, by several orders of magnitude, the impact we can make by merely voting, paying taxes and giving.

Further, the time for decontextualized, self-indulgent inner work is over.

Meditation and prayer are essential tools for anyone wishing to connect with a larger identity or operate with a clean mental and psychological engine. These tools empower us to remain centered in the moments when life's circumstances seem beyond our control. However, our spiritual tools have been ineffective in stopping corruption in government, or the bombs in the Middle East, or the sex trafficking in Asia or the chainsaws in the Amazon, nor have they built sustainable transit systems or sent the disenfranchised to college. Some even are accompanied by the advice to "live and let live", "give unto Caesar, what is Caesar's", or that "it's all maya", or that "the only real battle is the one fought in our own hearts". Rubbish.

Additionally, common tools for greater psychological health, emotional balance and socialization, like psychotherapy and personal development seminars (e.g., Tony Robbins, Landmark) are of great use in understanding the nature of our discontent and empowering us. However, these are also not enough. As famed psychotherapist and purpose pioneer, James Hillman PhD noted in the title of his book, *We've Had One Hundred Years of Psychotherapy - and the World's Getting Worse* (Hillman, 1992).

Despite their many gifts and uses, therapy and personal development offerings are generally deeply lacking in context and prescriptive action. They empower people, but do not do so within an intellectually broad worldview, rather they empower people to take any action they choose within their default worldview, which as we will explore in "Chapter 17: Humanity's Midlife Crisis", humanity's default worldview is killing us all. Moreover, these traditions lack a path for discovering and living our life's purpose; they do not compel us to act, addressing the broader dynamics that continually create and expand suffering in our lives, society, the economy and our environment.

Therapy and personal development programs do not root us in our soul's identity. They don't ignite the rockets. Although incredibly useful, these approaches do not provide explicit guidance as to how to do more than cope with a dysfunctional world, how to reach our fullness as a human being, how to actually be ourselves, how to express and embody our unique powers in the world, how to unlock our leadership, or how to make the world a better place. In a sense, mediation, therapy and personal development (sans purpose and context) are merely a salve, a saffron-flavored moral self-license, a way to feel calm and empowered, but not in action creating a better world.

Like the market for charity, the markets for spiritual retreats, therapy and personal development grow in lock step with the dysfunction of the world. Unless inner work includes a contextual awareness of the political, market and institutional dynamics that create suffering, AND a means to put people in action transforming dysfunctional institutions, they run the risk of profiteering and colluding with the dysfunctional institutions that generate this suffering. In a sense, without this context and action orientation, spiritual practices, therapy and personal development have much more in common with veterinary medicine than general medicine, in that they are there to distract, numb, soften and placate a wild beast, to make her and him docile, ready for burden, entertainment or slaughter.

So, clearly something is missing. This is where purpose is needed. It connects what's within you and an accurate understanding of what's going on in the world, binding your deepest personal heartbreak with its systemic causes. Purpose is the nexus of the macro and micro, the universal and particular, the head and heart, the doing and being. Purpose is your descent into action, into your leadership, your call, virtues, vision, mission, story, powers and craft. It is your seat assignment here on Earth, it is what you must do to both achieve your fullest potential as a single human and step into your leadership of humanity in solving our most pressing problems.

Never before in human history
has the quality of your life and the well-being of humanity
been linked with one single task:
FINDING YOUR PURPOSE.

CHAPTER 8

Your Path to Purpose

"I'm getting a divorce," said Ariel.

"Wow. Tell me more," I said with trepidation, as many of my clients want to make radical life changes during their purpose journey.

Ariel was only six weeks into her journey with me. Like so many of my clients, she came to me with the desire to find a job she loved. And as soon as she started to inquire into the broader purpose of her life, she saw that it wasn't just her job that needed to change. She discovered that her marriage didn't serve her and that neither she nor her husband really had the will to make it work. She also saw how disconnected and isolated she was from people, and she came face to face with her lack of self-confidence, as well as her muted desires to start her own healing center and to be creatively self-expressed.

She continued, "We love each other, but this relationship has run its course, and my husband agrees. We are both ready for something new."

Of course, I cautioned her not to make any bold decisions before her purpose work was over. However, as her sense of purpose awareness grew, and as she overcame many of the obstacles that previously kept her quiet, inert and disconnected from others, she felt empowered to take bold purpose-aligned actions. As much as I might have wanted to, it wasn't for me to stop her. She was on fire and wasn't going to play small any more. Over the course of the four months of our work together, she:

1. amicably left her husband,
2. quit her job,
3. took a month off,
4. found a new job with a better work environment and fewer hours,
5. moved out of her house, and found a new place to live in the hills, overlooking San Francisco Bay,
6. took a big risk and shared with a friend her romantic feelings for him, and
7. joined two meditation communities and made new friends.

Best of all, shortly after our work together, she applied, was accepted and enrolled in a Master's program in psychology to launch her new career and bring her vision to reality.

Not every one of my clients has such a dramatic number of life changes occur during this work. Most folks slowly deepen into the discovery experience and take a few months after our work together to make just one of these big purpose-aligned changes, like quitting smoking, changing jobs, finding love or launching a purpose-driven venture or project. You might be asking, what is it exactly about the discovery process that gives people access to the clarity, confidence and power to make these big changes?

Your Purpose Expedition

Although every human is unique, most (but not all) purpose discovery journeys follow a similar pattern. An apt metaphor to describe the process is crossing a chasm - moving from one place of stability to another. Your life as it is now and your life fully lit up by purpose are separated by a space that is unknown, complete with hidden obstacles and the exciting possibility that new, even more desirable destinations may reveal themselves after you begin your expedition. Just as Ariel did not know her love life was going to go in another direction, your journey may also surprise, challenge and delight you.

Your life-with-purpose will be a new way of life, not an incremental improvement, but literally a new way of being and operating on purpose in each of the key areas of your life (health, romance, family, career, community, finances and spirituality) that greatly expands your fulfillment, impact, joy, connection and success. On any expedition into the unknown, you have to summon your courage and willingness to make necessary sacrifices, to leave behind that which does not serve you. You'll need your resources, wonder, curiosity, faith in yourself, and, if you have it, your connection to spirit.

To make the journey from your current life and way of being to your new life expressed by your high-resolution life purpose, a couple of things are required.

First, you have to know that the journey is possible. It has to exist as a very real and worthwhile undertaking. Usually this means that at least one person you trust has said that the journey exists and that it is worth it. Reading books like this or connecting with a trained Guide or someone who is on the journey can be extremely helpful in clarifying your understanding of what purpose is, why you should connect with it, how to find it and how it will show up in your life.

Secondly, you have to be clear the time is now. Not everyone needs to do purpose work all the time. We all need it at different points in our lives, but not all of us need it now. To know the time is now, you must be clear that (1) your current life and way of being no longer suits you and (2) that even if you don't know what it might be, you have a bigger game to play in life, a game you can no longer ignore. You must get present to the physical, social, emotional, spiritual, ecological and economic impacts of being disconnected from your life's purpose. You must also feel, trust or perceive that finding, living and leading with your purpose will empower you to play that bigger game.

Once you are clear on the possibility of the journey, as well as the necessity to cross chasm between your current way of being and your future life on purpose, you are ready to begin your purpose expedition.

Preparation

You cannot do this alone, so you'll need a trained Guide, proven purpose discovery program to follow, or a group of mature, high-integrity friends who share a commitment to helping you find your purpose. By establishing a solid structure, you will markedly improve your odds of success on the journey and the chances that you will move through each of the parts of your journey with as little confusion, pain and resistance as possible.

Although the impacts of living disconnected from your purpose are no longer acceptable, you must first establish that your life, although unfulfilling, is indeed stable. You will need all of your surplus mental resources for the journey, and if your current life is unstable and uses all of your surplus mental resources just to keep the wheels on the bus, now is not the time. Signs that your current place is unstable might be: you cannot meet your monthly expenses, you indulge in overwork, you are psychologically unstable, you have dysfunction in your home, or you have debilitating addictions or other health crises. If any of these are present, now is not the time for your purpose journey. Beginning your journey with any of these conditions present would be like forgetting to pack your bags or renew your passport before you head to the airport. You have to make sure your current life is stable, so that you are ready to leave it.

To ensure your success, it is important to have a baseline of economic, social, psychological and physical stability by completing this Systems Check:

- **BIOLOGICAL SYSTEM CHECK:** I am in good health or am in action with my known health issues.
  - o   If not, begin a regimen to get in shape, join a gym, see a nutritionist or see a doctor.
- **ECONOMIC SYSTEM CHECK 1:** I am able to meet my monthly expenses and feel confident that I will continue to be able to do so for at least the next six months.
  - o   If not, increase your hours or get a job that pays more.

- **ECONOMIC SYSTEM CHECK 2:** I work and commute no more than 50 hours a week combined.
  - o If not, reduce your hours or get another job that allows you to earn a living with no more than 50 hours of combined work and commute time and allows you to leave your work at work. If this is not possible, then ensure that you are not sacrificing your health or important relationships by taking on your purpose discovery journey at this time.
- **PSYCHOLOGICAL SYSTEM CHECK 1:** My home is a peaceful place that allows me to attend to my needs for a good night's rest, physical safety and downtime.
  - o If not, create or move to a place that allows for this.
- **PSYCHOLOGICAL SYSTEM CHECK 2:** I am free from any debilitating addictions, e.g., drugs, alcohol, social media, gaming, gambling.
  - o If not, get into a recovery program.

Together, these conditions constitute a complete Systems Check, a stable home base from which to begin your purpose expedition. Once your Systems Check is complete, you're ready. Now, buckle up! You'll move through these four phases in your journey.

The Four Phases of Purpose Discovery

Phase #1:

Initial Discovery

Achievements:
1. Awareness of impact on others
2. Awareness of purposeful life moments
3. Vision for a full life of purpose

Phase #2:

Resistance Tools

Achievements:
1. Clear path to soul
2. Self-love, inner peace and hope
3. Ability to transform inner resistance

Phase #3:

Deep Discovery

Achievements:
1. Hi-res Purpose Revelation (all 10 aspects)
2. Confidence and clarity
3. Connection to life and people

Phase #4:

Integration / Action

Achievements:
1. Integrated soul-driven life
2. Gratitude for past traumas and challenges
3. Executable plan and team to lead

Phase One - Initial Discovery

The initial phase of purpose discovery is where you gain greater clarity on your vision, your optimal states of being, what most fulfills you and how you impact others already. During this phase, you'll do exercises which will uncover hidden pieces of your life's purpose. You'll discover how you show up for people, what you do that already makes a huge impact, and how your life would look if, from this point forward, you lived it mightily and on fire with your life's purpose. You'll use this intelligence to refine your navigation as your expedition continues.

As with any search, initially there will be times that are rich and exhilarating, and other times that will feel scary and shaky. You'll waiver. The further you get from home, the more you'll doubt how smart your decision was to go on this expedition. You'll question whether this is what the expedition should feel like. This is normal.

As your new life of purpose begins to come into view, you'll get confronted by it, doubt it and even try to kill it. This is your resistance - the old ways of being and doing that historically kill off possibility, that take you away from living your life's purpose and have you heading back home to safety. Collectively, these are *The Trials* of your expedition.

Phase Two - Resistance Tools

This phase has you meet *The Trials*, your resistance, a gauntlet of obstacles to living your life on purpose. Your resistance is a crucial function of your ego, your personality structure. The function of your resistance is to contain your expression and exploration by convincing you to go back home and play it safe. This is the part of the journey during which you will rely most heavily on your structure - your trained Guide, purpose discovery program, community or circle of mature, high-integrity friends.

Rather than turning back, rather than cowering from the discomfort of the unknown, of growth, purpose and the beyond, you must head straight into The Trials. You must work with every voice of resistance, each flavor of the message "Stop this nonsense. You have it good. Go back home." You'll meet, among other voices, your Critic, Skeptic, Image Consultant, Wounded Child and Risk Manager (Kelley, pp. 48-53, 2009). Much like any hazard you encounter on an expedition, you must learn about them, and discover their contours and behaviors. You'll learn each voice's origin story, needs and constraints, and begin to transform these voices into allies on your journey.

The process that Tim and his colleagues at the True Purpose Institute pioneered involves a permanent psychological reconstruction around one's soul/purpose. Tim's process is based on the Voice Dialogue Method (Stone, 1993), and resonates with other methodologies such as the Internal Family Systems Model (Schwartz, 2001),

Archetypes (Jung, 1969) and Psychosynthesis (Assagioli, 1965). This process entails deconstructing your ego into its multiple parts. By parsing the ego in this manner, you clear the space for new soul/purpose information to arise. Doing so opens the channel for new information from your soul to surface.

It bears mentioning that your ego is not wrong or bad, and you're not trying to get rid of it. It serves a vital function. Your ego is the felt sense that you know who you are, what your name is, what you did yesterday, how you feel about things, etc. And yet you also have a deeper identity, one that generally lies beyond this immediate ego awareness, beyond your resistance. I refer to this deeper identity as your soul - a felt sense of truth, openness, imagination, creativity, expansiveness and unity. Atheists might refer to this as deeper truth, or higher self, or intuition. For the sake of simplicity, let's refer to the soul as that part of you that knows your life's purpose (Kelley, 2009, p. 12).

Once you discover and understand the resistance offered by each of your ego parts, you'll be clear on the internal narratives and limiting beliefs that have historically stopped you. By navigating The Trials, you will understand your ego and establish the solid and secure foundation required for exploring the unknown. Beyond The Trials, you will be present to a new field of purposeful possibilities. You will be empowered to take in this new vista, take purpose-aligned action and use your new skills to navigate future obstacles.

Phase Three - Deep Discovery

With luck and grit, you will encounter each of the ten aspects of your life's purpose - your core, virtues, vision, mission, story, flow, powers, worldview, craft and the call (see "Chapter 2: What is Purpose?" on the Purpose Tree). With the space now cleared after the Trials, you'll dive more deeply into discovery with powerful exercises that reveal the remaining hidden or cloudy aspects of your life's purpose. You'll be clear on your craft, your mentors, your path to mastery, what you will accomplish, how your purpose will move into the world, how you will purposefully interact and reshape your world. You'll see what there is to do immediately and what must wait for later. You'll develop a faith in the journey itself and be excited to turn the next page in your story.

Most importantly, you will see there is no turning back. Looking back on your old life and way of being, you'll see that there's nothing for you there anymore. There is only forward momentum, only steps towards your purpose.

Phase Four - Integration / Action

This phase is the call to integrate, to bring all that you have discovered back home to make your life match your new sense of purpose. This integration phase is where your high-resolution purpose awareness begins to settle into your tissues.

Although you now are fully empowered to continue your purpose exploration, an endless exploration is no fun if it isn't punctuated by periods of repose and integration. Nobody says, "Hey, I want to live out of a suitcase indefinitely." At some point you'll want to pause, put down some roots and begin to embody and integrate all that you have discovered and achieved. You'll want to celebrate the achievements of your discovery journey, enjoy them, play with them, integrate them and build your life of purpose.

Now that your ego and soul are more internally integrated, you can take on the soulful reformation of your life. Your task is to take another hard look at each of your seven key life areas and upgrade them with your purpose. You'll ask, "How would my purpose enhance my fitness?", "What sort of love life is best expressed by my purpose?", "How can my family reach its purposeful expression?", "What is the purpose of my community and how can I evolve it?", "How does my purpose make, spend and save money?", "What is the relationship between my purpose and my spiritual orientation?". You'll immediately see behaviors that no longer serve you and begin to create more purposeful behaviors and relationships. You'll make promises to people in your family, community and workplace to take on new purposeful expressions, and you'll be held accountable to them. The result of this is that you will show up differently, not just more excited and enlivened, but also more wise, grounded and sovereign in your relationships, career, family and community.

This phase is also where the rubber meets the road, where you will learn firsthand that the price of your purpose just went up. You paid to find it with your courage, time and resources. To live it, you will have to forfeit another luxury - playing small. The price of living your purpose is your leadership. This is where you will confront what Shakespeare meant when he said in *Henry IV*, "heavy is the head that wears the crown". Purpose awareness is all fine and good, however what really makes the journey worthwhile, the reason why you started this journey, is that you now get to integrate, embody and lead with your purpose. You didn't start this journey to see nothing in the world shift or change. You wanted impact. You wanted results. You wanted to be known by your deeds.

During this phase, you will also take on the first of many Purpose Projects, a discrete project that you will complete in 30-60 days. This project will have you build a team to help you complete your project and share the project with numerous people in your life and many new folks. The result is that the world will begin relating to you as your purpose.

Additionally, the goal of this project is to give you the tactile, tangible experience of seeing how your soul's purpose meets the world as well as highlighting the ways your inner resistance to living your purpose shows up. All of your inner voices will still arise. Your Critic will tell you it's not good enough. Your Skeptic will tell you it's not possible. Your Risk Manager will tell you that you have too much to lose if you do the project and that you'll die poor. Your Image Consultant will tell you that you'll look foolish, everyone will leave you and you'll die not just poor, but alone, outcast and living under a bridge. Your Wounded Child will tell you that it's better to play, avoid your purpose, numb or zone out. All of these voices would otherwise end your Purpose Project. That is, unless you use the tools you acquired in Phase Two. You'll be able to listen to these voices, examine their concerns, incorporate their valid insights and continue to take purpose-aligned action towards the completion of your project.

With your first Purpose Project complete, you'll have the beginning of a purposeful track record and the confidence and clarity to execute your next Purpose Project, and the next one, and so on, until your life, your career and the world becomes the full expression of your life's purpose. Your purpose is a profound achievement that takes commitment, effort and time. It is not all hard work, however. Each step along the path reveals more beautiful, rich and complex textures in your life. Let's explore now what it actually feels like to find your purpose.

CHAPTER 9

The Five Ecstasies of Purpose

"Just promise me you'll never be gay," said my Dad.

I was six years old and had just asked my Dad to get me the Culture Club's *Karma Chameleon* 45 single on vinyl. In our small farm town of Morris, Illinois, smack dab in the middle of America's Wheat, Bible and Rust Belts, at a time (1983) when "man" meant John Wayne, Neil Armstrong and Ronald Reagan, I had found the record section in the general store and located *Karma Chameleon,* my then favorite song.

I ran up to my Dad and through my gap-toothed grin exclaimed, "I really like this song, Dad! Can I get it?"

He examined the record, looked at me and said, "Sure. Just promise me you'll never be gay."

My big smile flattened. I did not know what gay was. In that moment, I made meaning of this and shock and confusion washed over me. In an instant, the excited, creative and boundless joy in my heart had vanished. I inferred that my Dad didn't like "gay", whatever that meant, and that my Dad did not like me.

I allowed his words in and felt the contours of fear and shame. In this moment, my Image Consultant was born. I decided that what I was excited about was not welcome. Something was wrong with me and I needed to act differently so that people would like me. To survive, I adopted the strategy that I should ignore my own wishes and act the way I thought others thought I should. I ignored the subtle pings of youthful purpose, enthusiasm, love and creativity, in service of being what others wanted, to please others in order to receive their love and acceptance.

I built a wall around my own thoughts, desires and emotions, and throughout grade school, I became what I believed others wanted me to be - an A-student, an athlete, and a hard worker. As I moved into junior high school and high school, this hidden fear of being gay resurfaced. I was a late bloomer and did not look like the other boys in the locker room. I decided that I was not a real man because I didn't have pubic hair and hadn't yet started fooling around with girls. So, the old fear came back up: I might be gay, something is wrong with me. I doubled down on my

Image Consultant's strategy by "manning up". I lifted weights, played sports, told dirty jokes and suppressed any remaining authenticity. I conditioned my psyche with porn, guy comedies and violent movies. I exaggerated my interest in girls, told the hateful jokes and was sometimes overtly cruel to others.

When the possibility of an authentic life finally entered my awareness in my late twenties, there was a palpable electricity, a sense that I would be able somehow to recapture the joy and truth that had died in that general store, that somehow, I could love and accept myself as I was and live an authentic life.

In the early stages of this awakening, I saw how messed up the world was and vilified racists, sexists, homophobes, consumerism, capitalists and the American Dream. I took out my anger on everyone, especially my Dad. One of the most powerful results of my purpose journey was that I realized I no longer needed to do this. Purpose work allowed me to truly begin the healing process, stepping deeper into self-love. With every gain in self-love, I was able to more deeply love and accept my Dad for who he is. And this was a relief, a joy even.

I have come to understand that my Dad did nothing wrong in that general store. He was and is an excellent father, a loving mentor, a supportive athletic coach and a generous humanitarian. He was operating from love on that day, as on all other days. What I could not have known then was how the world occurred for him. I did not know that America was in the grip of the AIDS epidemic, and that a culture war had begun between homosexual and conservative Christian culture, and I did not know what it was like for Americans to deal with this new expression of male sexuality. What I didn't know was that Boy George, the creative force behind the Culture Club, was openly homosexual, and that my Dad had erroneously collapsed homosexuality, with the music created by homosexuals and the then terminal AIDS diagnosis.

With little to no information on what AIDS was and without an awareness of the Kinsey Report (revealing that most people are significantly more bisexual than many cultures permit), my Dad made the best possible parenting choice given the information available, by projecting his fears onto me. I accept that and am now grateful for it. Yes, grateful. As poet, Mary Oliver, so beautifully penned, "Someone I loved once gave me a box full of darkness. It took me years to understand that this too, was a gift."

Like all children, I received a sacred wound in that general store, an inescapable initiation, one that every child receives from a caregiver in one form or another, wherein I was forced to psychologically individuate and generate a socially acceptable identity (beginning with my Pleaser/Image Consultant) and a way of navigating the world. Although it came at a cost (self-loathing, fear of abandonment, repressing my soul, my emotions and creativity), this was a necessary step in my psychological individuation. Without this wound, I would not have learned how to navigate society. I would not have developed the social skills of being agreeable, funny and generous. These traits brought me friends, girlfriends and leadership opportunities.

As the pain of this wound was too great to bear at the time, I also birthed my Wounded Child, who chose to escape into the private world of books in my youth, strategy games as a teen, and in my 20's with adventure, sex and drugs. Because of this wound, I partied really hard, had lots of fun, traveled the world and pushed the limits of my body and mind. Although my Wounded Child at times had a serious death wish, I'm grateful for all of these experiences. I'm grateful I lived to tell the tales, at least the ones I remember.

Further, in my teens and twenties, this wound propelled me to carefully observe group dynamics in team sports and social cliques, to know who the leader was and what I needed to do to fit in. The social facility/awareness that this afforded me made me a frequent choice for social, academic and corporate leadership roles.

In my thirties, this wound also made me especially sensitive to the plight of my gay, bi-sexual, transgendered and questioning brothers and sisters. When puberty finally hit and I realized my very real infatuation with the female body I was, on one level, very relieved. However, the deep groove of shame formed by this closeted decade would cast a long shadow over my sexuality and sex life. Living as a function of shame for ten years brought me face to face with the experience of feeling like I was fundamentally defective, like I didn't belong, like the world wasn't designed with me in mind. It was for only "normal", straight, manly men.

And this too was a gift. Feeling this estrangement had me experience myself as an outsider, even as I did everything I could to be an insider. This gave me access to my Skeptic, allowing me the vantage point to see the patterns and dynamics of society. Without feeling this estrangement, I would not have had the ability to see, and to distance myself from, the American Dream and our materialist, success-driven culture.

My Skeptic afforded me a powerful perspective and fueled my thirst for knowledge of what it means to be a human being. In my thirties, my Skeptic heartily explored the disciplines of psychology, philosophy, economics, comparative religion, politics, ecology, literature and history. This wound provided me with the energy, drive and perspective to understand what was going in the world, and why I felt so isolated from it.

As you can see, purpose work is not just about purpose discovery: it contains entire worlds of self-discovery, joy, healing, forgiveness and self-love. For me it gave me access to compassion for myself, my Dad, my Midwestern roots and capitalism. This journey is about embracing and loving what is, seeing how there are no wrong or "throw-away" moments in our lives. Each moment, and especially each painful moment, is a vital element of the story, one that allows each of us to develop in new ways. [This is not to condone any injustices, perpetrators of harm, abuses or violations of personal sovereignty.]

When you choose to discover your purpose, you will also start seeing your life anew. Specifically, you are likely to experience five distinct ecstasies - five discrete joys that make your path to purpose also a journey of joy and self-love. Living purposefully is more than just living fully and intentionally. The process includes a series of horizon-expanding, heart-opening moments that give you the confidence to keep after it, to continue digging through your ego, blasting through old patterns and forms of resistance to live your life's purpose.

Although many folks experience these joys sequentially, they don't always happen that way, so please consider these ecstasies less as a trail of breadcrumbs that must be followed in a specific order, and more as a collection of neon signs that say, "Yes, you are getting warmer. Keep following your path of purpose."

The First Ecstasy: Purpose Exists

Of course purpose exists, right? If you didn't believe that, why would you be reading this book? Out of curiosity? Or to arm your Skeptic with knowledge to argue against the existence of purpose? We all have a Skeptic, but there's also a part of you that truly hopes there is something in this work that can awaken the joy and excitement you remember from childhood, that can rekindle the fire inside you - the idea of you that you faintly remember and yet know is still possible.

And yes, I intentionally say "rekindle" because the fire that is your purpose never dies; it's always there. So, no matter how you're feeling right now, wherever you are emotionally - from feeling on top of the world to wondering if there is really a point to anything - you have a purpose, something that you and you alone can offer to the world. This journey is about remembering and rekindling: it's about removing what is in the way of you stepping fully into your purpose and greatness.

Still unsure? I was, too, at first. When I began my inner journey after graduate school, I read a lot. I crammed my head full of new concepts and ideas. I armed myself with philosophical and spiritual frameworks to attack a world I felt had wronged me. Unfortunately, I had also become stuck in a worldview that asserted there was no meaning in the human experience, that everything in the material plane was illusory, and the only thing we can do is to become Spiritually Enlightened.

This is commonly known as a "spiritual bypass", which is using new age, spiritual and philosophical language to justify one's avoidance to doing deeper work with the ego and soul - healing dysfunctional relationships and awakening one's life purpose. Perhaps you are familiar with this phenomenon. Perhaps you've used or heard the terms, "It's all good", "We are one," or "Only God is real" as an excuse to not look at oneself or refuse to take bold action.

When I first entered into the question of my life's purpose at age 34, I was operating from this place. I believed that all my wounds, powers, joys, and sorrows were insignificant and meant nothing whatsoever in terms of the Cosmos or the well-being of my fellow humans. I used this belief to ignore anything that alluded to individual meaning, soul, purpose or responsibility. I ignored my values, my desire to make the world a better place, and even the validity of my own personal peak experiences in nature and during sex. I discounted or invalidated the very real joys I regularly experienced by engaging with the mystery of the Cosmos, giving and receiving love, and in moments of service and creativity.

I held tight to my belief that there was no meaning, no possibility of a richer, more meaningful life here in the world of matter. I believed all I could do in this life was to try like hell to transcend my human form and become "Spiritually Enlightened." While I enjoyed this pursuit, I suffered greatly for it. My career was lackluster, my marriage was dysfunctional, and my health was terrible.

Following my divorce in 2011, I was broken open. I was aware that my spiritual bypass orientation wasn't working out too well for me. In walked Jonathan Gustin, my Purpose Guide™. He reintroduced me to the possibility of purpose - not just Spiritual Enlightenment, but also a soul awakening, the descendent path to a manifested life purpose. He made a very compelling case that I was ignoring two of the three purposes of life. I was well developed in the upper realm of purpose, transcending the world as a meditator, scholar and philosopher. But I had wholly ignored the middle realm of purpose, of purpose manifested and materialized as an emotional adult, enjoying the human experience, being responsible, giving and receiving love and crafting a purpose-driven livelihood. I had also ignored the lower descendent realm of purpose, in which I might receive a soul initiation, discover the various aspects of my soul's purpose, and my unique place in the Cosmos. As a result of not having had a soul initiation, I had no access to my purpose-driven livelihood or to an integrated life.

And for a moment, amidst the din of my existential malaise, spiritual bypass and spiritual nihilism, I listened to him. He told me that I couldn't truly ascend to become Spiritually Enlightened unless I also descended into my soul and became whole at the level of ego. I needed to have a healthy ego in order to transcend it.

He showed me that humanity was rich with people living their purpose, living authentically in the world and making great changes to it, while simultaneously pursuing a spiritual path. While my Skeptic said, "No! Stuff this wishful thinking and anthropomorphic self-importance up your arse!", my Soul said, "Give it a try, you've got nothing to lose."

In that moment, I felt hope for the first time in many years. I was overjoyed at the possibility of finally ending this many-sided internal war among my ego parts. I was delighted to learn that there was a path to having it all - to having a spiritual yearning, a passion for changing the world, a career that allowed me to be well-paid for doing so, a reason-based understanding of the world through philosophy and the Cosmos, to honor my carnal desires, my love of intimacy and my desire to be a husband and father. However, all my fears of inadequacy and limiting beliefs had, thus far, kept me safely cloistered and inactive, far away from an active life of purpose.

So, I jumped into Jonathan's expert arms and said, "Yes!" to the world of purpose. He led me through a number of powerful exercises that deepened my awareness of my ego structure, led me to own my unique powers in a meaningful way, and taught me to have compassion for my deepest wounds. On each step of the path, my confidence in the existence of my purpose strengthened. At some point, a critical mass was achieved and my Skeptic finally relaxed. I no longer doubted the existence of my purpose. I was pitched forward, awakened to the possibility of purpose and excited to create a fully integrated, on fire, purpose-driven life.

The Second Ecstasy of Purpose: Validation

Once your purpose discovery path begins - once you believe in the possibility of living a life of purpose and choose a path towards its revelation - you set in motion sequential revelations about your life of purpose that all come as a version of this powerful message:

Your purpose is unique beyond measure. Others love you for it, humanity needs you for it and the Cosmos rejoices in it!

In your finest moments, you contributed your core, virtues and powers, impacting others through your energy, love, service, and creativity. You touched, comforted and inspired others in their time of need. You blew them away with your creative expression. At times, you may have even made them glad that the Universe exists.

This validation reveals itself in many forms, beginning with a process of seeking feedback from others as soon as you begin your purpose discovery path. You'll receive feedback from your community that reveals your greatest powers - how you already live purposefully and change the lives of people you love. This continues as the rest of the world recognizes the expanding expressions of your purpose that you bring forth.

I love this exercise, and so I come back to it again and again, simply because I love learning how I show up in other people's lives. This really landed for me when The Huffington Post covered the company I created, EVR1 - a company that was purpose-born, authentic and committed to creating a better world. The validation I received in this article fueled me at a time when my path seemed dark and difficult, when my relationship with my Dad was in trouble, when I'd been devastated by a break-up, when I'd run out of savings, and began to question my path. Although I knew at some level I was making a difference in people's lives, my old patterns of self-doubt emerged, took this new data and started to take over.

And yet, just as soon as I entered this nosedive, I was able to pull myself out of it. I knew the impact of my life and purpose on others, by seeing the validation from others who were moved by what I was creating. Every time EVR1 would get a positive mention in the press - whether it was from TechCrunch or USA Today or Fox News - I felt another cosmic jolt, or sometimes the whisper, "You're doing it right. Thank you."

Unlike the first ecstasy, this second ecstasy is recurring. It is the jelly-of-the-month club of purpose, showing up consistently on your path. Once you tune into the frequency of your purpose, and get the impact that your existence and purpose has on the world, you permanently establish a listening for it and will receive this feedback, filling up your tank of self-love, a resource that is available to tap when you need it the most.

As soon as you start to get the impact you have on others' lives, you will be overwhelmed. I did not say that it can or might be overwhelming - it *is* overwhelming!

When you receive this feedback, you will see the whole picture of the accumulated effects that "just being you" has on the people you most care about. Truly validated, you will experience that you are powerful. You will know that who you are makes a huge difference in the lives of others. All that remains is for you to own your greatness more deeply, and commit to what has always been true your entire life: your life's purpose.

The Third Ecstasy of Purpose: Freedom

The third ecstasy of purpose is freedom - a jail break, a progressive liberation of your soul (that part of you that knows your purpose) from the jailer (your unexamined, untransformed ego). This is an unparalleled delight that every human can have with purpose discovery work. This is not to say you get to live without your ego, but rather, you get to live in right relationship to your ego, and eventually in right relationship to the whole world.

When I discovered that my ego isn't a single entity (as indicated per the Tim Kelley/Voice-Dialogue method, it's a number of different voices - Critic, Skeptic, Image Consultant, Wounded Child and Risk Manager, etc.), I felt a surge of hope.

Before I began my purpose journey with Jonathan, I felt trapped by these voices and their cacophony of conflicting narratives, desires and fears. On one hand, I felt compelled by my spiritual path to leave society, to dive deep into gurus and solitary spiritual retreats. On another hand, I felt compelled to act on my social, economic and environmental justice aspirations. On yet another hand, I felt compelled by my biology to be perpetually single. And on still another hand I felt compelled by my Midwestern conditioning to be a husband, a father, coach Little League and just ignore the world.

But how did any of that fit with my reason-based understanding of psychology, philosophy and physics? And even if I could find a synthetic position or a middle ground, the cognitive dissonance of this possibility rendered me hopelessly immobile.

Yep, I was stuck, broken down, disempowered, thinking I was damaged, confused, maybe even certifiably crazy for having all of these different parts of me with different desires, values, affectations and character traits. I was confined to hearing these voices in solitary confinement, unaware that my jailer was me - or rather the parts of me who would take the reins at random intervals and contexts and keep me inert, off the court of my life, small and safe, and a healthy distance away from my soul and purpose.

I was at the whim of this "Lord of the Flies" chaos of mind, wracked with anxiety and confusion. Unclear as to what was the real me, I jumped from ego part to ego part, acting out of alignment and out of integrity with my soul. During this ego deconstruction process, I engaged with these parts one on one, began to understand them, and learned how to negotiate with them. By honoring my ego parts, I began to truly know in my heart that discovery of my purpose was possible; it was now only a matter of time before I found it.

As I began to unearth these voices and create cohesive character profiles, they began to feel a lot less scary. The messages of my ego parts showed up like little passive-aggressive post-it notes, e.g., "It's pointless!" (Skeptic), "You'll look foolish!" (Image Consultant), "There is too much at risk!" or "You'll get hurt again!" (Risk Manager), "You can't do it!" (Critic). And they would all finish with the same sentence: "Therefore, you can't and won't live your purpose."

As I dug deeper, I found that although these voices could be loud and obnoxious, they are also well-intended. They want to keep me safe and protect me, albeit sometimes in misguided ways.

Once you engage with your ego parts, you'll start to see that they are just part of your ego and not the whole experience of you. They are not your most central and sacred part - that is, your soul and its message, your life's purpose. As you begin to understand these parts, honor them and work with them, you'll be surprised at their willingness to yield the floor to your soul.

Of course, at first, they'll protect their territory with everything they've got. They'll fight tooth and nail to make everything in your life more important than ego deconstruction and finding your life's purpose. And this is important to presence - if it hasn't happened already, it will. Soon you'll start to create all sorts of reasons to put down this book and eschew the subject of purpose altogether.

However, if you are able to stay with the process and finish the deconstruction, you'll be able to partner with these parts and create the silence and space for your soul to enter the void and speak.

Once I completed this part of the journey, I knew that purpose revelation was on its way because all the resistance I had experienced in my life thus far was not an objective reality I was correctly perceiving from the world, but was entirely generated from within. And now that it was known, I was no longer a schizophrenic jumble of desires and fears, but instead I was a blank canvas upon which to paint my purpose.

With this new opening and possibility, I immediately felt six inches taller; I felt the inclination of my sternum rise by 15 degrees. I started walking tall. I knew that the purpose work I was doing was working, that I was free, that the die was cast for purpose revelation.

The Fourth Ecstasy of Purpose: Revelation

The fourth ecstasy of purpose is revelation. It's that moment of repose after the steepest part of the ascent (blasting through your resistance, organizing your ego parts), when your soul beats its drum most loudly and lets you know what you have to do. It's a series of precious, exhilarating, unbelievable moments when your soul speaks, "Thank you for clearing out the attic of your psyche. Thanks for organizing your ego. Thanks for putting me in right relationship to your ego parts. Thank you for hearing what I've been screaming at you your entire life. Your purpose is X."

The first time my soul spoke to me in definitive terms was during a massage on February 12, 2012. I began the morning with my assigned purpose work, went to a yoga class and devoted my practice to purpose revelation. I grabbed a bite to eat and went for a massage. As I lay there on the massage table, feeling every knot gradually uncoil and release, an electric image formed on the screen of my mind.

The image was of a 6"x8" pouch made of 550 lb. - test nylon cord, woven in a spiritual pattern, at once a functional bag for tools, itself made of a multi-tool (rope that could be unwoven) and a spiritual totem. This would be the first of hundreds of prototypes and eventually over 50 products I designed and created at EVR1, a company I founded that very day. Upon revelation, I felt energized, called forth into immediate action. I went home and started creating the site, designing prototypes, and telling the story about why we need fewer, but more powerful, sacred and useful objects in our lives.

As I was building EVR1, I also accidentally started a career as a Guide. I shared the power of this work with everyone I knew, and eventually was asked to coach my friends and family. My first clients were my mom and two of my aunts. Suddenly after 18 months of growth at EVR1, a new revelation struck. We weren't making the difference we wanted to make. Even though we were building a worldwide customer base and distribution partnerships, and receiving fantastic press, it became clear to me and my business partner, Dane Zehrung, and that this path wasn't our greatest contribution. After a few months of discussion, we realized our greatest contributions were not in making products, but in awakening people to their lives of purpose.

Your purpose breakthroughs may follow a similar pattern of emergence and surprises. The language of your soul can be verbal, but it is just as likely to be a symbol, a poetry fragment, a feeling, an image, a sound or a sensation. When it comes, it will rumble and vibrate within you.

When this happens, you will trust it. With your resistance firmly behind you, you can fully trust the soul wisdom of your body. As you let this truth rumble and vibrate throughout your whole body, this moment joins other moments of truth in your life. In the way that your soul has let you know in the past when something is right and powerfully aligned, so will your purpose revelation. This is your birthright; you've earned it.

The Fifth Ecstasy of Purpose: Coronation

"You're so grounded," said Jamie, a new friend and the producer of a sustainability conference she founded and we were attending.

"Really? No one has ever said that to me before."

I was shocked, as my understanding of myself was different. Having spent seven years meandering through spiritual and personal development programs, reading radical political philosophy and social commentary, my experience of myself was more of a new age iconoclast, a free-spirited thinker and destroyer of orthodoxy, or as my rugby mate, Kyle, said, "You're a random number generator." In course of a single sentence, I could I jump from conspiracy theory to spiritual practice to existential musing. Something had changed, however. I was at this conference one year after having done my purpose discovery work with Jonathan. Although I had new awareness, my narrative of myself was in need of updating. I wasn't as prone to whimsy. I wasn't as critical, but more accepting. I was on a mission, purposefully rooted, charged with a global vision. As Jamie had reflected, I was occurring to her as very grounded.

After your purpose discovery work, and in large part due the liberating effects of deconstructing your ego, you too will start to occur differently to yourself and others. Not only are you clearing the path for purpose revelation, what Bill Plotkin refers to as "soul encounters", but in doing so, you are revealing the ways your purpose is already present. Without the limiting beliefs, constraints and constant infighting of your ego parts, what is left of you? It is your true self, an ease, a centeredness in the ways you are, when you are free of those encumbering obstacles.

Dr. Richard Schwartz PhD, the creator of the Internal Family Systems model, discovered that his clients, having dissected their ego structures (but prior to doing any soul encounter/purpose discovery work) began to exhibit eight qualities of what he calls the true self (and what I refer to as core): calmness, clarity, curiosity, compassion, confidence, courage, creativity and connectedness (Schwartz, 2001, pp. 47-65). These 8 C's release an individual into fullness.

1. **Calmness** - a release of tension, the ability to be with one's emotions and conflicting beliefs without identifying with them, and a sense of groundedness, acting in a way that reflects that there is indeed a ground underneath, and upon which one's experience dances and rejoices.

2. **Clarity** - the ability to decide, freedom from overwhelm, to see the situation clearly without story, extreme emotions or limiting beliefs.

3. **Curiosity** - an orientation towards wonder and novelty, towards seeking a greater understanding of self, others and the ways the world works, the result of which is that people have the experience of being heard and deeply listened to when they are asked clarifying questions and acknowledged.

4. **Compassion** - being able to feel someone's pain and share it with them, to understand their experience, feel it, honor it and hold space for it.

5. **Confidence** - being whole, healed, and rooted, knowing that regardless of whatever circumstances or triggers arise there is no actual threat to oneself, the knowing oneself as capable of responding with wisdom, grace and compassion, rather than reacting with anger or judgment.

6. **Courage** - the desire and ability to take bold, compassionate and nonjudgmental action in the face of injustice, suffering and inequity, towards a generative outcome for all concerned parties; the desire and ability to go towards one's own pain and shame, to heal and resolve integrity leaks and inauthentic ways of being so as to step into greater fullness as a human and make a greater contribution to others.

7. **Creativity** - the natural emergence of the unfettered soul, wherein the desire to self-express, to push beyond the current limits of reason and possibility, manifests through novel works, generating more joy, harmony and flow in relationships and creative pursuits.

8. **Connectedness** - the state created by an undefended heart, one that has been broken a thousand times before, one that is enlarged, open and willing to receive and be with others, free from reaction, free from the desire to look good or judge, free to connect with the experience, with true self and with the longings of others, free to connect with all of existence, experiencing unity in nature, deep relating, creative emergence and physical intimacy.

Now, these are just the results of the deconstruction process. When you do purpose discovery/soul encounter work after this step, these aspects of your true self will radiate and align under the banner of your purpose.

I've had many moments where one of the eight C's newly erupted in me. The most powerful occurred in one day on a 9-day intensive training retreat with the Purpose Guides Institute. About three months prior (and five years into my purpose journey), I recognized that I still had anger holding me back. Although I had made peace and practiced forgiveness a number of times, I was still holding onto anger, anger towards my parents, towards capitalism and towards all the forces that perpetuate suffering in the world. At that time, this book was called "Purpose Revolution" (you will encounter this energy in "Chapter 17: Humanity's Midlife Crisis"). The book was focused on using the power of purpose to overthrow the orthodox establishment, to "eat the rich", dispossess the 1% and do a *Fight Club* style takedown of modern, technological, globalized, industrialized capitalism. A better name for it may have been the "Make Wrong Manifesto." I threw my parents under the bus, the Midwest under the bus, America under the bus, and basically everyone who wasn't a declared change agent under the bus. They were part of the problem. And this book had become a predictable, angsty postmodern coming of age treatise.

This didn't serve me or the people I judged. More importantly, this book would not have made any difference, as versions of the "Make Wrong Manifesto" had already been written by Michael Moore (*Stupid White Men*), David Korten (*When Corporations Rule the World*), and Howard Zinn (*The People's History of the United States*). The book needed to change, but I needed to change first. So, I surrendered to my soul.

On the PGI retreat, we did a 24-hour process called the Soul Quest, where we fasted, took a vow of silence and spent eight hours on the land performing a self-designed ceremony. The night before the Soul Quest, we performed the Fire Ceremony, where I ended my love affair with anger, injustice and the postmodernist view that hates all power and hierarchies. My last words before entering silence were to thank postmodernism. Postmodernism had helped me awaken my intellect and discover the world. It had broken open my heart to receive the world's suffering. It had expanded my worldview, an attempt to include the entire human and ecological condition. It had driven a decade of efforts to make the world a better place. I stated how this relationship no longer served me, how this anger was burning a hole in me, that I was called into what I now call Shambhala Leadership, and that I would have to set down my anger to truly lead. So, in the ceremony, I spoke to postmodernism as if it was a lover whom I valued, and loved, but nonetheless had to leave. I then burned the paper that held these written sentiments. Upon completing the ceremony, we entered silence.

The next morning, we silently left camp and found our remote ceremony spots in the woods and within which we would stay during the eight-hour lament. I found my spot and carefully arranged sticks and rocks to form my circle. I prayed, cried, sang, screamed and danced. I talked to trees, leaves and bugs. I smoked and sacrificed tobacco. I listened to the wind as if each gust was a sentence possessed of new soul information. I screamed and pounded on the Earth as I begged my soul for a new name. I demanded a name that would call me into my Shambhala Leadership. The words that came through were "Buffalo Heart". And immediately my Skeptic chimed in "Yeah, right. Of course you are. Everyone's spirit totem is a buffalo or jaguar or wolf or bear or some nonsense. Where are the spirit aardvarks, rats and weasels?"

To honor my Skeptic, I did as I had done earlier in the ceremony and talked to the trees. I left the circle and went to the nearest tree and touched it. I said, "Am I Buffalo Heart?" Nothing came through. So, I moved to another, and yet another without any confirmation. On my way to the fourth tree, the second part of the name came through: "who loves and wholes the world". Immediately my knees buckled and I fell to the Earth crying. I was trembling with recognition, gratitude, excitement and also fear, for I knew the scope of this charge and that it wasn't going to be easy. I had to forgive everybody. This was just the beginning. I had to rewrite this damn book, already three years in the making. More importantly, I had to forgive myself, my generation (X/Y), my parents and their generation (Baby Boomers) for our participation in the destruction of the human and ecological condition.

Inside this name, "Buffalo Heart Who Loves and Wholes the World", I began to step into a far greater sense of the eight C's, specifically compassion, courage, connectedness and curiosity. I felt compassion for the suffering of those who only know how to exploit and perpetrate violence. I was connected with the whole evolving state of humanity - so beautiful and creative, yet so flawed and lacking integrity. I took responsibility for matters as they were, for the human condition as is, and declared my leadership. I humbled myself before this task, knowing that I would have to grow tremendously and get really curious about myself and others and the best way forward for our species. When I returned to civilization, I put to paper who I now am and what I must now do. For reference, it's included in "Appendix D: The Buffalo Heart Manifesto".

Now that you have built a cognitive foundation exploring the real results and felt experience of the path of purpose discovery, you are likely connected to the possibilities of a life of purpose. So, let's do this thing! In Part Two you'll learn about the Global Purpose Expedition. When you go online, register and join the global community of purpose-awakening leaders, when you complete each of the exercises, you will discover new aspects of your purpose and align your internal ego structure around your soul. You will be empowered to align your core life contexts (love, family, career, community, finances, spirituality and health) with your purpose. Most exciting of all, you'll begin to feel the stirrings of the five ecstasies in your own life.

PART TWO

Your Purpose

CHAPTER 10

Your Global Purpose Expedition

More than anything, this book is an invitation to actually find, live and lead with your purpose. Additionally, the words written after this chapter will only be useful to you if you begin your purpose discovery journey now. If you are inspired by the science of purpose and possibility of what purpose could do for you, your career and the planet, if you want to uplevel your life with purpose and join the millions of purpose-driven leaders around the world, you are in the right place. There are two paths you can take - you can work one-on-one with a trained Guide to create a customized purpose discovery journey (this will usually take 3-6 months and a few thousand dollars; see "Appendix C: Purpose Transformation Resources"). Or you can begin with a lower-priced online purpose course, like the Global Purpose Expedition (http://GlobalPurposeExpedition.com).

This chapter is an overview of the Global Purpose Expedition (GPE), preparing you to stop reading and start discovering. When you do, you will immediately begin to build a deeper relationship to your purpose. When you're finished with the GPE/purpose discovery program, please pick this book back up and continue the exploration of what your career, leadership and humanity could look like if we all knew our life's purpose.

Think of the GPE as a living laboratory, a place to explore and expand your life, through the lens of purpose, and a place to build authentic community and soulful professional relationships. The exercises in this course yield more than purpose awareness. They will anchor you in hope, possibility and self-love, empowering you with the confidence, clarity and courage to make big changes in your purpose-driven life and career.

Does the GPE work?

Thousands of people from over 50 countries have taken this course (and its predecessor, the Purpose Challenge). 95% of those who have completed the course reported a deeper connection to their life's purpose, and said they would recommend this program to friends and family. Furthermore, each participant took the Meaning and Purpose Questionnaire (MPQ), developed by Gleb Tsipursky PhD at Ohio State University, before and after the program. In the MPQ, participants were asked to share their agreement on a series of statements on a scale of 1-10. For the statement, "I am satisfied with my sense of meaning and purpose in life," participants reported an average 1.91-point increase over their pre-course score (Tsipursky, 2015). As we all know, even numbers can be misleading, so I invite you to learn about the experiences of the actual participants in their own words, located at GlobalPurposeExpedition.com.

What is the structure of the GPE?

The 10-week GPE contains exercises designed to incrementally expand and deepen your purpose, propel you on your path of purpose, expedite the realization of the many fruits of purpose (health, success, love, a better world) and connect you with a global community. It is an immersion into both the nature of your life's purpose and the actual experience of living your life on purpose. The course contains:

- 10 short teaching videos
- 10 powerful exercises
- 10 purposeful conversation exercises
- 10 Q&A recordings
- Private online forum
- Lifetime access to the exercises, plus updates
- Lifelong alumni group of purpose awakened people around the world

How much time does it take?

The GPE can be done in as little as 3 hours a week:

- 15 minutes watching the teaching videos,
- 30 minutes having an optional accountability call
- 60 minutes listening to the weekly Q&A session
- 30 minutes doing the exercise,
- 15 minutes having your purposeful conversation with someone important to you
- 30 minutes contributing on the online forum.

That's a 30-hour investment over the course of ten weeks to create decades of impact, fulfillment, success, joy and connection. Upon completion, you will have a deeper connection to your purpose, the power to overcome resistance to living it, and lifelong alumni community of graduates.

Why is the GPE different than other purpose course?

The GPE is comprised of the 10 most powerful purpose exercises I have created, based on the contributions of my key influences (Bill Plotkin, Clarissa Pinkola Estes, Thomas Moore, Michael Meade, Jonathan Gustin, Tim Kelley, Rod Stryker, etc.) and other leaders in the soul/purpose space. The GPE is designed to be your first stop on your purpose journey, a progression of exercises moving you deeper into your purpose.

Secondly, unlike most purpose courses, the GPE is an expedition. It is an active endeavor. It is not about sitting in a cave and contemplating. Sure, there are exercises that are done alone, but every week, you have a purposeful share conversation to bring your life and relationships into alignment with who you really are. You'll share what you are discovering and begin to transform the key relationships in your life, such that they express and support your life's purpose.

Although this course is one of the most effective online purpose discovery programs, your experience will be unique to you. You will immediate love some of the exercises, and some may take weeks or months to fully land for you. That is just the nature of this work. There is nothing wrong if you don't get a big breakthrough with each and every exercise. However, there is a great chance (95%) that by the end of the course, you will be much more deeply connected to your purpose and have the clarity, confidence and courage to take action on it.

Moreover, you don't have to take this course only once. You come back to it as needed to refresh your purpose, discover new aspects of it and connect with the global purpose community. Also, the GPE has its own purpose and evolutionary growth path, so what follows is only the current version of curriculum. As we consistently improve the course based on participant feedback, please explore the latest exercises in the GPE at GlobalPurposeExpedition.com.

The stages of the Global Purpose Expedition follow the progression outlined in "Chapter 8: Your Purpose Expedition":

Pre-course Work:

Before you begin, you will get clear on where you are right now on your journey. You will also get clear about your reasons for starting and completing the Global Purpose Expedition.

Preparation: *Purpose Assessment Tool #1* - you'll discover how connected you are currently to your purpose, how empowered you are to take action on it and how purpose-aligned your life is already. You'll also get clear on all your reasons to find, live and lead with your purpose, everything that could go wrong if you decide to live your purpose, and all the reasons you will give to stop doing the Global Purpose Expedition. You will retake the Purpose Assessment Tool at the end to see how far you have come.

Hearing the Call (Weeks 1-2)

During this phase, you'll get connected to what is pulling you into a big life of purpose and how humanity stands to benefit from you coming fully online with your purpose.

Week 1: *Entelechy* - you'll connect with your fully actualized, perfected self who will reveal new aspects your high-definition life's purpose

Week 2: *Community Diagnostic* - you'll learn from the wisdom of 10 people in your life on your core, powers, and clues to your purposeful future

The Search (Weeks 3-4)

During this phase, you are leaving home and exploring the beyond. You are searching for signs of what your life's purpose might be, looking more deeply at what breaks your heart. Also during this phase, if it hasn't happened already, the new possibilities for a more purposeful life will arise and you WILL encounter resistance to this work, to the perceived implications, considerations and constraints this new information reveals. You will begin to confront your purpose and get hooked by reasons why you cannot do this, or why now is not the right time. This is collectively referred to as "The Trials" - your resistance to change, your fear of leaving home. We will address all of your concerns, implications, constraints and considerations in the following phase, "The Trials".

Week 3: *Messages from the Future* - you'll envision the totality of your full life of purpose, achievement and impact from the end of your life on purpose back to today

Week 4: *Purposeful Titans* - you'll gain the wisdom of three purposeful titans, by interviewing three people who are living lives on purpose or have achieved mastery in a field you are passionate about.

The Trials (Weeks 5-6)

This phase is the most intense and rewarding part of the expedition. Your pre-purpose life is protected by a formidable web of resistance. To actually find and embody your purpose, you'll need to be tested, to endure and navigate The Trials of your resistance. In this phase, we'll look at all the ways you have historically been stuck or blocked from finding your purpose and taking purposeful action.

Week 5: *Default Purpose* - you'll discover the core types/themes of resistance and how they show up in your life.

Week 6: *Overcoming Resistance* - you'll get tools to uncover, transform and overcome future forms of internal resistance to taking purpose-aligned action.

Revelation (Weeks 7-8)

Now that you have passed The Trials, and your resistance is catalogued, you have two new powers: 1. you have the power to overcome your resistance to living your purpose and 2. you've got a wide, clear channel to uncover more purpose information. In this phase, you'll do powerful soul encounter methods to reveal hidden aspects of your life's purpose.

Week 7: *Soul House* - you'll deepen your connection to your soul and learn the wisdom of various incarnations of soul - young, healed, activated, ancestral and universal.

Week 8: *Jungian Journaling* - you'll gain greater clarity on your craft, who you are meant to serve, how you contribute to them and the next step on your journey, your mission.

The Return (Weeks 9-10)

With this new information about your purpose, your task is now to integrate this awareness and then move it out into the world. This phase is where you descend to your roots and ignite your Purpose Project. You'll get connected to the people you are meant to serve in the world, experience what it feels like to communicate from your life's purpose, and see your Purpose Project come to fruition. In seeing your purpose live in the world as a project, you will be ordained into a full, rich life of soul. As Mark Zuckerberg illuminates, "Ideas don't come out fully formed. They only become clear as you work on them. You just have to get started." (Zuckerberg, 2017)

Week 9: *Future Walk* - you'll get clarity on the next step on your path, as you will visually move into your future and reflect back to the present moment on what you need to do next.

Week 10: *Purpose Project* - you'll craft a 30-60-day project that is the expression of your purpose and have the opportunity to powerfully deal with resistance that comes up in completing the project. *Purpose Assessment Tool #2* - you'll see how far you have come since the beginning of the course and receive your certificate of completion.

What happens when the Global Purpose Expedition is over?

Whatever your purpose dictates that you should do, you will begin to do. Here are a few options:

1. **GO DEEPER:** After you graduate, you can go deeper and do an advanced program, where you will align and integrate your purpose into every key area of your life, transform your key relationships, and move your Purpose Project into action with the support of the GPE community.
2. **CONNECT:** Build connections with other graduates on fire with their purpose.

Alumni Groups

Once you are a GPE graduate, you will have the opportunity to connect with your global tribe of purpose-awakened leaders, other people who are committed to the same things as you, by joining a purpose-driven alumni group that supports you and your purpose project. In this group you can share articles, developments and best practices, ask for advice, and connect and collaborate with your fellow purposeful leaders around what matters most to you, your life's purpose. Once you complete the program, you can join any of these alumni groups (or start one of your own) to take on big purposeful projects and create a purposeful movement in your field:

- GPE Local Chapters - connect with other local purposeful folks for fun, culture and adventure
- GPE Entrepreneurs - connect with other folks who are building, or aspire to build, a business fueled by their purpose
- GPE Environmental Leaders - connect with other GPE graduates out to impact humanity's relationship to the planet
- GPE Social Justice Leaders - connect with other GPE graduates out to foster equality, empathy, freedom and understanding
- GPE Democracy Reformers - connect with other GPE graduates out to create a better government
- GPE First Responders (military, police, fire, EMT) - connect with other GPE graduates out to make the world safer
- GPE Educators - connect with other GPE graduates out to impact education
- GPE Healers - connect with other GPE graduates out to impact human health, wellness and conscious evolution
- GPE Parents - connect with other GPE graduates to share best practices for purposeful parenting
- GPE College - connect with other GPE graduates out to create a more purposeful college experience

- GPE Revolutionaries - connect with other GPE graduates to bring purpose discovery education into major institutions, e.g., government, education, religion, business and media
- GPE Translators - connect with other GPE graduates to bring the GPE to non-English speakers

Ready? Go to http://GlobalPurposeExpedition.com to begin!

Once you've completed the Global Purpose Expedition, you now face the tasks of bringing your purpose into the world and into your relationships, family, career and community. These are difficult tasks. The remainder of this book explores how this increasingly integrated experience of purpose can be lived at the level of career, relationship, society, economics, politics, ecology and species.

CHAPTER 11

Creating a Purpose-Driven Career

"I'm not sure I'll ever have a regular job again. I'd be fine living under a bridge reading humanity's great works," I said to my then girlfriend in a fit of disillusionment.

"You can't be serious. That's not an option."

"It is for me. I have a deep suspicion, born out of real economic and ecological data, that if I put my MBA to use with any of these companies that are hiring, I'd be doing a grave injustice to all that I hold sacred. I'd rather be poor and on the right side of history, than be an accomplice in the downfall of our species."

Coming out of business school in 2004, I was disheartened and confused. I wanted to live my values at work and create a better world, but I was struggling to find companies that would hire me to do this. Sustainability, purpose and fair trade were not yet shared ideals in business and the halls of power. As we will explore in "Chapter 17: Humanity's Midlife Crisis", I found that in addition to producing many great things, our economy also rewarded some odd behaviors and outcomes, like long hours, low wages, ecocide, oppression and political corruption. Although our global economy creates increasingly more beautiful, useful and powerful goods (e.g., internet, smartphones), it also makes an incredible number of goods with questionable value (e.g., textile novelties like Snuggies, single-use packaged sugar drinks), and almost always at great cost to human health and well-being and the environment.

I discovered that many businesses trample on civil rights, lobby for the right to pollute our air, water and soil, and fight against fair wages. I learned that understanding the history of American capitalism is incomplete without the exploitation of labor (indentured servitude, slavery, subsistence wages), without the genocide of 50-100 million Native peoples, without the enslavement of 10's of millions of Africans and their descendants and without America's the current inequalities, such as its:

1. Prison-industrial complex/slave state, wherein companies like McDonald's, Chevron and Bank of America, benefit from paying prisoners (mostly people of color) pennies on the dollar for their efforts. (Abdulrauf, 2017)

2. Discriminatory hiring and income practices, paying African-American women $0.63 for every dollar paid to white men (American Association of University Women, 2016).

3. Gross economic inequality resulting in 51% of American children now qualifying for poverty-assistance school lunches (Southern Education Foundation, 2015), and one out of every 30 American children is now homeless, or 2.5 million homeless children (American Institutes for Research, 2014).

These consequences are not just confined to people of color or children, nor are they just limited to the United States: they are globally and economically devastating, severely damaging poor and immigrant populations, the ecology that our biology and economy depends upon - our planet's watersheds, topsoil, air quality, water tables, plants and animals. Over the last forty years, we've reached historical levels of food, water and air toxicity, as well as record deforestation. As a result, between 1970-2012, it is estimated that Earth has lost 58% of its wildlife (World Wildlife Foundation, 2016).

As my awareness of this dynamic grew, I moved beyond shock and outrage and into full blown shame – I felt shame for being in business.

Was I on the wrong side of history?

I was at a complex crossroads. On one hand, I was excited about exploring and changing the world and on the other had I was also deeply ashamed by my lifestyle and career choices to date. When I looked at what my career and the worlds of high finance and technology startups were actually doing for the human and ecological condition, I did not like it. I was stuck. I wanted to do what was right, but did not know how. I wanted to understand how best practices for human life intersected with economics, and how my life and career could include both.

Of course, I didn't decide to live under a bridge. But I also couldn't think my way out of this pickle, so I decided to stop thinking about it and do something. I wanted real world experience working with other people who were confronting this data and questioning what to do about it. In the years following business school, I worked for many young companies in search of something that could be called generative. I was lucky to contribute to social and ecological enterprises, such as Lifefactory, SunTechnics, ReadSocial, and Babycenter/Johnson & Johnson. These formative experiences allowed me to see what was possible in purpose-driven business, and gave me a vision of what honest economic progress looked and felt like.

These experiences still inspire me and drive the work I do, developing purposeful leaders of successful startups (Net Driven/KKR, AnnMarie Skincare, Dr. Hops Kombucha Beer and SnapMobile) as they step into their purpose. I've also worked with executives at large Fortune 500 companies such as Morgan Stanley, Google, Apple, Illumina, Zeiss, Sapient, and Johnson & Johnson, to take on the task of living their purpose at work. I've seen leaders transform themselves, their organizations and their performance through the power of leading from their unique purpose.

On this path, I've witnessed leaders reconcile the hard facts of existence with the powerful mechanism of commerce and develop novel approaches like triple bottom line accounting - accounting for the financial, ecological and social impact of the business. I have also encountered many things that make a mockery of the intention, where companies apply a new coat of conscious paint to increase market share, e.g.,

1. Greenwashing - Companies that promote that they are pro-environment, while stuffing their products full of toxic chemicals, e.g., Clorox's "Simple Green" brand which received a rating of 3.8/5.0, midway between "suspect" and "bogus" on the Greenwashing Index (Greenwashing Index, 7/12/17).

2. Pink-washing - Companies that promote they are pro-women's health while doing little about it or in some cases working against it, e.g., Susan G. Komen Foundation's relationship with the cancer industrial complex, taking money from enterprises that profit by selling goods that contain chemicals linked with cancer, diabetes, heart disease and ecological destruction. The Susan G. Komen Foundation has been paid to license its "pink ribbon" to sell fast food (Kentucky Fried Chicken and Coca-Cola), promote sedentary spectator sports (NFL) and promote gas fracking (Baker Hughes painting drill bits pink) (Benfit, 7/12/17).

This is not to say that greenwashing and pinkwashing endeavors don't drive the conversation forward or generate awareness, only that these practices don't function organically as purpose-driven concerns who have aligned their businesses with their core values.

However, this chapter is not about what does not work, but what does work. I'm going to introduce you to some successful and inspiring purpose-driven enterprises, like Johnson & Johnson, Patagonia and Canon, who do business with the organic and explicit goal of improving the human and ecological condition (I don't suggest they are perfect, only that they try to express their purpose and values). You'll also meet a humble guy from Chicago, Illinois, Ryan D'Aprile, who took an otherwise traditional business – a real estate brokerage – and created an inspiring organization that unlocks the purpose-driven expression and leadership of its employees as a strategic advantage to drive growth. Before we meet Patagonia and Ryan D'Aprile, let's take a couple steps back and look at where we are in the purposeful evolution of our economy.

Purpose as Economic Redemption

As I deepened my exploration of the history of capitalism, I started to see a light of hope. I saw that over time, our species was making considerable progress in improving capitalism and dealing with its social, economic and ecological externalities. I found that over the past 400 years, capitalism has been transformed by four successive evolutionary waves:

- Free enterprise wave – liberating entrepreneurial capital (1776 - present)
- Dignity wave – accounting for human capital and dignity (1842 - present)
- Ecology wave – accounting for ecological capital (1962 - present)
- Purpose wave – accounting for psychological capital (1994 - present)

The fourth wave – the purpose wave – is a quest for authenticity, for honestly representing the truth in the hearts of the founders and reconciling that with our vision for the world via economic activity. It includes the previous three waves and ushers in a new, more personal, creative, fulfilling, and abundant economic model.

The First Wave: Free Enterprise

During the first wave, Adam Smith argued in *Wealth of Nations* (Smith, 1776) that free market capitalism is built upon a bedrock of brotherhood and moral behavior, which he elaborated in his previous work, *Theory of Moral Sentiments* (Smith, 1759), and that collectively, free markets comprised of highly informed moral actors are a vehicle for greater individual freedom, fulfillment, and self-determination. Rising on the thought of Smith and other Enlightenment thinkers, this wave empowered entrepreneurs to liberate themselves from the bonds of tradition and class. Along with representative democracy, free enterprise afforded citizens the time and capital they needed to participate in government and to rapidly transform their communities.

Today, millions of enterprises are still making headway with a first wave focus, and continue to offer consumers numerous useful home products like soap, textiles, toilets, and washing machines that free them from many hours of manual labor. This wave continues to generate productivity tools for communication (email), information (Google), navigation (Trimble), entrepreneurship and business operations (eBay, PayPal, Mailchimp, Asana, Google Docs), connection (Facebook) and mobility (smartphones). This wave also gave us the fail-fast start-up culture, e.g., *The Lean Startup*, as well as the belief and courage that we can and should use best practices to disrupt antiquated power structures to create better outcomes for all, e.g., Netflix, app stores.

Smith considered that the market functioned as an "invisible hand", efficiently allocating resources and creating better outcomes for all parties involved. As history has revealed via countless labor riots, ecological disasters, and financial bubbles and crises, this part of Smith's theory has not been borne out. The majority of businesses have incurred expenses that they have not yet paid, what economists call negative social, cultural and ecological externalities, e.g., air, water and soil pollution, unfair wages, subsidized carbon energy, media/brand culture pollution.

The Second and Third Waves: Dignity and Ecology

The next two waves addressed these misgivings, specifically the relationship of capital/land owners to humanity/labor and the environment.

The second wave began the process of restoring dignity to humanity through the Labor and Socialist movements (beginning with the 1842 *Commonwealth vs. Hunt* case which legalized labor unions), the Women's Rights movement (beginning in 1848) and the Civil Rights movement (beginning with the 1954 *Brown v Board of Education* case). The lasting gifts of the second wave are expressions of equality and dignity: collective bargaining, worker-owned cooperatives, affirmative action, the Occupational Health and Safety Administration, the 5-day/40-hour work week, child labor laws and anti-discrimination laws.

The third wave, the ecology wave or the Green Movement (1962-present) has also contributed many lasting gifts such as ecological conservation, renewable energy, sustainability, climate change accords (2016 Paris Agreement), ecological accounting, government agencies that regulate pollution, social enterprises, e.g., Tesla (electric cars), Sunrun (solar energy), Kiva (social enterprise financing), Lyft (on demand transportation), and Sun Basket (on demand organic meals).

The Fourth Wave: Purpose

The Fourth Wave of capitalism takes into account a new type of capital: authenticity and purpose, the creative and psychological capital of every human to create the life, career and planet they want. This wave empowers publicly traded Purpose-Driven Enterprises (PDEs) like, e.g., Johnson & Johnson, to outperform the stock market 15-to-1 (Collins/Porras, 1994) and triple their growth rate (McLeod, 2012). As we explored, what drives this performance is people - purpose-driven human creativity, collaboration and leadership that gets unleashed inside PDEs. As we explored, unlocking the power of purpose inside an organization increases employee engagement by four times (Gallup/Healthways, 2013), employee fulfillment by 64%, and employee productivity by 500% (McKinsey, 2013).

So, what does a PDE actually look like?

A PDE emerges from the soul's purpose of a company's founders and team. As purpose is a bridge between the inner and outer world, leaders of PDEs treat business as a spiritual practice, in that they commercially transact with other people and businesses on the basis of not only economic values, but purpose and authenticity, seeking a soul resonance, a shared vision between both parties for a better world. PDE's have more than an organic and transcendent purpose, including a commitment to create sustainable and equitable value, honoring the complexities of the first three waves and making business personally meaningful.

A PDE is defined as having:

1. **Purpose-driven and embodied leadership (aka Shambhala Leadership, see the next two chapters).** A PDE begins with the purpose, heart and mind awakening of the executive team. Once soul-awakened, the executives craft and evolve their business to allow them to embody their purpose at work, to realize their vision, live their virtues, express their individual powers, craft, core, mission and story. PDEs create a bridge between the souls of the founders and the world, rendering the words "work" and "retirement" meaningless, creating irreplaceable value for customers and empowering each employee with the full expression of their life's purpose and progression through the stages of their own integrity and leadership (next chapter).

2. **Integrity.** A PDE is more than a soul-centric enterprise, but one that meets and interfaces with the world. A PDE is integrous, holistic and generative, in relationship to all of humanity, future generations and the Earth's biodiversity. It is also evolutionary as it expands its planetary context and evolves its organizational purpose.

When founders and CEO's unlock their purpose, and create a PDE, they are able to more deeply connect with their customers. As mentioned previously, 55% of customers will choose a product that has a higher purpose over one that does not (Nielsen, 2014). Roughly, 35% of US consumers (Ray, 2010) and approximately 50% of EU consumers (Ray, Anderson, 1999) primarily make purchase decisions based on their purpose and values resonance with the companies who make the products and services they purchase.

Yet, your inner skeptic still might be thinking that purpose is just fluffy marketing designed to keep crafty marketers shilling the same useless and toxic wares with a new coat of paint. Rest assured, the purpose economy properly defined does not include toxic businesses that green/pink-wash themselves with celebrity endorsements and PR. Although this happens and needs to be carefully watched, this is not what PDEs do.

Rather, a PDE is a business with an inspiring genesis story, namely the sacred purpose of its founders. Johnson & Johnson, Canon and Patagonia are beautiful examples of for-profit, for-benefit PDEs who strive to continually expand their founder's purpose and values through generative business practices. Patagonia is the soulful expression of its founder, Yvon Chouinard. Yvon started Patagonia with the desire to create innovative outdoor gear for its customers, while simultaneously marching forward to increase human dignity, standing for employees to live their fullest expression at work as he articulated in his book, *Let My People Go Surfing*. Patagonia also stands for the rights of animals and plants, and was the first company to implement a fully transparent supply chain and use traceable, torture-free goose down.

This is not just a phenomenon available to specialty apparel companies, but also a strategy that drives the growth of large publicly-traded companies. Johnson & Johnson is such a company. I have had the pleasure of working with Johnson & Johnson and helping them deliver upon their purpose, put forth in their famous *Credo*, written by Robert Wood Johnson in 1943. Their credo places customers, doctors and patients first, suppliers and distributors second, employees third, community and environment fourth, and shareholders last. Not surprisingly, this approach has worked, as Johnson & Johnson is ranked #35 on the 2017 Fortune 500 list and #13 on the 2017 Fortune list of most admired brands (Fortune, 2017).

The PDE is also not just an American phenomenon. The Japanese electronics company, Canon, was founded in 1933 with a spirit of "kyosei", of living in harmony and interdependence with the world. Canon regards itself as a "fourth stage" company - standing firm its commitment to serving all of mankind in its philosophy, purpose and activities. To achieve this, Canon continually sets up labor-friendly operations in poorer countries to develop and train their workforces, transfer technological know-how and empower local economies.

Other notable PDEs include Clif Bar, Eileen Fisher, Tesla and Whole Foods, and there are tens of thousands of lesser known PDEs who craft soulful, local, sustainable goods and services. However, PDEs do not have to be sexy consumer brands, tech companies or feature artisanal cuisine. Nor do they have to come from hip cities like Portland, San Francisco, Boulder or Austin.

Ryan's Story

Anyone, anywhere can build a purpose-driven business. Meet Ryan D'Aprile, a man who built a thriving purpose-driven real estate business in the heart of America's rust and wheat belt, Chicago. In 2011, Ryan started D'Aprile Properties, a company that would become one of Chicago's fastest-growing, highest-performing real estate agencies, one whose purpose, as you will soon see, is purpose itself.

Yet Ryan didn't set out to become a pioneering purpose-driven entrepreneur, or even a real estate agent. He wrestled in high school, got average grades and, like many children of blue-collar parents, Ryan's initial idea of success and life trajectory was quite conventional - get a job, get married, have kids, retire and die. Deep inside, however, Ryan had another plan. He wanted more out of his life.

By age 26, and with more than his share of tenacity and charm, he made partner at his executive search firm and was earning $250,000 per year. Yet he knew that being a high-performing salesperson was not his life's purpose. Although he loved working with and inspiring people, his role in executive search didn't allow him the creativity and the impact he craved. He saw real estate as a blank canvas, as an open space upon which he could create his own destiny.

In his late twenties Ryan became a real estate broker. He wanted to join a well-known firm, but was told he wasn't a good fit. He was told he was "too hyper" and "too energetic". So, predictably, he started his own firm. Within six years he joined the top 1% of Chicago's real estate agents, doing $40 million a year in volume.

But even this level of success and autonomy wasn't the fullest expression of his purpose, so in 2010 he began training and developing other real estate agents. He took on six agents, three of whom were brand new and three of whom were about to quit the business, to see if he could help them become successful. In two years of working with them, five of the six agents entered the top 5% of real estate agents in the State of Illinois in terms of revenue. The sixth was hired away as a Vice-President of a real estate development company in San Francisco.

One day, he received a call from one of his mentees who told him that their work together had changed his life permanently for the good. In the rawness of this moment, Ryan saw that his purpose had evolved from his own self-expression, autonomy, success and creativity, to service. He became clear that his role was to help people see that real estate wasn't just a path to autonomy and financial success, but that with the right training and development, it was so much more. It could be a path to self-awareness, fulfillment and purposeful self-expression. Ryan saw that he was more than a salesman or even coach, he was a leader of leaders.

So, Ryan rebooted his company in 2012 to focus on the inner-game of real estate, rebranding as D'Aprile Properties, a real estate agency with a primary focus on training and development, whose agents now receive more training and development than 85% of the industry. As a result, they are on their way to producing $1 billion in annual volume and $15 million in annual revenue across four states (Illinois, Indiana, Michigan and Wisconsin). Ryan says, "This is just the beginning." And he is likely right, as D'Aprile Properties was recognized as one of *Inc. 5000's* Fastest Growing Companies of 2015 (Inc., 2015).

Of course, Ryan did not do any of this alone. Through their own continual purpose evolution and company revisioning, Ryan and his leadership team, Lindsay Miller (Co-CEO) and Jaid Ritter (EVP Operations) consider themselves spiritually connected to each other, and are invested in each other's purpose, learning and development. To effectuate this shared purpose, they created a quarterly leadership team book club, dissecting books on leadership, purpose, psychology and spirituality, such as *The Four Agreements, Delivering Happiness, Start With Why, The Toyota Way, Destiny of Souls*, and *A Whole New Mind*. As a result of this intense embodied commitment to purpose, growth and development, the trio revealed a new company purpose and values statement in 2015:

Vision: "Our purpose is to create experiences that inspire growth from within and the confidence to dream."

Core values:

1. Do what's right.
2. Develop yourself + others.
3. Discover your dharma.

Ryan fought with Jaid and Lindsay to include "dharma" in the company's statement of values. Dharma is a Hindu word that means many things, including order, law, divine connection and purpose. Perhaps rightly so, they feared the Eastern/new age connotations of this powerful word for purpose, in a very traditional industry and in the Midwest's Christian culture. But Ryan felt that dharma was so distinct and empowering, and necessarily shocking, that it would set the firm far apart from its peers. And indeed, their dharma has attracted high-performing, growth-oriented agents who continually grow, develop, perform and go on to be great coaches and leaders themselves.

Ryan's own dharma dictates that he treat his agents as his clients. As such he has crafted a full curriculum that is designed for their personal and ethical development (critical in an industry with so many moral hazards), as well as their financial success. In the first year of work with D'Aprile Properties, the firm functions as a university for its agents, providing dozens of online courses and one-on-one coaching sessions, and in year two, it functions as a consulting firm to the agents, helping them accelerate their business.

As Chief Morale Officer, Ryan focuses on creating an atmosphere and culture for the whole company, one that allows for every agent to be empowered to succeed, and to take their self-awareness, leadership and success out into their communities. Whether it's in the office or on their internal messaging group on Facebook, Ryan and his team explicitly create a culture of purpose, sharing successes, leadership lessons and inspiring quotes, and asking for support. As such, Ryan and his team are on the front lines of the purpose movement, developing purpose-driven entrepreneurs who are as much agents for cultural transformation as successful real estate brokers.

As you can see, PDEs can be a fun, personal and creative way of doing business, fulfilling many of our human needs, all the way up to self-actualization. They operate with what traditional business folks would call an unassailable competitive advantage, and with what marketers would call the "brand of you." This PDE ethos permeates every transaction and supports the founders, their employees, their suppliers, and their customers to contribute their greatest powers, to be fully self-expressed, engaged and creative at work.

How can you surf the fourth wave?

As a purpose-driven business person, you have the unique opportunity to make purpose the center point of your career, your strategy and decision-making, actively infusing your purpose into your business practices, culture, worldview and community. Among many other things, the path to doing these things empowers you to:

1. **CHOOSE** which companies you work for, partner with, buy from, invest in. Ensure that they are also driven by purpose. Explore companies who are registered B Corps, members of BALLE (Business Alliance for Local Living Economies), the Social Venture Network or Game Changers 500.

2. **LEAD** with your purpose by crafting a purpose-driven foundation document with your team (Vision, Mission, Values).

3. **SHARE** purpose discovery and leadership development work with your team, customers, partners, investors and suppliers (e.g., the Global Purpose Expedition), training and developing your employees, partners, communities, investors and customers to awaken their purpose.

4. **EXPAND YOUR CONTEXT** by developing a broad understanding of the latest thinking on purpose-driven business, e.g., Aaron's Hurst's 2016 book, *The Purpose Economy*, Frederic Laloux's 2014 book *Reinventing Organizations*, Robert Anderson and William Adams' 2016 book *Mastering Leadership*, Dave Logan, John King and Halee Fischer-Wright's 2011 book, *Tribal Leadership*, and Robert Kegan and Lisa Laskow's 2016 book, *An Everyone Culture*, as well as through the academic fields of history, psychology, ecology and economics, so that the worldview of your PDE includes, unifies and amplifies all four waves.

5. **BUILD COMMUNITY** by cultivating a circle of purpose-driven, high-integrity peers, whose goal is to support you in living truthfully, fully and on purpose (e.g., men's and women's circles such as The ManKind Project or Woman Within), and cultivating networks of other purpose-driven entrepreneurs such as through Conscious Capitalism, B Corps, Bioneers and Net Impact.

But which of these should you do first? Should you first find a new purpose-aligned job? Or should you hunker down and try to make your current role more purposeful? Should you share your purpose with your friends and colleagues? Should you take on a year of study to expand your context? Or start right now and build a new community? Yes! All of the above and more! Of course you can only do one thing at time, so I'd like to suggest a simple structure, one that gets you into action every day AND meaningfully transforms your relationships:

1. We live in relationships, in conversations, so for your purpose to move into your life and career, it must be spoken about. Review all of your communities (work, family, gym/sports, hobbies, friends, college mates, professional organizations, community groups, spiritual groups, etc.) and choose 10 people who you believe to be the most likely to support you in living purposefully. Schedule a time to speak with each of them individually, share in confidence what it is you are creating with your purpose, and ask them to check in with you about it from time to time. This creates a social context for you to continue to speak about your purpose, to keep it alive and also, a warm set of relationships to celebrate wins and explore the edges of your purpose.

2. Although it only takes three weeks to build a new habit, it takes more sustained attention to purposefully reformat your life and career. You'll need at least two months of daily and achievable actions to begin seeing results. Begin by creating a 60-day action plan where you take one (and only one) new action a day towards your purpose. As we explored, purpose touches your whole life, so these actions should not just be limited to your career. Your whole life has to rise with this new center of gravity and commitment. Review the five bullets above (choose, lead, share, expand, build), as well as the other six key life areas (health, love, family, community, finances and spirituality), and list 60 actions that you could complete in 30 minutes or less. Now put time in your calendar to complete one action a day each day for the next 60 days. It is important to have an accountability partner, one person with whom you can share your progress with each week. Pick someone from your list of 10 above who is a person of high integrity (they do what they say). Ask them if they'll send you a note once a week for the next eight weeks inquiring about your progress from the previous week and what you're committed to completing in the following week. You'll reply to each note within 24 hours, and share everything you achieved (or did not achieve) along with the 7 new actions for the following week.

By speaking your purpose and taking one new action a day, two things will happen. First, you'll have a purpose habit that will be hard to break, as taking purposeful action is now your new normal. It will be very hard to fall back to the old ways. Secondly, you will be surprised how quickly your life and career will align around your purpose. This does not mean that the world will roll out the red carpet for you- it will not-, nor that you will not have breakdowns and resistance - you will - however, you will begin to see progress and experience a measure of serendipity, wherein aligned insights and opportunities that are not in your current realm of possibility, e.g. job offers, words from songs, advertisements or bathroom books, chance conversations on the subway or around the watercooler, will begin to lead you down new more purposeful pathways. When you choose this path of purpose-driven business, you not only open yourself to greater levels of personal fulfillment and financial success, as Johnson & Johnson, Canon, Patagonia and D'Aprile Properties have discovered, but you also become a leader in the evolution of our species, reconciling your career with the interconnected reality expressed in our sciences and wisdom traditions, as you'll discover in Part Three.

As you'll explore in the next chapter, by stepping into your Shambhala Leadership you will find yourself on the right side of human history. Your career will become an authentic, cogent and inspiring answer to these questions your children and grandchildren are sure to ask:

How did you live truthfully and create a more equitable, sustainable and peaceful human presence?

How did you lead in humanity's darkest hour?

With these provocative questions, let's dive into an evolutionary understanding of leadership.

CHAPTER 12

An Evolutionary Model of Purpose and Leadership

"Brandon is going to bring this whole movement down," wrote Sandy, a former colleague, to a group of people I trained to lead the Purpose Challenge, the precursor to Global Purpose Expedition.

She continued, "He's delusional if he thinks we're going to publish and translate the book into Spanish by the end of the year, and run another Challenge in January. He has got to walk his talk, slow down and do this right. If he doesn't do that and just focus on the priorities for the near-term, the Global Purpose Movement is going to fail before it even starts."

As the Purpose Challenge and the upswell of support for a Global Purpose Movement began to rise in 2015, I didn't have sufficient leadership skills to meet this growth. I wasn't listening to Sandy or really tuned into what the team was experiencing. I was overwhelmed by all the projects, and defaulted to my warrior-like leadership strategies. The first was to damn the torpedoes, to work as hard and fast as I could and ask everyone else to do the same. The second reactive behavior was control. I put myself in the center of it all as the bottleneck. And the third was to abdicate, to deny responsibility when things went wrong. These are the three of the most common leadership follies: (1) to overwork (vs. delegate and empower), (2) to become a tyrant (vs. mentor), and (3) to deny responsibility (vs. assume responsibility for all of it). And, yes, I was doing all three.

As a tyrant, I tried to control and manipulate this mutiny among the fifteen trainers. I made Sandy wrong, tried briefly to re-enroll her, then quickly announced her exit from the team and began looking for her replacement. Yeah, ouch. Embarrassing.

In my abdication, I perverted the self-management principles from the book *Reinventing Organizations*, telling everyone that the movement was a volunteer effort and that anyone who participated must either be enrolled and inspired to act as owner/CEO or stop participating - basically blaming others for any lack of performance or enthusiasm. Combined with my boyish idealism/megalomania, I believed we would be able to achieve all I intended to - publish a book, translate the Purpose Challenge into five languages, train fifteen people to deliver the Challenge (while reworking the Challenge), and run it again, all within about three months. Crazy.

Although I was four years into my purpose journey and I had success running teams in the past, I had yet to do any intense leadership development work, so I was working with my old, pre-purpose, command-and-control leadership programming. I wasn't being my purpose. At that time, I did not yet understand that leadership is the fulfillment of purpose. Leadership is the on-the-court access to being one's purpose. It is easy to be a monk in a cave, cultivating soul awareness and practicing peace. But we did not come here to sit the game out. The game is on the court of life. It requires us to lead, be challenged and remain steadfast, grounded in purpose.

"The sharp edge of a razor is difficult to pass over; thus, the wise say the path to 'enlightenment' is hard."

-Katha Upanisad

Once alive with purpose, one is then tasked to lead as, by, for and through it. Which is exactly what I did not do. I was selfishly attached to glory, to being "the one" leading a Global Purpose Movement, who accomplished all these things in an insanely short amount of time. As such, when things went wrong, I neglected to listen and look at myself, and instead doubled down with my old ways of being - work hard and fast. I closed my heart, veered from my purpose, abandoned the inner game and thus, forfeited both my leadership and the desired outcome. Without a focus on the inner game (on who the leader is being) as well as what she is doing, leadership is deeply handicapped and teams do not work well.

When the inner and outer game are explicitly cultivated, high-trust relationships develop, high-integrity teams are built and a culture of distributed leadership rises to realize the team's vision. As I was doing none of this, my work ground to a halt. My team left to pursue other projects. In this dysfunction and chaos, my one-on-one Purpose Guiding business also took a hit, I had a number of breakdowns in my health and relationships, and I went another $10k in debt.

I was the problem. My inner game needed work. I needed to be my purpose. I needed to focus on opening my heart, living in integrity, becoming the walking embodiment of my purpose, and empowering others. As I knew the movement, as well as my life on purpose depended on embodiment, I enrolled in three sequential immersive leadership development programs over the course of two years (1,000+ hours of leadership training).

Of course, leadership development is not an easy thing. It's not learning new concepts and being tested on them. It's a lived experience - a series of breakdowns and breakthroughs. So, my life actually got a lot worse before it got better.

The low point of this breakdown was that I had to take a job waiting tables, which is about as far from my highest contribution as you can get. It's not that it's bad work or beneath me - I've worked at McDonald's, as a caddy, landscaper, painter, construction worker, caterer and bartender. But I was almost 40, and I like to talk about things like human potential, revolution and mythopoetic identity over a glass of peaty scotch. I don't really care to engage in small talk, discuss tasting notes, share my opinions on what the term 'locally-sourced' means or mythologize farmers with philosophy degrees. And I had to, to keep paying my bills. It was fast-paced and humbling hard work, a perfect stew of mismatch and shame for me to sit with as I wrestled with the massive leadership transformation being called forth from within.

This work empowered me to more fully embody my purpose, develop an expanded relationship to my word (integrity), step into being fully responsible, empathize with the experiences of my team members and be at the source of my team's success, growth, satisfaction and empowerment.

As I started being more responsible, empathizing and operating with increasing integrity (giving my word and keeping it), who I was being in the world shifted. I restored integrity where it was out - all my broken promises, white lies, trespasses and their impacts had to be addressed. I was just as purpose-driven and creative as before; however, a new level of rootedness began to emerge. I began to know my word as myself (as sacred as my purpose), I had the confidence to borrow money to invest in a business coach. I quickly retargeted my marketing, improved my client conversion and started charging premium fees. And this, of course, allowed me to start paying back my debts and invest in this book.

Shortly thereafter, I hired an assistant and an editorial team to finish the book and rejoined with my colleagues in the Global Purpose Movement to bring this important work to the people through their purpose programs, summits, conferences, trainings and speaker networks. I had begun to taste what it meant to be a leader among leaders, leading with my purpose, as my purpose, and empowering others.

Of course, I'm nowhere near finished with my purpose embodiment/integrity work, and see that what is next for me on my path is to dive more deeply into my feminine, my receptivity, my empathy and be able to fully open my heart as I lead.

But why develop your leadership?

Aren't there other ways to get ahead? No, not honestly anyways. As I discussed in the introduction, authentic, purpose-driven leadership may now be the only game in town. By this I mean that the other efficiencies of the free market system have already been realized and wrung out. As a global economy, we optimized manufacturing efficiencies throughout the 1970's, financial and operational efficiencies throughout the 1980's, organizational efficiencies throughout the 1990's and information technology efficiencies throughout the 2000's.

There is very little left to optimize in the system except the games of purpose-driven leadership and culture. As we explored in "Chapter 5: The Science of Purpose - Career", I believe this is now the current frontier of growth and value in the economy, correlated with higher levels of performance, engagement, profitability, income and wealth.

The Science of Leadership

As Robert Anderson and William Adams explore in their critically acclaimed leadership book, *Mastering Leadership* (Anderson, Adams, 2016), when leaders do their inner work, root themselves in their purpose, actively listen and open their heart, their effectiveness and productivity increase. In their study with Notre Dame's Mendoza College of Business, of over 500,000 leaders (Anderson, Adams, p. 72, 2016), they found that when leaders move from reactive leadership (what I call sociocentric leadership, below), where reactivity characterizes 70% of their behaviors (overwork, controlling, abdicating), to creative leadership, where only 30% of their behaviors are reactive, their business performance (revenue growth, profitability, stock price) moves from the bottom decile to the top decile.

When you move from reactive/sociocentric to creative leadership, your leadership effectiveness increases by 25%, from 10% below average to 15% above average, as Robert Anderson and William Adams discovered in their Notre Dame study. When you move from reactive/sociocentric to creative leadership, you are granted access to much more than expanded financial performance and managerial effectiveness; you gain access to your true legacy. Your higher purpose provides you with your bone-rattling identity, transcendent vision, clarity, conviction, desire and confidence to make the world a better place, and the ability to communicate and inspire such that others reach their fullness through your leadership, contribution, presence and commitment.

As Anderson and Adams demonstrate in their book, organizational change efforts always fail unless leaders do their inner work. In this process, what begins to drive the leader's inner game is their life's purpose, and specifically, their call and vision. They move from reacting to social constructs and economic forces, and they start creating their own game, becoming the authors of their lives and careers. As Anderson and Adams show, when leaders do this, every action taken towards creative leadership increases their overall leadership effectiveness score by 0.93, almost a one-to-one correlation. But what does this actually look like in the day to day occurrence of leadership? To answer this question, I offer another: Who comes to mind when you hear the word 'leader'?

An Evolutionary Understanding of Leadership

Odds are you'll come up with a few different types of high-achieving examples. You'll likely have one group of folks who achieved tremendous success through deception, violence, theft, and/or by exploiting or hurting others. Leaders like Al Capone, Andrew Jackson and Genghis Khan might come to mind.

You'll likely encounter another group of high-achieving, well-meaning, but notably flawed leaders - people like Steve Jobs, John F. Kennedy and Richard Nixon. These leaders have notably mixed legacies:

- Job's amazing iPhone on the one hand vs. the toxic production processes involved in the production, the willfully ignored epidemic of factory worker suicides, the command and control organizational structure and his fear-based leadership legacy.
- Kennedy's rousing Civil Rights rhetoric, NASA achievements, Bay of Pigs negotiation vs. election fraud.
- Nixon's China diplomacy and his championing of the Environmental Protection Agency and Medicare vs. his legacy of impeachable offenses, e.g., collusion, corruption and lying.

You'll also likely see another group of folks, folks who stayed true to their ethics, expressed our species' most prized virtues, who functioned with a high level of integrity, who were respectful to those whom they opposed and have a less complicated legacy. Folks like Elon Musk (Tesla), Eileen Fisher (Eileen Fisher Clothing), Yvon Chouinard (Patagonia), Oprah Winfrey (OWN) and John Mackey (Whole Foods) might come to mind.

Lastly, you'll likely have another group of leaders who not only expressed our species' highest virtues, but advanced them, and meaningfully moved the ball forward for the human condition. Folks like Nelson Mandela (compassion), Jane Goodall (interspecies affinity), Ashoka (mindfulness), Marcus Aurelius (wisdom) and Martin Luther King Jr. (courage) might come to mind.

To arrive at a useful evolutionary model of leadership, one that reveals an authentic and whole expression of your personal purpose, empowers you to expand your impact and success, as well as serve humanity's deepest needs and highest virtues, we need to explore what distinguishes these different "buckets" of high-achieving leaders. We must flush out a definition of leadership that includes a progression from Jackson to Nixon to Fisher to King.

What distinguishes these groups of leaders?

Purpose, or rather their particular connection to, *and* embodiment of, purpose.

Just as the evolution of purpose moves from no purpose to declared purpose to higher purpose to embodied purpose, leadership follows a similar progression from:

1. **Egocentric leadership** - marked by **no connection to purpose**, only the quest for power driven by unprocessed childhood wounding, and choosing to cope with one's wounds through achievement, domination and blame, by manipulating others for personal gain through tyranny, deception, abdication and denial of responsibility for impact of one's actions, e.g., Al Capone, Andrew Jackson and Genghis Khan.

2. **Sociocentric leadership** - marked by a **declared purpose**, reactively and opportunistically setting goals to fulfill on the vision of someone else (American Dream, wealth gospel, being #1, creating the best product, saving the Earth, *noblesse oblige*) and managing and motivating others with extrinsic rewards to achieve their goals, e.g., President Richard Nixon, most modern CEOs, Steve Jobs.

3. **Creative leadership** - marked by an explicit connection to **higher purpose**, to most if not all of the ten aspects of one's soul purpose (vision, virtues, core, mission, story, flow, powers, craft, worldview and the call), inspiring others with the purpose and meaning of the endeavor and standing for and empowering the self-expression, purpose, fulfillment and leadership of all concerned parties, e.g., Oprah Winfrey, Elon Musk, Yvon Chouinard, Eileen Fisher.

4. **Shambhala Leadership** - marked by the **unitive and embodied expression of higher purpose**, an open heart and an integral worldview that accelerates their impact. These people move through the world effortlessly from their core. They do not make anyone wrong; they are empathetic and stand for making a difference with anyone they meet. They *are* their purpose, and have a continued commitment to personal and spiritual growth, an always-evolving purpose to meet their always-evolving, integral understanding of the world. The result is that the identity of Shambhala Leaders rises to meet and include the world as it is: they take full responsibility for the world as it is, and offer their leadership in service of a world that works for all beings, e.g., Nelson Mandela, Jane Goodall, Marcus Aurelius, Ashoka, Martin Luther King, Jr. This is not to say these leaders have no character flaws or inner demons, merely that they have a stand for the world that continually calls them to transform.

As Anderson and Adams discovered, when you start to live and work with integrity, embodying and expressing your purpose, opening your heart and developing a broad, holistic and integral worldview, you move from creative leadership to integral leadership (what I call Shambhala Leadership) and your leadership effectiveness moves from 15% above average to 40% above average. In doing so, you cultivate a deep well of compassion for all beings, harness an intellectually broad and philosophically defensible context, continually step into an expanding identity with, and affinity for, the world and position yourself to meaningfully improve the whole human condition. Let's take a deep dive into Shambhala Leadership.

CHAPTER 13

The Four Commitments of the Shambhala Leader

"There comes a time when all life on Earth is in danger. Barbarian powers have arisen. Although they waste their wealth in preparations to annihilate each other, they have much in common: weapons of unfathomable devastation and technologies that lay waste the world. It is now, when the future of all beings hangs by the frailest of threads, that the kingdom of Shambhala emerges.

"Now comes the time when great courage is required of the Shambhala warriors, moral and physical courage. For they must go into the very heart of the barbarian power and dismantle the weapons."

"...the battle is not between good people and bad people, for the line between good and evil runs through every human heart. We realize that we are interconnected, as in a web, and that each act with pure motivation affects the entire web, bringing consequences we cannot measure or even see."

"The Shambhala Prophecy" A Tibetan Legend, as told by Joanna Macy (Awakin.org, 6/1/2017)

To live and embody your purpose and move into Shambhala Leadership, you will need to activate much more than just your soul's purpose. As we explored in the Introduction, awareness without action is not what humanity needs right now. Much more is required to ensure the survival and flourishing of our species. Humanity can no longer afford to have anyone sitting on the sidelines, with their purpose neatly folded and tucked away in their pocket. Nor can your purpose only come alive some of the time. Nor can we merely have another generation of inspired activists hating the establishment, fighting what's not working and burning themselves out. Nor can we have action rooted in anything less than a holistic, compassionate and integral worldview. We are all in this together and have to lead from this place.

This is an all-hands-on-deck moment for our species, a moment that demands that every able-bodied human harness the power of their purpose, grow deep roots of integrity to embody their purpose, open their hearts and minds and awaken their Shambhala Leadership. To do this I offer the Four Commitments of the Shambhala Leader:

1. Awaken and evolve your higher purpose
2. Embody your higher purpose
3. Open your heart (compassion)
4. Open your mind (integral worldview)

The First Commitment: Awaken and Evolve Your Higher Purpose

In Part One, we explored the importance of purpose. Your higher purpose is what gives your leadership authenticity, velocity and direction. It is the fire under your ass, the impetus for all that you do. However, as we've seen, purpose discovery work is not a one-and-done affair. Your purpose will continually evolve, so to be a leader also means that you connect with your life's purpose daily, and that you regularly dive back into your soul, using books, Guides, retreats, vision quests and medicine ceremonies for new purpose information and guidance.

The Second Commitment: Embody Your Higher Purpose

A Shambhala Leader must be the walking, talking, eating, breathing, fornicating, defecating embodiment of their life's purpose. She actively engages with each day to create greater alignment with her life's purpose and be the public expression of not only her life's purpose, but the possibility of purpose itself. Her purpose and integrity serve as an inspiration to others. She builds trust by holding herself accountable to her purpose, ethics and all commitments.

She can do none of this alone. To embody her purpose, live in integrity and engender trust, she must regularly and openly submit herself to rigorous training programs and demanding masters, mentors and coaches. These are programs and people who hold a bigger vision for her fullness as a leader. Masters, mentors and coaches provide a critical capacity to push and challenge her to die from her smallness and die into her bigness - the destiny of her purpose-driven life and career.

Further, embodiment means that Shambhala Leaders have no secrets, admit and address all wrongdoing, seek to live in full alignment with purpose, actively encourage others to point out their flaws and integrity leaks, and take full responsibility for all relationships, dynamics and results. A Shambhala Leader knows the ends do not justify the means. She knows that how you do anything is how you do everything. As such, she is also holding a stance as an open, transparent and courageous leader and nurtures the process, virtues and culture that manifest her vision. This also means standing for and actively creating a transparent organization that has no secrets, that communicates above board, while honoring personal boundaries and professional commitments. While firmly rooted in her soul's identity, she is also porous and flexible, allowing others in, allowing others to contribute to her, be present with her, encourage her growth (towards purpose and full potential) and be committed to the question and implementation of what is needed to be sustained, destroyed or created in the moment.

To fully embody your purpose and Shambhala Leadership, your primary tool is integrity. Let's explore the two most important aspects of integrity:

1. Integrity is a condition of functionality contingent on concern and perspective.
2. Integrity moves from the inside out.

Integrity is a condition of functionality contingent on concern and perspective.

Integrity is the process of maturing, of becoming oneself, of being aligned, of bringing more of your life and the world into alignment and fullness through the expression of your life's purpose. There are many definitions of integrity, which usually equate integrity with honesty, ethics and morality. From Merriam-Webster's Dictionary, integrity is:

1. a firm adherence to a code of especially moral or artistic values: incorruptibility
2. an unimpaired condition: soundness
3. the quality or state of being complete or undivided: completeness
-(Merriam-Webster, 7/21/2017)

Integrity comes from the Greek root word, *integer*, meaning a thing complete in itself. So, to function with integrity means to operate with completeness. But how do we know something is complete or if it is partial? It depends on what your mental concept of what the complete thing is. It depends on your context, or your understanding of the purpose of the object, machine, human or organization. For example, a piece of wood that measures two inches by four inches by 24 inches can be seen as either a complete "2x4" (pr. *two-by-four*, a construction term used to describe a standard-sized piece of lumber), thereby having integrity as a 2x4, or as an incomplete house, in that by itself it fails to fulfill on the purpose and function of the house (adequate safety, shelter, comfort, privacy, structure), and thereby it lacks integrity.

Integrity is a function of perspective and concern. If we're concerned with a house, our 2x4 lacks integrity, but does not lack integrity if we're only concerned with a 2x4. The 2x4 is not wrong if it is not part of a house, or if the house is falling apart. There is just a sound, complete and perfectly functioning 2x4, from one human perspective, AND an incomplete, malfunctioning house from another. No character defect here, just a difference in perspective and concern. Same 2x4, different concerns, and thus, different human stories to describe the state of integrity.

The same can be said for human behavior. A human behavior that is self-destructive, like eating to excess is a behavior that doesn't work for the long-term concern and well-being of the human. So, it is the human that lacks integrity, not the behavior. The behavior is complete, but from the larger perspective, it does not serve the function of the human. It is not wrong, it just doesn't work towards the optimal functioning of the human.

Integrity moves from the inside out.

The only reason to expand your concern and add integrity to your life or the world is because your purpose compels you to move beyond one level of concern to another. Integrity does not matter unless you are up to something bigger than you. An apt metaphor for integrity is a ring of concentric circles, where integrity grows from the inside out. In this sense, integrity is a process, emerging from the center and expanding outwards to the next ring and so forth. Based on my experience with the value and function of integrity in my own life and that of others, I believe that we move through (at least) seven rings of integrity on our way to a fully embodied and unitive purpose.

You can have can simple integrity by keeping your word and restoring your word, e.g., honesty and accountability (Ring One below), and then, once your higher purpose is alive within you in Ring Two, you have access to the third, fourth, fifth, sixth and seventh rings of integrity, reaching ever greater levels of fullness, soundness and completion.

A Shambhala Leader publicly brings greater integrity to her life by keeping and honoring her word (Ring One), doing regular purpose discovery and personal development work (Ring Two), explicitly rooting each day in her purpose through ritual and generating herself as a purposeful leader (Ring Three), bringing each area of her life into full integrity (Ring Four), crafting a purpose-driven livelihood that brings greater integrity and generative impact to the world (Ring Five), creating space for the experience of unity consciousness (Ring Six) and welcoming the opportunity to die a good death when her life is complete (Ring Seven).

Much like with Maslow's needs hierarchy, wherein one is never finished meeting a particular need, integrity is an inclusive progression. Once a level of certainty, completion and stability is achieved with one ring of integrity, there is capacity to focus on the next ring. In this fashion, the center of gravity or awareness moves from the inside out, from one ring of integrity to the next, but never forgetting or taking for granted the previous rings or dismissing the importance of the following rings. This model attempts a whole spectrum integrity awareness, whose locus of activity gradually moves from the inside out.

Now, let's explore each ring of integrity.

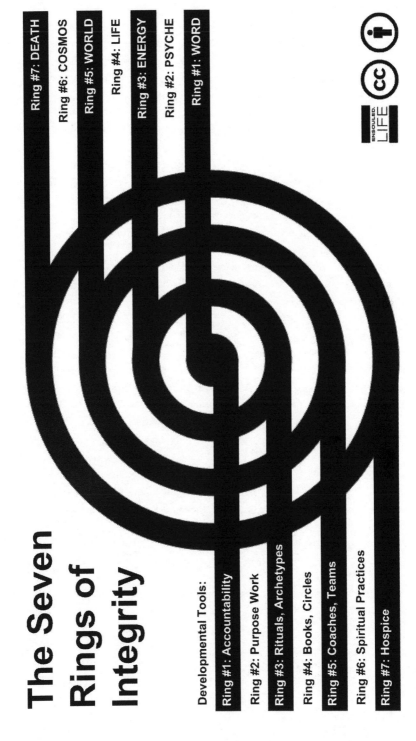

The Seven
Rings of
Integrity

Ring #7: DEATH
Ring #6: COSMOS
Ring #5: WORLD
Ring #4: LIFE
Ring #3: ENERGY
Ring #2: PSYCHE
Ring #1: WORD

Developmental Tools:

Ring #1: Accountability
Ring #2: Purpose Work
Ring #3: Rituals, Archetypes
Ring #4: Books, Circles
Ring #5: Coaches, Teams
Ring #6: Spiritual Practices
Ring #7: Hospice

Ring One - Verbal Integrity

The first ring of integrity is verbal, the common understanding of honesty and accountability. Anyone, regardless of their awareness of their purpose, can exercise their honesty and accountability and realize the first ring of integrity. Although it helps if you know your purpose, especially your virtues and vision to achieve this first ring of integrity, it is not necessary. You can muscle your way through Ring One by committing to be honest and fulfill on your commitments with sheer determination and willpower.

In this ring, you have likely experienced yourself as more powerful and aligned when you give and keep your word. Keeping your word is frequently accompanied by the experience of personal power, service and personal connection. Your word is your power to create. When your word becomes an inviolable expression of intent, creation, and fulfilment on that intent, others will relate to you and the things to which you give your word in that way.

This is a ring of integrity that becomes available to young children as they develop a relationship to their word. Children develop relationships with their parents and friends and have to use their word as a means of getting what they want, e.g., I'll do my chores by Friday to get my allowance. As children, we become people on whom others can rely by increasingly giving and keeping our word. Keeping your word is just that. Tell no lies, do what you say you are going to do. However, sometimes you cannot or choose to not keep your word. In this case, it is important to restore your integrity to your word and the situation, by following these ten steps (inspired by the ManKind Project's Accountability Process):

1. You must first admit to yourself that your word has been broken or that it will or might be broken,

2. Then communicate with the affected parties, acknowledge that the act or lack of action, as well as the impacts of breaking your word are inconsistent with your life's purpose or broader commitment,

3. Then share that you will take a new action or create a new method for keeping your word, to ensure that your word will not be broken in this manner again, for example, setting a reminder to complete the action at the specified time, or having a friend text you at a certain time and ask you if you have completed the task,

4. Take the appropriate action(s) until integrity is restored with the affected parties.

5. Now we begin to use this integrity breach as an access point to do deeper inner work. With a close friend, coach or in a men's/women's circle, re-presence all the impacts on yourself and others of having broken your word,

6. Then look and see if this is a pattern, to determine if it shows up in other parts of your life,

7. Then look at what you must believe about yourself or others such that breaking your word was the best option,

8. Then commit to transforming the root cause of the belief, e.g., through therapy, shadow work, men's/women's circle processes,

9. Do that process, and

10. Then declare and take a new action expressive of your purpose/commitment.

However, if you are purpose-aware, you know the vision and mission you are committed to and thus, what you must do to express it, so verbal integrity becomes an expression of your life's purpose. You know from experience you cannot lie and still achieve sustainable progress. You know you cannot rob Peter to pay Paul. You know you live your purpose by being honest and accountable. When you relate to your word as sacred, as an all-powerful tool to live your purpose, others will do so as well. They will begin to trust you, and you will find that your word starts to cause your life and the world, to move in an unprecedented fashion. When combined with your higher purpose, you can now access further rings of integrity, step into your Shambhala Leadership and make a huge impact in the world.

Ring One Tools: Coaches, accountability processes, such as those offered by the ManKind Project

Ring Two - Psychological Integrity

When you know your higher purpose, and have identified and begun to integrate your ego parts, the second ring of integrity is now available. You can now live and express the marriage between your soul and your ego. With an integrated ego, you are in relationship to all of your ego parts, such as your Skeptic, Critic, Risk Manager, Image Consultant and Wounded Child. You can witness their ongoing concerns as input rather than as demands or reasons to stop taking action; you can move through the world with their support and input, but primarily under your soul's guidance.

This ring of integrity is the missing piece for most people, it is where they get stuck and hit the limits of their effectiveness, success, impact and fulfilment in life. Without this ring of integrity, people are moved by these varied voices and operate at cross purposes with themselves. Since they are not connected to their higher purpose, they generally take action based on the commands of the loudest ego part, which are inconsistent with who they really are and what they really care about. Inside of this tension, they frequently get stuck, have breakdowns and engage in emotional rationalization, in which if they don't feel like doing something (like keeping their word, fulfilling on New Year's resolutions, etc.), they make up a reason to justify and rationalize the feeling and blame something or someone.

In emotional rationalization, people often use psychological or spiritual terminology like intuition or self-care or soul-guidance or another serious-sounding term, rather than what it really is - the resistance generated by their unexamined and unintegrated psyche. This ring is why purpose discovery work and men's/women's circles exist. It is why this book was written. Once connected to higher purpose, every human being can reach fullness, create a high-integrity soul-infused ego, and move into the outer Rings of integrity, so they can lead, and inspire others to change the world.

In this manner, your purpose works in the opposite fashion of modern consumer society, which relies upon an unexamined and unintegrated psyche to scan the market and society for solutions to fill a purpose-sized hole. Consumer society thus has a lack/taker orientation, wherein consumers take meaning from products, services, experiences, food, drugs, alcohol, media and relationships in order to fill a bottomless pit, an insatiable purpose-sized hole.

With purpose, the opposite is true. Purpose has a fullness/giver orientation. Purpose effects a reversal of the flow of energy, from lack and incompletion, from dependency on external validation, consumption and distraction to autonomy, to completion, integrity, sovereignty of soul and giving, creating and contributing. Store-bought meaning and happiness no longer can flow in, as the outflow of your personal purpose fills the width of the channel.

The wellspring of your purpose bursts forth from the inside-out, as you express your sacred truth, your integrated psyche and give away your craft and powers, and live your mission. You must give your purpose away, because there is always an even more purposeful expression coming behind right it. You can feel it. You are constantly pregnant with purposeful expressions, and must make a life of giving birth to it, of making way for your sacred purpose to flow through you. In so doing, you no longer need to purposelessly consume, you no longer need to fill, to patch or to numb, but you now need to release, to express, to give from your purpose. You become a servant to your purpose, awakening your leadership and continually expanding the ways you serve with purpose, from the inside out.

This ring is expressed as a soul-infused ego, a conscious identity that empowers you to heal and complete egoic wounding/trauma, and act from your purpose. I believe crafting a purpose-driven ego structure is the beginning of true adulthood, wherein a person knows their purpose, continually explores it, heals the remaining wounding that impedes it, and cultivates a growing capacity to function with integrity, powerfully living and leading from their soul's purpose.

Ring Two Tools: Purpose discovery work, mother/father-wound work, Voice-Dialogue Method, Internal Family Systems Method, gestalt psychotherapy and somatic healing processes such as those offered by the ManKind Project and Woman Within.

Ring Three - Energetic Integrity

With a sacred relationship to your word (Ring One) and a healing and increasingly high-integrity self, a grounded soul-infused, purpose-driven ego structure - (Ring Two), you now have the power to authentically express and create your purpose in the world. No longer impaired by a loose relationship to your word, unprocessed wounding, an unintegrated psyche, disempowering narratives, emotional rationalization, or all-consuming emotional states that keep you from taking action, you can now choose who you are in every moment. You are self-authoring. You say who you are in every moment.

This third ring of integrity operates at the level of energy, archetype and intention. Depending on the context, moment, time of day, time of year and time of life, you can now purposefully and effectively create who you are and how you show up. You choose who you get to be in any situation. Each context might call for a particular archetype, and you can choose to express that, e.g., express the "Lover" with your friends and family in their time of need, the "Golden Child" when playing, exploring, enjoying and celebrating life; the "Warrior" with your morning routine, self-care and personal boundaries; the "Mistress" or "Seducer" with your romantic partner; the "Magician" with your inquiry into your own purpose, the mysteries of existence and your evolving vision for the world; or the "Sovereign" in your careful consideration of the big picture as you act upon your mission (Moore, Gillette, 1990).

Ring Three Tools: Morning rituals (meditation, prayer, vision board, somatic practices), archetypally-driven programs from the Mankind Project, Woman Within and the Animas Valley Institute.

Ring Four - Life Integrity

Once you have this creative power, your task is to ensure that your life is a match for your soul. To do this you begin the path of embodiment, of being your purpose in every moment of everyday, in every context (health, love, family, career, community, finances and spirituality) and leading others as the embodiment of your purpose. This means having a broad and expanding worldview and understanding best practices in every single area of life. This means cultivating the best body of your life, achieving optimum health, creating a physical structure that best allows you to live your purpose, contribute your powers and realize your vision.

This ring of integrity includes the desire for purposeful romantic partnership, to define and work towards a union that serves a purpose greater than the sum of its purpose-awakened constituents. This desire moves out from partnership to every successive level of cooperation - to the family, the community, and eventually to the economic organization, the political organization, the species imperative and towards ecological resilience (Ring Five).

This also means developing a career that achieves increasing coherence with your purpose, and especially your expanding worldview, such that your career eventually becomes the playful expression of your worldview and vision for an evolved world.

Integrity at this level cultivates the physical, intellectual, social, economic and spiritual sustenance to live your purpose. It is expressed as an abundant, high-integrity livelihood. This also means having fun in a way that doesn't inhibit or contradict your life's purpose, your worldview and vision for the world.

Ring Four Tools: Worldview-expanding books and films on systems theory, integral philosophy, economics, ecology, spirituality, politics, Big History, and training programs such as the Collaborative Operating System, spiritual disciplines, mentors, apprenticeships, life coaches, accountability partners, intentional communities, and groups, such as those from Woman Within and the ManKind Project.

Ring Five - World Integrity

As your individual life (mind-body-soul) becomes increasingly sound and integrated, and especially as your career and relationships become the reflection, expression and embodiment of your life's purpose, you become a purpose-driven, high-achieving individual, someone who noticeably changes the world. Internally you are aligned, and increasingly in the ways in which you relate to other people, your body, the marketplace, the realm of public discourse and your political decisions.

This ring of integrity desires to express and realize purpose at every level of human cooperation. It is a desire to empower every human with their life's purpose, to enable them to draw from their own internal wellspring and achieve liberation from smallness and dependency on external validation.

> "Only one who can do it with love is worthy of being the steward of the world."
>
> -Lao Tzu, *Tao Te Ching*

This ring of integrity is when Shambhala Leadership reaches its fullness, and you become one who lovingly deters purposeless people, organizations and ideas from letting these forces take you off purpose, and works to compassionately transform their purposeless action into a greater expression. This ring is a fight for the hearts and minds of humanity, purposefully and compassionately transforming power structures, markets, companies, governments and individuals who do not yet know their purpose (and as a result only know how to work against the realization of purpose and integrity). This ring of integrity reveals the unity of the call, vision, virtues and core in the awakened heart. It creates communities, teams and companies of purpose-aligned souls to express a larger purpose out in the world.

Soon, this experience of being someone who purposefully creates one's life, relationships and community effects a further expansion in identity. When every part of your life is aligned with your purpose, you start moving through the world as both your purpose and the world's purpose. You will begin to personally identify with, and act on behalf of, the well-being of the whole world, of each person's full expression within it and the health of the Earth's ecology. At this ring of integrity, your interconnected cognitive understanding of the world - the context of your purpose and your career - and your physical and economic expression of your purpose descend into your tissues, such that you move through the world with grace, politically, socially, ecologically and economically as, of, by and for the world.

From this ring of integrity, your purpose starts to move towards Unitive Purpose. You start drawing your purpose on a planet-sized canvas, seeing your purpose as empowering a global movement and, in doing so, effecting a shift in humanity towards a fuller expression of itself. In essence, your purpose becomes a vehicle for humanity to be in integrity, to step into its greatest potential (as you'll explore in Part Three), to live its purpose as Earth steward, as the emerging central nervous system of the Cosmos, and as the evolutionary edge of the Cosmos itself, deepening its interconnection and expressing its beauty in increasingly diverse ways.

Ring Five Tools: Mentors, coaches, teams, covenants.

Ring Six - Cosmic Integrity

The escalating accumulation of these moments of world integrity, of unity, and those experiences and relationships that serve that understanding and identity, results in a more deeply established integrity - being in integrity with all of existence, the flow of Cosmic evolution, and as a steward of its creative expression. At this ring of integrity, you are the Cosmos itself, all of humanity's "good" and "bad". Your cognitive context for your life's purpose and identity expands to include all the processes, relationships, hierarchies/ holarchies and all of humanity's scientific and spiritual traditions. The whole biography of the Cosmos and humanity becomes your personal autobiography.

At this ring of integrity, you identify as every point in space-time and all concepts that relate these points. You are the subject, the object and the process by which the subject perceives and acts upon objects. You are the background of being and field of all that arises. You are all of human knowledge, all of the unknown (exo-knowledge), and all of the unfolding creativity and exploration that connects these two bodies of knowledge. You are the emerging, sustaining and destruction of the Universe. You are all that is, was and will be.

Having established a healthy ego structure in Ring Two, creating your life and world as the expression of your life's purpose in Rings Three, Four and Five with the power of your word (Ring One), you have experienced numerous peak experiences and made an enormous contribution to humanity, the Earth and Cosmos. In effect, you have lived life mightily. You have charged into the unknown with love and courage, consistently expanding your integrity and impact, and have reached completion and fullness as a human being. You have finished the task of becoming a mature human.

Ring Six Tools: Spiritual practices, psychotropics/plant medicine ceremonies, meditation, teachers, mentors, books and retreats.

Ring Seven - The Integrity of Death: *Zoi entelechia, evgenis thanatos* (a realized life, a noble death)

Once your purpose has become flesh, once integrity has worked itself all the way through you, once it has burned away your smallness, made your word sacred, accelerated your works in the world and given you the power to identify with and create the Cosmos, there is nothing left for you to do except die a good death.

The final gift of integrity is to die as you have lived. The noble death is best exemplified by Socrates. He devoted his life to truth, spoke his truth to power, exposing the folly, misdeeds, corruption and hypocrisy of Athenian politicians, and inspired, mentored and "corrupted" the Athenian youth with the fullness of their potential. He was, of course, jailed, tried and sentenced to death by poison. This did not bother Socrates, so he drank his hemlock with joy, knowing that this death was the perfect expression of his life. Having played his life full out according to his purpose, he realized the fullness of his life, his entelechy (his soul's full realization), and left an enormous mark upon his successors - Plato, the Symposium and all of humanity who would follow. As such, Socrates was gifted by the court a way to die as he lived, devoted to truth, to die in complete alignment with himself.

This is the final ring of integrity, to die a noble death, to die in the fullness of self-expression, in a full and final way that serves your life's purpose. This means not to die in a psychologically painful fashion, or with regret or resistance. This means to have had died long before as a solitary ego-driven, human. Having begun the process of abandoning egoic/individual biological identity and addiction to pleasure and pain avoidance in Ring Two (dying from smallness into the bigness of purpose/ soul), and experiencing an increase in identity, integrity and impact in Rings Three, Four, Five and Six, there is only one thing left to do, to biologically die as you have lived, with grace, joy, surrender and gratitude for having had the pleasure of realizing the fullness of your soul (entelechy) during the course of your brief, but powerful, purpose-driven human life.

Ring Seven Tools: Biological dying and death, hospice, practices of surrender and gratitude.

When a leader commits herself to integrity as a human, a species, a planet and Cosmos, and uses these tools to live in ever greater alignment, she steps into her Shambhala Leadership, and creates the space for others to trust her and succeed through her.

Commitment Three: Open Your Heart (Compassion)

The awakening of compassion begins in Commitment Two, specifically in Ring Two, Psychic Integrity. When you do the hard and noble work of deconstructing your ego, meeting all of your ego's parts, the process of healing begins and self-love deepens. I say begins, because it never ends. There are many reasons to heal, such as to feel better, to effectuate your purpose, or because it's fun and exciting, but the reason that most matters to the Shambhala Leader is that she needs to move through the world with an undefended heart.

An undefended heart is an enlarged heart. It is enlarged because it has been broken and repaired so many times it is used to it and welcomes it. With each fracture, new insight and healing arises and a greater capacity to love emerges. The undefended heart is the result of years and decades devoted to personal healing and transformation. There are no shortcuts here. No techniques. An open heart is an expression of being. It allows you to embrace every human with love and acceptance, to heal her with your compassion and concern and inspire her to move into her healing and step into her own bigness. As mentioned in Ring Two, men's and women's circles are powerful ways to transform shadow into strength, to heal and re-parent old wounds, and increasingly move through the world with love and compassion.

Commitment Four: Open Your Mind (Integral Worldview)

The awakening of an Integral Worldview also begins in Commitment Two, specifically in Ring Five, World Integrity. One cannot be of, by, for and as the world if one is ignorant of it. The 4th Commitment, to open your mind and develop an integral worldview, deserves some focused attention. Once your wounds of the past are healed in Ring Two, your view of life opens to reveal whole swaths of reality that were formerly obscured. To adjust to this new capacity to see, it's helpful to have a powerful framework, one that is designed to hold all of reality together, love it as it is and make nothing about it wrong.

This is what is referred to as integral, holistic or 2nd tier thinking. This type of thinking sees all of reality as an interconnected whole and a process of becoming. There are dozens of integral philosophers including many living thinkers, such as Ken Wilber, Erwin Laszlo, Terry Patten and Steve McIntosh, but the line of thought stretches back to the 20th century to the work of Pierre Teilhard de Chardin and

Aurobindo, and has its roots in the 9th century work of Shankara and 3rd century to the work of Plotinus. By reading Part Three, you'll meet some of these folks, expand your mind and develop a worldview that can include all of reality.

With these Four Commitments in place, trust is present and a Shambhala Leader is created. Of course, it all begins with purpose. Without purpose (all ten aspects of it), one cannot embody it, nor lead with wisdom and love.

Using this framework, you can begin the path of your Shambhala Leadership in a world that aches for it. Are you ready to take this on? I ask this question because the world will not fix itself, nor will it empower you with the responsibility to lead either, unless you are 100% committed. This means that you have to surrender to the unknown, to your mentors, masters and coaches, to expand your worldview, heal your wounds and be open to continual purpose awakening and embodiment. Are you all in?

If so, go boldly into Part Three, wrestle with the expanding worldview of your Shambhala Leadership. In Part Three, you will get connected to the possibility and responsibility of what it means to be a leader in our complex, interconnected and often chaotic world.

> "The new leadership must be grounded in fundamentally new understandings of how the world works. The sixteenth-century Newtonian mechanical view of the universe, which still guides our thinking, has become increasingly dysfunctional in these times of interdependence and change. The critical shifts required to guarantee a healthy world for our children and our children's children will not be achieved by doing more of the same."
>
> -Peter Senge (Jaworski, p. 9, 1996)

> "Recognize that the very molecules that make up your body, the atoms that construct the molecules, are traceable to the crucibles that were once the centers of high mass stars that exploded their chemically rich guts into the galaxy, enriching pristine gas clouds with the chemistry of life. So that we are all connected to each other biologically, to the earth chemically and to the rest of the universe atomically. That's kinda cool! That makes me smile and I actually feel quite large at the end of that. It's not that we are better than the universe, we are part of the universe. We are in the universe and the universe is in us."
>
> -Neil de Grasse Tyson, Astrophysicist, (History Channel, 2007)

"It's a planetary movement and together we're going to find our way into what it means that we are deeply interconnected with everything. What kind of economics do you build when you start off with such an idea? What kind of religions do you have?"

-Brian Swimme
(quoted in Martin, *Cosmic Conversations*, pp. 31, 2010)

PART THREE

Humanity's Purpose

CHAPTER 14

The Power of Context

"Are we rich?"

"Well that's a good question. I would say we have more money than most people," said my Dad while shaving. My parents and I had a morning ritual. Or rather, I had a morning ritual and they were my victims. As they were getting ready for work, I would follow them around their bedroom and bathroom and pelt them with questions and they would do their best to answer. As soon as I'd get a response, I'd hit them with another question...

"Why do you love Mommy?"

...

"How come Ryne Sandberg steals more bases than Leon Durham?"

...

"Is it worse to die from fire or freezing to death?"

...

"How come people are poor?"

...

"What does it mean when a car is called 'turbo'?"

...

"Can you die if you get shot with a BB gun?"

...

As my parents discovered, my quest for knowledge was really important to me. What I was in search of was context, an understanding of the deeper patterns of life, why I'm here, how the world works and what I'm supposed to do. I wanted to know what I didn't know. And so, I'd ask them questions. Lots of them.

As my parents walked in the door after work, I'd pelt them again. Finally, my Dad made up a rule, no questions until he sat down and enjoyed his Dewar's scotch on the rocks with a twist. He took to calling me the "Question Man" and made up a song about me, "Do you know the Question Man?" (based on the nursery rhyme "Do you Know the Muffin Man?") to make fun of me a little, but I suspect it was just to make the questions stop for spell.

From my perspective, adults were a magical source of knowledge, mystery and adventure. My questions were less often answered with facts, and more often thoughtfully answered with consideration and other questions that opened whole new realms of possibility and inquiry. I asked my parents questions about their childhoods, our family history, why they voted for Carter over Ford and Reagan over Carter, and the fundamentals of sexual intercourse, marriage and childbirth. My questions plunged us into the realms of financial markets, sex, war, physics, slavery, history and politics, revealing the incredibly mysterious dynamics at play - power, wealth, compassion, exploitation, justice, greed, creativity, racism, genius and sexism. I also enjoyed conversation with my parents' friends, with whom I got to keep pushing the limits of my reality, opening portals to whole new realms of perspective, existence and expression, stretching my context as far and wide as I could take it.

As I began to explore the different worlds of the adults in my life, I discovered that in one context an action can be seen as optimal, and in another context, it can be seen as suboptimal. Killing someone on the street was bad. Killing someone in a war was good. Buying drugs in an alley was bad. Buying them in a pharmacy was good. Telling dirty jokes in front of women was bad. Telling dirty jokes in front of men was good. For me, this tension of differing contexts was confusing. I felt compelled to choose which of these contexts I would use to govern my behavior. Some days I would follow my Dad's example; other days, my Mom's; and sometimes I would just do whatever I felt like and justify it with something I once heard. All of this is normal kid stuff - being a sneaky little SOB, playing with context, ethics and reference points and trying to get away with my sneakiness.

As an adult, however, I now have the ability and responsibility to generate my own worldview, to root my life and livelihood in my purpose.

And, never before in human history has developing an awareness of context been more critical. We find ourselves in a world torn not between good people and bad people, not between values and selfishness, but between worldviews.

My experience tells me that we are all good people. We are moved by our deepest concerns and express those concerns in the best way we know how, given our worldview. This is to say that human beings always choose optimally, *given their worldview*. Each of us is a human with a big heart, wild soul and vision for the world. Each of us, if prompted to list our top 20 values, would generate roughly the same list. The values would be in a slightly different order, but the lists would look pretty similar in aggregate.

"This not a battle of nations, this is a battle of ideas."
-Mark Zuckerberg (Zuckerberg, 2016)

What accounts for the wide difference in decisions made in the world is not values, but worldview. Presently, our species sits in the tension between two major worldviews, a worldview of unity and cooperation versus a worldview of isolation and individualism; a worldview of wonder, connection and mystery versus the worldview of a zero-sum, king-of-the-hill game; a worldview of creativity, emergence and love versus a worldview of reactivity and fear.

"A human being is a part of the whole called by us the 'Universe,' a part limited in time and space. He experiences himself, his thoughts and feelings as something separated from the rest, a kind of optical delusion of his consciousness. This delusion is a kind of prison for us, restricting us to our personal desires and to affection for a few persons nearest to us. Our task must be to free ourselves from this prison by widening our circle of compassion to embrace all living creatures and the whole of nature in its beauty."

-Albert Einstein

The cooperation/unity/creativity/emergence/wonder/love/mystery worldview is one supported by hard facts in physics, ecology, psychology, sociology and economics. The fear/reactivity/isolation/individualism worldview is given to us by our formative childhood experiences, in which we took on views of cynicism, separation and persecution and also the unexamined cultural influences of our increasingly factless media, of politicians, society and "gotcha" Facebook posts. However, this second worldview, despite its pervasiveness, is actually no longer valid. Isolation and individualism are reflections of an outdated view of the Cosmos, namely the determinism and mechanistic materialism of Newtonian physics.

As Albert Einstein showed, modern physics has revealed that we are actually all interconnected, that the Cosmos is full of mystery and wonder. As Peter Senge, Neil deGrasse Tyson and Brian Swimme illuminated at the end of the last chapter, and as you will explore for yourself shortly, we now face the task of a worldview upgrade. If it hasn't already occurred to you, your personal worldview must now rise above the modern, mechanistic and out of date assumptions governing most of our institutions and culture. Your worldview must evolve beyond this Newtonian worldview that posits the universe as an aging lifeless clock full of selfish actors competing for limited resources (Social Darwinism). Your worldview must rise above the false dichotomy of liberal versus conservative. Your worldview must rise above the media's simplistic narratives of bad actors working malevolently to oppress helpless victims. Your worldview must rise to meet this new mysterious, interconnected, creative and highly emergent Cosmos as it is.

Questions that value, explore and cultivate worldview are not merely intellectual exercises, but reflect a reverence for the beauty of existence, and a love of what could be, for all beings and for our Earth's ecology. We have already seen that integrity is a function of perspective and concern. We tend to want to improve matters (make them more complete and sound) only for those things, people and dynamics we feel connected to. We cannot effectively improve something unless we understand what it is, can conceive of its history, nature and have a vision for its fullness.

As we explored, embodying your purpose as a Shambhala Leader, and moving through the rings of integrity, the key to the fulfillment and evolution of your purpose lies in the expansion of your worldview. We must now turn our eyes to the context of all of existence and inquire into the nature, history and fullness of the Cosmos itself, as it is the largest foundational context in which your individual life purpose arises.

What is the Cosmos? How did it arise? Will our Cosmos terminate in a fiery collapse, or endless expansion into cold lifeless oblivion, or are there other possibilities we can create? Can we alter the evolution of life in the Cosmos? Should we even use our higher intelligence to make things better for humans and the Earth's ecology? Can we access undiscovered dimensions of being and cultivate new capacities? Is there a way to evolve our essential humanness such that we can transcend the current limitations of biology, the Sun's eventual consumption of the Earth or even our current understanding of physics?

Part Three of this book is an invitation to dive into the Cosmic waters of context, to root your life's purpose and your leadership in a philosophically broad and intellectually defensible worldview, to hear what the Cosmos is calling for. This will also empower you with a much more grand and inspiring narrative for your life. It will grant you certainty where you need it - in your actions - and curiosity where you need it - in your understanding of yourself, others, their worldviews and the nature of reality. My hope is that you find delight in this paradox, that your dance with context reveals new magic and joy in your life and it empowers you to create more impact, fulfillment and abundance in your career.

Many notable thinkers (Joanna Macy, Ken Wilber, David Abram), poets (Drew Dellinger, David Whyte) and Underworld Guides (Bill Plotkin) write and speak eloquently about the importance of the worldview/call of your life's purpose and its vital importance to the survival of humanity. To root purpose in worldview and worldview in purpose, The Purpose Tree makes worldview explicit, not as something to be studied separately, but something to be cultivated organically. The Purpose Tree is itself a context, relating all aspects of your life's purpose, and also orients you to the very real, necessary and difficult task of locating your soul's purpose inside the world as it is (inside your worldview and the call of the human community/the Earth/Cosmos). Your worldview puts you inside the question of what the purposes of the Cosmos and humanity are asking of you. In this sense, your worldview is crucial in determining what theologian Frederic Buechner refers to as "the place where your deep gladness and the world's deep hunger meet."

But, what is the world's deep hunger? Ask one person, and they'll say cheeseburgers. Ask another, and they'll say love. Ask another, and they'll say jobs. Ask another, and they'll say truth. Ask another, and they'll say sustainability. Ask another, and they'll say domination. All are true and all reflect the governing worldview of the person who says it, and all will yield radically different outcomes.

This is why worldview must be included in any model that explores a life's purpose, why as a purpose-awakening individual you have to cultivate, expand and integrate your worldview. Part Three gives you access to the Cosmos-sized context required to powerfully and authentically express your life's purpose, lead and purposefully recreate humanity, as we'll explore in Part Four. But, first there are some hazards you need to consider:

HAZARD #1: It is highly recommended that you do not read this part until you have completed the Global Purpose Expedition or have worked with a trained Guide, and you have dealt explicitly with your ego parts, have discovered your purpose and have created an integrated soul-infused life. Without such work, without your life's purpose being central - your primary love relationship and true religion - you will only be able to view the rest of this book within the context of your pre-existing (pre-purpose) psychological filters, your default social structures, your parental wounding, and social, religious and political identities, and this will prevent you from any expansion in how you understand yourself and the world. You'll be reading this from the question, "Does this resonate with my current identity?", not from the perspective that your worldview is always expanding. This section presumes that you are purpose-aware and awakening, that you are inclined to deconstruct your limiting beliefs, any social and cultural conditioning that doesn't serve you or your people, and that you are excited to amplify the impact of your purpose by expanding your worldview and increasing the scope of your identity.

HAZARD #2: DO NOT read this part unless you are open to playing the BIGGEST possible game, to embody your life's purpose and step into your Shambhala Leadership, to create a world that works for all beings. As such, this part will not allow any remaining ideas you may have about your smallness or insignificance to survive. If you are feeling primarily called to continue your purpose exploration and are not yet ready to live your purpose in the world, please explore "Appendix C: Additional Purpose Resources". Part Three is for you only if you feel ready to embody your purpose, step into action, and contribute your leadership towards the greatest good.

HAZARD #3: Parts One and Two of this book were written for a college educated urban professional. Parts Three and Four are written for emerging Shambhala Leaders. As a Shambhala Leader, you must be a lover of ideas, one who actively explores the possible, asserts the unreasonable, and moves through the world expecting magic. This requires some significantly more advanced language. Especially as we unpack the purpose of the Cosmos and the human species, you are now expected to be more than a consenting, purpose-driven adult, but a scholar. Because of what we know about the Cosmos, humanity's place in it and the place that the Cosmos is within you, and if you are paying attention, this part will blow your mind. This part stands only for your greatness in the world, in human history and the unfolding beauty of the Cosmos. This means not moving forth with this book unless you agree to look up unfamiliar terms, check my sources and note your points of dissonance. Because of what is at stake, your leadership, success, survival and the survival and flourishing of the human species and the future of Cosmic evolution, you have to read as if the future of the species is on the line. If my arguments are weak, you must wrestle me to the ground and pound me into submission with your own logic and sources. Can you take this on? Will you hold me accountable? If you answer no to either of these questions, what follows was not written for you. Please come back when are ready to lay it all on the line.

Still here?

Congratulations! This is great news for you and our species! This puts you in a special place, on the leading edge of human evolution. In fact, you are among the 13% of humanity that is engaged in their life and career (Gallup, 2014), part of the arm-in-arm, one billion strong inner-uprising of purpose-awakening humans.

Part Three provides you with the necessary tools to step into Commitment Four of your Shambhala Leadership, empowering you to expand and evolve your life's purpose and connect you to:

1. **A Large Worldview** – guiding you into a broad, deep and historical perspective from which to live your purpose in the world.
2. **The Call for Your Shambhala Leadership** – establishing a compelling, scientifically-informed mandate for you to unleash your life's purpose NOW, not only to realize your full potential as a human being, but also to awaken your leadership and create a world that works for all beings.

#1 A Large Worldview: An Evolutionary and Unifying Context for Your Purpose

Your purpose is evolutionary. Your understanding of yourself through actions (e.g., your purposeful projects and leadership) and your worldview will always reveal new ways for you to live your purpose. Your purpose gives you a license to create your worldview. Beginning with an understanding of the purpose of the Cosmos and humanity, you will understand yourself as part of this interconnected Cosmos and play your part as a Shambhala Leader in the global human political economy and the Earth's interconnected ecology.

#2 The Call for Your Shambhala Leadership

"Chapter 17: Humanity's Midlife Crisis" is an invitation to consider the cold hard facts of human existence, and to firmly challenge you to act, lead and live your life's purpose in the world – updating every relationship and area of your life with your life's purpose. With the interconnected context of reality in place, you will be invited to be 100% responsible, not only for your actions, the extent to which you live your life's purpose, but also for the extent to which every other human on Earth lives their life's purpose. ***Wait, whaaaat? Yes, that's right.***

> With great power comes great responsibility.
>
> -Spiderman

You have now unlocked the freedom and power to live your life's purpose and to realize all of its benefits: a long life of vitality, impact, abundance and love. However, this power is not for you alone and it comes at a price.

The price of your purpose is leadership.

Because your purpose is rooted in the inescapable, interconnected reality of the Cosmos, you are now called to use your purpose to steward the whole of reality towards a greater expression of its purpose. If you accept this challenge, any distinction between the personal and the political will vanish, as you find yourself increasingly defined as being of, by and for the people and planet that put you here. Your Shambhala Leadership is the product of 13.88 billion years of a combination of physics and ecology, the hard work of your ancestors, our wisdom traditions, and the scientific method. You and your purpose are no accident.

Are you willing to lead and take 100% responsibility for all that is, including man's inhumanity to man?

This is not to say that you are to blame, or that you must feel guilt and shame for everything that has happened, but that you declare that you are the result of, and responsible for, everything in existence. If you say yes, your leadership starts right now. If you say no, that is fine, but know that assigning blame will diminish if not altogether stop your leadership in its tracks.

Your first task is to summon the courage and resolve to move forth into the unknown, to embrace your discomfort and meet (possibly for the very first time) the grandeur of your purpose and your vision for humanity. Fear is always present when we are about to do something big, something our soul craves, and so our ego resists taking new action, such as reading any more of this book. Just sit with that, acknowledge and welcome your resistance; but then keep reading provisionally, as if this discomfort is the most nourishing food imaginable. In this discomfort, you are expanding, tilling the soil for the deeper roots of your soul to take hold and preparing you for an unprecedented amount of growth, impact and achievement.

CHAPTER 15

The Purpose of the Cosmos

(whack)

"Nice one!" said my Dad.

I was twenty years old and on a golf trip with my Dad in Hilton Head, South Carolina. My golf ball exploded off the tee and found itself 320 yards away, and just a chip shot to the pin. Except my ball wasn't on the fairway. I had hooked it so bad, it wasn't even on the right hole.

"Tee up another one. We're not in any hurry," my Dad said with a mixed look of amusement and confusion. We were both clear I was not playing the game as it was intended to be played. I wasn't playing the inner game of mindfulness that I would go on to learn in my late 20's, the practice of "true gravity" from Michael Murphy's *Golf in the Kingdom* (Murphy, 1971) and "being the ball", cultivating a natural swing rhythm, playing the hole conservatively and intentionally, yet unattached and relaxed into the experience of golf. I was an addict in search of long drive glory.

So, I tee'd up another. This time my ball took a flight pattern that looked more like a high-trajectory wedge shot and sliced far out of bounds to the right.

"Tee up another, Chief Sleeve-a-hole," my Dad said, chuckling and still shaking his head from my first tee shot. My Dad called me Chief Sleeve-a-hole because I was capable of losing a sleeve of three balls each hole in pursuit of what he terms my "flair for the spectacular", my desire to damn the torpedoes, push far into the unknown for the chance at a moment of glory.

So, I tee'd up another, this time it was a long straight drive, but I pushed it right and also very far out of bounds. We got in the golf cart and drove first to my Dad's ball, a respectable 250 yards down the right side of the fairway. After his approach shot that landed on green 30 feet from the pin, as per custom, I handed him his putter for the long walk that his wizened play afforded him, while I took the cart on an adventure to find my first ball on another hole.

On any given hole, I had just as good of chance of making a birdie (one under par) as a 12 (eight over par). My drives were a grand gesture. I'd swing so hard, I'd come of out my shoes and spin myself around. The way I tee'd off made Tiger

Woods, then the reigning king of golf and notable master of the long drive, seem like he wasn't trying very hard.

This is all to say, I love going big. I love risk, the unknown, and pushing my mind and body to its limit and some of the time far beyond that limit. And, I believe boundary-smashing is what humanity needs right now. The world isn't working. It is aching for courage and imagination.

Now is not the time for marginal improvements from neoliberal technocrats. Now is not the time to work harder. Now is not the time for partisan politics and waiting your turn. Now is the time to go big. Now is the time for grand gestures. Humanity needs ALL of us to go big. Now is the time for revolutionary efforts, full exertion and entirely new frames and possibilities for what it means to be a human being on Earth.

My hope is that this section of the book lays out an intellectual foundation for you to go big, such that your understanding of the Cosmos, allows you to play the biggest possible game with your life, to craft a purposeful life that meaningfully advances humanity.

In addition to widening the canvas upon which to paint your life's purpose, Part Three is included as an academic foundation for Part Four, which lays out a vision for a purpose-driven human society. Just as spiritual traditions have foundation stones, e.g., Christianity's Book of Genesis, we need to lay down our own foundation narrative, before we can begin to imagine how we can create a purpose-driven society. We must now lay these foundation stones in terms friendly to a modern Western reader.

However, much as the Golden Rule ("do unto others as you have them do onto you") stands on its own without you needing to agree with the historical veracity of the Book of Matthew, know that you do not have to read Part Three in order to try on a vision for a collective purpose. You can skip it. For most folks, this level of rigor is unnecessary and likely laborious.

SPOILER ALERT: If you choose to skip Part Three, know that what we discover is that the Cosmos has done, is doing and will likely continue to do three things over time (and not without glaring counterexamples). The Cosmos creates:

1. More **unity** (more goodness, interconnection – more ethical behavior);
2. More **beauty** (more syntropy, more rare, richly complex, interdependent and beautiful things and concepts over time); and
3. More **truth** (via an expanded relationship to certainty and uncertainty).

The Cosmos and all of human experience is a reflection and expression of these three themes. These three themes are engaged in a trialectic discourse, revealing evermore goodness/unity/spirit, truth/uncertainty/soul and beauty/syntropy/matter over time. And this is not a new idea, just one that now has much more scientific evidence which we will explore in this chapter. The first known expression of the good, the true and the beautiful dates back to the Platonic transcendentals in the West ~380 BCE, and, in the East ~500-200 BCE in the Bhagavad Gita (Eswaran, Ch. 17, v. 15,1985).

Moreover, the purpose of humanity is to step into this good, true and beautiful Cosmic identity, and act as, of, by and for the human species, the Earth's ecology and the whole Cosmos. We are not just humans; we are also Earth and Cosmos. As such, our purpose must express these identities. Specifically, following the Mission Statement Model from "Chapter 2: What is Purpose?", our purpose as a species is:

1. As an apex ecosystem steward of Planet Earth, an evolutionary community of Shambhala Leaders and the emerging *Cosmosapien* central nervous system of the Cosmos (core),
2. We awaken, heal, bring order to, express, create and celebrate the beauty of existence (powers and craft),
3. In service of an abundant, just, sustainable and peaceful presence on Earth and with a story and message of acceptance, love, achievement, wonder, learning, creativity and joy throughout the Cosmos (call, virtues, vision and mission).

If you are curious to see how these conclusions were arrived at, please continue on. If not, I will see you in Part Four.

Now it's time for you to put on your space suit, lab coat, smoking jacket or tie-dye, or whatever costume suits your ventures into the unknown.

A Note on Humility

It may seem outlandish to consider that the Cosmos is a real thing, something that informs your everyday experience of life. Most people don't ever think of the Cosmos, except during movies and TV shows that deal with this seemingly separate, foreign and distant concept and reality. After all, isn't the Cosmos just a huge expanse of space, that final frontier that really doesn't have a lot to do with us here on Earth, and even less to do with your purpose? And who are we, as mere humans, to make such proclamations that we know the nature of the Cosmos? It is only with a massive dose of humility that we can move forth into this incredibly mysterious question.

According to the calculations of our species' brightest astronomers and astrobiologists (those who study non-terrestrial life in space), it is highly likely that that there is other complex life in the Cosmos. Dr. Frank Drake, SETI Astronomer and Emeritus Professor of Astronomy and Astrophysics at the University of California, Santa Cruz, developed an equation for estimating intelligent life in the universe, from which he has deduced that the range of other advanced civilizations in the universe is between two and 280,000,000 (Tate, 2015). Within this wide range, current estimates calculate the number of intelligent civilizations with the capability to communicate at between 100 and 10,000:

- 100 per Neil de Grasse Tyson, PhD (Tyson, Strauss, Gott, 2016)
- 500 per the National Radio Astronomy Observatory (Scoles, Heatherly, 2011)
- 10,000 per Dr. Frank Drake (QST, p. 38, August, 1995)

What this means is that it is only with a healthy measure of humility that we move forth, as it is highly likely that we humans are not the only ones with the question, a perspective and a say in the matter of the purpose of the Cosmos. If there are, indeed, other conscious entities, surely their perspectives, models, stories, theories, philosophies, religions and science would be useful in understanding the purpose of the Cosmos. As of yet, these aren't in the public domain. What we do have is our human/ Earth models, theories, philosophies, religions and science, so it is with this humility that we proceed to ascertain the purpose of the Cosmos.

A Note on Perspective

It's also important to note, as a preliminary matter, that as we currently understand it, the Cosmos is ubiquitously expanding and omnicentric, meaning we cannot find its center. What this means is that its center is everywhere, including inside of you. Since the expansion of the Cosmos seems to be happening everywhere, in very physical terms there is no ground, no rule of measure, no concrete owner's manual, nothing by which to say something is absolutely near or far, better or worse. In this way, the Cosmos is foundationally multiperspectival, all perspectives are needed to understand its emergent purpose, and the more perspectives we have the greater the understanding of the purpose of the Cosmos we can perceive. As Einstein revealed in his famous "clock on a train" thought-experiment, time is more an experience than a law - the experience of time slows and quickens depending where you are and how fast you are moving in the Cosmos. As such, anything said by me or anyone/thing else is also a perspective. Nothing more, nothing less.

However, some perspectives themselves take multiple perspectives, such as the integral theories of Ken Wilber and Erwin Laszlo and the Big Histories of Cynthia Stokes-Brown and Brian Swimme reveal, and thus these theories have greater explanatory power over the observable phenomenon in Cosmos than other theories. For example, in physics, quantum physics explains more of the nature of energy/ matter, e.g., including particle-wave duality and Heisenberg's Uncertainty Principle, than Newtonian physics. This doesn't mean Newtonian physics is wrong or bad, just that as a model it has less integrity, because it is less complete and comprehensive. It also is my intention in this chapter to weave multiple perspectives together in order to reveal as much as we can of the underlying patterns and purpose of the Cosmos.

The Purpose Holarchy

We exist within the purpose, context and constructs of other purposes. We don't exist separate from the Cosmos and its purposes, we are every bit a part of it, just as much as galaxies, stars and planets are. Think of it this way. Your body is made up of billions of cells. Each one of your cells is discrete and has a unique purpose, meaning a particular role in the system in which it functions. Yet, each cell is also part of a greater whole, an organ or system that has a purpose, which is part of the greater whole (you) that also has a purpose. This whole cannot function without each tiny, seemingly insignificant cell living in integrity with its purpose.

So on and so forth, all the way down the scale of complexity to molecules, atoms and quarks, and back up that same scale to relationships, family, community, corporation, nation, humanity, planet, and TBD galaxy federations, etc. In this regard, you can only reach the fullest expression of yourself as a human – living a fully integrated life of purpose – when you also express and serve the well-being of the other wholes (which may also mean destroying, reforming or starting new wholes) of which you are a part, which for you includes your romantic relationship, your family (*gulp!*), your community, your place of employment (*double gulp!*), your country (*triple gulp!*), our species, all the way up to the greatest whole you can conceive of with your current knowledge, which for most of us is the entire Cosmos or our concept of God.

Your personal purpose is the bridge that joins what's inside (your soul, your corner of the Cosmos) with what's outside (the rest of Cosmos). To have a life purpose that is fully aligned with and expressive of reality necessarily implies that you know something about your soul as well as something about the Cosmos, so you can align your soul with the Cosmos, building a bridge between them with your powers, craft, flow and mission. As such, the totality your life purpose, to a great extent, depends on the extent to which you understand the Cosmos and its purpose, i.e., your worldview. This is a tall order, and a lifelong task. This chapter merely attempts to outline a framework for exploration, and to deliver you the beginning of an inch-deep, mile-wide understanding of the Cosmos.

Our understanding of the Cosmos has expanded rapidly in the last twenty years. Just over a hundred years ago, we began developing tools like carbon dating, radio telescopes, rockets launched from Earth carrying research equipment, and new mind-blowing fields of study like theoretical physics and astrobiology. As a result, we have brought much more of the Cosmos into view. With the help of these tools and fields of study for exploration, we now know that the Cosmos has created increasingly more complex structures over time (e.g., from a hydrogen atom to a molecule to an organism to an organism's way of cooperating and tools like an iPhone).

Consider this progression: algae, worm, bird, ape, human, artificial intelligence. All are the Cosmos at different stages of complexity and interdependence. Another way to say this is that:

Over time, the Cosmos has become increasingly self-aware through the evolution of life and life's increasingly complex consciousness structures that are uniquely and increasingly geared to connect with each other and express their unique purpose.

As far as we know, humans are among the most advanced (complex) lifeforms in the Cosmos. Collectively as a species, and potentially in cooperation with other species in the Cosmos, we are forming the central nervous system of the Cosmos. We are able to network knowledge across space and time, accumulate and evolve best practices, and cooperate economically, socially and politically to advance and connect the Cosmos with itself through our tools, technologies and fields of inquiry (e.g., the telegraph, TV, and the physical tools for capturing and expressing the noosphere, such as the Internet, Wikipedia and artificial intelligence).

> "And now, as a germination of planetary dimensions, comes the thinking layer [the noosphere] which over its full extent develops and intertwines its fibres, not to confuse and neutralize them but to reinforce them in the living unity of a single tissue."
> -Pierre Teilhard de Chardin (Yong-hee, 2015)

In essence, the Cosmos is becoming increasingly self-aware over time, with basic forms of self-awareness arising with protons and microbes, all the way through more complex forms like us, *homo sapiens sapiens*. We are the Cosmos in the flesh, but unlike protons and microbes and fish and horses, we are aware that we are aware and, thus, the Cosmos is aware that it is aware. Of course, the whole Cosmos isn't yet aware that it is aware, just its more complex structures and networks.

This raises questions, lots of questions. As a four-dimensional consciousness structure (the four dimensions being height, width, depth, and time), what is this Cosmos thing that is expressed through us? Why did we become self-aware? What purpose do humans serve within the Cosmos? What forms and themes within each human and the whole Cosmos are reaching fuller expression over time? This inquiry will help us explore the contours of the purpose of the Cosmos, to expand our worldview and missions.

Let's begin our exploration with a few selected moments in the known and theorized history of the Cosmos, and then dive into the three key themes (syntropy, unity and uncertainty) that have reached greater expression in the Cosmos over time:

- **~13.88 billion years ago**
  The most generally accepted theory is that the Universe exploded from an inconceivably tiny point, aka The Big Bang. Immediately after The Big Bang, the Universe expanded rapidly, and some data, from Nobel Prize Winners in Physics, Saul Perlmutter, Brian Schmidt and Adam Riess, suggests that the Cosmos is still accelerating in its expansion (Reiss, et al, 1998). This may have happened before, and may happen again, aka The Big Bounce or Big Crunch, although recent evidence suggests there will be only be expansion, and no future contraction. This phenomenon may also currently be happening in other universes. It is possible that our Universe has been bruised four times (Gurzadyan, Penrose, 2010) in its history by banging into something else beyond itself, such as another universe or a gigantic wall of pudding – we don't know exactly what, only that our data reveals that this may have happened and could happen again. This raises the question that there is something larger than our Cosmos – that we have yet to discover – something that, perhaps, even our Cosmos serves with its purpose.

- **~4.5 billion years ago**
  The Earth formed, gaining all of its heavier elements from at least two prior explosions of stars like our Sun.

- **~3.8 billion years ago**
  The Earth became cool, temperate and hospitable enough for carbon-based life forms. Non-organic molecules sprung forth into organic carbon-based organic molecules and then proto-cells. We're not sure exactly how this happened, only that it did. Just as the Cosmos came to being in a moment out of nothing (The Big Bang), life came into being out of non-life.

- **~200,000 years ago**
  We know humans evolved from our primate cousins in East Africa, or potentially Eastern Europe, but how and why are still conjecture.

With this in mind, let us explore the radical shifts of the Cosmos within the very recent human era, witness what it means to be a human in the Western world, and how this understanding has shifted over the last 11,500 years. (As this book is written in English for a modern Western reader, and with the aim of expanding our collective understanding of what it means to be human in the modern world, which owes much of its current form to Western developments, I've focused primarily on the key developments in Western civilization. This does not diminish the significance or importance of other cultures, worldviews or developments which flourish in Asia, Africa or South America.)

- **Urban Shift: ~11,500 years ago**

  With the advent of agricultural production in the Fertile Crescent, economic volatility decreased. The necessary expenditure of human calories to procure food calories decreased, resulting in more economic surpluses, and more time for leisure, the arts, spirituality and economic specialization, e.g., crafts, trades, and services. This engendered the creation of more permanent settlements, structures, transportation systems, bureaucratic functions and eventually complex city-states and kingdoms.

  Humanity became capable of experiencing the distinctions of identity in novel socio-economic ways, to experience the subtleties of life that could exist between a farmer, a blacksmith, a courtesan, an artist or a priest. Human identity then shifted to include more than just one's tribe, but one's socioeconomic role and status.

- **Best-practices Shift: ~5,000 years ago**

  As complex economic kingdoms arose, we developed symbolic language many times over the course of our 200,000-year history (Ong, 1982). It is hypothesized that language was initially used to meet the need to express vital political and economic information, e.g., to be able to communicate about movements of enemy troops, and taxes, herds, fish, technical know-how, exotic foods/spices, etc., and to be able to move across larger geographic areas. When these pre-agrarian kingdoms declined, so did their use of symbolic language. But, somewhere around 40,000 years ago, symbolic language became something that would survive the booms and busts of complex human civilizations. And, somewhere around 5,000 years ago, symbolic language matured into written languages capable of capturing and expressing the complexity and core of human life, and of sharing what we would now call best practices.

  For the first time in human (and, possibly, Cosmic) history, the intellectual, cultural and spiritual wealth of our species was able to survive the passage of time, and our love affair with the concept of best practices began to come alive. For the first time, the core of humanity could live in an abstract form as text, as information outside of our biological form, and thus transcend time by means of cave paintings, pressed papyrus, parchment and clay tablets that outlasted their creators. As a result of economic specialization and increased time for leisure, certain humans started specializing in cultivating knowledge.

  This love affair with transgenerational best practices meant that human development no longer was dependent upon grandparent/parent to child transmission. If children were lucky, they had access to these texts and the adults who read and cared for them. Today a child can simply walk into a library, talk with a teacher or surf Wikipedia to become better informed than her parents and discover numerous best practices for life, like yoga, meditation and purpose, without their parents even being aware or involved in the exploration.

Co-arising with economic specialization, spirituality became a discrete discipline of study and practice. Although it was likely transmitted orally for thousands of years before, the first evidence of humans meditating appears in the Hindu Vedas (5,000-6,000 BCE). Numerous somatic, breathing, vocal, sexual, psychopharmacological (opiates, stimulants, entheogens), ethical, dietary/fasting, meditation and awareness practices were cultivated in order to transform and elevate individual human consciousness. This effort greatly expanded through the use of text and eventually through epic myths that aided spiritual and personal development, such as the *Epic of Gilgamesh* (2,500 BCE) and the *Mahabharata* (800 BCE). These best practices were shared among tribes and religious sects, demonstrating that human consciousness was plastic, that one could apply oneself in a particular fashion and be transformed.

For the first time in human history and for the lucky few, human identity was no longer necessarily determined by birth, economic role or social order. People had the choice to engage in consciousness altering practices and expand their consciousness, transform and write new futures.

- **Cognitive and Political Empowerment Shift (The Enlightenment): 1540 CE**

Seeded by the age of Empire, and the spread of Latin, Greek, French and English around the world (owing a great deal to the Western intellectual tradition that had begun in Greece 3,000 years prior), a rapid democratized personal awakening occurred, sourcing personal human identity and responsibility inside the individual and within the framework of shared best practices, aka science and the Western intellectual tradition. With increasing scientific objectivity, we began to examine our place in the Cosmos. Copernicus' *On the Revolutions of the Celestial Spheres* (1543) placed the Earth in space. Darwin's *On the Origin of Species* (1859) placed humanity within the Earth's ecology. Numerous Contributions from Enlightenment philosophers such as Voltaire's *Essay on the Customs and the Spirit of the Nations* (1756) and Rousseau's *The Social Contract* (1762) began to speculate on the connection between the individual and collective, eventually rooting each human inside the human species, as well as inside of our individual purpose and ethics. Originating in the proto-psychological musings of Montaigne's *Essais* (1580) and Descartes' *Meditations on First Philosophy* (1641), the Enlightenment radically empowered society's literate with long forgotten tools like contemplation and debate to expand their personal knowledge, power and effectiveness. This questioning eventually gave rise to dozens of democratic revolutions.

The Enlightenment shifted human experience into an expanded sense of personal, economic and political power along with varying measures of collective responsibility and purpose awareness. Humans had re-awakened the capacity to purposefully cause changes in their consciousness and experience of life as well as in their political and economic power. Their fates were no longer merely at the mercy of the power of God-ordained feudal monarchies.

- **Psychological Empowerment Shift: 1900 CE**
  At the beginning of the twentieth century, the field of psychology began to extend the focus of our scientific inquiry more deeply inward, empowering us to begin to understand the mysteries of consciousness using the language of science to lead more fulfilling lives. The works of William James, Sigmund Freud and Carl Jung radically illuminated the inner workings of the human mind/soul.

  Those who had the access, time, money and inclination (admittedly a very small segment of society) could use these tools (psychotherapy, spiritual retreats) to more deeply understand the inner workings of their minds and make changes in their thoughts and actions which could enable them to expand and deepen their experience of life. The seeds were planted which would give rise in the later 20th century to an emphasis on self-awareness that would enable millions of people to expand and deepen their experience of life.

- **Evolutionary Shift: 1940 CE**
  Leveraging the work of Hegel and his dialectic model for human evolution, notable integral thinkers began conceiving of the whole of the Universe and the evolution of humanity as following certain evolutionary patterns. The fields of evolutionary psychology (Kegan, Piaget, Kohlberg, Gilligan) and evolutionary philosophy (Aurobindo, Teilhard de Chardin, Wilber, Laszlo) were born. These approaches expanded on developmental psychology, which was primarily focused on the psychological development of children, and examined the way adults develop new capacities by transcending and including old capacities.

  Through their philosophy, theory and research, these luminaries demonstrated that the adult psyche is not fixed, but rather does evolve over time to transcend and include old ways of being, to become more whole, complete, effective and fulfilled. These thinkers also began to see correlations between adults who evolved quickly and the practices they employed (integrating cognitive, psychological, physical and spiritual developmental techniques).

- **Cosmic Shift: 1950 CE**
  The space race turned our eyes to the sky in a brand-new way. Aided by developments in modern physics as well as technological advances such as radio telescopes and rocketry in the early 1900's, in the 1960's we began to physically explore the Cosmos and embrace it as a context for our lives. Many countries, most notably the United States, Russia, China, The United Kingdom, France, Belgium and Chile, began public and covert endeavors to explore space, document anomalies and establish contact with intelligent life beyond our atmosphere. In the United States, numerous initiatives were launched, such as the U.S. Air Force's Project Blue Book (1952-1959), NASA, SETI (Search for Extraterrestrial Intelligence), Area 51 and the Advanced Aerospace Threat Identification Program. In December of 2017, the New York Times reported that the U.S. Defense Department declassified "The Advanced Aerospace Threat Identification Program", revealing a dossier of hundreds of unexplained encounters in Earth's atmosphere and beyond, as well as a stockpile of materials and artifacts recovered from alien aircraft, now located in a facility in Las Vegas, NV. (Cooper, Blumenthal, Keane, 2017) The field of astrobiology eventually emerged to explore the nature of life beyond our planet. Beyond a mere curiosity, the existence of complex extraterrestrial life has been advocated by numerous notable figures, including high-ranking government officials and heads of state, such as:

  o   Former U.S. President, Jimmy Carter, "I am convinced that UFOs exist because I've seen one." (Telegraph, 2009)

  o   Former U.S. President, Ronald Reagan, "I looked out the window and saw this white light. It was zigzagging around. I went up to the pilot and said, 'Have you ever seen anything like that?' He was shocked and he said, 'nope.' And I said to him: 'Let's follow it!' We followed it for several minutes. It was a bright white light. We followed it to Bakersfield, and all of a sudden to our utter amazement it went straight up into the heavens. When I got off the plane I told Nancy all about it." (Telegraph, 2009)

  o   Former U.S. President Bill Clinton, "If we were visited someday, I wouldn't be surprised." (Jimmy Kimmel Live, 2014)

  o   Former President of the Soviet Union, Mikhail Gorbachev, "The phenomenon of UFOs does exist, and it must be treated seriously." (Telegraph, 2009)

o   Former NASA Astronaut, Edgar Mitchell, "UFO cover-ups must end." (Bloomberg, 2013)

o   Former Canadian Defense Minister, Paul Hellyer, "UFOs are as real as the airplanes flying over your head." (McGuire, 2013).

The experience of being a human and the context for our existence is now not only inside the Cosmos, but it now comes with the possibility that we are not alone, that our governments may already be in communication with intelligent life that originated beyond our solar system.

- **Self-improvement Shift: 1970 CE**

  Leveraging the tools of developmental and evolutionary psychology, as well as the fields of philosophy, religion and various scientific disciplines, new tools were invented to expedite the psychological and spiritual development of adults. Humanity began to see that a better experience of life is possible, not just by having more stuff, but by also upgrading our consciousness. New approaches were hypothesized and tested, eventually driving a host of transformational schools, techniques and processes throughout the latter half of the twentieth century to transform human consciousness, e.g., Landmark, The ManKind Project, Woman Within, Women in Power and Alcoholics Anonymous.

  A culture and appetite for personal transformation began to emerge. The human experience started to become more fluid and expansive, and tools for evolving consciousness were being rapidly distributed, leveraging widely available books such as Dale Carnegie's *How to Win Friends and Influence People* (1936), Norman Vincent Peale's *The Power of Positive Thinking* (1952) and Eckhart Tolle's *The Power of Now* (1997). Personal development books, workshops, courses and trainings can now be found in virtually every city on the planet, and their principles are making their way into mainstream culture, via TV shows like *Lie to Me, Treatment, Seinfeld, Sex in the City* and *The Sopranos,* and children's movies such as *Inside Out, Moana, Guardians of the Galaxy* and *Coco.*

- **Purpose Shift: 1994 CE**

  The purpose movement in the West emerged via the rediscovery of the shamanic practices of indigenous societies, (e.g., vision quests, Ayahuasca medicine ceremonies, guided visualization practices) and cultivation of these ancient techniques by schools such as the Animas Valley Institute and the School of Lost Borders. Purpose discovery work is becoming known once again as a way to induce personal, spiritual experiences and to facilitate psychological re-ordering, to align ego and soul, and to empower individuals to reach greater fullness in life.

Purpose also became a scientifically measurable factor, through a metric known as Purpose in Life (PIL), developed first in 1963 by James Crumbaugh and Leonard Maholick. It became a measurable factor which can now be correlated with the use of causative purpose discovery practices and other quantifiable outcomes: physical (organ and cellular health), neurochemical (levels of cortisol, dopamine, serotonin, oxytocin), behavioral outcomes (lifestyle choices), economic success (impact, effectiveness, leadership, engagement, income, wealth and title), as well as a variety of social indicators (health care spending, educational achievement, civic participation).

The question of one's life purpose was no longer a backwater interest of psychologists, shamans and self-help junkies. It is an increasingly common discussion, one explored by numerous *New York Times* best-selling books like Thomas Moore's *Care of the Soul* (1994) and James Hillman's *The Soul's Code* (1996). It is now also an increasingly achievable and predictable result through proven practices. Leveraging the Voice-Dialogue Method (Stone and Stone,1993) and the Internal Family System Model (Schwartz, 2001), Tim Kelley (Kelley, 2009) created a powerful method to clear a path to our soul's purpose, and integrate our ego structures around it. These techniques empower each of us to understand the genesis of our personality as having multiple parts, empowering us to understand our egos and reconstruct them around soul, to become wound/shadow aware, so that we can increasingly live our lives from soul rather than from ego or in response to external conditions.

In 2015, twenty colleagues and I launched the Purpose Challenge (now Global Purpose Expedition) and around the same time, the Global Purpose Movement sprang forth from Greenheart International, to help each of Earth's 7.5 billion people find their life's purpose using our most powerful methods from the perspective of the greatest contexts known: the human species, the Earth's ecology and the Cosmos. Our shared goal is to rapidly distribute purpose discovery education, ignite a generation of purpose-driven leaders and create a just, peaceful, abundant and sustainable human presence on Earth.

During this progression, many themes have emerged to articulate the possible purpose of the Cosmos. Of course, much more has happened than this short list of developments can include. These represent only a few highlights, but they begin to tell a powerful story of how we got here, and they help us begin to intimate what we're supposed to do.

En route to discovery of the core personal take-aways (finding your purpose, remaining in relationship to it, expanding your worldview, living your purpose and leading with it in the world), as well as the core collective take-aways (best practices for expressing Cosmic, Earthly and human purpose through economics, politics and culture), I want you to get from this book the three most evident themes in this progression: syntropy, unity and uncertainty. By understanding these three themes and incorporating them into your worldview, you can ensure that your purpose rises to meet the world and Cosmos as it is, that your purpose doesn't become an irrelevant passion project of a 21st-century eccentric, e.g., amassing a collection of PEZ dispensers or blogging about novel ways to use groom your cat, but rather your purpose aligns with the deeper desires of the whole Cosmos.

Theme #1: Syntropy

Syntropy is derived from the root *syn*, meaning together and *tropos*, meaning a tendency; syntropy is thus the tendency of the Cosmos to create individual organisms, systems and ideas that are more complex, unique and interrelated over time. Although human beings are unique in so many ways, what stands out most is that we are expressions of the deeper syntropic order and nature of the Cosmos. We are evolutionarily novel organisms capable of ever emergent expressions.

Syntropy is a concept that was developed by physicist Erwin Schrodinger in his book *What is Life* (1944) and refined and popularized by other 20th-century thinkers such as Buckminster Fuller, Sri Aurobindo and Pierre Teilhard de Chardin. It describes the escalating complexity, novelty and creativity of matter and energy and the structure of the Cosmos over time. This is not to say that the Second Law of Thermodynamics, Entropy – things regress to lower levels of complexity, energy and mass – is invalid. Entropy is merely a cyclical phenomenon in the course of a far grander syntropic narrative of the Cosmos.

Entropy fits nicely into the syntropy model in the sense that the death of every Cosmic artifact isn't an absolute death; rather, it is the end of a particular cycle for a particular structure or system. Entropy removes that which no longer serves. As the Cosmos winds up, someone has to take out the trash. To see the fuller meaning of this cycle, we must observe many cycles in sequence. In doing so, we find that the Universe produces increasingly complex structures as it destroys less complex structures.

> One of the stunning developments of 20th-century science is that we can actually say that the universe seems to be in search of complexity… What we can say with some certainty is that the sense of the universe being entirely random would lead to the expectation that after 14 billion years there wouldn't be much complexity in the universe. So, it's interesting that whatever it is

that we're enveloped in is getting somewhere more quickly than it would if it were simply random... it's not just random, but I want to emphasize the fact that it's *also* random...

-Brian Swimme (Martin, pp. 26-27, 2010)

Simply put, over time things get more complex, more connected, interdependent, creative, novel and more expressive of the vastness, chaos and complexity of the entire Cosmos. Much like fractal geometry, over time the Cosmos seems to be imprinting an increasingly larger pattern of the whole Cosmos onto smaller particular parts of it.

To put it in today's technological language, more of the function and potential of the whole is built into each part; each new line of Cosmic code becomes a greater expression of the entire Cosmos. Humans are a perfect example of such syntropy. As a species, we have:

1. biologically evolved to incorporate an increasingly larger percentage of the Cosmos, now including the 10 trillion diverse organisms within each human (human microbiome) that form a complex, interdependent whole that only survives through cooperation towards a common purpose;

2. genetically evolved along with our microbiomes and are more accurately described as a hologenome, wherein the genomes of a human host and its microbes evolve genetically together, encompassing thousands of different types of bacteria in the skin, digestive system and reproductive organs;

3. economically evolved to become more and more economically interdependent, incorporating an increasingly larger percentage of the Cosmos, as we've expanded across the planet in our search for resources, energy, labor and customers;

4. intellectually evolved the capacity to represent the complexity of the Cosmos (as well as continue to evolve it) with language, concepts, science and a fascination with developing and sharing best practices;

5. technologically evolved to more efficiently create and share knowledge bases for aggregating and improving species-wide best practices, and communicate those practices with ever greater speed and at ever lower costs;

6. psychologically and spiritually evolved to identify with the entire fabric of space-time with increasingly academic language, e.g., "supernormal/ non-ordinary states of consciousness", "quantum entanglement", "Big History".

Each of us is a distinct being, yet also a line within this Cosmic code. The result of this progression is not only more syntropy, but more ways of experiencing syntropy, new mediums, tools and fields by which the Cosmos, through humans, can create ever greater beauty, representing an infinitely fractal relationship to beauty, imbuing the Cosmos with more beauty per square inch, over time.

In addition to greater complexity, interdependence, and cooperation at larger and wider scales, we also increase evolvability. Life keeps getting better and better (and faster and faster) at evolving, Indeed, in us, life is now learning how it has evolved for billions of years. We are in the early stages of learning how to align ourselves with this process and will, in the decades to come, begin to consciously evolve, rather than just muddle through unconsciously.

-Michael Dowd, Evolutionary Theologist (Martin, p. 115, 2010)

At the individual level, over time we move towards more syntropy, or what the religious among us might call grace – the embodiment of wisdom and compassion or the nature and will of God. We experience this as a call towards living our own code structure, our purpose, our own conscious/psycho-spiritual core, toward biological health, and in cooperation with the collective code structure, the Cosmic purpose, towards greater economic and social prosperity, ecological diversity, creative self-expression, and social actualization. With a syntropic orientation, we yearn to be what we are at every level: living our purpose, exercising our powers, so that the next lines of human code can be written for the greatest benefit of all, reaching ever higher levels of integrity, beauty, and actualization, Syntropy is not merely an individual human phenomenon, but a collective one as well.

...we've seen throughout cultural history... ...that we keep finding ways of cooperating that supersede the needs and wants of any one individual. We've created larger scales of cooperation through beliefs, through moral codes, and through scripture, sacred stories, laws, constitutions, and so forth. If we are to move into a just, healthy, sustainable, life-giving future, then we have to recognize *how* life has created these greater spheres of complexity throughout time. We need to find ways to align our laws, our medicine, our politics, our economics, and our education with the way that life really works...

-Michael Dowd (Martin, p. 121, 2010)

When we look at evolutionary patterns, we see that humans are a part of a long line of increasingly novel and syntropic evolutionary advances. However, if we are honest with ourselves, we will see that we too will most likely perish as a species at some point, just as 95% of all species that have ever lived here on Earth have perished in service of the larger purposes of the Earth, humanity and the Cosmos. If we are also to perish, we should ask ourselves to what end should we give our lives (purpose)? For what Cosmic purpose were we instantiated?

We don't know how it will end. We don't know if it will be a literal extinction, or a figurative one, wherein we move into an entirely new form of being and cooperating. It's possible that we could evolve beyond our current understanding of the physical constraints of the Cosmos. Humanity's core may continue to exist in other dimensions, (such as in the 2013 movie *Her*, in which human-created artificial intelligence/consciousness dissociates both from human biology and possibly matter altogether). We could experience singularity, wherein all realms of existence evolve to incorporate each other and become one - a singular entity of spirit, matter, energy, machine, technology, culture and economics.

With our understanding of syntropy, we have a new appreciation for what it means to be human, as we hold two notable Cosmic distinctions: 1. We are Cosmically average, and 2. We are Cosmically extraordinary.

We are Average

In many ways humans are just plain average, and this is actually a very cool thing in Cosmic terms. Dr. Joel Primack, Professor of Physics and Director of the Theoretical Advanced Study Institute at the University of California, Santa Cruz, posits that we are the Cosmic average size, halfway between the tiniest thing and the largest thing, seemingly perfectly placed and equipped to understand, incorporate and express the complexity of the whole of existence within ourselves. (Martin, p. 42, 2010) We have a unique middle path, a Goldilocks perspective from which to examine and know really small things, like atoms and quarks, and really big things, like galaxies.

Moreover, we live on a planet with just the right conditions, just big enough and warm enough to sustain and evolve life. The astrobiological conditions by which we exist physically and biologically are quite perfect, as if finely tuned using precise, perhaps even zero tolerance, specifications. Known as Goldilocks conditions, human life could have only been possible with a planet sized just as ours is, at the exact distance from the Sun that it is, having been formed by physical laws exactly as they are with zero margin of error. Any nearer to or farther from the Sun, or with a Sun any older or younger, and the Earth's surface would have been extremely hostile to life, and humans would not have arisen and evolved.

It seems that from this Goldilocks bowl of porridge, we have the ability to eat, digest, appreciate and possibly become the scale, complexity and purpose of the whole Cosmos. However, this "just right" phenomenon is not unique to our biology and atmosphere: we experience and observe Goldilocks conditions in many of our terrestrial pursuits, such as:

1. Economics: in macroeconomics, moderate growth and moderate inflation are optimal conditions, and in behavioral economics, a purchase most naturally occurs as the middle choice;

2. Spirituality: the Buddha's Middle Path, the idea of being in the world, but not of it;

3. Communications: the optimum effectiveness of communication tends to be via media of moderate length and depth;

4. Developmental and flow psychology: optimum human experience is correlated with moderate complexity;

5. Medicine: optimum effects are achieved in the balance between inhibitory and excitatory properties of compounds; and

6. Human recreation: optimum sexual experience results from variations around a moderate friction and speed; optimum sensory experience and performance due to ingestion of chemical substances increases up to a point and decreases thereafter (aka the bell curve/beer-pool playing effect).

We are Extraordinary

Yet, despite this talk of moderation, we are also quite extreme. We are unique in a number of ways, such as our energetic throughput and complexity. Humans have the highest energy rate density in the known Cosmos (Chaisson, 2010). That means, we have more energetic throughput (as well as the structural, biological and the social complexity that holds it) per square inch than any other type of mass in the Cosmos, including stars. (Note: that we need to exclude black holes in this assertion, as we don't yet understand them; it's even possible that they may be or may contain entire universes themselves and/or are the Cosmos' sex organs, continually producing new Cosmoses.)

We are comprised of some of the rarest elements in the Cosmos, formed from the explosions of at least two previous stars, and have gone on to create really cool tools and technologies like lasers, lamps, batteries, rockets and electronics for further creation, novelty, connection and exploration, that make use of rare earth elements. It appears that over time the Cosmos, through us, wants to experience, appreciate, connect and metabolize more of itself. Why it has endowed us as its vessel for this function is, of course, is still a mystery.

As we explored, something awesome accelerated our evolution 40,000 years ago. We developed a sustained relationship with symbolic language, and in so doing, we transcended our biology. We created a mechanism for capturing and improving the informational, cultural and spiritual payload of our species. Through symbolic language we cultivate best practices for behavior and cooperation as well as art forms. 5,000 years ago, as symbolic language matured into written text, the human species entered into a new realm of existence, extending the purview of our existence beyond biology and sociology, to include the vector of time itself. As Brian Swimme observes, unique to humans...

> ...is the ability to hold conscious self-awareness in a form that is exterior to the human body, and more particularly in language that can be given cultural forms, such as paintings, books, and libraries. This change can be talked about in various ways, but one way to say it is that the DNA, which has operated brilliantly for three and a half billion years, has through humans spilled out into an exterior trans-genetic form that we call culture...

This calls us into a much more mysterious and mutualistic relationship with meaning and culture. No longer can culture be considered a byproduct of, or curious phenomenon in, a mechanistic universe. It's a tool for the creation of the Cosmos. Brian continues,

> ...if we live to be a hundred years old, it's not fair to say that we have a hundred-year-old mind. Rather, even when we are young children, we are involved with a mind that is a hundred thousand years in the making. Through cultural artifacts, we enter into a continuously accumulating mind called humanity. In a real sense that continuously accumulating mind is currently shaping the planet more powerfully than anything else in nature.
> -Brian Swimme (Martin, p. 35, 2010)

And, with the advances in the use of carbon combustion, nuclear energy and radio communications, we have begun to transcend the other dimensions in the fabric of space-time (i.e., height, width and depth), by being able to move human bodies, artifacts and information faster (more distance, less time). Because we constantly update our best practices, humanity is much more a process of software updates than a distinct piece of replicating evolutionary hardware. The rate at which our software goes through these cycles - our intellectual, economic, psychological and spiritual advancement - far exceeds the rate of advance in our hardware - our biological evolution. Therefore, if the future of human evolution is anything like the past, it will be driven more by internal and collective, systems-oriented evolution than by biological evolution.

Through this progression of syntropic biological, cultural and technological advances, we have evolved to wonder on behalf of the whole Cosmos, to play with what the future holds. In this way, part of us can continually embrace and enjoy a healthy adolescence in its highest form, exploring and playing with curiosity and creativity, ever-searching and ever-hopeful of what will unfold and who we might be.

To accomplish this and begin to create authentic and increasingly novel lives and modes of human cooperation, it is helpful to deeply embrace adolescence, not as an awkward, perfunctory holding pattern between childhood and adulthood, but as an important and evolutionarily significant phase of life and a rich mode of being.

Not surprisingly, we now know that humans have the most variable Hox genes of all mammals. These are the genes responsible for determining the length of adolescence, the time it takes to biologically mature into an adult. Under the right economic and social conditions, our time to biological and psychological maturity can increase from age thirteen in impoverished and war-torn areas to age thirty in safe, abundant and healthy areas (Swimme, 2006), providing almost two decades primarily spent in wonder. It appears that the Cosmos wants to increase our period of adolescence, wherein we (it) can stay in wonder, play with and explore the Cosmos and cultivate our role and purpose within it.

> The universe is not a thing or an event, but is the living process of revelation and questioning itself. Not only is the universe what is revealed by asking the question, but it is also the *process* of inquiry itself... The universe is what is seeking, what is being sought, and the seeking itself.
>
> -Stephan Martin (Martin, p. 274, 2010)

Using our current knowledge and experience, we have the capacity to imagine not only what is next for us in the coming week, but also what lies ahead for us in a decade, for our species in a hundred years, for the Cosmos in a billion years. *Given our incredible ability to evolve, our creativity, our compassion and our desire to actualize, to what end will we apply our imagination?*

Our options are startling. As mentioned, we have begun to understand and explore concepts like singularity – the phenomenon in which biology, machine and consciousness/spirituality become deeply intertwined and mutualistic, collectively forming a more than biological, a more than machine co-evolutionary organism. We have the engineering capacity to create biomechanical appendages and Artificial Intelligence mechanisms like Google's Translate and IBM's Watson.

Most importantly, we are capable of updating our entire psychological operating system, with more evolved and more elegant ways of being. Consider a human driven by a Purpose Operating System (purpose-driven humans like Gandhi, Eileen Fisher, Martin Luther King Jr., Jane Goodall, Seane Corn and Oprah Winfrey) and the Enlightenment Operating System (spiritually awake beings like St. Catherine, Buddha, Eckhart Tolle, Jesus).

So, we might well imagine a future of syntropically advanced beings who might combine these operating systems (and others) to create a universally-identified, purpose-driven, spiritual entity that is partly organic chemistry and biology, partly actualized human psychology, partly electrical machine and partly Wikipedia/ Google/Watson – an entity now capable (mechanically, biologically, intellectually, psychologically, and spiritually) of ceaselessly guiding and evolving the Cosmos into its fullest expression.

And now, we get to generate the selection of possible futures and also choose among them. What we do know is that for the first time in this long march of Cosmic evolution and human history, we can consciously unite with and powerfully express individual, species and planetary purpose. As we exit this exploration of syntropy, a question to ponder:

How will the now evident syntropic evolution of the Cosmos influence the expression of your life on Earth?

As we shall see, deeply related to our syntropic understanding is another important theme of Cosmic evolution, one that deserves special treatment, even though to a large degree it is inseparable from the other themes of syntropy and uncertainty: Unity.

Unity

Unity is a condition of things being joined. It is expressed spiritually as Spiritual Enlightenment, as well as the more tangible cognitive awareness of the interconnectivity and complexity of existence. Before we get into the weeds philosophically and scientifically, let's just note the expanding unity we feel and see around us. In the United States, we've witnessed an expanding sense of cultural unity, despite predictable countercultural and radical populist movements of separation. We've seen our political identity dance with greater forms of cooperation, shifting from that of our specific state to the United States, then back to North vs. South states (1800's/Civil War), then the difficult struggle to find and embrace a national identity (pre-WWI and pre-WWII isolationism, early 1900's), join with other Allied forces in WWII, form the United Nations and NATO, and now our identity is stretching to include all beings with supranational for-profit and non-profit entities.

In the last sixty years our identity has begun to increasingly include our whole planet, with the advent of worldwide movements for suffrage and civil rights, multilateral organizations like NATO and the United Nations, space programs, or the efforts to deal with financial crises (1987, 2008) or climate crises. There have been failures (Kyoto) and successes (Paris Climate Agreement), as well as the rise of a distributed, instantly connected and aware media network that highlights world affairs with unprecedented alacrity and saturation. Even the United States, long a nation regarded for its individualism and exceptionalism, is now tending to move to a planetary identity: 79% of Americans believe Nature is sacred and 71% of Americans agree with the statement, "I see myself as a citizen of Planet Earth, as well as American" (Ray, 2010).

This is more than a curious sociological phenomenon; it is an increasing cultural expression of the reality revealed by our sciences, philosophy and wisdom traditions.

The Cosmos is held together by forces both seen and unseen. Quantum physics, Einsteinian physics, Newtonian physics, biology, ecology and our social sciences have all failed to fully isolate anything that functions alone. Nothing is self-contained, nothing is self-driven or self-aware without interacting with similar organisms or as a vital part of another whole organism or system. The rationale or order of the Cosmos is thus an unending progression of increasing unity, of wholes – all the way up, and also all the way down in scale.

This unifying scale of wholes is what philosophers Arthur Koestler articulated in his book, *The Ghost in the Machine* (1967) and Ken Wilber offered in his book *Sex, Ecology and Spirituality* (1995), as a "holarchy." This means each whole consists of smaller wholes. Each whole is also the building block of a larger whole. As we explored, the human body is an example, with its whole molecules like proteins, forming whole substances like blood, forming whole systems like our circulatory system, forming a whole being - a human. This holarchical structure is also found in human consciousness. We master things sequentially. For example, humanity mastered the whole concept/act of how to pound a nail before we mastered the whole of building a frame. We followed that mastery with the whole of designing a house and then the whole of building a house, then neighborhood, urban plans, regional economic entities, and so forth.

Our consciousness, ideals and purpose also evolve in this way, as we conceive of, identify with and participate in increasingly larger wholes within the Cosmos. Through the sacred function of integrity, as we explored in "The Four Commitments of the Shambhala Leader", the whole of our identity expands, expressing and mastering whole ways of being. For example, we learn to set boundaries and express love to each other in psychological and social relationships, to surrender to mystery in spirituality, or to master domains in intellectual, political and economic realms, and these together continually create a larger whole identity.

Over time, we incorporate a greater understanding of the Cosmos (self, family, society, species, planet, star systems) into our awareness, identity and ethics (Loevinger, 1987). At the quantum level, the Cosmos has the capacity to connect every part of itself instantly. Mathematically speaking, the four observable dimensions of our Universe (height, width, depth, and time) are themselves a whole that can, under the right conditions, connect each and every part of the Cosmic body with itself. As theoretical physicist David Bohm illuminated in his concept of "holomovement", the Cosmos is best described as an undivided whole in universal flux. It is unity in motion.

> The relationships constituting the fundamental law are between the enfolded structures that interweave and inter-penetrate each

other, through the whole of space, rather than between the abstracted and separated forms that are manifest to the senses.

-David Bohm, (Bohm, 1980)

This space-time "whole" is a continuum that contains all that is, was and ever will be. It is only within this fabric of space-time that cause-and-effect, evolution, syntropy, politics, economics and consciousness occur. Although concepts like consciousness, spirituality or culture may seem outside of the realm of physics, nothing is entirely exogenous to the whole of the Cosmos. Thus far, we've been able to establish that everything in the human experience of the Cosmos – even ideas, love, and our experience of God – possesses some sort of energy-mass signature in the fabric of space-time (e.g., neurons firing, neurochemicals reacting, brain-wave frequencies, somatic and neurochemical expressions of thought patterns). This is not to reduce the unique fields of spirituality, consciousness and culture to physics, only to demonstrate that they occur within the whole of reality, not outside of it.

As we saw in our exploration of syntropy above, humanity, as currently conceived, is a software product/update process that continually updates itself. As we understand and know humanity today, we acknowledge that this understanding is dependent on the existence of time and space. Our existence, if it is time dependent, must also rely on and express the whole spectrum of space-time. As we cannot physically separate (or stop, reverse, or accelerate) the present from the future or past, we cannot isolate time from the space dimensions (height, width and depth) of the space-time fabric.

If humanity is dependent on the whole spectrum of time and space, it exists at all points in the space-time evolutionary continuum, from this moment in time back to the Big Bang, from this moment to the end of time and from every physical point inside of us to every point in the Cosmos, as well as between all points in the Cosmos, as well as in the expanding edge of the Cosmos and in the process by which our identity meets this understanding. Humanity, because of its space-time location AND its dependency on the continuum, is thus an expression of, and dependent upon, the whole Cosmos.

Your understanding of your own human experience is greatly dependent on the place and time of the human condition in which you find yourself. Who you are is dependent on how this place and time serves and doesn't serve you economically, psychologically and socially. To truly know and be your purpose, you must also know and be the place and time in which your find yourself in humanity as well as the Cosmos.

Moreover, because all points in space-time are connected, this means that the story of each human is the story of humanity (the software progression) as well as the story of the Cosmos (the hardware progression). We are all that is, was and ever will be. We are the Cosmos in its entirety. Every trip to the market is a Cosmic event, both physically and evolutionarily. As we update our own understanding of best practices, we update and thus express, expand and evolve the whole Cosmos. This is not just philosophy and logic, but an expression of our understanding of quantum mechanics - we are nonlocally interconnected and inseparable.

Now this assertion of unity is not to diminish the richness of our experience, nor the uniqueness of our purpose, nor our significance or worth, nor the validity of our distinct realms of inquiry, e.g., psychology, theology, religion, philosophy, physics or chemistry. None of these realms is reducible to the others. Chemistry cannot wholly account for ideas and theology cannot wholly account for physics and so forth. This is only to say that we cannot really ignore any realm of inquiry. Each distinct realm tells us something important about the unified whole. To truly understand art, we must know a bit about science. To truly understand certainty, we must know a bit about mystery, uncertainty and epistemology. To know matter, we must also know energy. To truly get the concept of reason, we must also know faith. To know masculinity, we must know femininity. To understand stillness, we must understand action. To know equality, we must know privilege and discrimination. To know causality, we must know acausality.

Most troubling and more mysteriously, matter is increasingly difficult to pin down, as the more we observe it, the less of it there seems to be. Solids are merely energy patterns held together by an electric charge. The more we examine atoms, electrons, quarks, and strings, the more the Universe seems to be made of energy rather than mass.

In fact, the Universe is mostly devoid of matter. Our world is much more accurately described as holarchic energetic patterns of increasing scale and unity: quarks, strings, atoms, molecules, organisms, social systems, star systems, galaxies, galaxy clusters. Some are stable. Some are growing. Some are dying. All follow the ever-mysterious and continually revealed rationale or order of the Cosmos, a few strands of which we believe to be syntropy, unity and uncertainty.

Each human possesses and emits a consciousness or energy pattern that contains and explains a portion of the Cosmos. Each human identifies with, expresses, empathizes with, and is connected to the Cosmos, to the extent that they understand it. In practical terms, this means that:

1. Our evolution as a whole human being is limited by the extent to which the unity, scale and complexity of the whole Cosmos manifests in our understanding of self, purpose and ethics.

2. Our purpose can be consciously cultivated and expressed as the chosen governing principle of our whole human energy-mass pattern. Without an organic, soul, revealed and higher purpose, we only have the ability to express nearby, inherited and default purposes, or energetic-mass patterns, for example, those which we derive from media, economics, culture, and our parents.

3. Our purpose is always in space; it is always Cosmic. We cannot escape this. What distinguishes our experience of life is the extent of our purpose awareness and our understanding of, and felt connection to, the Cosmos.

Despite the evidence pointing us to a unified reality, we cannot with total certainty say this is the case. Indeed, the Cosmos also seems intent on our remaining uncertain or open to evolution and deeper understanding. It seems to want us to hold all of this lightly as we engage with it heartily. As we transcend and include greater wholes, we are called to re-mystify ourselves, to embrace the emerging edge of truth, the next whole beyond our awareness, as we expand the frontiers of both our own cognitive knowledge of the Cosmos and our soul's identity.

Uncertainty

> Uncertainty is an uncomfortable position, but certainty is an absurd position.
>
> -Voltaire

Future generations may well regard the 20th and 21st centuries as the period of "The Great Unknowing." The Enlightenment, which began in the 1500's, took square aim at the intellectual underpinnings and raison d'etre of our orthodox political, religious and cultural institutions. The Enlightenment asked, "do these systems create human flourishing and excellence?" The answers revealed massive inadequacies. Especially hard hit were feudal monarchies and institutional religion. Emerging discoveries challenged a human- and Earth-centered Cosmos with an intimation of an infinite realm of space beyond Earth's atmosphere. As most religious cosmologies did not adapt to include the groundbreaking contributions of Newton, Descartes, Freud, Copernicus and Darwin, they lost power and relevance. Although their morals, myths, rituals and cultures still have enormous value, their creation cosmologies no longer accurately explained the origins of what was now recognized as a vast and evolving Cosmos and of our increasingly mysterious psychological experience.

The Enlightenment gifted us new access to the fields of physics, psychology, history, philosophy, and astronomy (through a revival of humanity's intellectual tradition, found across the world's cultures, e.g., Greek, Aztec, Egyptian, Inca, Arab and Hindu). Collectively, these fields have now taken religion's place, as they more capably express the observable nature of reality (although not our spiritual impulses, ethics, experiences, possibilities and achievements). This decoupling of the Church's worldview from our understanding of reality provided an opportunity for unheralded realms of achievement, personal liberty, self-awareness and scientific understanding. In the space created by this decoupling, and by admitting our unknowing, we have been able to economically, technologically and politically advance as a species (not without significant sacrifice and tragedy, of course).

As the core themes of Enlightenment (reason, achievement, self-determination) continue to penetrate human awareness and reach fullness (there are many who remain fixed on ancient cosmologies and ways of organizing socially, politically and economically), we now have brand-new realms of inquiry and fields of study (e.g., theoretical physics, neuroscience) that make cognitive certainty impossible. In 2009, neuroscientist, David Eagleman coined the term "possibilianism," an attitude that recognizes that mankind knows too little about existence (especially with respect to physics, the origin of the universe, neuroscience, perception and DNA) to support a position of atheism, and far too much about existence (comparative religion, socioeconomics, history and mysticism) to believe that any one organized religion can be the sole possessor of truth.

Nor could philosophy, despite its many merits, furnish any certainty to take religion's place. Consider the famous expression of Descartes, "I think therefore I am," or the most certain statement purported by philosophy: "I am." Even these are riddled with mystery. *What exactly am I? Who is the 'I' – a human? A line of code in a computer program? The whole Cosmos? A divine spark? A bioelectrical organism? A sentient being possessed of free will? A node of Cosmic Consciousness?* The reality is, we do not know. Science and philosophy have failed to provide any clarity on this matter. All that can be said with an absolute level of certainty is that because we are here and something appears to be happening, something exists whose exact nature, location, purpose and function remains largely mysterious. Even the aforementioned themes of syntropy and unity are (despite the efforts of humanity's intellectual titans) unprovable hypotheses.

Still, Western intellectual and scientific traditions remain useful, having progressively expanded our understanding and giving us scientific language to quantify and share best practices. And yet, our progress in advancing a complete understanding of reality has actually regressed, in relative terms. Yes, each discovery carves out a piece of the unknown, by making it known. However, ask any scientist about their latest research and you'll learn that each discovery also yields 10-100 more questions. So, while some of the unknown is brought into light, the expanding edge of mystery - the size of the darkness - continues to expand by at least an order of magnitude with each cognitive discovery.

Our total cognitive knowledge expands while our relative cognitive knowledge decreases. This is the core teaching of uncertainty. As we learn more, we come ever closer to the age-old wisdom of Socrates, who said "I know that I know nothing."

There may be said to be four realms of knowledge:

1. Conscious known (what you know you know),
2. Conscious unknown (what you know you don't know),
3. Unconscious unknown (what you don't know you don't know), and

4. Unconscious known (what you know, but don't know that you know or have misplaced)

With regard to these, a few things are happening. The first is that, over time, #1 and #2 are expanding. We are constantly learning new things about the Cosmos (#1) and establishing even more new questions we need to explore - increasing what we know we don't know (#2). In the process, we also discover entirely new realms of inquiry and ways to the explore them. This presents a problem. We are faced with the possibility that what we don't know we don't know (#3) might also be expanding over time or, to put it another way, as we move into the unknown, cognitive certainty seems all the more further away.

Moreover, our ability to penetrate into and perceive truth in the unconscious unknown, to break through the formidable mountain of data and information blasting its way towards us seems to be decreasing. We are rich in data, but starved for wisdom. As a species, we generate billions of bits per second, and with each day exponentially expand our ability to do so, and seemingly our appetite to consume it. Much of which makes it into our individual and collective consciousness, aka the "fake news of the mind" is outdated, unverified and/or unuseful information, e.g., celebrity gossip, top ten lists, reality TV, sensationalized "news" and propaganda. This firehose of trash obscures our access to the other realms of knowledge and our ability to discern truth. This onslaught of rubbish, combined with humanity's largely unexamined psyches, impairs, if not impedes, our ability to have a relationship with truth, to open ourselves to the mysteries of life and beyond.

One thing of which we are certain is that much more research and many more theories are required to frame the new questions now emerging (e.g., *If reality is holarchic, then what role does the Cosmos play in a larger whole? Is the Cosmos a computer simulation manifesting energy patterns for the delight of some other universe or supreme entity? Do we have a responsibility to empower humanity to access verifiable information, and the ability to distinguish rubbish from merit via a cultivated intellect and examined psyche?*)

Lastly, the unconscious known (#4) includes senior moments of course, but more germane to our inquiry is that this is the realm of soul and purpose. It seems to be a core function of the ego, as well as the unintended consequence of mainstream human culture to make us forget our soul's purpose. This requires an initial excavation (purpose discovery/remembering) to bring soul back into the light of awareness and consistent ritual to re-presence what you know about your soul. However, the knowledge excavated and re-presenced from this realm, unlike that of the other realms can never be proven or justified to another, only internally recognized as true and remembered by an individual.

While we can achieve more certainty about particular theories over time with new data, experiments and results, due to the aforementioned variables, cognitive certainty about the nature of the whole Cosmos seems to be increasingly elusive.

Could it be that science is an endless Sisyphean endeavor? This isn't to suggest that our scientific pursuits have no use, but rather to point out that, with regard to reconciling human knowledge with the totality of knowledge available, science has failed and continues to fail in relatively larger terms each day. *So, are there other, non-cognitive, ways of knowing? Should we spend more time exploring the unconscious known?*

Before we explore these questions and what they might mean about the purpose of the Cosmos and our role in it, however, let us continue our slaughter of certainty, and the false god of the Western intellectual tradition, the Scientific Method.

Uncertainty in Neuroscience & Psychology

So far, we've been unable to locate the self, either electrically, chemically or via psychological observation. We've discovered a number of systems, organs, pathways, and neurotransmitters related to our experience of consciousness, but not consciousness itself. We know that certain physical conditions (such as hunger, disease, brain injury, diet) impair consciousness, and that consciousness (especially the experiences of psychological trauma, our psychological states and thought patterns) can change the physiology of our brains and bodies. What we haven't learned is anything conclusive about the primacy of energy, matter or consciousness. Like the chicken and the egg, neither the exact relationship between energy, matter and consciousness, nor the location of the physical source or center of a self has been deciphered.

Through the exploration of the controversial and not widely accepted field of paranormal psychology (PSY), and its alluring reproducible experimental results such as precognition, extrasensory perception (ESP) and near-death experiences (NDEs), we've begun to intimate that consciousness and the mind are not perfect partners. For example, when a human experiences biological brain death, theoretically there should be a perfectly paired and completely irreversible psychological death. However, a person's consciousness (or perhaps, soul) often continues to experience and add data to their life record in a manner congruent with that of others who are still alive and embodied in the same room where their now "biologically dead" brain and body rest. Studies of NDEs demonstrate that when the electrochemical brain reboots, the consciousness reattaches itself to the person who "died," but the memory of the period between brain-death and reanimation (often several minutes) are not lost (Moody, 1975).

Further, when we try to observe human behavior we find not one rational algorithm or set of rules for constructing a person. Instead of an entity, let's say "Jim", we find a neural network throughout the body that is involved in many unconscious micro-decisions of the body. In this instance, body and speech movements occur

169

without once communicating with the physical "brain" in the skull. "Jim" makes automatic decisions in (from? as?) other parts of his body, then uses the brain in his skull to create logic (often poorly constructed) to support the actions he just automatically took, as if it were a linear progression beginning in Jim's brain, following a pattern such as:

1. sensory stimulus from the outside;
2. physical brain observation;
3. mental brain contemplation;
4. mental brain decision; and, finally,
5. physical action.

But, this isn't what actually happens. What actually happens is:

1. physical stimulus; and
2. physical action; then
3. mental justification/rationalization.

Even more troubling are the conclusions from studies at the Institute of Noetic Sciences (Mossbridge, Tressoldi, et al, 2014) on precognition (knowing what happens before it happens), which suggest that what actually happens could really be this:

1. physical stimulus;
2. physical action (contingent upon a future brain decision, per #5 below);
3. physical brain observation;
4. mental brain contemplation;
5. mental brain decision.

Their experiments have revealed that decisions made in the future literally change the actions of the past.

> Well, the evidence strongly suggests that precognition exists. And if precognition exists, then we don't have a very good understanding of time. Time is essential to how we experience the everyday world, and if we don't even understand that, then basically all bets are off.
> -Dean Radin, PhD, Senior Scientist, The Institute of Noetic Sciences (Martin, p. 87, 2010)

Moreover, as we explored in "Chapter 8: Your Path to Purpose", we also find that our understanding of self is dependent on a number of factors. In fact, we might more accurately describe the experience of being "Jim" as being many "sub-Jims" or sub-egos, each with a different value array of impulsive reactions. It is the crazy-making task of "Jim" to make sense of his unruly band of his "sub-Jims." Speaking from personal experience, jumping from "sub-Brandon" to "sub-Brandon" is difficult, unsettling and creates anxiety, because my "sub-Brandons" constantly contradict each other, operate with different logic rules. This unpleasant and unworkable tension between unexamined ego parts is what I believe creates both the spiritual impulse to transcend and escape the insanity, as well as the descendent drive for purpose, to descend and find a ground of being, of non-cognitive, non-egoic soul truth, of a central identity by which to live one's life.

As we explored, the Psychosynthesis work of Roberto Assagioli (Assagioli, 1965), the Voice-Dialogue Method of Hal and Sidra Stone (Stone and Stone, 1993) and the Internal Family Systems model of Richard Schwartz, PhD (Schwartz, 2001) provided powerful new insights for understanding multiple parts/voices within our ego structures. This understanding has been used by many people, most notably by Tim Kelley (Kelley, 2009), with great success over the last two decades to help people investigate their multivariate ego, create the space for exploring soul/purpose and creating a coherent personality structure, an ego-soul marriage.

It can be argued that without an examined, properly ordered and soul-infused psyche, what we have is a loose consortium of selves, a barely sane multiple personality structure that claims otherwise.

Quantum Weirdness

The field of physics reveals less ambiguous, but equally disastrous, flaws in our experience of certainty. With respect to uncertainty, there are four important things to know about the realm of physics:

1. **Nested wholes.** We and all matter (energetic patterns) in the Cosmos are connected as nested wholes (as explored in the previous section on Unity) and thus the scientific method, which requires a physically detached observer, may no longer be able to furnish a detached observer, as demonstrated by the Bell Test Experiments (Aspect, 1982).
2. **Observational hindrances.** Heisenberg's Uncertainty Principle makes it impossible for us to observe any matter (energetic patterns) in the totality of its space-time existence. We can only know its location *or* its vector in any given moment, but never both (Heisenberg, 1927), and the act of human observation changes the result.
3. **Processive Nature.** The Cosmos is better explained as a river, never the same in any instant or place. The Cosmos is whole and also in flux as an evolutionary process, rather than a collection of stable things that we can observe. There are no stars per se but, rather a like a river, there is a

multitude of relatively predictable processes that express a common pattern that we call a "star". Matter is more than anything a convenient shorthand for a process of arising energy patterns.

4. **Relational Nature.** Because the Cosmos has no one center, but is omnicentric, the Cosmos is better explained as a collection of relationships between space-time "points". These "points" are related to each other via evolutionary processes, energetic patterns, and the information that expresses these relationships and phenomena.

Think of it like this: imagine you are a "scientist" who wants to observe a car driving between point A and point B, but what's really happening is that the car is attempting to drive a straight line while being on a tilt-a-whirl, going around in a circle while spinning on an axis. You are also on the tilt-a-whirl, sitting in a different seat and experiencing a slightly different set of forces. Every time you attempt to observe the car, you and the car change course as result of your observation, and the car also changes its nature, flipping back and forth between energy and matter, between wave and particle. And the instrument of measurement itself suffers from the aforementioned flaws in perception. Another way to say it is:

> One of the implications of quantum brain is that you are no longer dealing with individual particles in the head. Rather, you're describing a substance that has both particle-like and wave-like aspects. In its wave-like mode, it reaches out to infinity, and not only that, it goes out to infinity faster than the speed of light. So, what we call gray 'matter' in the brain is made of neurons, but it is also something that extends to the edges of the universe and plays fast and loose with concepts like time and space.
> -Dean Radin, PhD (Martin, pp. 98-99, 2010)

This is what our current understanding of evolution and quantum physics has done to the Scientific Method. The Scientific Method was developed with the Newtonian worldview of matter and force in mind, not a worldview of the Cosmos as a nested whole, a process or set of relationships and an exploding library of information that describes it. The scientific method requires a sane, competent, detached observer, "solid things" to observe and a controlled environment. We don't really have this at the level of neuroscience (a detached observer), psychology (a whole self) or physics (discrete things, a controlled environment).

> And yet the nature of psi phenomenon suggests that separability at deep levels of reality really is an illusion. There is no separability.

And if there is no separability, then how do you study anything? That's the puzzle.

-Dean Radin, PhD (Martin, p. 90, 2010)

In this way, our intellectual and scientific progress has significantly undermined the scientific method. We are not detached observers, and yet the entire Western intellectual tradition assumes as much. The Western intellectual tradition is constructed of layered disciplines, each dependent upon the previous layer. We need to understand physics in order to understand chemistry, chemistry to understand organic chemistry, organic chemistry to understand biology, biology to understand the social sciences and the social sciences to understand how to cooperate collectively (e.g., democracy, justice, law, economics, etc.).

Both physics, the foundation of knowledge, and science, the primary tool of Western Civilization, seem to be less stable the more closely we look. This is not to say that the Scientific Method is futile, just that its relevance and utility is becoming increasingly more narrow. This is also not to say that science is dead, only that to remain relevant in light of these revelations, its nature must shift towards a more humble, process/relationship/information/systems-centric and more epistemologically-curious (how we know things) expression. Brian Swimme believes that 21st-century science,

> ...will not be in the direction of the 17th, 18th, 19th and 20th centuries where science aimed at discovering the 'fundamental' equations that governed particular phenomenal domains. A number of leading scientists believe that search is over and done with. So, what new way of interacting with the universe will surface, especially in terms of scientific investigation of the universe? ...21st-century science will be focused on the study of... particular systems such as Earth's climate, or a spiral galaxy, and will attempt to learn not the fundamental equations, but the basic habits of behavior of such systems.
>
> -Brian Swimme (Martin, p. 30, 2010)

This is a long way of saying that we don't really know what we think we know, what we're doing right now or what we're talking about when we talk about science, especially as a vehicle for exploring the truth or purpose question. With the revelations in the section on Unity (above) and Uncertainty, we now need new chemistry, new organic chemistry, new biology, and new social sciences before we can use scientific language to describe what it means to be a human on Planet Earth today, much less to determine how we should cooperate economically, ecologically or politically.

Philosophy

In philosophy, Wittgenstein's *Philosophical Investigations* (1953) demonstrated the futility of conveying absolute meaning between two humans, so that the totality of one person's understanding can never meet another's. We can come to a consensual agreement representing the overlap of the individual experiences of an object (say a blue chair), but to each of us the meaning and context of the blue chair will be different, as our reference points for "chair" and "blue" mean different things in our unique psychologies (e.g., one person's most relevant memory of a blue chair was being tied to it and tortured, versus another person's most relevant memory of a blue chair was sitting on it during their first kiss). Thus, although we can get close to a shared understanding of an artifact or idea, we cannot reason our way into a completely shared understanding of anything.

Philosophy, physics and psychology may each fail to bring us certainty; however, there are other realms of knowing which may indeed succeed. This is suggested by upper world spiritual masters and lower world shamans from numerous traditions. Meditation, plant medicine, purpose work, and other disciplines have been reported to deliver people an experience of certainty – a bone-rattling spiritual and/or soul identity – that even their mind cannot express or justify. Yet these means of knowing still cannot create a fully shared knowing. I will never be able to impart my spiritual experience or purpose awakening fully onto you and vice versa.

Michael Murphy, in his major work, *The Future of the Body* (1992), he details numerous practices, rituals and witnessed occurrences that (claim to) create access to absolute knowledge, knowledge beyond human cognition and the limitations of human observation. Different from faith, these experiences are actual and unique, and not based on hope or wishful thinking (although heavily influenced by the inescapable context of culture). Instead, these experiences are somatically registered as intuitive or spiritual wisdom, and recognized by others as such, as being true without the need for science or philosophy to prove their truth (like, for example, the Golden Rule), or deeply personal, like how you know you love the people you love.

Thus, over the last 100 years of Cosmic evolution in the realm of human inquiry, the Cosmos seems to have asked us to look beyond science, philosophy and psychology for answers, as these realms can take us only so far. The rest of the path lies within each of us.

We can certainly use the gifts of science (the Scientific Method), theology (the possibility of personal Spiritual Enlightenment), psychology (our multivariate egoic constitution), and philosophy (skepticism, logic) as tools to maneuver our way into the unknown, into our individual experience of consciousness and the Cosmos. However, we can no longer believe in the absolute authority of any of these disciplines. We can develop the skills and knowledge these disciplines offer but, ultimately, we can only trust ourselves, our own experience, our own going within.

It is best to think of our academic disciplines as training programs for an evolving intellect, not as means of access to truth.

As we explored previously, in order to express one's purpose a human, as a Cosmic artifact/consciousness structure, must also endeavor to express the order of the whole Cosmos. We must understand this connection, this unity of wholes, while we are acting here on Earth and simultaneously holding the mysteries of perception, knowledge and existence dear. And yet, we must do this without sacrificing any of our individuality, any of the contours of our unique life purpose.

Collectively, these three themes (Syntropy, Unity and Uncertainty) do more than explain what is happening in the Cosmos; they influence human behavior, your life's purpose and how you choose to express it. Moreover, they give your purpose a greater significance, as your purpose cannot ever be proven, quantified or validated cognitively. It can only be realized as true by you.

Purpose work thus has a deeper significance now than at any time since the advent of the Enlightenment. It comes with new knowledge that you are literally seeking the deepest possible truth, and perhaps the only possible truth. In doing so, you also do the work of Cosmic evolution. By finding and living your life's purpose, you discover that mystery is not outside of you, but that evolution is emerging through you and in every purposeful moment of your life.

Moreover, we now have these Cosmic guideposts for expressing our species' collective purpose. Regardless of whether or not we like it or feel empowered by it, how do we use our awareness of these themes (Syntropy, Unity and Uncertainty) to create a society that is in greater alignment with the Cosmos? How do we realize a more full expression of each Cosmic being here on Earth?

The Purpose of the Cosmos and You

Now that you've had a deep, incomplete and intentionally unsettling dive into the nature of the Cosmos, what are you going do with this knowledge and lack of certainty, here in Earth's atmosphere? Will you fight to hold onto your religious, scientific and terrestrial certainty? Will you believe that someone has more answers than you, idolize them and put them on a pedestal? Will you continue to defend the supremacy of science as a path to truth? Will you deny what you have just read and regress altogether into a religious identity and code of ethics? Will you stick your head in the sand and abdicate your responsibility and purpose? Or will you say yes to it all, say yes to being the emerging edge of the Cosmos, full of possibility, wonder, love, connection, creativity and joy, and nearly void of cognitive certainty? Can you hold faith and reason in equal regard? Can art and science cuddle more closely in your heart? Can multi-perspectival curiosity and metaphorical promiscuity be your baseline approach to truth?

Will you say yes to meeting your need for certainty by courting your own purpose? The Cosmos seems to be begging us to do so. It seems to be asking us to abandon everything that isn't absolutely or personally true, to find and live our purpose within the evolving purpose of the Cosmos: to express greater curiosity (uncertainty), to expand our awareness of reality, to craft the connective tissue of the Cosmos (unity), and to perfect every life function and every creative moment to express a more elegant and evolved expression of this whole, of the Cosmos (syntropy).

Practically speaking, you can embrace the opportunity to be the Cosmos in any given moment. You can live in accordance with your deepest truth, your purpose, while also living in accordance with the purpose of the Cosmos, provided you exercise great curiosity, humility and intention. Living with purpose – with soul and Cosmic awareness – can be effectuated by holding these fundamental questions dear, considering them as you move through life:

1. *What am I not seeing here?* (Uncertainty)
2. *What is the deeper truth that connects this moment, relationship, context or dynamic? How can I express and connect the whole world?* (Unity)
3. *How can I more elegantly and creatively express the Cosmic purpose and greater harmonic wholes as I live my life purpose?* (Syntropy)

These are lifelong inner work questions that allow you to connect with the entire Cosmos: to express it, to ask what it is evolving into as you move through your day and take on new opportunities. This, however, is not all you must do. You are also called to be human, which is to say to enjoy your human experience, to have fun, to give and receive love, to be a part of and generatively contribute to humanity, in relationship to other humans politically, economically and culturally, as well as to be in ecological relationship to Planet Earth. From this perspective, how do we express and evolve the purpose of humanity?

Before we dive into in the next chapter, my recommendation is to pause and attempt to grow something in this field of wonder, to turn over the mystical humus you have just laid down. Consider meditating, taking a long walk in nature, stargazing, or just sitting there, turning these questions over in your mind.

Now we can talk turkey. Now we can explore what purpose looks like at the level of the human species, culture, economy and government. To do this, we first must arrive at our purpose as a species, for we must serve our species' purpose, which must also be a function of the Cosmic purpose. As Brian Swimme suggests, embracing the order and questions of the Cosmos gives us a radical license to reinvent the human experience:

The human is certainly a place in the universe where the entire vast story can burst in awareness of itself. The human is this place where 14 billion years of evolution is reflecting upon itself. One way to think about us is to think that we are the way Universe reflects upon its own majesty and mystery.

It means that it's possible that our primary role as humans is that of celebration. We have this destiny - and even duty - to become astonished by the universe!

-Brian Swimme, PhD (Martin, p. 32, 2010)

However, as Brian continues, this is not how we are currently organized. Our systems are not optimized for human consciousness, purpose or awe.

It sounds almost ridiculous to say this when our industrial society is oriented towards getting a job and producing stuff. But, it's a perspective that we need to take seriously. What if we began to organize our school system and educational process so that humans could move more deeply into an understanding and celebration of existence itself?

... (W)e are here to marvel over existence and to celebrate it and to extend to those less fortunate the great privilege of being alive and healthy.

-Brian Swimme, PhD (Martin, pp. 32-33, 2010)

CHAPTER 16

The Purpose of the Human Species

The task of telling the story of humanity, articulating its purpose and defining its future is a difficult one, yet it is needed now more than ever as we find the gap between the triple purpose of the Cosmos and our default institutional purposes widening. Our default purposes, as you'll explore in the next chapter, are rapidly bringing our economy, culture and ecology – of which our species is the leader – to an end. So, there is a huge opportunity and existential call to listen for and create a species-wide purpose.

The opportunity for a species-wide purpose

With a unified species purpose, countries and regular citizens can achieve the unimaginable in terms of implementing best practices for living here on Earth, and can create new ways of connecting, exploring and creating beyond Earth. Such a vision would allow and enable each human's purpose-awakened potential and, collectively, the enormous, soon to be sustainable, economic surpluses of humanity to be deployed toward grand achievements, e.g., transcontinental rail, space exploration, human consciousness/purpose optimization, global infrastructure for education, healthcare, urban beautification and ecological restoration. Heaven on Earth is indeed possible with such a vision. Where do we begin? We must first ask the question, "What is a good vision?"

What is a good vision?

For any vision to take hold and inspire the creation of a better world, it has to fulfill on two tasks. First, it needs to draw humanity into a greater collective realization of itself than would otherwise be possible without the vision (aka the default setting of adhering to old identities, economic incentives, cultures). This means that the vision has to hold out, express and articulate a felt experience of life that is better, more rewarding, more fulfilling, more self-expressed and more powerful than anything else offered. In light of the allure and promise (but not efficacy) of the "American Dream"/ wealth gospel/ more is better narrative, this is a very tall order. The second task is that the vision has to be communicated in a way that includes, inspires, empowers and unites every human. It must be spoken in a language that everyone can hear and be delivered by individuals and groups they respect.

The last time this truly happened was when the Enlightenment began to emerge, when leading thinkers began to do what we are attempting to do here in Part Three: redefining what it means to be human, articulating how government, economics, education, spirituality, personal freedom, community, health and love could look if we expanded our view of reality and began to do things differently. What was articulated, first by Montaigne and Descartes and then by dozens of Enlightenment thinkers (Voltaire, Rousseau, Paine) and Transcendentalist thinkers (Emerson, Whitman), was that if every human cultivated her or his intellect, unlocked the power of reason, and used it to navigate not only the external world but the internal realms of consciousness and psychology, we all could live happier, healthier, more connected, self-expressed, and powerful lives.

Prior to the Enlightenment, the primary vision articulated in the West was offered by the Catholic Church and its appointed feudal kingdoms, a vision that said, "Surrender and sacrifice before royal and religious authority and one day you will die for the glory of your King and live with God in heaven." When offered the ability to create one's own political destiny (democracy), social status and economic advantage (the free market), and spiritual life (religious freedom/mysticism), a tolerant (relatively) representative democracy and capitalist economy was an easy choice for folks to make. People stepped into this vision for their lives rapidly. This vision took fewer than ten generations (1700-1900 CE) to reach mainstream cultural saturation and political expression in the West, and it is still being adopted throughout Asia, Africa and South America.

Since the Enlightenment, our species has attempted two other species-wide visions or revolutions, but each time we failed. Both the International Labor and Socialist Movements (1800's) and Green/Environmental Movement (1900's) tried to bring about global revolution. Despite their many merits and tactical wins, they were unable to claim total victory because their visions were reductive, neither inspiring nor additive to the Enlightenment vision of liberty and economic abundance. The vision offered by organized labor, unionists and the Socialists reduced the experience of being a human to a struggle for economic power, making the clarion call of the movement a reactionary fight against the owners of land, money and the means of production. Now this wasn't without good reason, as industrialization created on the whole some pretty terrible economic outcomes (sub-survival wages, 100-hour work weeks, poverty), social outcomes (child labor, blacklisting, workplace discrimination) and political outcomes (corruption, federally-sanctioned monopolies).

While the possibilities being offered by organized labor were radically new and the abuses of capitalism increasingly widely documented, the socialist vision of state/communally-owned enterprises failed, as it expressed merely the fight for justice itself and represented a *reduction* in the possible abundance, achievement and unique expression of life promised in the alternatives they presented - the commune or planned economy factory. This vision offered only justice, but no more freedom, and less possibility and self-expression. The creative capital of humanity never really got behind the Marxist project in ways that could accelerate and realize it, as evidenced by the poor execution of this vision – the diminished quality of life experienced by most Soviet bloc countries during the 20th century.

In the way Marxism reduced humanity to economics, the Green Movement reduced humanity to biology. As with socialism, the Greens could only see what wasn't working and demonized Western civilization and capitalism, ignoring the evolutionary merits of humanity's intellectual and cultural achievements: the progress of civil rights, technological innovation, art and the cultural wealth created during the industrialization of the West. Instead, the Greens remained focused on the ecological destruction and diminishments to human health that it produced. As such, there was no new vision offered, no means of accelerating human expression, only a quasi-spiritual Gaia hypothesis and sometimes a nostalgic plea to go back to the land, to do less harm, to lessen the destruction and poisoning of our Earth's fragile ecosystems.

This is not to say the concerns of the socialist and Green movements are not valid. They are. It is also not to say that there were not important victories to be had. There were. Indeed, there were many victories of ecological and social justice (e.g., workplace discrimination laws, collective bargaining/unions, 40-hour work weeks, the Environmental Protection Agency, the Occupational Safety and Health Administration, the Paris Climate Agreement, child labor laws, etc.) and there will be many more. However, both movements failed to offer a unifying and enhanced vision of what an individual human could achieve, nor what the whole of humanity could look like if we operated with more fairness, justice and sustainability.

Of course, there are plenty of rational and spiritual reasons to protect the environment and treat our fellow humans with dignity; however, these reasons alone were not sufficient to unlock the creative drive of each human to see something new for themselves, step into their personal greatness and create a better future for everyone.

So, let us explore a vision that does these things. Let's create a world where everyone reaches their fullest potential, enjoyment and experience of life. Let's develop a vision of humanity on purpose, one where each human is fully realized, living a 100% authentic life, crafting an abundant and sustainable livelihood and transforming our world. To be successful, this vision must be the most comprehensive and elegant vision on Earth – one that will leave every human and living being better off physically, psychologically, socially and spiritually, as well as more creatively self-expressed. This vision must also be easily communicable to every subculture, such that it can inspire people to realize their own greatness within and get to work on living it.

If history is any indicator, this job is too large for one person (consider the dozens of Enlightenment thinkers and hundreds of thousands of revolutionaries the democracy movement required). This vision will take shape with much collaboration and evolution over time. This is a shared quest for a vision, not Brandon's vision, as together we will evolve our purpose-driven visions of humanity to put the most amount of power, freedom and self-expression in the hands of the greatest number of people in as little time as possible, without injuring the Earth ecology that we all depend upon and steward. Nonetheless, I believe we must start somewhere, and share a vision that we can then challenge, beat up, smash to pieces, evolve and improve.

I believe that a vision of purpose - at the level of the individual, company, polity and species - will address all the concerns of capitalists, socialists and environmentalists, and put our whole species on a track to create a more pleasurable, creative, abundant, just, sustainable, and peaceful human presence. Together, we will explore how to arrive upon this vision and use it to inspire ourselves to create the planet we all want.

This brings us to the second task of a successful vision; it has to be delivered in a simple and relatable manner. The vision has to be packaged for the ready consumption and metabolism of people with different value-sets. By which I mean that the vision must not only incorporate and enhance all other ideals in humanity, it must also be capable of being expressed in terms every human can understand and still be distinct enough to leave people feeling inspired, empowered and included. As such, the vision must transcend and include all of humanity's ideals, including its three values/culture groups:

1. Traditional (valuing God, country, nature, family)
2. Modern (valuing reason, material progress, science, individualism)
3. Postmodern (valuing community, justice, environmentalism, equality, collectivism).

I realize that sharing a vision in terms friendly to each of these groups is difficult. Indeed, it is a tall order. But, because it is hard, it does not mean we should not try. There is too much at stake to abstain from the challenge. I share this vision with humility, as I know that even if I were to toil for the next 30 years evolving this vision, it will still be woefully incomplete. This vision will always be incomplete and will thus require your personal embrace, sober assessment, creative destruction, and evolutionary contribution to reach its fullness.

A Vision Battle Royale

To arrive at a vision that elevates us all, and is embraced by us all, a number of compelling starting points and voices must be explored. To get a handle on this vision, we should look at what has been done before, in such approaches as Integral Theory and the philosophical systems that preceded it (Plotinus, Sri Aurobindo, Teilhard de Chardin, Alfred North Whitehead, Ken Wilber, Steve McIntosh, Terry Patten), Systems Theory (Erwin Laszlo, Fritjof Capra, the Santa Fe Institute), history (Herodotus, Francis Fukuyama, Jared Diamond) and Big History (Carl Sagan, Thomas Berry, Cynthia Stokes-Brown, Brian Swimme). All of these fields and thinkers have taken on the task of telling the biggest story they can imagine. It would take years to summarize their work and conclusions, so I will not attempt to do that, but will encourage you to read their books yourself. However, I will share a few big themes/visions that I've encountered in their work and in the work of their colleagues, popularizers and evangelists. My friend and colleague, Sam Clayton, terms these "the four awakenings" – four distinct visions that are already changing our species and planet, pulling us into the future, whether or not we are aware of them:

1. **The technotopian/singularity vision** (Kevin Kelly, Peter Diamandis, the Long Now Foundation), favored by proponents of globalization, neoliberal technocrats, and technology entrepreneurs, in which we merge our biology and psychology with machines, and innovate our way via technology and entrepreneurship out of our current economic, social and ecological problems;

2. **The spiritual/consciousness vision** (Michael Murphy, Eckhart Tolle, Bill Plotkin, the Institute of Noetic Sciences), favored by traditional and "New Age" spiritual communities, wherein we transcend our egoic desires for commercial products and approval through personal and spiritual growth disciplines;

3. **The ecological resilience/sustainability vision** (Charles Eisenstein, Joanna Macy, Paul Hawken, Lynne Twist, the Pachamama Alliance), favored by ecopreneurs, activists, and back-to-the-landers, wherein we restructure our society and economy to protect the environment and expand ecological biodiversity; and

4. **The social justice vision** (Martin Luther King Jr., Gandhi, Riane Eisler, Cornel West, Bernie Sanders, Occupy, Black Lives Matter), favored by social justice activists, wherein we restructure our society and economy to ensure tolerance, diversity, peace, abundance, and social and economic justice for all humans.

Odds are you are already feeling one or two of these present in your own vision for the world. Each of us has such a vision; few of us, however, recognize that these visions need each other and cannot express the whole of the human experience alone. As such, each of these, if adhered to strictly, will continue to make the other visions wrong, leave people out and thus fail to unite and bring humanity into an expanded expression.

Accordingly, we need a unifying narrative, one that weaves all of these together, one that allows humanity to express its totality in ways that every human can understand and eventually embody in their lives, careers, communities, and political actions. As of yet, no unifying vision has thus far caught fire.

A Note on Privilege

I realize that this lineage of visionaries is comprised mostly of men and mostly heterosexual, white, Western men. And yet, as an Ivy-educated, mostly heterosexual, white Western male, I would do a disservice to my purpose, our human community, Earth's ecology and our Cosmic identity if I stayed quiet on this issue. If I didn't transcend my own postmodern values (which are only a part of my values), that would have me step out of the conversation in hopes that someone with a more diverse background would come forth, I would actually dishonor my purpose and my commitment to you and every being on Planet Earth.

If I stayed quiet, I would dishonor the privilege of having received so much from so many (while acknowledging the many injustices that made it all possible). And, I would dishonor my stand for a just, sustainable and peaceful human presence on Earth. With this in mind, I will now share what I think is an empowering, abundant, inspiring and equitable vision for humanity, one that allows each of the "four awakenings" to reach full expression, one that empowers every human, and welcomes their creativity, participation and enjoyment.

The Rise of the *Cosmosapien*

The larger our concern, the more powerful our vision and its expression can be. If we care a lot, we create a lot. If we care little, we create little. For example, if we're renting an apartment, we might spend a few bucks making it look nice, such as painting or hanging some art. That is because our concern is just for our near-term comfort and utility. We know we'll be out soon. Whereas if we owned our home, we'd be thinking about many more things in addition to comfort and utility, like resale value, our long-term family needs for space, what the neighbors think, energy efficiency, upkeep time and cost, our property taxes, who is on the city council, and how much we would use that new deck vs. how much it costs, etc. The result is that we're going to make different decisions that are likely to have a more generative outcome.

As mentioned, now is the time for big ideas, so why not redefine what it means to be human? Why not tell the biggest possible story? Why not be responsible for everything in existence? Why not scrap the rule book and outdated social norms? Why not regenerate ourselves entirely from a current understanding of what is actually happening in the Cosmos?

In our search of what it means to be alive, what would be the largest possible expression of concern we can offer? I believe that if we become concerned with the whole Cosmos, we can identify with it, express it, act on its behalf and create more generative and inspiring outcomes for all beings on Earth than would otherwise be possible. As such, I would like to offer a Cosmosapien vision.

Based on my understanding of the works of the aforementioned visionaries and intellectual heavyweights, and many more, the four already-evident strands of awakening in process - towards greater syntropy (technotopian), unity (social justice and ecological resilience) and uncertainty (consciousness) - and following the Mission Statement framework (from "Chapter 2: What is Purpose?"), I believe a starting point for our purpose as a species is:

1. As an apex ecosystem steward of Planet Earth, an evolutionary community of Shambhala Leaders and the emerging *Cosmosapien* central nervous system of the Cosmos (core),

2. We awaken, heal, bring order to, express, create and celebrate the beauty of existence (powers and craft),

3. In service of an abundant, just, sustainable and peaceful presence on Earth and with a story and message of acceptance, love, achievement, wonder, learning, creativity and joy throughout the Cosmos (call, vision and mission).

But, what is a *Cosmosapien*? In short, I believe humanity has begun its evolution into a new species. A *Cosmosapien* is a Cosmic citizen, one who identifies with all points in space-time, whose understanding of self and purpose spans the vector of time - past, present and future - and dimensions of space - height, width and depth. I believe that we are just beginning to grasp this new identity. I believe that our species is one of the first expressions of the Cosmos within itself that has developed significant mastery over both space and time. However, this speciation did not happen all at once. It has happened slowly and in fits and starts, beginning first with the vector of time.

Specifically, when agriculture set in (in different places around the world 13,000 - 5,000 BCE), the future started to matter in ways it didn't before. Because land and plants and orchards bore fruits for hundreds of years, what happened to that land and those plants and orchards due to the environmental, political, religious and economic climate also started to matter. In this moment, we burst forth into what the father of positive psychology, Martin Seligman, PhD, calls *Homo Prospectus,* a species with a fascination with the future (Seligman, Tierney, 2017). Recent research (Baumeister, Vohs, 2016) has revealed our fascination with the past is actually a desire to create and predict the future, with humans spending 3x more time immersed in future scenarios than past ruminations. Luckily, we already had some symbols available to document our past observations and make our future hypotheses. But, we needed better knowledge tools.

Enter written text. When written text first appeared as a sustained technology 5,000 years ago, our species not only gained an enhanced ability to predict the future and track the past, but some of us actually began to transcend time. Text allowed our intellectual best practices and cultural contributions to live outside of our biological organisms. At this moment, 5,000 years ago, we started to give more weight to text from the past over the hearsay of those in the present. We became *Chronosapiens*, a species of sentient beings that to be fully understood and considered in its wholeness as a species must be understood to be evolutionary, and thus must also include the history of evolution and the whole vector of time.

Moreover, due to this fascination and ability to capture intelligence and hypothesize, what it means to be "us" now dramatically changes with each year, decade and generation. Prior to text, what it meant to be a human was roughly the same 20,000 years ago as it was 100,000 years ago, where humans were concerned with finding food, water, sex and shelter and avoiding danger. Now we are different than prehistoric humans and also all other Earth species. For the most part, the experience of being a blue jay was the same in 2,000 BCE as it was in the year 2000 CE. There were no meaningful upgrades such as civil rights, democracy, and digital entertainment for the blue jay.

As our facility with text expanded and accelerated over the last 5,000 years, we deepened our identity as a new species, one that was no longer just *Homo sapiens sapiens* (aware that we are aware), but one that also now achieved greater expression and mastery over time. Because human expression is so dependent on the time in which it arises, we must include the whole existence of time into our understanding of what it means to be human.

This was an evolutionary leap, and thus for the first time we established an identity with the entire chronological history of not only our species, as we are products of species evolution, but the history of all species. And not only of our species and all species, but also that of matter, as life evolves from matter. And not only of matter, as matter evolved from non-matter/space.

Given that our current understanding of evolution and time does not stop in the present but extends out the future, to understand humanity we must also understand the past and future of the whole Cosmos. Every field of study that we know of was cultivated by humans, so to know humanity is to also know all the things that concern humanity, all of our disciplines and theories, whose sum total attempts to study, connect, express and, in many cases, evolve all points in the Cosmos. This sum total also pontificates on the unobservable realms and dimensions beyond it.

Our *Chronosapien* identity and expression continues to expand daily, such as through our theoretical framework for human time travel, and our awareness of particles colliding at the quantum level with former versions of themselves.

This isn't just a Western or written text phenomenon. Throughout the world, cultures have evolved to include a concern for the future (e.g., the Greek proverb "society grows great when old men plant trees whose shade they know they shall never sit in"). Although dramatically expanded with text, this capacity to embody *Chronosapien* awareness even has its seeds in cultures without a written language, as the Iroquois First People's Great Law suggests. The Iroquois society was governed by laws handed down verbally, one of which is the Great Law that includes a decision-making framework to include the next seven generations, or about 140 years. This expansion of *Chronosapien* identity and governance seems to want to evolve in cultures around the world, regardless of their information technologies.

We reached a more somber technological milestone in our *Chronosapien* expression on August 6, 1945, when the United States deployed nuclear bombs in Hiroshima, and later in Nagasaki, in an ironic attempt to end the violence of World War II. On this day, and in the six years that led up to it (the Manhattan Project), humanity began making existential decisions not only for the current cohort of humans (those alive on August 6, 1945), but on behalf of all humans and beings for the next few hundred thousand years. Aside from the massive civilian casualties of the decision to use these bombs (129,000 deaths in Hiroshima and Nagasaki), and now along with the 31 nuclear test sites the world over and the nuclear meltdowns at plants such as Chernobyl, Three-Mile Island and Fukushima Daiichi, our nuclear weaponry and power technologies have affected an irreversible shift in the human and ecological condition for hundreds of thousands of years in these areas.

Not only do we have nuclear capabilities to assert influence and destroy our current cohort of humans, abilities that prior to 1945 were heretofore unimaginable, we have the ability to render useless vast swaths of our planet for future generations and other species. With great power comes great responsibility, and the jury is still very much out as to whether we have sufficiently evolved *Chronosapien* consciousness to meet our *Chronosapien* tools (text, nuclear technology, the internet).

As result of her remarkable environmental and humanitarian work around the world, her poetry and her anti-nuclear activism, I consider Joanna Macy to be one the flag bearers of *Chronosapien* consciousness. Joanna not only considers the future generations in her actions and cultural creations, but calls to the unborn for spiritual guidance. In her poems, Joanna prays to the future unborn to guide us in this critical juncture in their, as yet unrealized, lives. Here, she captures the emotional sentiment of what it means to be enchanted by, and tasked as, a *Chronosapien*: "You live inside us, beings of the future... Your beat in our hearts... Let us feel your breath in our lungs, your cry in our throat... We are your ancestors. Fill us with gladness for the work that must be done." (Macy, 2007, pp. 201-202)

Just as we began speciation 5,000 years ago into *Chronosapiens*, I believe we have begun speciating again, this time into *Cosmosapiens*. Although the theoretical underpinnings of this identity began much earlier, with the Big Bang and unified Cosmos theory traced back to the Middle Ages in Grossetestes' *De Luce* (1225), and the scientific language that describes it began in the 1920s (Hubble, Einstein, Lamaitre, Friedmann), evidence for *Cosmosapien* speciation became clear in 1958, when the United States government launched NASA. Shortly thereafter, in 1960, Dr. Frank Drake, PhD, then an astronomer at Cornell University along with Carl Sagan, PhD, began SETI (Search For ExtraTerrestrial Life - listening to and receiving information from the stars with a radio telescope).

As far as we know, we are the first sentient Earth species to leave the atmosphere and see our home, planet Earth, from a distance, and bring these images and our reflections back to the land. In 1968, American astronaut William Anders, aboard the Apollo 8 mission, observed and described his feelings of awe, unity and gratitude, watching the Earth rise over the horizon of the moon. Anders would be the first of many astronauts, such as Edgar Mitchell, to experience this "overview effect". This phenomenon occurs as a human sees the whole of the Earth and passes through a door of mystery, connection, wonder and awe. In this moment, the astronaut's consciousness instantaneously expands, her/his single human identity recedes, and awareness merges with the grandeur of the whole species and our Earth's interdependent ecology. This phenomenon resonates with a theoretical understanding of quantum physics, one that connects and expresses all points in space-time.

> "You develop an instant global consciousness, a people orientation, an intense dissatisfaction with the state of the world, and a compulsion to do something about it. From out there on the moon, international politics look so petty. You want to grab a politician by the scruff of the neck and drag him a quarter of a million miles out and say, 'Look at that, you son of a bitch."
>
> -Edgar Mitchell, NASA Astronaut

As evidenced by our Cosmic prose, poetry, spiritual practices, science and tools, I believe we are becoming a species of, by and for the whole Cosmos. That is, to know what it means to be us, we must understand what is means to be connected to and in service of the whole Cosmos.

Between 1958 and 1977, the United States and the Soviet Union implemented policies and programs which we could call *Cosmosapien* in order to accelerate humanity's technological ability to travel beyond the Earth, to connect with, embody and transcend points in space-time with increasing effectiveness. Although there were clearly Cold War political motivations at play that accelerated the technical expressions of our speciation in this way, our ventures across space and time can no longer be said to be merely defense-related.

The year 1977 marked another big point in the cultural and technological maturation of our *Cosmosapien* identity, as it was the year NASA launched the *Voyager II*, and took humanity's cultural payload out to the stars, with *The Golden Records*, a payload of information for intelligent life forms about Earth (the languages, history and culture of humanity). That year we also received the now famous and still unexplained "Wow! Signal" from the Sagittarius constellation at the Ohio State University's SETI Facility. And, let us not forget 1977's blockbuster movie, *Star Wars*.

Culturally, we have begun popularizing the scientific body of evidence for Cosmic citizenship, our *Cosmosapien* identity, and creating the cultural bridge to this identity via Carl Sagan's *Cosmos* book and video series (1980) and, in the 21st century, *The New Story* (Brian Swimme, 2006), and Neil deGrasse Tyson's remake of the *Cosmos* video series (2015).

Moreover, the mainstream media has taken a leadership role in our *Cosmosapien* cultural evolution by nurturing our imaginations and accelerating this speciation with thousands of comics, books, television series, and movies, most notably: *Buck Rogers* (1933), *Star Trek* (1966), *2001: A Space Odyssey* (1968), *Star Wars* (1977), *Battlestar Galactica* (1978), *ET* (1982), *Contact* (1997), *Men in Black* (1997), *The Fountain* (2006), *Avatar* (2009), *Cloud Atlas* (2012), *Gravity* (2013), *Interstellar* (2014), *The Martian* (2015) and *Arrival* (2016).

As this new awareness moves beyond scientific facts (as we explored in the previous chapter, supporting our unified Cosmic identity) and media, we are starting to see its expressions in many parts of culture and economy, e.g., Burning Man, Space X, Virgin Galactic, Mars One.

We are becoming, as cosmologist Brian Swimme has illuminated, the awakened Cosmos, simultaneously aware that we are aware (*sapiens sapiens*), and increasingly aware that what is aware is not just a human, but the Cosmos itself. We are now engaged in a giant intellectual and physical waking up process, a feline morning stretch across all dimensions of space-time (time-height-width-depth), getting oriented to our body (the Cosmos) and just now beginning to think about what to do with our careers and the Earth's political economy from this new awareness. As we create new technologies to observe ourselves (Arecibo Observatory in Costa Rica, and the FAST: a Five-hundred-meter Aperture Spherical Telescope in China), to network knowledge (the internet, advances in software and artificial intelligence) and to transport human bodies (space travel), I believe we find ourselves at the emerging edge of Cosmic evolution.

We are the waking Cosmos, networking itself, developing its central nervous system, one breath, one moment at a time. As our eyes adjust to the morning light, and with a hint of Christmas morning excitement, we awaken from our pre-purpose, terrestrial dream that we are merely humans defined by our careers, opinions, nations, races, genders, sexual orientations, and creeds with limited personal desires and terrestrial concerns.

As a *Cosmosapien* species, we now stretch, awaken with our wisdom traditions, with purpose discovery work, dancing with art and science, faith and technology, mystery and reason, creating the synapses and muscle memory required to ambulate as this new identity, *Cosmosapien*.

So what?

I believe this Cosmosapien identity and perspective is one of the many missing unifying visions in all our quests to make the world a better place. As the emerging central nervous system of the Cosmos; and as the multi-perspectival beating heart of existence - we are now unified and empowered to achieve collectively what would otherwise be impossible. We now have a new planetary and species mythology, a code of conduct and declaration informed by science, a new reason to find and live our purpose individually, to be a stand for others to find their purpose and make their greatest contribution, to restore integrity, through the vehicle of purpose, to every unit of human cooperation and create a planet that works for every living being.

Imagine a whole planet of humans on purpose, in purposeful romantic relationships, parenting with purpose (nurturing, challenging and evolving the purpose of their children), deepening our connection to our species, planetary and Cosmic purpose! This is a new perspective from which to evolve economic and political activity, to cooperate as companies and nations on purpose, making our highest contribution towards breakthroughs in human achievement, sustainable economic development, ecological resilience, and Cosmic exploration.

Translating our *Cosmosapien* identity into a Common vision

However, we now face the second task of a good vision. We have to bring it out of the ethers, bring this identity back into our atmosphere, into our trips to the supermarket, our ways of being with the people we love, our careers and our cultural filters. We have to meet humanity where it is. We have to put this new identity in terms anyone can understand. What matters most to any given person is not outer space or philosophy or quantum physics or non-dual consciousness or syntropy or uncertainty or rockets or sci-fi fantasy novels. What matters to people is improving their lives and those they care most about, their families and friends.

It is a tall order to root our *Cosmosapien* identity inside of this concern. To do this, we have to both describe our vision in terms friendly to others, and show them an idea of what the vision looks like when it is successful. Part Four is an exploration of what a *Cosmosapien* planet could look like at the level of culture, economy and government. Before we get there, however, we have to come up with a language that can be heard.

Because the bulk of humanity (~95%, per integral philosopher Ken Wilber) has a values center of gravity that reflects their individual desires and tribal collective (e.g., race, family, gender, sports team, nation, age, sexuality, etc.) and is not primarily identified with our species, the unborn, the planet or the Cosmos, we need to make a practical move and eschew all Cosmic language, making purpose the leading edge of our vision. As much as it pains me to say "forget everything you just read," all this space talk and highfalutin' philosophy will be of no use to you in inspiring people to find their purpose, to make their greatest contribution to our species, or to join you in manifesting your purpose. As mentioned, purpose is a trojan horse, because it includes the invitation to expand one's worldview. It is only a matter of time before a purpose-awakened person becomes curious about the world and Cosmos.

Dare I say, it can be argued that even "purpose" is irrelevant to most people. However, what is supremely relevant and communicable are the documented benefits of purpose, such as great health, fulfilling relationships, a meaningful career, and a life of abundance, aka "the good life". Because the bulk of humanity has arisen in a modernist, science-driven culture, and yet also has a tribal identity (e.g., Christians, Burners, skaters, capitalists, hipsters, Raider Nation, Rotarians), we have to lead with our new scientifically-informed best practice, purpose. This is why this book is rooted in science. This is why it is called *Planet on Purpose,* and not the *Aquarian Rising,* or a *Five Point Plan for Interstellar Public Policy,* or *Let's Go to Space with Excruciatingly Painful Personal Development Work.* So, to make purpose palatable, we've got to use obvious, uncontroversial language that will move people to pick up a book like this or do purpose discovery work.

Let's dive into how a life on purpose could appeal to the diverse values of people in the United States:

Purpose for People with Traditional Values, aka Traditionals (~25% of the U.S. Population)

Traditionals are people who generally identify as religious, who stand for God, country, family values, community, nature, divine order and consistency. For them, the door to discovering their purpose is spiritual. For Traditionals, their life's purpose is a personal expression of their divinity, an internalized rapture, allowing the wisdom of Ecclesiastes "Walk in the ways of thine heart." (11:9), the Parable of the Talents (Matthew 25:23-30) and the words of Jesus Christ from the *Gospel of Thomas*: "If you bring forth what is in you, what you have will save you; If you do not bring forth what is in you, what you do not have will destroy you," (Miller, 199, p. 316) to take on new practical application. Purpose allows each of us to surrender to Spirit, while embodying our powers as expressions of Spirit in the world, and to make our highest contribution to our families, communities and employers in service of God.

Purpose for People with Modern Values, aka Moderns, Yuppies (~50% of the U.S. population)

Moderns – the primary audience for whom this book is written – are people who primarily value science, reason, best practices, pragmatic material progress, technological innovation, individual self-expression, creativity, entrepreneurial achievement and global impact (in addition to many traditional concerns). For Moderns, purpose is a scientifically-informed best practice for life, as you explored in Part One.

Further, purpose is one of the most effective, personal and practical internal applications of modern science. The Enlightenment and the Scientific Revolution gave us many powerful tools to use, e.g., engines, phones, textiles, soap, etc. Now they are starting to provide us with powerful software upgrades. Inside purpose awakening, the Enlightenment can actually reach its fullness, delivering each human incredible autonomy and freedom, empowering each of us to create our own meaning and destiny and to achieve full emancipation from foreign sources of meaning and control. Purpose puts every human in the driver's seat of their own lives, empowering each of us to become an authentically self-expressed master of our internal experience and economic and political future.

Purpose for People with Postmodern Values, aka Greens, Socialists, Postmoderns (~20% of the U.S. Population)

Postmoderns are people who primarily value sustainability, peace, social justice and equality (in addition to many traditional and modern concerns). For Postmoderns, purpose is the final civil right – the full expression of the human experience. In terms friendly to the postmodern person, without purpose humans are exploited by others who oppress them or sell them meaning that keeps them controlled, inert and small. This civil right can be won and cultivated not through Postmodernism's traditional tactics (i.e., the fight against capitalism, the cultural mainstream and all forms of authority), but rather through creativity and service – by sharing the possibility of a life of purpose, and purpose discovery education (e.g., the Global Purpose Expedition), as a means to awaken and empower all humans. Purpose teaches a man to fish and builds capacity, passion and resilience for all movements. Purpose thus levels the playing field, placing each human on equal footing, ready to contribute their unique brilliance to the commonwealth.

Further, individual purpose is the psychological precondition that is missing to actually create peace in the world, a core value of postmoderns. By first helping each human craft a personal life narrative and create peace within themselves (ego-soul marriage), purpose empowers people to fully love themselves and embody wholeness, a necessary precondition to acceptance of, and love for, humanity and modernity as they are. Purpose is the necessary precondition for not only personal empowerment and economic independence, but political effectiveness. Purpose allows us to embrace and express the unity so beautifully articulated by science (quantum entanglement,

Big History) and religions (e.g., the Holy Spirit, Brahman) while holding a larger vision for, and working toward, a world that works for all beings.

Lastly, purpose liberates the postmodern from the tyranny of choice, from all the activist standing outside of Whole Foods begging them to take action. Purpose is internal and organic and gives the postmodern person the clarity and certainty they need to focus and achieve the greatest impact, to say no to the other important concerns that are not expressions of their unique life's purpose.

Now the question remains, who are your people and with what language will you share the power of purpose?

Before we step into our *Cosmosapien* identity and create our purposeful world we need to first get a lay of the land, a map of the territory upon which we'll lead and create our planet on purpose.

CHAPTER 17

Humanity's Midlife Crisis

HAZARD: Now that you have a had an experience of possibility, of exploring the purpose of the Cosmos, the purpose of humanity and your place as their evolutionary edge, you must now come back to Earth. You have to know the terrain of the human and ecological condition as it is before you can reconcile your now Cosmos-sized purpose with your terrestrial actions. This chapter is also the "Buzzkill Betty" of this book, so steel yourself. You are about to encounter/reconnect with some truly unsettling things about what it means to be alive today on planet Earth.

"Mom, capitalism is murder."

"What do you mean by that?" my mother inquired.

"The game is rigged. Our whole society and economy doesn't work for anyone. The poor are getting poorer, and the rich are only getting richer, not happier. According to the Easterlin Paradox (Easterlin, 1974), after ~$30k/year, wealth doesn't actually improve the quality of life. Maybe business school was a mistake. Maybe I should have gone into politics."

Fresh out of business school, and equally deep into Marxist philosophy and my existential crisis, I was in dangerous territory, about to launch a *Fight Club*-style rant on my Mom. I felt she needed to know what I knew, my new understanding of humanity through the lenses of ecological economics, politics and the Cosmos from thinkers like Paul Hawken and Hunter Lovins' *Natural Capitalism* (1999), John Perkins' *Confessions of an Economic Hitman* (2004), Brian Swimme's *The New Story* (2006) and Howard Zinn's *The People's History of the United States* (1980).

These commentators share a story that most of what is considered profit is actually the spoils of fraud, theft and in many cases, murder (even if not all of them use this language). What my Mom and I had bought into, what our respective generations (Boomers and Gen X) had bought into, was the American Dream, and Wall Street's belief that it is possible to have exponential growth in a closed system. This not only doesn't work, but is physically impossible. I had come to understand that my career in finance, media and technology and her career in finance, existed and profited only due to the American exceptionalist myth, one that blinded us from

193

the true nature of how the world worked. As I felt my stomach and balls tighten and my breath quicken, my shadow warrior and tyrant king awakened - the vindictive parts of me that want to shame and punish others. I was ready to unleash a shower of fact-driven shame on her, the likes of which she'd never seen.

"Without the accurate pricing of key resources like oil, coal, sugar and cotton, inclusive of all costs to society, environment and the people we bomb to shit to get them, these key economic inputs are deeply discounted, sometimes to the tune of 90% off fair market value. And, this does not include the priceless lives we oppress, marginalize and kill to get them. This means everything that goes into our economy is 30-1000% more expensive than the price we as consumers and businesses actually pay. Thus, there is no actual profit being created by the system. And, if there is no profit, we don't have a capitalist system at all, we have organized crime, a legal wealth transfer from labor, future humans and the Earth's ecology to the living wealthy. This transfer enforces some very familiar power dynamics, power transfers from women to men, from rural to urban, from brown to white people, from Gen X, Y, Millennials and future generations to the Baby Boomers."

"Well I don't see it that way."

"Of course not. You can't. Your livelihood and sense of worth as a human depends on you actively ignoring these facts. You are not alone - everyone is responsible. Knowing and accepting these truths, and continuing to support this dynamic would at best make you a willing accomplice in fraud and theft, and at worst, murder. If you truly sat with these facts, you'd do something about it, and not just sit there like the rest of your self-contented generation, playing golf and sipping margaritas while the world fucking burns. This shit happened on your watch."

"You think I'm a murderer?"

I was disillusioned and disgusted with the American Dream and lies my Mom and I had been fed for decades by Reaganites, our business schools and the financial news media. Blinded by my own shame and pain, I continued hit her with facts, to knock her off her block with an argument that I was sure would destroy her identity and sense of worth. I wanted this woman who had given me life and selflessly all of her love, who kissed my boo-boos, built me up whenever I was down, who had worked tirelessly to help me pay for college and graduate school and all the big books I read, to feel my pain. I wanted her to know how little I respected her career, and by extension, my career and myself. I wanted her to know which side of history the two of us stood on. I wanted her to get up close and personal with how free market sausage gets made.

Of course, as a tactic for persuasion, a conversation with the intent to shame is futile. Shame is simply not a condition for workability, persuasion and progress. Her identity was at stake, she had not apprised herself of Howard Zinn, Rachel Carson, Upton Sinclair or the numerous 19th century economists (Marx, Ricardo, Veblen) that disproved free market capitalism's hypotheses from the start, that articulated what capitalism would actually to do people when it reached full steam in the 20th century. She wasn't aware that capitalism doesn't just mean electricity and household luxuries, but it also means that 51% of American children are now below the poverty line and qualify for state-assisted food programs (Southern Education Foundation, 2015). She didn't know that the global capitalist system she fed and convinced others to feed meant that the rich get richer, while worldwide, half of the world's 2.2 billion children live in poverty, with 300 million children going to bed hungry each night and 5 dying of malnutrition each day (UNICEF, 2017).

She hadn't looked at these questions, nor had she done any self-awareness work to root her identity in her life's purpose, or anything other than her opinions, circumstances and the right-wing echo chamber of her colleagues and the *Wall St. Journal* IV drip of American exceptionalism.

"Not that you would identify as an accomplice to murder, or take pride in it, but yes, you are, as am I, as is everyone participating in our current model of capitalism in every moment of every day. It's science and fact, not my opinion or political philosophy." As I amplified my point, I told her that over the last 40 years, there had been a radical wealth transfer from the middle and lower class to the wealthy equity holders, aka her clients. Due to real year-over-year inflation of 9%, real unemployment of 23% (stadowstats.com, 7/24/2017), due to offshoring manufacturing jobs, decimating social services and education and enacting deep tax cuts for the rich. I told her she was a pawn in game played by the wealthy to hurt the poor.

I charged at her with statistics, such as that with every 1% increase in unemployment, 1,500 more Americans, and 30,000 more humans globally, die each year (Roelfs, Schor, et al, 2011); that the resources and services provided to businesses by the environment is estimated between $125-145 trillion dollars per year (Costanza, et al, 2014); and that global GDP is $78 trillion (CIA World Factbook, 2014), resulting in a negative world profit of at least $50 trillion. And, that's before any other unpaid economic externalities in the production process are accounted for, e.g., labor.

"Of course," I said, "there is no one alive to lend us this $50+ trillion to make up the difference, so we just take it from the environment and the poor and leave the remainder of this bill to future generations."

As I was hooked, outraged, I continued bully her with my rant.

"And to keep this ruse going, we send our nation's youth to the Middle East, South America, Asia and Africa, for cheap oil and rare earths, to make the world safe for corporations, to kill on our behalf and return, at best, only psychologically damaged, and at worst, in pine boxes. Your entire career and mine, and as well the meaning of who you and I believe ourselves to be, and as inspired as you are by the difference you made in people's lives during your career,…" I paused for effect, "actually made the world worse! Every check you brought home to feed and house us was dirty, filthy with deception, fraud and murder. Every tax bill you paid was a contract to kill. I don't blame you uniquely, because you could not have known this, but this is what is so. I now choose to know this. I now choose to change this. I take responsibility for it. Now what are *you* going to do about it?"

She was stunned, as the implication of this arrangement put her much closer to the trigger than she wanted to be. It put her whole life firmly outside of her values. It put her next to the bodies floating in the bayou after Hurricane Katrina, it put her face to face with the hundreds of thousands of women and children we napalmed in Vietnam, with the 100 million first nations of people we wiped clean from the Earth to "settle" the "New" World. It put her eye to eye with the drone exploded faces of children in Syria, Palestine, Afghanistan, Iraq, Libya and Yemen, and the apartheid we still fund in Israel.

Of course, there were no quick answers to my question, nothing that would create less harm and suffering, so we did as we were raised to do in the Midwest. We took another drink and changed the subject.

What I was failing to do in this period of my life was to recognize that chaos begets creativity, that our current model of "late stage" capitalism is actually an initiation, a developmental stage necessary for the next boom in human creativity. Capitalism optimized our manufacturing capabilities, rapidly advanced our information and communication technologies, developed our organization strategies, created massive surpluses for art and culture (some of it quite good and enduring, e.g., Picasso, The Beatles' *The White Album*, *A Hundred Years of Solitude*, *The Sopranos*) and is now largely responsible for revolutionizing human consciousness, making inner work such as purpose discovery and leadership development a strategic economic imperative. There would be no purpose movement without the fruits of purposeless capitalism. And this is the moment in which we now find ourselves, moving from one stage of life to another, from the consumptive caterpillar to the generative butterfly. As John Mackey and Raj Sisoda, authors of *Conscious Capitalism,* expound:

> ...a caterpillar does little more than eat; that is seemingly its only purpose. Some caterpillars eat so much that they grow to one hundred times their original size. However, eventually the amazing process of metamorphosis begins. When the time is right, certain cells become activated in the caterpillar and it enters the cocoon phase, from which it emerges a few weeks later unrecognizably transformed into a creature of enchanting beauty, one that also serves an invaluable function in nature through its role in the pollination of plants and thus the production of food for others to live by. (Mackey, Sisoda, p. 25, 2012)

And, as we are starting to see, over the last 30 years individuals and companies like Whole Foods and Tesla are rising on this transformation. John and Raj continue:

> ...We are also capable of evolving to a degree that is no less dramatic than what happens to a caterpillar, transforming ourselves into beings who create value for others and help make the world more beautiful. The same is true for corporations... they can reinvent themselves as agents of creation and collaboration, magnificent entities capable of cross-pollinating human potentials in ways that nothing else can, creating multiple kinds of value for everyone they touch. (Mackey, Sisoda, pp. 25-26, 2012)

Capitalism 1.0 performed a sacred function, preparing humanity economically, ecologically, spiritually and culturally for a rapid phase of evolution. Much like a person going through a midlife crisis or a caterpillar undergoing metamorphosis, we are dissolving our current of way of being in order to make room for something new, something altogether more purposeful, elegant and abundant. But, before we get there, we need to really immerse ourselves in the decay, to see fully and finally that no aspect of the human experience as it is today can survive without a radical transformation. We cannot become a butterfly without realizing that there is no turning back to simpler caterpillar times and accepting that every caterpillar cell must now give way to death.

The Decay

In Western culture, our decay is marked by sluggish consumption. We are encouraged not to become self-aware and purposeful, but to consume. Our governments, societies and economies are geared to privileging approval, status and indulgence in ever more exotic experiences and sensory delights, and to encouraging us to stay ignorant and avoid responsibility for our actions.

Most of us were raised in a culture that did not have an abundance of soul-initiated elders or trained Guides to guide us, nor an educational system or marketplace that provided soul-initiation for its young adults. So, most people are raised and parented by well-meaning biological adults who are actually psychological and emotional adolescents, with little to no sense of their soul's purpose. As such they could only parent from what they know, having also been raised by socially-conditioned purpose-ignorant humans and a society that emphasized esteem, materialism, conformity and acceptance and the indulgence in pleasure and escape, e.g., alcohol, shopping or media.

As mainstream Paulist Christianity pushed shamanism, paganism and Gnosticism out of mainstream Western civilization (more on this in "Appendix B:

The History of Purpose"), the soul conversation has been largely silent in our culture and parenting. The soul of a child is typically not actively acknowledged, cultivated or encouraged by parents, other family members or teachers. What has filled this void is inherited socioeconomic conditioning, using purpose substitutes such as chemicals, religion and advertising/consumer goods to pacify or distract children (and adults) from their real human need for purpose. This creates a generational epidemic, a parenting approach/ cycle that keeps people on a hamster-wheel of seeking pleasure, avoiding pain, and searching for the social approval of others. This dynamic also makes for a world of eager and pliable consumers. This hamster-wheel of consumption has become all we know, our primary identity and the basis for our moral, career and lifestyle choices.

To jump off the purpose-substitute hamster-wheel, certain conditions must be present. Purpose awakening requires more than proximity to soul-initiated adults, elders or access to a trained Guide or purpose discovery programs; it requires the time for purpose exploration and cultivation.

Ideally, purpose awakening requires an initial investment of time, usually a few months, as well as space - both in nature and as time on the calendar in which to do the exercises (~3 hours a week), reflect and receive insight. This becomes exceedingly difficult in light of the economic pressures of modern life (50-hour work weeks, 15 hours of commuting) and the cultural norms that encourage us to stay busy and glued to screens, email inboxes and social media feeds. The inevitable result of being always on, of being biologically mature humans who are disconnected from our life's purpose, is that it is usually only a life-changing event, a purpose or midlife crisis, that slams shut the door to the status quo, conformity and pleasure seeking, and demands that we ask and answer the 'big' questions. Here is where the quest for purpose begins.

Behind the Crisis

In the face of the horrors of modern society I have described above, one might be tempted to take a misanthropic point of view, to drift into despair, hopelessness or resignation, or to stay inert and on the sidelines of the greatest show on Earth - the simultaneous death/re-birth of the human species. However, horror is not all that has happened during capitalism's reign. We have also birthed Civil Rights, the internet, Wikipedia, Burning Man, smartphones, and amazing art. We turned TV into not just a wasteland for fake news and reality programming, but also a place for high art, like the critically-acclaimed filmed series on HBO, Showtime and Netflix. Despite all the violence and abuse of power in our history, we have also had numerous purpose-driven leaders, and numerous micro-expansions in what is possible (although not ideal) in equality, self-expression, freedom and achievement.

Although purpose hasn't been an explicitly acknowledged cultural value in the

West, it has always been there in some form, such as through a handful of inspiring books (*The Razor's Edge, Jonathan Livingston Seagull*). Indeed, as we explored in "Chapter 1: Purpose, the New Normal?", the call to find and live one's purpose is as old as humanity itself. In fact, most wisdom traditions advise us to live truthfully, do the work to find our purpose, live it in the world, and find a career that expresses it.

Historically, we've always had this inherent urge. It's a quest some intentionally embark upon, and one others seem to follow through an innate knowing. So, why is now any different? Why do we now require a purpose movement? Why can't we just chill out and let our purpose come to us and our community in its own sweet time?

The reason that it is different this time is that our disconnection from purpose at the personal, cultural and systemic levels of politics and economics has compounded upon itself, creating exponentially larger and now existentially threatening costs of ignoring our purpose.

> "We have created new idols. The worship of the ancient golden calf... has returned in a new and ruthless guise in the idolatry of money and the dictatorship of an impersonal economy lacking a truly human purpose."
>
> -Pope Francis

Although, culturally, purpose is emerging as a new normal, the purposelessness of our collective systems has reached the level of an epidemic. We are in a collective purpose crisis, one that creates and glorifies economic and political leaders who do *not* know their life's purpose. Remember the *Harvard Business Review* (Snook, 2014) study we talked about in "Chapter 1: Purpose, the New Normal?", the one that revealed that 80% of our economic leaders (CEOs) do not know their life's purpose? These are the people we have placed on our magazine covers. If you were a cynic, you might argue that they *do* know their purpose: it is to make money and screw anyone who gets in their way. That's certainly their implicit and often declared purpose, but that is not their higher or unitive purpose.

Although a large majority of corporate employees believe the top responsibility of a company exists within a larger context - to provide goods and services that positively impact society (Deloitte, 2014) - in practice nothing could be further from the truth. In its fullness, higher and unitive purpose enhances humanity and Planet Earth; it doesn't recklessly destroy it. 80% of the world's CEOs in the Harvard study and 87% of the world's workforce (Gallup, 2014) are not living their higher or unitive purpose, but rather are living the default purpose of our economic and cultural consumption machine.

This occurs not as a function of corporations being run by evil people, but as a function of good, but largely purpose-ignorant people with an outdated worldview, doing their best in a system they do not really understand, one whose core function, despite all appearances, is actually to oppress humanity and destroy the environment. This is not a moral judgment, and is not an indictment of corporate America or business people. It is just a way of describing the lack of integrity with our system of laws and economic incentives. Is just what is so in the world. People are innately good, potent with tremendous latent purpose potential, joy and goodwill. However, the system within which our good people are educated and employed keeps this potential unexpressed. With the potential in the system unrealized, the system is doing more than oppressing us, but is actually killing us.

The last thirty years of compounding institutional purposelessness has also begun to break one of our species' greatest contributions - democracy. According to Martin Gilens, PhD and Benjamin Page, PhD at Princeton University (Gilens, Page, 2014), the United States, arguably the loudest voice in the conversation about democracy, is no longer itself a democracy and has become a *de facto* oligarchy. With the rise of the ultra-wealthy and now the unapologetically kleptocratic Trump administration, it is clear that the American model of democracy has some fundamental flaws, that it is no longer living according to its founding documents or serving its constituents. It is no longer serving as a model for political participation and economic empowerment. As it is - purpose-agnostic and worldview-crippled- it is thus no longer capable of leading the so-called free world.

Well-meaning but purpose-ignorant wealthy individuals and corporate interests have perverted the United States political system to such a large extent that the will and best interests of the people are ignored. "The central point that emerges from our research is that economic elites and organized groups representing business interests have substantial independent impacts on U.S. government policy," write Gilens and Page, "while mass-based interest groups and average citizens have little or no independent influence."

Princeton's report further states that the proven way to get what you want is to have the money to buy democracy. Over a 5-year period, "Between 2007 and 2012, 200 of America's most politically active corporations spent a combined $5.8 billion on federal lobbying and campaign contributions… what those same corporations got: $4.4 trillion in federal business and support." (Alison, Harkins, 2014). This represents a 759% return on investment over 5 years.

And this isn't just a case of unscrupulous business people making outsized profits. It's life and death for many. For example, in 2016, Big Pharma made $108 billion in profits (Speight, 2016) and they spent approximately $240 million on lobbying congress (Opensecrets.org, 10/13/2017). What did they get for that tiny investment, a mere .2% of their profits? It can be argued that they also purchased a license to kill. According to Donald Light of Harvard University (Light, 2014), 328,000 American and EU citizens die unnecessarily from pharmaceutical drugs each year. Every year.

What this means is that we cannot solely rely on the government to pass laws to make it illegal for corporations to kill us, or pollute a watershed, or charge corporations for the carbon they used in the process. Many politicians are loathe to do these things, as corporate money is too often a politician's ticket to power and job security.

In some sense, this is the way it has always been. We can well imagine politicians in ancient Greece or Rome being privy to an extra jar of olives or a few nubile nymphs.

So, *what's the big deal?* The big deal is that, in years gone by this behavior was not existentially threatening; it was just irresponsible, localized corruption, it was just morally corrupt and would eventually run its course, as each self-serving politician - a Caesar or a Hitler - and every empire, e.g., those of Egypt, Greece, Rome, Persia, Spain, France, Great Britain, collapsed under their own weight. As ye sow, so shall ye reap. But, now we know we are an interdependent planetary ecology and global economy, with no new lands to despoil or other nearby planets to colonize. We now have transnational super-sovereign corporations that are not beholden to voters, but to shareholders, and work to actively subvert democracy via controlling influence in electoral and legislative politics. As their influence is not just problematic in the United States but all over the world, the next collapse won't be solely regional, or simply morally lamentable.

Under this purposeless political-economic scheme, not only is the bulk of humanity comprised of unrealized purpose potential, but it is dangerously close to ecological, economic and cultural collapse. A recent study recently revealed that 32 complex human civilizations have collapsed in the last 5,000 years (Motesharrei, et al, 2014). As detailed by Jared Diamond's book *Collapse*, human civilizations routinely extinguish themselves when they ignore their purpose and reason for existence by mismanaging economic growth and despoiling the environment (Diamond, 2006). As Thomas Piketty demonstrated in his book *Capital in the 21ˢᵗ Century* (Piketty, 2014), unchecked free market capitalism creates incredible inequality as a feature of the system, not as a bug or mistake of its design.

The kind of capitalism we have today is an incentive structure for individuals to give up their rights and the promise of their unique purpose, and to sell all they have (time, resources, clean air/water/soil) in exchange for subsistence level wages and the amusements of the market (purpose substitutes). In this dynamic, corporations take raw materials from nature (through extraction - harvest, mining, etc.), and from the poor (through labor), and turn it into something that's quickly consumed, 99% of which finds its way to a landfill in six months (Leonard, 2007). Often these toxic remnants are shipped back to another poor country as trash to be sorted, recycled, reused and resold to consumers in the West. There are whole towns that now live, work and exist entirely within these toxic waste dumps in Latin America (e.g., La Chureca in Nicaragua) and India (e.g., Karuvadikuppam). Inside these toxic waste dump towns, babies are born, children grow up working as scavengers, mining scraps from trash. They find love, marry, have children, get a preventable disease in their youth and die in their middle age.

The costs of this purposelessness are not measured only in human terms. Species extinction rates are 1,000 times pre-industrial levels (World Wildlife Foundation, 2016). Habitats are being polluted and vanishing entirely. Water tables are being irreparably drained. Ecological catastrophes like Deep Water Horizon, Fukushima, Chernobyl and Union Carbide's Bhopal explosion are destroying our natural world. Ninety percent of the big fish in the sea are gone (National Geographic, 2003). 58% of our wildlife has disappeared in the last 40 years (World Wildlife Foundation, 2016). There will be no reversal in this trend unless there is a radical shift in our connection to our purpose as a species, in how we define success, live our lives, and use and share resources.

This is the disparity that unrestrained capitalism fundamentally creates by focusing solely on financial returns instead of functioning from its purpose and the purpose of humanity. Instead of considering actual value generated for each stakeholder, it optimizes only return on financial investment to one group of stakeholders - debt and equity holders - thus creating downward pressure on wages at home and abroad and an increased demand for cheap resources. Although the specifics of this arrangement are becoming increasingly horrible and public, this dynamic and the underlying fundamentals of this system have been known for 300 years, from the time that industrial capitalism was just taking off.

Devastating critiques of unrestrained capitalism have been around since the beginning, with Ricardo/Lassalle's *Iron Law of Wages* (Marx, 1875) in the 1800's (wages always seek subsistence levels), Marx's *Das Capital* (Marx, 1867) in the mid-1800's ("commodity fetishism" and "accumulation of capital"), and Veblen's *Theory of the Leisure Class* (Veblen, 1899) in the late 1800's ("conspicuous consumption"). Each of these thinkers concluded that, as it reaches its fullness free market capitalism worsens the human condition for the many while accumulating financial wealth and luxury experiences in the hands of the few. They saw that without proper checks, capitalism centralizes wealth and oppresses the many as its core function.

However, this isn't just the conclusion of dead economists. It is also the conclusion arrived upon by many of our current leading economists, like Joseph Stiglitz's *Globalization and Its Discontents* (Stiglitz, 2002) and Robert Reich's *Saving Capitalism: For the Many, Not the Few*, (Reich, 2015). In his groundbreaking 2011 book *Crash Course*, Chris Martenson demonstrates how an exponential economic growth model (which is what we have with our current model of capitalism) must keep generating exponentially larger financial returns every year, and use exponentially greater amounts of raw materials (oil, coal, cotton, soy, beef, corn, sugar, wood, etc.) just to keep the system alive and in stasis (Martenson, 2011). As anyone knows, an exponential growth model in a fixed closed system destroys the system, just like cancer's exponential growth model destroys its host. Unchecked, purposeless capitalism is unique, as it diminishes not only most of the present inhabitants of Earth, but decreases the likelihood of a future for all humans.

This is why the purpose conversation is more than merely making decisions about how to spend our leisure time. Purpose is no longer a nice-to-have luxury item for people inclined to gaze at their navel. The purpose movement is now an existential necessity.

That's why this isn't just the latest self-help movement. It can't be. It must be more.

We need a rapid awakening of every member of our species to discover our individual life's purpose AND, within the context of this global awareness and the emerging purpose of humanity, a purposeful reformation of our institutions and sovereign nations. In so doing, we answer the twin calls of purpose: (1) to discover and live what brings us most alive, and (2) from a sober understanding of reality, to listen to the call of what humanity, our ecology, the unborn, and the Cosmos are asking us to do to survive, thrive and evolve.

We have the power to fix this problem. This "perfect storm" of broken democracy, economy, ecology, and culture presents the solution. As we've reached peak oil, water, copper and phosphorous in a number of locations, there is increasingly very little left on this planet to extract, produce, grow, or exploit to turn into purpose-substitutes. To grow – as we must, as must all forms in the Cosmos – we must now grow into the richness of what is, by fractally descending into the richness of our souls, creating ever more syntropic and elegant expressions. We must descend into meaning, discovering our purpose, and then ascend together towards a shared vision, cooperating economically, socially, ecologically and politically with deep personal and collective purpose awareness.

How do we do this? We awaken our higher purpose, embody it and lead with it in our careers, relationships, families, communities and lifestyle choices. As we'll explore later in "Chapter 21: The Declaration of Soul", we can redirect our day-to-day finances away from purposeless companies towards purposeful companies. We can reuse and repurpose durable goods. We can buy only what is necessary and then only what serves the greater purposes of humanity, e.g., local, organic, grass-fed, pasture-raised, sustainably-produced food, and durable goods from purposeful companies. We can stand firm on every single front: in our personal homes by making purposeful economic choices, in our communities by protecting our local ecosystems, by making exploitive wage policies illegal, by making local economics and fair trade the law of the land, and demanding that corporations articulate a life-giving purpose and a net-benefit business model.

Although these are specific ways to express a deeply informed, contextually rich purpose in the world, this movement follows no actual prescriptive path and must be a natural unfolding of the uniqueness of every human soul. As we've explored, and as Jesus of Nazareth alluded to in the Gospel of Thomas, the stakes in this purpose game are absolute. If we bring forth and live our purpose, it will save us. If we do not, the purposelessness of our institutions will destroy every last one of us.

In the following chapters, we will explore purposeful governance, economy and culture, and illuminate the possibilities for creating a more just, sustainable, peaceful, and evolutionarily exciting human presence on Planet Earth and throughout the Cosmos.

PART FOUR

Answering the Call

CHAPTER 18

The Possibility of Collective Purpose

> Finding your purpose isn't enough. The challenge of our generation is to create a world where everyone has a sense of purpose... For our society to keep moving forward, we have an additional challenge ahead, to not only create additional jobs, but to create a renewed sense of purpose.
>
> -Mark Zuckerberg (Zuckerberg, 2017)

"Much like each human has a soul and ego structure, so does humanity," said Tim Kelley, founder of the True Purpose® Institute and author of the foreword of this book. He was outlining the landscape of humanity's purpose in a lecture given during my training with the Purpose Guides Institute.

Tim continued, "Each of our sectors of society and each of our institutions is a part of humanity's ego, each with its own purpose and each with its purposeful role in supporting humanity's purpose."

I hung on every word, as if Tim was revealing the deeper structure of my own worldview in very succinct language. I knew that every person, institution and country was vital to the whole, but I didn't have the macro/micro psychological language for it. Intuitively, I knew that humanity had its own soul, one that burst forth into my own awareness in the powerful oratory of Martin Luther King Jr., through meditation, Jim Morrison's lyrics and Melville's prose. As I weighed this knowledge against the tragic state of humanity, it became clear that the only reason for a soulful species to act otherwise is if it is disconnected from its soul.

Humanity wasn't leading with soul; it wasn't as loud, fun, loving and creative as I know it can be. As the majority of human experience is governed by shared beliefs, beliefs in all sort of ideas that bind us and govern our behavior, our beliefs in God, capitalism, the Dollar, the Euro, the afterlife, gender, race and sexual identities, and a wide variety of scientific, market and religious cosmologies, I began to see that humanity's current set of beliefs was in need of a soul upgrade, a cosmology more friendly to the development of the individual and collective soul.

Tim continued, "Not only are humanity's institutions not serving the purpose of humanity, but they no longer serve their own purposes. Without a purpose awakening at the level of our ten most influential institutions - humanity's ego parts: government, economy, healthcare, education, religion, media, culture, agriculture, transportation and energy-, as well as that of each individual sovereign (Israel, Colombia, the United States, China, Russia, et cetera.), we're toast.

"Without deconstructing humanity's ego and awakening its soul, and a new, deeper, more generative and purposeful order to human cooperation, without institutional and country purpose awareness, our institutions will continue to work at cross-purposes to their own purposes, as well as to the survival, purpose and continued evolution of the human species. The path forward begins with the purpose awakening of a critical mass of world leaders to steward the purposeful integration of humanity's institutions/ego parts."

I was filled with excitement. Finally, we were getting to the core issue of all things, of all of human suffering, the point of existence, being alive and the roadmap for the future of the species.

Tim had illuminated new possibilities for my craft and had enrolled me in his vision for the future of humanity. I saw the Cosmic evolutionary role that purpose now must play, not only to ignite the lives of our brothers and sisters, but also to radically reshape the way we function politically, economically, culturally and environmentally, in order to create the structures that support each human being to realize, express and contribute the fullness of their soul's purpose.

This is how Tim spends his time. He trains and develops world leaders to awaken their own purpose and works directly with sovereign nations, such as Israel and Colombia, to craft their national purpose. As a result of the numerous, recent, critical failures of state, a handful of countries are finally starting to ask the most important question: why are we here? Yet, we are very much at the beginning of this movement. At present, based on the studies cited in "Chapter 1: Purpose, the New Normal?", I surmise that we live in a world marked by:

1. Emerging individual higher purpose awareness (~ one billion people), but
2. Minimal world leader higher purpose awareness (<10 people)
3. Minimal sector purpose awareness, at least the ten big ones (economy, government, education, media, health care, agriculture, religion, transportation, culture, energy). Such awareness exists only in a few holistic health care modalities, a handful of spiritual traditions that explicitly cultivate soul purpose, and several thousand purpose-driven, positive net impact businesses.
4. Minimal country purpose awareness (emerging - Israel and Colombia), and

5. Minimal species and planetary purpose awareness. There are perhaps a few thousand people connected to the basic evolutionary themes of Cosmic purpose - syntropy, unity and uncertainty.

The collective result of this is the "purpose gap." We are a species torn between the new normal - the best practice of purpose discovery - and humanity's midlife crisis, the purposeless means with which we politically, economically and ecologically cooperate. This chasm between what is possible for our species and the experience of most people has never been greater. By what means will we bridge this gap?

Now that we have some understanding of the purpose of the Cosmos and of our species, we can get out our building blocks and start to have some fun! Throughout Part Four we will explore a culture and a political economy that could support every human being in finding and living their purpose (and having a livelihood that allows them to make their highest contribution), and restores integrity to our relationship with our planet. To do this, we will re-examine a long-forgotten form of political economy, the city-state, to allow a tangible realization of purpose at the foundational local/community level including:

1. Your purposeful livelihood (**career**),
2. Your purposeful civic participation, (**government and location**)
3. Your purposeful relationships, family and culture, and (**community**)
4. Your purposeful enjoyment of and interdependence with all living things (**environment**).

Together, we will explore how purpose, once awakened at the individual and collective levels, ensouls our daily life. We'll take a trip to Chattanooga, Tennessee, a mid-sized American city that is ten years into its purposeful re-visioning. If we are to be successful in embodying purpose collectively, we will need new methods for cooperating (economically, politically, ecologically and culturally) that will allow each of us to be well-compensated for making our greatest purposeful contributions.

Although the arc of moral progress bends towards love and unity, I join many in thinking that humanity is not yet ready for a world government. Purposeful planetary governance will require significant preconditions, beginning with a nucleus of purpose-awakened world leaders, and networks of purposeful city-states and companies. Especially if purpose-ignorant planetary governance looks like anything we've seen in the EU, NAFTA, TPP or the United Nations (or that has been illuminated in science fiction), I am fearful of any central controlling entity for Earth's citizens in the near-term, without first seeing the purpose awakening at the level of individual leaders and local political economies. Since the purposeful company and leader questions have been explored exhaustively over the last 15 years, with landmark books such as Frederic Laloux's *Reinventing Organizations* (2014), and

Robert Adams and William Anderson's *Mastering Leadership* (2016), we will focus on the broader, structural political economy and culture questions.

As I touched on above, I believe the starting place for this discussion is the purposeful city-state. A city-state is a semi-autonomous or autonomous political and economic territory, usually no larger than a few hundred square miles, although some did spread into full-blown empires around their central city-state core, e.g., Athens, Rome, London, New York. The advantage of a city-state is that, because it is a localized bureaucracy, there is a greater sense of cultural identity, ease of cooperation around shared concerns, shorter feedback loops for political, economic, cultural and ecological decisions and a scale that is better able to holistically and soulfully govern human behavior (inclusive of all social, economic, cultural and ecological impacts).

This is not to say that romantic purpose, family purpose, community purpose, corporate purpose, national purpose, species purpose, and Cosmic purpose are unimportant. Quite the contrary! Those purposes are in many ways much more important than that of the city-state. However, at the level of the purpose-awakened city-state, we can begin to see a tangible expression of a full life on purpose, the ensouled integration of love, livelihood, leisure, family and community.

To do this we need an intellectual foundation for the purpose of the Cosmos and humanity (Part Three). To conceive of what the purposeful city-state and the lived-experience of a person on purpose would look like, we must reconcile the expression of a purposeful city-state with the purposes of the Cosmos and humanity. Otherwise, one might imagine a plethora of perfectly-functioning, ideologically-cohesive city-states such as Atlantic City, NJ; Dallas, TX; Fargo, ND and Phoenix, AZ, that may claim to know their purpose and govern themselves accordingly, but are not connected to the broader purposes of our species, planet and Cosmos. Without such a connection, there is a strong likelihood that city-states, despite being proud, hardworking and ideologically-cohesive political, cultural and economic units, could be a nightmare from the perspective of the purpose of optimizing human potential, or living in harmony with the Earth's ecology, or expressing the upper limits of Cosmic evolution. This is why we first had to wrestle with the purposes of the Cosmos, Earth and humanity before having this discussion on our purpose as a political economy and culture.

Purposeful Conflict

I believe we will have little difficulty agreeing on a general vision for our communities, companies, nations and species. We all have roughly the same values and want the same things - some version of a fun, just, creative, prosperous, peaceful, and sustainable human presence on Earth. We all want to make our highest contribution, have freedom and autonomy, be with the people we love, enjoy life and make an impact. Although each human has a unique soul and purposeful expression, it is not what we all *want* that is the issue. The issue is by what means we will achieve it. And this is good.

We need healthy, engaged, purpose-aware conflict to achieve the best result for all concerned parties. Every great achievement is a Goldilocks solution, forged in the tension of opposites, such as social democracy (responsibility vs. freedom, collective vs. individual purpose), the smartphone (size vs. power, ease vs. choice), romantic partnership (personal vs. collective purpose) and Olympic athletics (strength vs. agility).

When the fighting is fair, when parties are grounded in purpose and a shared commitment to the betterment of mankind, when we respect and honor each other's virtues and powers, the outcomes are far greater than those created or initially envisioned by any faction. These more-beneficial outcomes call us into expanded expressions of self, environment and society, such as the environmental conservation movement (protecting game for conservative hunters, protecting biodiversity for liberal nature lovers, and fostering shared concern for the future of our species), or purpose-driven enterprises like Patagonia and Tesla (creating unparalleled customer value, shared purpose, human dignity, economic prosperity AND a more sustainable economy).

> "In order for things to truly change, the tension of the opposites must intensify and be tolerated long enough for a third energy to appear. The bird of good omen must emerge in the midst of all the tension and opposition just long enough to reveal the hidden patterns and motivations of the clashing forces. Then, in the moment of revelation everything must be risked at once and everyone must somehow pull together or else the dilemma will return and likely do so at a deeper level."
> -Michael Meade (Meade, pp. 56, 2016)

So, let us have faith that we will always be creating new visions for our institutions and city-states. We will evolve them through the dynamic tension of healthy conflict. However, having a provisional vision (or, at a minimum, being committed to creating one) is extremely helpful in moving things along, in negotiating how we will make progress and engage in healthy conflict. A healthy provisional vision for our political economy and culture, one that expresses the multitudinous desires and interests of the planet, although subject to continued evolution, puts a stake in the ground for what we want our species and planet to become. It empowers us to take ourselves and our personal fears and desires out of the equation for a moment and to create a world that works for everyone. It will also, undoubtedly, require unforeseen sacrifices.

Imagine what would be possible if our cultural mainstream valued the importance of being connected to one's life purpose? How awesome would it be if our scientists, business owners and politicians knew their life's purpose and acted only in accordance with it?! Imagine turning the world's greatest minds onto their life's purpose! What might become possible if the economic, technological and research institutions they worked for were likewise turned on to their organizational purpose?

Inside these exciting questions lies the path to the survival and flourishing of the human species. However, in practice, this will be messy. We will have to contend with existing power structures, wealth centers and political identities. Luckily, purpose provides another vital utility - liberating us from old identities.

Purpose is Transpartisan

As your vision begins to take hold and move into the world, it will meet all sorts of resistance from those whose identity is still sourced in race, gender, age, sexuality, geography, politics, economics and religion. Without purpose, these good people will continue the same ways of being and acting, and they will produce the same results - dividing our species against itself, perpetuating and escalating our known problems. In all likelihood, they will create mind-blowing new problems as well. So, I urge you to consider that purpose discovery education, when widely distributed, will source every human's identity internally, in their soul, and markedly decrease their resistance to progress, to best practices and to your vision specifically. This fundamental upgrade will create a new listening for your ideas and empower your vision to gain traction.

When purposeful living is the standard, we will each no longer be a Democrat or a Republican or an Independent, or even disaffected by politics. From this place of purpose awareness, we can finally transcend identity politics (e.g., "I'm a liberal, so I vote for all expansions of the federal government" or "I'm a conservative, so I vote against all expansions of the federal government"), and instead focus on the issues at hand and use the best tools available to make the largest impact using the fewest resources. We will all be Shambhala Leaders, stewards of the whole of reality – the Earth's ecological and global polity.

Thus, bringing forth a purpose-awakened culture and political economy is fundamentally a transpartisan issue, one that can be embraced by conservatives (as it engenders individual freedom, personal responsibility, authentic economic prosperity, and reduces demand on the state for resources and services), as well as by liberals (as it empowers a broader collective identity and a transcendent personal vision in service of a more sustainable, just and peaceful planet). Purpose is, then, a unifying anthem, one that makes everyone more themselves (individually), as well as more connected to the whole (collectively).

Purpose provides the connective tissue between the individualistic, economic values of the right and the egalitarian, communal and ecological values of the left. Purpose allows each human to achieve power and liberation – embodying an authentic life purpose, crafting their purpose-driven livelihood in service of the greater good, and embracing a vision of prosperity that is a victory over the smaller narratives of either political faction.

Let's start this exploration by imagining what a purpose-driven global economy could look like.

CHAPTER 19

An Economy on Purpose

"Mr. Peele, your son's umbilical cord is wrapped around his neck and every time your wife contracts his heart rate slows," Dr. Curtis said to my Dad.

On Labor Day of 1976, my mother struggled to give birth. However, with every push, my umbilical cord tightened its grip around my neck and my vital signs declined. There was no easy way out. I couldn't stay and I couldn't leave. The only way through was total surrender and asking for help. Luckily, we were not alone. With his deft and veteran hands, Dr. Curtis was able to slip the umbilical cord off of my neck and allow my mom to make her final push and ensure my safe passage out into the new world.

This is now our task as a species. We have to sacrifice the comfort of our good enough, but increasingly toxic and dysfunctional, society for a great one, and we can only do this with each other's help. No human is an island, and we now enter what Charles Eisenstein terms the era of "we need each other". We must leave the known for the unknown, choose purpose, connect, lead and surrender. We must surrender the emptiness, inequality, ecocide and toxicity of our current political economy and culture.

We must also surrender *to*. We must surrender to our brothers and sisters. We must surrender to the wildness in our hearts, to our soul's purposes, to being buoyed by the faith in our own souls and in the generative, soulful expressions of our fellow brothers and sisters. We must surrender to the nobility of the human spirit, and have faith that we will be successful in crafting our world of purposeful cooperation.

So, what could this economy on purpose look like?

To bring about a purposeful economy, beyond finding our individual purposes and creating purpose-driven careers, we must also act upon the structural level of our entire economy to encourage a new expression of humanity. There are many levers we can pull to make a purpose-driven economy not only possible, but also way more fun and rewarding than our current system. We have at our fingertips all of the technological, economic, information and consciousness tools we need

214

to individually and collectively craft a purposeful economy to maximize human potential and ecological biodiversity.

To create a purposeful economy, we must accept that **the current economic system is broken.** We cannot stay in the womb. Our amniotic sack is tight, cramped, unworkable and toxic. If we do more of the same, we will get more of the same, which (as we explored in "Chapter 17: Humanity's Midlife Crisis") is killing us. More purposeless technology and economic "growth" is a death march for most, if not all, beings and achievements we hold dear.

Just as with a birth or a butterfly's metamorphosis, our political economy must radically and rapidly evolve such that it unrecognizable to its former self. As such, our vision must inspire us and help us create a better future, but it need not justify itself against this status quo. The infant doesn't carefully consider the pros and cons of a tight and toxic home vs. the unknown, it only knows it must leave. Thus, our visions need only prove their merits against other new visions, according to their ability to generate purposeful, just, abundant and sustainable outcomes. The power structures, intellectual capital, wealth dynamics and pre-purpose concerns of the status quo/ orthodox establishment are rich with valuable elements that we must repurpose; however, the adverse effects of their purposes - the consequences of their actions - are now in clear view, and thus, their claims, power and worldview are no longer valid.

This is not to say, that we act with cruelty towards politicians, businesspeople or the wealthy in our implementation of our vision(s); we must implement any vision with creativity, compassion, understanding and generosity. We are only talking about the vision itself, the goal, the next chapter of humanity. It will look radically different than our current chapter, so we will have to compassionately ease the transition, while not sacrificing our vision.

How do we create an economic system to ensoul, empower and ennoble people, to utilize the power of purpose-driven enterprise to steward the Earth's ecology and to evolve and express our unified and syntropic Cosmos? To build such an economy, it must include:

1. **Cosmically-Derived Economic Ethics**

   As we are always in, of, by and for the Cosmos, we need to express the nature of the Cosmos in our economy, specifically by optimizing it for connection, justice and ecological biodiversity (**unity**), human autonomy, empowerment, excellence and creativity (**syntropy**) and wonder and understanding (**uncertainty**). The individual realization of purpose awareness must also be recognized as an expression of all three themes and cultivated as a civil right, one made possible through our spiritual and cultural traditions, and our education systems and company cultures, such that all humans reach their highest potential and make their greatest contribution. However, ethics alone are not enough. We need new structures that incentivize us to express them.

2. **A Policy Framework for Organizing Economic Activity and Investing Economic Surpluses**

The current free market paradigm defines profit as whatever financial capital an enterprise or individual can accumulate legally. As we explored, this paradigm rewards financial sorcery, job cuts, pension fund raids, lobbying, ecocide and labor exploitation. A purpose-driven economy expresses our Cosmically-derived ethics so that our purpose-driven enterprises (PDEs) can honestly achieve profitability. PDEs must be run by Shambhala Leaders who generate financial profit by optimizing the human, ecological and Cosmic condition, through creating just and sustainable enterprises that express ever-greater creativity (syntropy), connection (unity) and wonder (uncertainty) over time.

The profits of PDEs should be used, at the discretion of the owners, to fulfill on the PDE's vision, within the shared economic, social and environmental constraints of our planet. To serve our human, ecological and Cosmic purposes, economic enterprises must act in a manner that:

- honors our interdependence with Earth's ecology,
- meets every employee's Maslovian needs and expresses our civil rights, and
- generates ever-greater feats of beauty, elegance and human achievement.

As all PDEs improve the human and ecological condition, it would be counterproductive to tax their sales or profit. The only taxes that make sense in a purpose-awakened world are taxes on resource usage, such that entities are rewarded for doing more with less. These tax revenues would be spent by the appropriate governing entity to create a just, sustainable and biodiverse planet, funding initiatives to ensure that every living being has free access to clean water, air and soil, public education (which would include the cultivation of mindfulness, creativity, purpose discovery, systems awareness and emotional intelligence - more details below), and the opportunity to live and profit by serving others with their purpose. These taxes would also reform and enhance global education, through awakening each educator to their purpose, and to the proven best practices developed by our greatest educational innovators (such as Waldorf, Tracker,

Reggio Emilia and Montessori schools), and through state-funded liberal arts university education and purpose development programs.

Economic Policy Framework

To achieve this, we need an economic policy framework that restores balance ecologically, socially and democratically, and makes the aforementioned purpose-driven economy possible. Since my professional experience (investment banking, venture capital, non-profit, consciousness transformation, education, and technology industries) has been centered in the United States, what follows is a list of ten economic reforms to begin with, to expedite the realization of a purpose-driven economy in the United States. By no means is this only an American discussion, however. This discussion must happen everywhere in the world, though some of these ideas might not be appropriate everywhere.

Following this list of reforms is my suggestion for a practical next step: an economic policy framework that would get the ball rolling towards this overhaul, and be a communicable economic platform for U.S. political campaigns. Further, this plan is not a cohesive lock-tight paradigm to step into, but rather the starting point for purposeful economic reform. Any one of these reforms, when brought to life, must by necessity evolve through the efforts of many committed citizens who compassionately marry this framework with the prevailing economic and political realities of their time and place. Further, it follows that any set of policies that does get implemented should also be obsolete in five years, because by then we'll have a new reality, and thus, need a new plan. So, I urge you to try this on hypothetically, and see if it resonates with you; see if the resulting world could allow humanity to thrive.

Plans are useless, but planning is indispensable.
-President Dwight D. Eisenhower

These reforms may seem radical and/or limiting. That is actually the function of a structure, to optimize outcomes and limit behavior in order to express a set of radical ideals (radical, meaning at their root), by imposing boundaries and limitations. Lest you think this is some kind of fascistic imposition, it is important to realize that we already have a reality given to us by the radical economic beliefs, boundaries and structures that we created and implemented (invisible hand of the free market, white man's burden, social Darwinism, etc.). As we've explored, the result of this current construct is income inequality and poverty along gender and racial lines, ecocide, oppression, etc. We're used to our racist, sexist, free market morality construct (this is not to say that we are nature-haters, racists and sexists, only that this is the outcome of our current construct). And, many of us do not notice it. But it was, nonetheless, our own creation, evolving slowly and marginally and, often, without our conscious awareness.

As tempting as it might be, if we are to put forth a new vision of the human species, we cannot simply do without a structure. We must instead create a new one to replace the old one. Some of these ideas may be considered impractical, but I assert it would be difficult to create a more impractical set of structures than the ones we have now. So, let's dive into a hypothetical set of structures intended to maximize our economy for purposeful human excellence and biodiversity.

Ten Reforms to Create a Purpose-Driven Economy

So, what is it like to do business in an economy that encourages you to find and live your purpose? What is it like to do business according to your soul's purpose? What is it like to lay your head upon a pillow at the end of the day, knowing your efforts are cherished, amply compensated and have advanced the wellbeing of our species, planet and Cosmos?

To create this scenario, we must bring our economic enterprises and the felt experience of the workday into alignment with our deepest identity as a species, planet and Cosmos. These ten proposed reforms, which may take years to implement at the national and state levels, can begin to provide the right incentives for humanity's entrepreneurial and creative potential to be purposefully, equitably and sustainably utilized.

As mentioned, we're going to reimagine the whole economy, and root it radically in the purpose of the Cosmos, Earth and species, beginning with the purpose of the firm and the purpose of money. I have two requests: 1. I request that you CTRL+ALT+DEL your current understanding of what money is, what a job is and how the economy works, and have an open mind, as if you were curiously discovering a new civilization that had governed its economy according to the laws of the Cosmos. Secondly, please note all of your "what-ifs", "yeah-buts" and "who pays for this?" in the margins and reserve final judgment until you have moved through all of these 10 reforms. Then standing in that new world, see if a new vision emerges. See if your life would be better off. See if you could picture the end-game realized, and only then dive into the mechanics of how to bring it forth.

Reminder: Your feedback is invaluable and we need it! A second edition is planned, so please send us all of your criticism and feedback via the ensouled.LIFE website.

1. **All corporate entities, including sole proprietorships, LLCs, LPs, and C-corporations will become Purpose-Driven Enterprises and "For-Benefit" B Corporations.** As mentioned in "Chapter 11: Creating a

Purpose-Driven Career", a Purpose-Driven Enterprise is one in which the executives are purpose-aware, which is to say that they have done deep purpose work and have revealed a high-definition life purpose (higher/soul purpose). The B Corp, a distinction of B Labs, is a for-benefit enterprise, a commercial entity that is explicitly crafted to improve the human and ecological condition (inclusive of all social and environmental impacts). There is a rigorous application and audit associated with becoming a B Corp that measures the impact of its purpose and accounts for resource usage. As such, I recommend that each current organization will have a 2-year implementation period during which all key executives will become rooted in their individual purpose, recraft their company vision, offer purpose discovery education to their employees and then apply for B Corp status. Before being granted the right to trade as a Purpose-Driven Enterprise/B Corp, each organization must:

- Articulate the individual purpose of each founder, executive and investor, along with the methods they used to discover their life's purpose. This means that every founder, executive and investor would have to do purpose-discovery work, e.g., a vision quest, a course like the Global Purpose Expedition, or work with a trained Guide, before revisioning their enterprise and recrafting their careers as expressions of their purpose. (Without this inner work, a venture will ultimately devolve into one motivated purely by fear, greed and profit.)

- Articulate the purpose of the PDE as it relates to Maslow's hierarchy of human needs, demonstrating a unique plan/method/product that makes a net improvement in the human, ecological and/or Cosmic condition. Offerings that serve humanity and the planet may include, but are not limited to, those which:
  - advance human longevity and wellness
  - address the root causes of poverty, disease, illiteracy, malnutrition
  - educate people, and advance consciousness via personal development technologies
  - develop sustainable transportation services
  - create walkable and bikeable communities
  - create knowledge management, search and networking tools
  - create art, cultural expression and communication platforms
  - develop renewable and distributed energy technologies
  - develop sustainable/distributed farming methods
  - develop renewable/recycled/reusable material processes
  - build sustainable housing and work spaces
  - nurture the global human community through service, spiritual and/or sustainable tourism

> o   treat and recycle (locally) water and sewage
>
> o   provide specialized services to other B Corps/PDEs, such as high-speed internet providers, marketplaces, research institutions, consultancies, productivity software and service companies, non-governmental organizations and transportation authorities (e.g., ports, airports and rail).
>
> • outline a plan by which the PDE will economically support the biological, psychological, spiritual, and social needs of the organization's employees and their households, with fewer than 40 hours of work contributed to the organization per household.
>
> • acquire insurance for all commercial activities.
>
> • Companies falling outside of these requirements, for example, mass producers of unsustainable fashion or apparel items or single-use consumer goods, will not receive a charter to trade and henceforth will no longer operate.

2. **Fiscal reform: Abolition of usury (financial interest) and corporate income tax, to be replaced by consumption and land taxes and currency demurrage (negative interest).** As all companies are now PDEs whose goal is to improve the net human and ecological condition, taxing their cashflow (their ability to invest in their mission) would be a disservice, not only to the PDE founders, investors and employees, but to humanity. The abolition of corporate income tax in favor of resource consumption and land use taxes (vs. taxes on income and property value) will create the strategic and financial incentive to invest cash flows and align the activities of PDEs with the interests of the commonwealth, to treat people fairly, and to use natural resources sparingly and land wisely. Thus, this system encourages PDEs to reduce the resource use/carbon footprint of their properties. Land use taxes tax the value of the land, not the property, and provide incentive for real estate developers to make the most of each parcel: to create dense, walkable and bikeable communities, to build up (vs. out) around community/commercial centers, to open up sustainable development on unused but valuable property near the commercial centers and to return parcels to nature if they cannot be economically utilized. Further, as money has no purpose other than to serve the needs of humanity the Earth and the Cosmos, it must be reimagined and function from this perspective. Thus, financial interest and the "time value of money" are concepts that are no longer needed, as energy and value are not finite in the Cosmos, but rather are infinite and evolving. Money as a concept must now be re-visioned as an infinite and emerging flow of energy, whose role is to move energy and resources as efficiently and purposefully as

possible to where they are most needed to achieve the soulful ends of humanity, the Earth and the Cosmos. From this perspective, the purpose of money is to empower creative, generative, just, sustainable and emergent economic activity, by measuring the exchange of value and enabling the velocity of transactions. To achieve its purpose, money must be abundantly supplied and exponentially depreciate the longer it is held in any account, a concept called currency demurrage, e.g., losing 1% of its value in month 1, 2% in month 2, 4% in month 3, 8% in month 4, etc. This creates the financial incentive for money to move quickly, to be paid out to suppliers and employees, and invested in research and development, professional development and capital improvements. This makes it unattractive for monetary wealth to be accumulated, and shifts the entire concept of the value of an enterprise or investment portfolio, from a static to a dynamic measure, wherein the value of an entity is primarily driven by its actual sustainable and generative economic throughput for meeting the needs of people, the planet and Cosmos.

3. **PDEs are communities.** We are social animals, who thrive when we are connected and develop deep relationships. As such PDEs, or autonomous divisions within PDEs, may comprise no more than 150 employees, such that the social contract, collective purpose, culture and ethics are easily maintained. This isn't an arbitrary figure, it is known as "the Dunbar number" (Dunbar, 1992), the number of people with whom an individual is able to maintain stable social relationships, ethics and culture. This naturally-occurring, human dynamic allows for company culture and purpose to be naturally maintained without burdensome, ongoing culture projects, training, enrollment, or bureaucracy. In teams up to 150, people naturally feel connected to each other, remain committed to the team's success and have the experience of being woven into the fabric of the community.

4. **All PDEs adopt a Cradle-to-Cradle product life cycle.** Each PDE adopts a cradle-to-cradle product life cycle whereby all products produced and materials used are durable (intended use of 10+ years), updatable or reusable, and can be easily deconstructed and reused, or will naturally decompose without a negative ecological impact at the end of their usefulness. Doing so makes each PDE fully responsible for the use and termination of its services and products. This dramatically shortens the feedback loop between economics and environment, making it impossible to externalize hidden costs of doing business upon suppliers, customers, the environment and future generations.

5. **GAAP reform: Labor becomes a line item on the Generally Accepted Accounting Principles (GAAP) balance sheet, AND biosphere services**

becomes a line item now found on the GAAP income statement.
Currently, labor is an income statement expense, and businesses have an economic incentive to minimize it, and thus exploit labor. Moreover, as we explored in "Chapter 17: Humanity's Midlife Crisis", the costs of raw materials (extraction/harvest, production, distribution, use and disposal) do not include many of the costs accrued to humanity, the environment or future generations. This results in the inevitable structural consequences of inefficient resource use, waste, and income inequality, ecocide, and animal exploitation and torture, many of which were presented in the 2008 documentary, *Food, Inc.* In our new economic paradigm, human capital would now be cultivated and accounted for as an asset on the balance sheet. Company leadership would then be motivated to retain their employees and invest in their potential, training, fulfillment and purposeful expression. Further, as each PDE is uniquely chartered to serve the goals of the species, planet and the Cosmos, ecosystem services consumed by the enterprise will be accounted for as an expense. At the end of the year, each PDE's resource use will be paid by tax payments made to local governments to restore and regenerate the supply of natural resources used by the entity, and to address the planet's most pressing global ecological problems and opportunities for regeneration, conservation, cleanup, biodiversity and ecological resilience.

6. **The brand of each PDE will be the aggregate brand of its team.**
As everyone in the economy will have completed some sort of purpose discovery program, marked by self-awareness, self-love, self-expression, and a big vision and mission, the fields and practices of brand marketing, advertising and promotion will have the ability to actually take on an authentic expression. PDE websites must now explicitly link to the social media profiles of each employee and honor the whole person in the organization, their interests and public expression. This public association ensures a deep soul connection between individual and collective purpose. This would allow anyone, anywhere to experience that an organization has a shared commitment to improving the human and ecological condition, one held by real people connected to their individual purpose and to the collective purpose of the organization. This would create the dual incentive for individuals to work for PDEs that are aligned with their purpose and for PDEs to hire individuals whose life purpose and self-expression resonates with the PDE's purpose. Making this connection explicit would now have every individual in the organization connected with the organization as a vehicle of self-expression and a sense of personal ownership. No longer could anyone hide behind the saying, "It's just a job," or "If I don't do it, someone else will," or "IBGYBG" (I'll Be Gone, You'll Be Gone - after the toxic impacts of our business are revealed), since folks will have to

publicly live with their association to the enterprise, its business practices and impacts on society and the environment.

7. **There is only purposeful brand advertising.** As all organizations are now PDEs, each brand reflects the purposes of the founders and the purposeful commitment of everyone in the organization. The practice of purposeless lifestyle brand advertising (glamorous people selling largely useless items) will no longer exist. And for good reason. Purposeless brand advertising validates and encourages an identity sourced outside of soul. Identity sourced in anything other than one's soul's purpose, and its connection to humanity, the Earth or the Cosmos is inauthentic, unfulfilling, unproductive and a waste of human potential (in the creation, marketing, purchase, use and disposal of purposeless products). This type of purposeless brand advertising does not tout the net social, economic and ecological benefits of a particular product versus the alternatives. Rather, it encourages people to fit in with a particular group or to stand out from others, via consumer status experiences, such as fashion labels, or food and beverages (aka purpose-substitutes). Doing so often occurs without regard to current best practices for meeting our core needs (from Maslow - sustenance, safety, shelter, connection, esteem, self-actualization) or the ecological, social and cultural impacts incurred in the delivery of said products or services. For this reason, PDEs may only communicate actual customer experiences, the purpose of the PDE, the purposes of their employees and the net Maslovian benefits of the product or service – the actual value to customers.

8. **All patents, copyrights and trademarks will be issued under Creative Commons licenses.** In that the reason that a PDE enters business is for the founder's authentic self-expression benefitting the common good, and given that we are part of a unified evolutionary Cosmos, the intellectual property (IP) generated by the PDE is thereby also for the common good and will be issued under a Creative Commons license. All other forms of IP will be abolished and reissued as Creative Commons. Historically, IP was developed to protect power, limiting innovation, service and impact. With a Creative Commons ethos, IP empowers humanity to adopt an open source mentality, allowing all of us to innovate and acknowledge previous contributions. This provides the incentive to innovate rather than develop a fiefdom, empowering us to take what was done before, generously attribute and source that work and make it better without fear of legal or economic recourse. This provides the further incentive to distinguish a PDE, based on the real, unique and practical value of the good or service, and the hard work and purpose/authenticity/story of the team that creates it. It also provides an economic incentive for those industries who feed on the current fiefdom of copyrights and trademarks (law, finance and research) to find

their true purpose. We are already seeing this culture in action as many organizations are experimenting with an open source/copyleft/Creative Commons approach to their IP, e.g., Patagonia, WordPress/Automattic, Mozilla, Whole Foods, NASA, Tesla, and Mercedes-Benz.

9. **Purpose Audits.** As part of their year-end reporting and accounting, all PDEs must justify their existence in light of the human, social and environmental resources they consume. Existing financial accounting/ audit firms will partner with B Labs (the organization that created the B Corp designation and B Impact Assessment) and add this new practice area, to ensure that the management's fiduciary responsibility reflects the purpose of the founders, and actually delivers a net benefit to humanity and the Earth's ecology. Though this may sound onerous, in practice the leaders of PDEs, such as the leaders of Clif Bar and Patagonia, take great pleasure in adhering to the company charter (that they, in most cases, created), which goes well beyond regulatory requirements. PDE leaders are proud and excited to demonstrate exactly how they innovate to live their purpose, exceed their legal obligations and create unique value for their customers, employees, suppliers, communities, humanity and the Earth, e.g., Patagonia's torture-free goose down and their efforts to publicize their values, business practices and achievements in the documentary, *Worn Wear*. These audits ensure that companies remain steadfast in their purpose-driven commitments and species, planetary and Cosmic identity.

10. **Fair compensation** As we've seen in recent times, while wages have remained flat or declined - due to average wage increases of 1-3% and inflation of 6-9% per year (shadowstats.com, 6/5/2017) - over the last 40 years, CEOs have made extraordinary amounts of money, often exiting with golden parachutes. The most well-known example is Walmart. Most of Walmart's 1.4 million full-time employees rely on government assistance, such as food stamps, Medicaid and subsidized housing, costing American taxpayers $6.2 billion/year (O'Connor, 2014), while the executives make millions and the founders make billions. *Forbes* reported that in 2012 CEOs were paid 331 times the wage of an average worker and 774 times minimum wage (Dill, 2014). On the surface, being rich is not a problem, as people who create lots of value should indeed be rewarded. However, gross system inequity has been proven to reduce social mobility, and to disempower those not born into the privileged wealthy class. As Robert Putnam, the Peter and Isabel Malkin Professor of Public Policy, at Harvard Kennedy School notes, "Smart poor kids are less likely to graduate from college now than dumb rich kids. That's not because of the schools, that's because of all the advantages that are available to rich kids" (Pazzanese, 2016). To resolve this inequity, our new purposeful economy allows CEOs

to take home no more than twice the average earnings (salary + options/ equity) of the other top five office holders. The average earnings of the top five office holders may be no more than twice the earnings of the lowest paid employee, such that the CEO can make no more than four times the lowest paid employee. This schema expresses brotherhood and creates a culture of dignity and appreciation for the purposeful powers of every team member, while still providing an economic incentive to achieve and lead. This also creates the incentive to build long-term strategic value in the way a business operates, investing in the purpose, leadership and generative output of each employee, raising the wages of the lowest paid employees and thereby raising the CEO compensation by $4 for every dollar paid to entry level employees.

Each of these economic reforms are massive undertakings that would radically change the way our economy works. It will take decades of hard work to realize these and hundreds of other necessary economic reforms. However, given that under the current structure we could be facing our own extinction in the course of a generation or two, we must start reforming our economy now. That means getting to work on distilling these big picture concepts into actionable policies and programs that are bite-sized and digestible, that can be easily communicated, legislated and that, when implemented, can provide a solid springboard for the next set of necessary reforms.

It is unlikely that our current politicians and decision-makers will embrace these reforms, as virtually all of these ideas threaten their personal wealth and campaign funding sources (especially those in the pocket of Wall Street, Big Oil, Big Ag and Big Pharma). As such, we need to immediately elect purpose-awakened and pro-purpose politicians to do the VERY hard work of implementing a purposeful economy.

Note to politicians and the 1%: If you have felt the poke of the pitchfork from Occupy, Black Lives Matter, Antifa, the rise of populist leaders, the Women's March or the Science March, living and leading with your life's purpose and screaming it from the mountain tops may actually be the best way forward for you. Further, you might consider that above all else, people value authenticity. They value the gifts of knowing your soul's purpose (being able to be vulnerable, soulful, integrous and relatable) and that these are more important to your success, leadership, fulfillment and impact than your pedigree, experience, network, capital or policy ideas.

To begin this transition and aid their election, I would like to offer a policy platform for an American political movement, for the election of a new generation of soulful executive and legislative politicians. This policy platform is a set of initial reforms to save our economy, ecology, culture, and species from the suicidal effects of institutional purposelessness, and to create a solid foundation for human and ecological flourishing, while fulfilling on our human, planetary and Cosmic purposes. In accordance with the requirement that a political platform be easily communicable, I have called this "The 5-20" – five powerful changes to be implemented in 2020. These five purposeful economic policies are designed to begin this shift, beginning with people's core concerns - career, happiness and health:

1. CAREER, MONEY AND SECURITY: Having meaningful work that allows each household to easily and reliably support themselves and their families, in less than 40 hours a week, being authentically fulfilled by their work in the world, and being able to invest/save a healthy portion of their income for creative, leisure, personal development and future expenses,
2. HAPPINESS: Having time to enjoy leisure activities, their relationships, home and communities, and
3. HEALTH: Being in good health.

To accomplish this, we must begin by shifting the five most important variables in the economy: energy, labor, infrastructure, entrepreneurship and scale:

- **ENERGY: $20/gallon of gas**
  When we factor in the real cost to the environment and society of a gallon of gasoline, the price rises from $3/gallon to somewhere between $5-20/gallon in 2017 dollars (Institute for the Analysis of Global Security, 7/31/2017), depending on the number of externalities we account for. These externalities include the cost of automobile infrastructure, human health (pollution/trauma) costs, highway patrol, ecosystem damage/cleanup, and military spending to secure a steady supply of underpriced fossil fuels. This may seem extreme; however, in reality we are already paying that extra $2-17 per gallon in the guise of federal taxes that fund our military to secure cheap oil - $584 billion per year (Congressional Budget Office, 2017) -, as well as what we spend healing our returning veterans, combatting air pollution, rehabilitating the environment, providing police and emergency worker wages (to monitor this dangerous activity and remove the dead and wounded) and infrastructure costs. Much of this cost we borrow and take from the unborn through two structural deficits, A. principal and interest payments on federal debt, B. ecological destruction. We can also incorporate many of these externalities into coal and natural gas usage. By localizing the actual cost of carbon-fuel combustion at the pump and energy bill, and giving people other incentives to switch to flex-time commuting, alternative-power vehicles, bikes and mass transit, we radically change the

incentive structure for our current economy and city-state plans. When carbon is accurately priced, it becomes more beneficial to develop smaller, better, less resource-intensive things (syntropy), to promote bicycles and public transportation over cars, to bring sources and production of food, water and goods closer to where people live, and to create more unity via a local and sustainable goods and services economy. This would provide a strong disincentive to centralize and mass produce, distribute and sell goods that have to travel beyond the 20-200-mile radius of a city-state's urban center. (See the next chapter on how this city-state could work, look and feel.) By implementing truthful carbon pricing and incentives for bikes, mass transit and alternative-power vehicles, we will re-localize the economy, strengthen the social fabric of our communities and provide the economic incentive to design better cities (more vertical, more walkable, bikeable communities and more immersed in nature). Further, it will reduce the compulsion to drive, decreasing the plague of tragic and expensive automobile-related injuries and fatalities, decreasing air pollution, and increasing daily exercise.

- **LABOR: $20/hour minimum wage**
  With fossil fuels accurately priced, and now much more expensive, the intrinsic value of human labor naturally rises, as it will be more cost efficient to hire people to do jobs that previously were done by subsidized carbon energy. No longer would the contributions of people be artificially devalued by machines powered by state-subsidized carbon. This is not to say that carbon fuels would be illegal to use, just very expensive. However, if we wait for rising gas prices to increase wages, we would be ignoring the massive wealth transfer, from the lower and middle classes to the upper class, that has already occurred over the last 30 years. We must address the compounded annual wealth transfer of 3-8% per year from the lower and middle class to the wealth - the difference between our 6-9% yearly inflation and our 1-3% income growth (shadowstats.com, 7/31/2017). 3-8% per year! For the last 30 years! Americans responded to this silent annual diminution of the value of their work by working longer hours, moving to two income households and piling on consumer and mortgage debt. As such, we need to immediately restore human dignity. To restore dignity and integrity, we must make a move to raise the federal minimum wage to $20/ hour, a level that reflects the productivity increases of the overall economy and keeps up with the last 30 years of 6-9% inflation. It would also mean that one person working a 40-hour workweek ($3,813 per month) would have a greater capability to support an entire family household. This in turn would allow another parent, caregiver or relative to attend to home

economics, the garden, and education of the youth, or both parents could work part-time while equally sharing in the domestic workload. Further, this move would also restore the most important middle and lower income safety net, by making available another capable worker per household, who can go out to contribute financially in difficult times. In essence, this would be a shift from a focus on "Work, work, work!" towards a more balanced lifestyle, giving everyone breathing room, the space to spend time with their families, invaluable leisure time on weekends and evenings for pursuing civic projects, quality relationships, personal development, time in nature and other activities that feed people's souls and the family's purpose. Numerous social democracies have implemented similar minimum/living wage policies and have realized positive outcomes in wealth, income and leisure (see "Appendix F: Starting Point for a Purposeful US Government").

- **INFRASTRUCTURE: Spend an additional 20% of the federal discretionary budget on city-state infrastructure, distributed renewable energy, clean water and low-impact organic food production.**
  With the focus on strengthening local economies and increasing economic resilience and energy independence, the U.S. Government can carve out a healthy chunk (20%) of the discretionary budget from the defense budget, currently over 50% of discretionary budget (Congressional Budget Office, 2017), to allow the Army Corps of Engineers to develop America's New "New Deal", a city-state and sustainable economic infrastructure. Through a coordinated effort among the National Energy Administration, Federal Trade Commission, Environmental Protection Agency, and the (reworked and lobby-free) Food and Drug Administration, we would use this budget to develop a nationwide, city-state-oriented bicycle and mass-transit infrastructure, distributed low-impact renewable energy solutions, and distributed organic food production systems. Local communities will then be able to provide for their caloric needs, while still having reliable access to mass-transit, to high-speed internet, and to clean soil, air and water.

- **ENTREPRENEURIAL LEADERSHIP: By age 20, every American will have earned an Associate Degree in Purpose-Driven Citizenship, Leadership and Enterprise.** This will also be made available at no cost to the individual (tax/state-funded, and including a modest cost-of-living stipend, as well as made available to everyone currently over 20 who wishes to partake). To create a purpose-aware, highly-functioning, sustainable innovation economy (and an effective democracy), we need a purpose-driven, creative, engaged and entrepreneurial workforce. To achieve this, we must radically expand and update public adult education to include an Associate Degree in Purpose-Driven Citizenship, Leadership and Enterprise, offered by local community colleges and paid for by city-state, state and federal land use and consumption taxes. Of course, the entire education system needs to be better funded, reformed and made more soul-friendly (more mindfulness, arts, nature, humanities). However, the purpose and society questions come into greater focus in one's teens, as this is the time that the first large decisions around education and career (as well as who pays for it) must be faced. As such, *before* encumbering young adults with these decisions and their financial consequences, we must first empower them with an experiential journey to a vision for their lives, the world and their contribution to society and the economy. To accomplish this, this degree would have five learning objectives:

1. guide each person in building an identity rooted in their unique individual purpose and our collective purposes as species, planet and Cosmos;

2. entrepreneurially empower every citizen with the basics required to live and craft a livelihood that expresses their life's purpose;

3. globally inform our citizenry (necessary for both the creation of a PDE-based economy and a democratic government);

4. embody personal purpose at the level of health, relationships/communications and community; and

5. foster each person's purposeful leadership capabilities in the community and economy.

To deliver on these objectives, each American high school graduate will embark on this personal and collective rite of passage/education journey. Before being admitted to any trade school, four-year college or university in the United States, or the Armed Forces, every U.S. citizen shall complete this two-year Associate Degree with coursework in purpose discovery, leadership, non-violent communication, critical thinking, ecology, Big History, entrepreneurship, classical mythology, comparative religion, martial arts, first aid, psychology, economics, change theory, community development, and a five-hour per week civil service commitment co-developed with their Faculty Advisor/Guide (who is tasked with nurturing their leadership and experiential purpose education).

The result of this policy would be a cultural shift towards purpose, planetary citizenship, leadership, civic action, community resilience, entrepreneurship, compassionate communication, personal empowerment and interdependence.

- **SCALE: 20 to 200-mile city-state incorporation.** To ensure that local economies take into account the local geographies and the impacts of economic activities in their communities, we need a governance structure that supports a purposeful local economy. As such, all towns and cities will be reincorporated as semi-autonomous city-states, absorbing all county and most state responsibilities within a 20-200-mile radius from the city center (depending on population size, geography, resources and weather). Within these new boundaries, city-states would have to:
  o Craft and articulate their city-state purpose,
  o Meet 80%+ of their demand for water, electricity and food
  o Meet 60%+ of the demand for their households' durable goods and for non-internet-related services.

One might be tempted to think this form of decentralization would raise the cost of goods and services. Along with the aforementioned shifts in labor and energy use, it might, but only because the actual value of goods purchased is not fully captured by the price paid, but rather hidden in taxes, or borrowed from future generations via fiscal debt or taken via ecological destruction. However, this move would encourage a greater diversity of local goods and services providers and, in conjunction with the aforementioned labor and energy policies, the price of goods would more accurately reflect their true value (the amount of resources and human life invested in it). Contrary to public opinion, America already is and always has been a network of small, local businesses; 89.4% of businesses have fewer than 20 employees (U.S. Census Bureau, 2014). Large companies that externalize costs and use subsidized fuels to make and distribute their goods and services would be the ones most impacted by this economic scale, and would therefore be forced to innovate and reconceive their supply chain, marketing and operations.

Collectively, these five policies would shift economic power from large centralized institutions to individuals and local communities. Although this structure would limit certain behaviors (e.g., wanton driving, soulless work, consumerism, pollution, exploitation) and encourage others (purpose discovery, soulful work, more tightly knit, walkable, bikable towns), I believe the net effect would be more power and freedom, not less. Freedom to be self-expressed. Freedom to have your purpose and livelihood be the same. Freedom to be healthy. Freedom to enjoy your life with abundance and spaciousness. Further, this would strengthen the autonomy of every American citizen, cultivate the experience of collective purpose at the level of the city-state, strengthen the moral and social fabric of American culture. It would strengthen democracy, alter the focus of the entire economy from sustaining the wealth and power of far away, inefficient and ineffective purposeless entities, and shift power back down into the local living communities of America. Under this schema, Americans would now have convenient access to, and control of, their essential economic inputs for living a life on purpose.

Collectively this schema would shift the country's energy portfolio from a dependence on fossil fuels to an appreciation of human labor and renewable energy. Land use would become a central concern; non-productive lots in urban areas would be re-zoned according to the city-state's purpose and economic development plan (e.g., for public use, agriculture, commerce, ecological diversity). This approach would align the economy with the community and the habitat on which it depends. (More on this in the next chapter.) Lastly, this would create an incentive for people to be closer to nature. Whether in the tending of city gardens or the choice to move from the city to the country, we would have a tighter bond to our environment (air, water and soil) and our enterprises would no longer be able to act in ways that would pollute or destroy ecosystems (e.g., "not in my backyard" – NIMBY).

As we make each step to this purposeful economy, the requirements we demand of the systems supporting us will undoubtedly change. Living on purpose embraces and welcomes this evolution.

I believe these structural shifts are necessary to realize the result of humanity living on purpose. However, as mentioned, this is merely an incomplete starting point for the discussion, shared with you to inspire, empower and prod you into action, to move you into crafting your own vision for your community and your career, to join the community discussion and contribute your leadership. The above isn't an exact prescription, of course: it is just one possible starting point for an economic structure that could be created when we all know our life's purpose. As to how that will actually unfold, well, that is the story we can now collectively begin to write.

CHAPTER 20

The Purposeful City-State

This isn't going to be decided at the UN... it's going to happen at the local level when enough of us feel a sense of purpose and stability in our own lives that we can start to open up and care about everyone else too. And, the best way to do that is to start building local communities right now. Change starts local. Even global change starts small.

-Mark Zuckerberg (Zuckerberg, 2017)

With a purpose-driven economic framework in place, rewarding and empowering the purpose awakening and expression of all Americans, we can now engage in a really fun task: crafting the expression and feel of political purpose at the local level. What is needed is a local and tactile means for citizens to express their purpose and create a community, culture and local political economy in line with their collective purpose. From this place, with every community member in touch with their soul and awakening their Shambhala Leadership, we come into the question of collective purpose. Who are we as a community? As stewards of our interdependent local ecology? As a culture? This chapter is an immersion into our local sandbox, a space to play and quickly see tangible, purpose-driven results in our city-states and communities.

However, in America, our city, county and state governments are structured to leave most of the people out of public life. We elect others to govern for us. I believe that this is a flaw, as it disempowers civic activity and connection to the community. Without citizen governance at the local level, some form of Athenian democracy, e.g. via mandatory voting, a government devolves into an oligarchy run by the interests of commerce and the wealthy, AND we lose our sense of brotherhood and collective purpose, devolving into a culture of selfish individualism, trading the commons for individual profit. Unfortunately, this is what has happened, as we've isolated ourselves from each other via gated communities and commerical centers, e.g. malls, outlets, that are accessible only by car, red-lined neighborhoods and underfunded mass transit, creating clear barriers between the rich and poor. It appears we have become a lonely, materialist and self-obsessed culture, as Adam Curtis explored in his BBC docuseries, *Century of the Self* (Curtis, 2002).

To recraft America from a soulful and integrous perspective, we need citizen governance at the local level. We need to resurrect the city-state and make it participatory and purpose-driven. Imagine a nation-wide patchwork of semi-autonomous city-states to celebrate our diverse local cultures and arts, and our resilient local economies, and to allow citizens to experience the joy of participatory governance. Such a city-state framework empowers an ongoing discussion and evolution of the tension between personal liberty and the commonwealth, and of acknowledging the past and creating our future. This structure could awaken the creative potential of every community through self-organization, citizen education, and the means to continually create and strengthen our local communities and economies. It was Thomas Jefferson's deepest desire to share the joy of governance with the people, to create a nation wherein participatory citizenship would become fundamental to the human experience.

And, this was more than just the heartfelt belief of Jefferson. Other American luminaries experienced the power of participatory local governance in New England's town meetings, wherein citizens spoke freely, were recognized and acknowledged, and felt connected and empowered in local affairs. The result of this face-to-face connection was a self-organizing commonwealth. And it got things done. As Ralph Waldo Emerson observed,

> A man felt himself at liberty to exhibit at town-meetings, feelings and actions that he would have been ashamed of anywhere but amongst his neighbors.... In a town-meeting, the great secret of political science was uncovered, and the problem solved, how to give every individual his fair weight in the government, without any disorder from numbers. In a town-meeting, the roots of society were reached. Here the rich gave counsel, but the poor also; and moreover, the just and the unjust. ... In this open democracy, every opinion had utterance; every objection, every fact, every acre of land, every bushel of rye, its entire weight. (Emerson, pp. 43-45, 1883)

American Default Purpose at the Local Level

As mentioned, most American cities and their surrounding suburbs are not organized to allow for participatory governance. The scale has become too broad and the matrixed complexity of overlapping entities (e.g., city, county, state) too burdensome for average citizens to understand, much less be empowered to vote or participate in council meetings. Even where there are opportunities to attend a town hall or city council, there is sparse attendance due to the strains of economic hardship, our mass media culture and an often disempowered and ill-informed populace. Even when well-attended, the experience often devolves into a shouting match. As a result, the purpose and power of workable, cooperative local government is not an experience most people either have had or believe can exist.

Although local governments are fairly good at providing some services (police, fire, schools, water, electricity, trash removal), in America, the default purposes of most towns and cities is to maintain the social and economic order. There are many structural reasons for this, but they all stem from one core cause: communities and community leaders are not connected to their purpose, they function largely from default purposes and almost benefit the entrenched interests of the wealthy and commerce. Over time, this has resulted in poor urban planning; constant traffic; road construction; uninspiring strip malls; big box stores/dilapidated town centers; poorly-funded schools, museums and hospitals; poverty; crime; pollution and addiction. This is not to morally indict American cities and towns, but to merely present how they are currently organized and what ends they serve.

City-states on Purpose

To counter this default manner of local political economy, the Jeffersonian vision has experienced a renaissance throughout the country. We are witnessing the rise of participatory, purpose-driven, creatively run and efficiently organized cities and regional economic development organizations, such as Portland, OR; Chattanooga, TN; Asheville, NC; Austin, TX and Madison, WI. Globally, this purposeful political economy trend is also referred to as the "slow city movement": a movement of over 230 cities in 30 countries, who have taken on quality of life as their governing concern. Cities in this movement have adopted a 54-point charter that seeks to improve the quality of life, protect the environment, encourage local businesses and improve human health (cittaslow.org, 8/25/2107).

Each of these cities has, in its own way, ignited the community purpose discussion. Each of these cities has implemented numerous proven best practices for urban life, such as celebrating and protecting their forests and natural water sources, focusing on their region's strategic advantages, managing a modest size and population density, and fostering a commitment to walkable, bikeable neighborhoods, robust public transit, and numerous cultural and academic institutions. So, how does this happen? Let's take a look at Chattanooga, a mid-sized American city.

Chattanooga

One thousand Chattanooga residents participated in a four-month re-visioning process in 2010. The result was a set of 40 initiatives to radically remake the city and surrounding region. These included a new distribution center to capitalize on Chattanooga's location at the intersection of Interstates 75, 59 and 24; an innovation district, the INCubator - a highly-concentrated start-up nest set in a 125,000-square-foot former ceramics factory; five miles of new greenway; a revitalized boardwalk; and the Tennessee Aquarium and Riverpark. Further...

> The [2010 Chattanooga] visioning process and the plan stimulated a number of subsequent redevelopment efforts, including creation of a private non-profit agency to facilitate redevelopment projects (RiverValley Partners/River City Company), and another private non-profit focused on eliminating substandard housing (Chattanooga Neighborhood Enterprise). The plan also resulted in a number of transportation improvements, undertaken by the Chattanooga Area Regional Transportation Authority (such as electric buses), and extensive environmental clean-up efforts. A number of attractions, including a stadium, an aquarium, a restored theater and bridge, and a cultural center, were developed as a result of the plan (Skeele, 2011).

The result was that Chattanooga transformed itself from an area with horrific air pollution and unemployment to a model of nature-infused urban life, low cost of living and an innovation economy, making it home to more than just startups, but also a great place to live and work - as employees of several companies, such as Tennessee Valley Authority, BlueCross BlueShield of Tennessee, Cigna, Volkswagen, and McKee Foods, have discovered. As a result of the environmental cleanup efforts, the area is now known for its attractive mix of urban and country living, making it a frequent destination for folks who love craft food, hiking, biking, kayaking and climbing. In 2011 and 2015, *Outside Magazine* proclaimed that it was the best American city for those interested in both city culture and nature. (Outside Magazine, 2015)

As part of citizen visioning processes like Chattanooga's, is that regular citizens get to engage in the Jeffersonian privilege of participation in governance, and can dive into the question of their city's purpose; what makes it unique. The results of this inquiry have been powerful programs to amplify and express a city's unique purpose, e.g., Portland - ports, sustainability, and mountain and water sports; Asheville - arts, consciousness/transformation, and National Parks.

The City-State

I believe the city-state best serves the purposes of ordinary citizens and their felt and lived experience of life, while simultaneously increasing economic independence, cultural expression and ecological resilience. This unit of political and economic cooperation would assume most county responsibilities and state responsibilities. This is not to say that we dissolve counties, states or sovereign nations, but rather that we move power down, decentralize it, and re-district political and economic activity in ways that give each town and city center expanded autonomy to create and express their city-state purpose. The idea would be to create a cohesive economic and political governing entity that would:

1. awaken, evolve and serve the purposes of the citizens,
2. empower every citizen to participate,
3. serve the unique, collective purpose of the city-state, and
4. establish a zone (20-200-mile radius) of economic independence and ecological resilience, within which most needs would be met and all waste would be ecologically assimilated.

There are two huge benefits to organizing ourselves this way:

#1 Autonomy, Efficiency and Scale

The first reason we should create purposeful city-states as a unit of concern, is that the city-state (more than county, state or federal government) can actually be reformed quickly with purpose. Within a short amount of time, say, five to ten years, we can create an immersive and collective experience of purpose faster than for other units of government. As the citizens and elected officials of Chattanooga demonstrated, a vast web of community organizations and social capital can be utilized and harmonized to effect a massive change in the community, in a short amount of time.

Imagine the power of every American community service organization, every church, every small business owner, every school and PTA engaged in creating a collective purpose and coordinating its expression economically, structurally, legally, culturally and spiritually! Imagine what would be possible with whole communities engaged in that purpose discussion, fighting for what they believe in, and having expert facilitators channel those passions into a shared goal?! Every town and city can have what Chattanooga has with the presence of shared purpose felt and experienced by all citizens. No longer would cities be impersonal places for commerce and entertainment, but living, co-created spaces that continually change what it means to be a human being in that city - a felt experience of being engaged, creative, honored and necessary.

#2 Economic and Ecological Resilience

The second reason the city-state deserves our attention is that the economic, social and ecological effects of uncoordinated individual and commercial actions are currently not properly accounted for. As we explored in "Chapter 17: Humanity's Midlife Crisis", many enterprises do not actually make any real profit (inclusive of all costs), but are only able to show profit due to their ability to externalize many costs of doing business onto the unwitting public, such as through their reliance on subsidized labor, energy and resource prices. This results in the liberal use of fossil fuels, traffic, air, water and soil pollution and a general depression in wages and quality of life for middle and lower income families. This is especially noticeable when the trash of the rich gets shipped away in a diesel truck and buried under or next to the poor, or when air pollution from our diesel trucks to move goods (in many cases, across the country, and containing quite useless goods, like bottled water, disposable fashion items, fidget spinners and Snuggies) causes respiratory illness, or when poor people can only afford to live hours away from their workplaces, or in toxic industrial areas. Within many of our cities, we witness the stunning discrepancy in the quality of life, life expectancy, income and education between residents of adjoining neighborhoods or just a few subway stops apart, e.g., New York's Upper East Side vs. South Bronx (Measure of America, 2013).

A city-state on purpose empowers cultural cohesion and the creation of closed-loop economic systems that rapidly decrease economic externalities (such as pollution, long commute times, food deserts, poverty/ghettos, resource overuse and cheap labor). City-states afford regular citizens control over their destiny. When done well, they provide each citizen the opportunity to step into their purpose and to make their highest contribution, one that also amplifies the purpose, efficacy and health of the greater whole, the city-state.

The result of this purpose-driven city-state structure would be an unprecedented richness and uniqueness, all of which would become a strategic and economic advantage for attracting residents, businesses and tourists, as Chattanooga has experienced. A well-designed city-state is a cultural achievement: collective purpose embodied at the level of architecture, urban planning, use of the commons, and convenience for its citizens, businesses and visitors. This can be achieved through a handful of local leaders coming alive with their unique life's purpose, then structuring a Chattanooga-style citizen visioning process, crafting a multi-year city-state economic and political development plan, and then crowdfunding or raising municipal debt to begin the transformation.

Plans like this are not an anomaly, nor something reserved for quirky, second and third tier cities. If a purposeful regeneration can be done in these American cities, surely, we can do it in larger cities. As urban planner Robert Moses demonstrated in the New York Tri-state Area, by networking New York, New Jersey and Connecticut via an interstate freeway system (1930-1970), with a clear purpose (albeit with many detrimental effects to air quality and ethnic neighborhoods, in this case), it was possible to transform a major urban area in a short amount of time. As urban planner Jaime Lerner demonstrated in Curitiba, Brazil (pop. 3.4 million), this can be done in a manner that also empowers and connects the community, educates and improves ecological resilience. Lerner implemented mass transit bus-train innovations, incentives for planting trees, and re-zoning and tax incentives to create a high-density urban center and restore to nature poorly used land. His public health and education initiatives transformed a sprawling slum into a dense, nature-rich, sustainable and resilient local economy (Lovins, Lovins, Hawken, pp. 288-306, 1999). To explore what this could look like in a large American city, please explore "Appendix E: Chicago on Purpose", and to explore a starting point for a nation on purpose, please have a look at "Appendix F: Starting Point for a Purposeful US Federal Government".

CHAPTER 21

Love, Family, Community
and Culture on Purpose

"Dad, here's my report card," I said entering the kitchen, barely containing my excitement.

During my first semester of high school, I set the goal of getting straight A's and I achieved it. Also having spent 15 hours a week in the water on the swim team, I awaited a king's feast, an "I'm proud of you", kudos, congratulations and possibly a cash bonus.

"What is this?" He pointed to *Studio Art A*.

"It's Studio Art, Dad. It's my favorite class. We sketched, painted and made jewelry, pottery and prints. I'm taking Studio Art B next semester. I'm really excited about it."

"No, you're not. What, are you going to work in the art factory? If you have an elective, take something useful like government or economics."

BOOM. I was sent back into the pain I remembered from that general store in Morris. Not good enough. Not enough, period. Back into the dark grey sticky shame surrounding my self-expression. Back to the belief that no matter how hard I worked, what I liked wasn't welcomed. My desires weren't important. My creativity wasn't valued. My soul went unacknowledged. I knew that I was good insofar as I advanced my Dad's standards and ideals. And so it was, I filled my remaining years in high school with electives geared towards my Dad's approval - government, sales, psychology, history, economics and sociology. And in college, I joined the top fraternity on campus, held leadership positions and declared the major that would please him - Finance.

[In my late twenties and early thirties, as I discovered the ceremonial role that my Dad had in effectuating my estrangement from soul, I raged at him. I called him every name in the book and deeply damaged our relationship. I have since apologized and acknowledged him for doing his best, doing what he thought was best for me. However, I am still in the process of repairing the damage I did.]

And thus went my soul. I pushed it back down to where it belonged, out of sight, out of mind, making only the rare appearance, and always under the influence of alcohol, on the dance floor and during sex. If you grew up in America, odds are you've had similar experiences, where you were told you are too much. Too emotional, too sensitive, too creative, too curious, too touchy, too witchy, too sexy, too opinionated, too quiet, too outspoken, too weird, too thin, too fat, too smart, too dumb. Too much! And so, for most of us, we push it all down and toe the line. We push down the language of the soul - our creativity, our carnal desires, our love of nature, our poetry, our fantasies, our emotions and our music. We accept the unwinnable bargain for acceptance; we placate, work, marry, procreate and consume. As such, largely we are nation of soulful hearts conforming to a soul-starved culture. We grow up to repeat these same soul degradations and deprivations as parents.

To truly live and embody purpose, we have to do more than reform our economy and political structures, we have to ensoul all corners of life, such that we welcome and embrace all our soulful expressions through every stage of life. We must reform every mode of human cooperation such that it embodies, embraces and cultivates purpose – from friendship to love to family, company, to our schools, our community, sovereign nations and global polity. We can't just have soul in some parts of our lives, like family and career, and not in others.

Soul doesn't work that way. It demands expression everywhere. Soul is persistent, multivariate, unpredictable and ubiquitous. In America, we've witnessed soul blast through the constraints of our protestant and puritan culture and soul-starved institutions as civil disobedience, carnal sin and decadence. Soul bleeds through our Rock 'n' Roll, Blues, Jazz, Bluegrass and Hip-hop music. It's there in every wild night out, every 3rd drink, every unsanctioned tryst. It's there at every local craft fair and in our great works of art. It's in Tom Robbins' prose, the Wachowski's films and Michael Jackson's moves. Its curvaceous sensuality is in every Corvette and summer dress. Its grief attends all funerals. Its justifiable rage is locked up in our prisons. It calls you into a three-way with your senses and what you desire. The soul is what "gets the *Led* out" and has you turn your seatbelt into a bass guitar and dashboard into a piano.

It is also in the ordinary moments. It thrives in the divine particularities of mundane human life, when your awareness falls upon the play of children, the seam of a well-made garment, a lover preparing breakfast and the juices of ripe fruit.

However, if it's not explicitly acknowledged and courted, it remains in the shadows, a silent witness and accomplice to shadow justice, the unwholesome expressions of our deepest wounds. As Jesus said in the Gospel of Thomas, "If you bring forth what is within you, what you have will save you. If you do not have that within you, what you do not have within you will kill you." (Miller, 1992, p. 316) When soul is ignored, shadow reigns and rages. It's still there, quietly watching every unkind word, genocide, addiction, murder, rape, domestic dispute and suicide. It lays dormant during the play of violence and horror in our art, TV, films, music and video games. Because of soul's enormous power for good and the destruction wrought from our estrangement from soul, we cannot ignore this core human capacity. We must invite soul into our homes, set a place for soul at our tables, welcome soul into our relationships, dance with and court our souls, be taught and lead by soul.

When we ensoul our lives, we allow soul's attachments to move us into the flow of our passions, the rapture of our carnal desires and through the contours of our emotional landscape. And in doing so, we move more creatively and purposefully in our careers and more curiously throughout the world.

However, your soul also seeks to create a world where you are not alone in living soulfully, but a world where everyone gets the opportunity to know and love themselves, where each child gets to explore their soul and make their highest contribution. So, how do we ensoul the world?

> It's not enough to have that sense of purpose yourself. You also have to create a sense of purpose for others... by redefining equality so that everyone has the freedom to pursue their purpose and by building community all across the world.
> -Mark Zuckerberg (Zuckerberg, 2017)

Let's look at our most basic cultural units and explore the possibilities for inviting soul into our lives. How would we couple? What sorts of families would we create? How would we parent? What kinds of communities should we build?

To answer these questions, let's first start with what culture is. Per Merriam-Webster's Dictionary, culture is:

1. *the integrated pattern of human knowledge, belief, and behavior that depends upon the capacity for learning and transmitting knowledge to succeeding generations*
2. *the customary beliefs, social norms, and material traits of a racial, religious, or social group; also, the characteristic features of everyday existence (as diversions or a way of life) shared by people in a place or time*
3. *the set of shared attitudes, values, goals, and practices that characterizes an institution or organization*
4. *the set of values, conventions, or social practices associated with a particular field, activity, or societal characteristic* (Merriam-Webster.com, 7/17/2017)

Culture is inescapable - like water is to the fish. We cannot see it with our eyes or measure it in a lab. But, we can study it, observe it and enjoy it. However, this quantification limitation is not grounds for dismissal, as culture provides much of the substance and background for everything we know about reality. It informs our worldview and our expectations and helps determine our actions and the meaning we make from those actions. Culture is not an afterthought, something that dances upon the hard facts of existence, something that we engage in once we finish our day as economic and political actors.

Increasingly, culture is the force driving these hard facts. Culture is an evolutionary advance in the Cosmos. As life evolved from non-life, culture evolved from non-culture, and as we explored in the "Purpose of Humanity", culture is not only the driving force of our experience as humans, but also the evolution of the Cosmos. As such, as Shambala Leaders, we must be responsible for the consequences of what can be regarded as a largely soulless culture. We must acknowledge the role that our culture has played in putting demagogues in power, millions of our brothers and sisters in poverty, debt, prison and early graves, and millions of our Earth's species out of business. We must acknowledge the role that our media plays in distracting us and wasting millions of hours of human potential every day.

Sure, there are headline grabbing economic, political and military leaders involved, as well as political ideologies (market royalism, lobbying) and economic drivers (resource imperialism) of these epidemics, but there are also cultural forces (cultural homogenization/hegemony, materialism, hyper-mediation, sexism, sexual oppression, racism, homophobia, poor communication, family dysfunction, poverty consciousness, addiction, soulless religions, soul-denying and mind-numbing education systems) that do not get enough attention. Before we take on ensouling our culture, we need to take our temperature, to see what we have to work with and acknowledge the cultural hell we have created.

America's Mass Culture Crisis

American culture is in the best and worst of times. On one hand our artists give us novel and breathtaking works of art, Burning Man, jazz, blues, bluegrass, rock and roll, documentaries, films and books. On the other hand, mass media culture makes a mockery of the intention providing us with surface-level amusements and trinkets - with reality TV, pop music, spectator sports, advertising and our political circus. The net result is the country and world we have, both the beautiful and tragic.

As we explored in the "Introduction" and "Chapter 17: Humanity's Midlife Crisis", the American culture and economy have tag-teamed to create a nation of good people who work tirelessly for five decades, playing an unwinnable game under largely false pretenses and enjoying a few amusements along the way. Most of us hope that somehow, through hard work and luck, one day our ship will come in, or that our children will have a better life. However, all we really do is hope.

While we hope for our children's future, collectively, we underfund public K-12 education (with the arts and humanities - the study, appreciation and creation of art, soul, music and culture - being the first to get cut) and pave over and pollute soul's favorite playground, Mother Nature. We have allowed college education to become so expensive that the bulk of Americans cannot afford it. For those who can afford it or are able to access student loans, the financial, social and parental pressures are such that most students waste the opportunity to explore their soul's calling and follow their genuine interests. All too often, they end up breaking under the pressure to get a job in a high-paying field, mistaking college for a trade school, and declaring a STEM major.

Further, we do not have cultural rites of passage that ensure our biologically mature adults also become soul-initiated (psychologically whole, culturally blessed and purpose-driven) adults, ones in possession of the self-knowledge required to choose on behalf of one's own purpose, interests, community and future. This is not by accident.

This is war. This is a culture war being waged by economic and political interests against our nation's youth, against soul itself, against humanity's soul, systematically depriving our youth of the education, nature, culture and artistic experiences required to pursue their interests, develop their soul's purpose, achieve actual adulthood and make their highest contribution. This war has made it impossible for our young people to become soulful and creative participants in the economy, civic affairs and culture. This war makes it possible to sell people things and experiences they do not need and vote for politicians who cannot effectively lead and serve the betterment of the realm.

As a result of many American generations having been encultured in this fashion, repeating this soulless cycle, the average American identity is not sourced in soul and our collective identity is not sourced in the collective American soul. Rather, we are a patchwork of disparate cultures trapped in narrow identities, along historical divides (gender, race, economics, sexuality, religion, age, etc.). News anchors, talk show hosts and politicians seize the opportunity to gain ratings and votes by deepening this rift, by turning us against each other, by dog-whistling us (using economic or moral rhetoric to incite anti-Semitic, generational, homophobia, Islamaphobia, class, racist and sexist beliefs). The result is that we find ourselves culturally inoculated, safe and unconfronted in predictable and politically inert culture pockets of hatred and fear.

Our fragmented culture is united only by a manufactured dream of a consumer suburban utopia, fueled by a false sense of power and free will (e.g., voting, consumer behavior, career and mate selection). What is really happening is that political, religious and commercial institutions maintain power, profit and cultural relevance by keeping Americans fearful, isolated, insecure, hate-filled, victimized, undereducated, uninitiated, indebted and soul inert, selling us false identities, distraction and limiting beliefs in the form of cheap credit, consumer goods, the promise of an afterlife, luxury experiences, religious, racial, economic and political ideologies and sports allegiances. Even the well-educated among us are not truly free, susceptible to merely different expressions of the same tactics, as I witnessed during my time immersed in the white collar urban culture of America's big cities: New York, Los Angeles, Chicago and San Francisco.

The result is, as much as it pains me to say this, as much as I love America and our numerous cultural achievements, our mass media culture has made us a nation comprised of soul-starved biological adults, drunk on narratives spun by politicians, religions and commercial advertising. Our culture encourages us to waste our nearly unlimited potential trying to win other people's acceptance, esteem and success games.

Broadly, the bulk of the cultural experience of America's rich is centered around overwork, consumerism, pharmaceuticals, restaurants, entertainment, gossip and political theater - the 'white fog' culture - while the bulk of the 'red fog' culture of America's poor is centered on living paycheck to paycheck, providing these raw materials, consumer goods and luxury services at subsistence wages, and enjoying a less expensive portfolio of distractions and vices. While these groups are captivated by roughly the same soulless ideologies (American Dream, American exceptionalism, consumerism and individualism) their cultures are markedly different and rarely co-mingle.

It is therefore time we accept that, just as our political and economic systems must rapidly and soulfully evolve, so must our culture delivery systems. We must address culture in our efforts to meaningfully instantiate a planet on purpose.

Culturecraft

Culture can be explicitly shaped. It doesn't just arise when two or more people are together, although naturally this does happen, but it can be intentionally cultivated to achieve particular experiences and behaviors through ritual (religions, rites of passage), within institutions (education, organizations) or media experiences (advertising, TV, social media). So, the question is, how do we ensoul culture in such a way that it supports each of us to make our highest contribution and to soulfully and creatively enjoy the brief experience of being alive, such that we improve matters, inclusive of all social and environmental impacts, for future generations and the Earth's diverse ecology?

To answer this question, let us assume that we are successful at the individual level, that we have succeeded in distributing purpose discovery education to every human being on the planet, and that every person's identity is sourced internally, in soul. Let us further assume that this purpose upgrade moves people to act, to embody our purposes and live soulfully in every moment of every day. We will find ourselves caught in a bind. Although we are awakened and on fire with purpose internally, we don't yet have well-understood models for purposeful relationships, families, communities. We don't have a model for a culture that celebrates souls. We have to create it.

What culture would support us living our purpose all the time? As culture is a "betweenness" that exists between two or more parties, let's look at the ways soulful culture can occur.

A Relationship on Purpose

A purposeful relationship shows up when a romantic connection is acknowledged between two people such that a distinct entity ("the relationship") appears – one that is greater than the sum of its parts, one that also is a vehicle for the full purposeful self-expression of each part. If this between-ness exists in the Cosmos, it must also serve the purposes of the Cosmos. Thus, from the perspective of Cosmic purpose, the purpose of a two-person relationship is threefold:

1. to express something greater, a relationship purpose – more wholeness (unity), elegance (syntropy), and understanding/curiosity (uncertainty) – than could otherwise be expressed in the absence of the relationship,
2. to soulfully inhabit space together, to share the richness of life, to muse, marvel and luxuriate in the joys of partnership, the circle of life and the mysteries of the Cosmos, and
3. to allow for a more purposeful expression of each part (albeit not without some initial sacrifice) than could otherwise be expressed or realized.

For example, I become more purposeful and whole as an individual human when I am able to express myself physically – through hugs, touching, kissing, sex – and emotionally through sharing my experience and having my lover's experience shared with and transformed through me. Similarly, when we court the Cosmos with sci-fi movies, or I express myself intellectually – when new ideas or questions exist in the between-ness, where my partner and I get to consider, create or evolve a notion together – I experience a deeper connection to my purpose, as well as to that of the relationship. Most mysteriously, it is in times of discord and conflict, when soul forces one or both of us to "give something up", to surrender an old way of being or unaligned belief, for the good of the relationship purpose, that we get access to the next evolution of our individual soul's purpose.

In this way, I become more whole, more "me" – *more purposeful* – when I am in the dance of life with another human being. When we are soulfully giving, receiving, healing and connecting with each other in ways only a partner can (unity), we create a more complex, interdependent and expressed life together (syntropy), and mutually explore each other's minds and shadows and the nature of the Cosmos (uncertainty). But, this isn't some roll of the dice, throwing caution to the wind, ignoring our own individual needs and just being in the grip of a codependent relationship. Rather, it is intentional, requiring a basic level of individual purpose awareness (e.g., completing the Global Purpose Expedition, doing a quest or working with a Guide), a desire to honor and cultivate the purpose of the other party, and also a desire to nurture the purpose of the relationship itself.

> We must be our own before we can be another's.
> -Ralph Waldo Emerson

However, most romantic partnerships are not initiated in this manner. Without both parties being soul-initiated, we have two oarsmen rowing erratically and occasionally in opposite directions. With neither the awareness of their own psychological constitution (the understanding of their wounding and internal filters that would be delivered by purpose discovery work), nor an awareness of their direction or worldview, we have deeply impaired perceptive capacities, and thus a very limited and likely contentious relationship. In this purpose-ignorant scenario, each partner is forced to do the impossible - reconcile the unexamined tangle of their desires and fears with the unexamined tangle of their partner's desires and fears.

It is for this reason that I highly recommend purpose discovery work *prior* to getting married and starting a family. If a person doesn't know their purpose, what is the purpose of getting married? Without a soul-initiation prior to marriage, what are we witnessing from the pews?

From a place of purpose awareness in both parties, a purposeful relationship involves an ongoing discussion, and sometimes a negotiation, between each party's purpose and the purpose of the relationship. In Part Two, we explored how to cultivate individual purpose; here we'll add three more tools to the toolbox for nurturing the soulful between-ness of a relationship and the twin goals of the relationship (its own purpose, and as a vehicle for the purpose of each party). These tools are:

- Purposeful Initiation
- Relationship Purpose Visioning
- Purposeful Communication

Purposeful Initiation

Once the initial exploratory phase of a relationship is complete (dating, sexual compatibility, vetting for long-term socioeconomic suitability), each party engages in the fish-or-cut-bait discussion. If they decide to keep fishing this typically means increasing their commitment to each other via exclusivity (deciding not to be with anyone else), cohabitation and/or marriage. This process of increasing commitment is typically done without the intention to purposefully initiate the relationship itself, without the intentional creation of a series of initiatory trials to deepen the long-term commitment. It is usually only embarked upon with a feeling of romantic love and a lens on sexual desire and conforming to the prevailing cultural narratives and achieving the associated socioeconomic markers of worth (enviable marriage, enviable wealth, enviable home, enviable children, enviable vacations).

Much as an individual purpose journey is an initiation, a romantic purpose journey also needs to be an initiation, where both parties commit to exploring (1) how the relationship will serve each one's individual life purpose, and (2) what exactly the purpose of the relationship is. To do this, emerging purposeful relationships need an engagement that is more than an opportunity to plan a party and deal with in-laws (although given the level of dysfunction in most families, these can be initiations themselves). What is needed is a series of rites and trials that reveal and consciously evolve the purpose of the relationship and illuminate the ways in which the relationship can best serve the purpose of each party.

For example, an engaged couple could craft a year of initiatory experiences leading up to their wedding that would be designed to reveal new contours of the relationship purpose question, unearth hidden wounds and triggers, and reveal new aspects of each other's character. Some examples might be a/an:

- 3-day backcountry camping trip
- Weekend babysitting two toddlers
- Tantric sex workshop
- Athletic endeavor, e.g., a triathlon/Tough Mudder/Spartan race
- Project compiling each other's family histories
- 10-day Master cleanse
- Art project
- Meditation retreat
- Weekend volunteering for the Special Olympics
- Weekend visiting an undesirable place to live
- Plant medicine ceremony, e.g., Ayahuasca, San Pedro, psychedelic mushrooms
- Personal development seminar, e.g., Landmark Forum.

The result of a series of initiatory experiences is a deeper understanding of each other's life purpose and a deeper awareness and compassion for each other's wounds. This strengthens the foundation of the relationship, instills confidence in the union's ability to endure extremes, and provides a rich trove of experience from which to divine the relationship's purpose.

Relationship Visioning

To be a powerful steward of the relationship, we first have to define the relationship, how it works, the future it is creating, as well as what the process is for evolving its vision. This usually requires having a structured, "relationship purpose" visioning session(s), initially guided by a trusted neutral party/trained facilitator to generate a co-creative relationship purpose (such as through a Catholic Pre-Cana or with a mentor, a pastor or a relationship coach). Following this initial visioning process, couples are encouraged to engage in quarterly visioning sessions to address the soul and health of the relationship, e.g., communication, sex, joy, pleasure, and the specific expressions of individual and relationship purpose (work, money, children, extended family, health issues, home economics, and responsibility sharing).

Purposeful Communication

Relationships thrive or perish because of the quality of their communication. Volumes have been written on conscious communication by masters in this field, such as David Richo's *How to Be an Adult in Relationships*, Marshall Rosenberg's *NonViolent Communication* and Gary Chapman's *The Five Love Languages*. I won't attempt to replicate or summarize their important work here, but will offer a synthetic position – five starting points to explore and expand purposeful communication in a relationship:

1. **A commitment to do physical, intellectual, creative, emotional, spiritual, and personal development work outside of the relationship**. When both parties commit to expanding their expression in life through personal, professional and spiritual development work, the result is that a new person keeps walking through the door, with new insights, new communication capacities and new awareness. There is a freshness, a sense of always having a new lover to embrace and seduce.

2. **Emotional authenticity**. Both parties welcome each other's wholeness, all the ways they are and are not, including the full spectrum of their emotional experience. They speak in "I statements", taking full ownership for their emotions (e.g., "I feel sad" vs. "you made me sad"), distinguishing facts from emotions, meaning and judgments. Both parties explore the source of their emotional triggers via personal work (#1 above) and make requests of the other to lessen the occurrence of these triggers.

3. **Entelechy stand**. Both parties commit to stand for each other's greatness, for their fullness, for making their highest contribution, and fully embodying their soul, aka their entelechy (a term from Aristotle, to indicate the fullness of form, e.g., the entelechy of the acorn is the oak tree, the entelechy of the violin is the Stradivarius). As such, they engage both with their partner's current experience of themselves, as well as their greatness, their entelechy. To do this, both parties agree to stand for each other's entelechy, to create a life together that works, using whatever best practices are available, and

248

to consistently expand the expression of the other's purpose with new experiments and structures.

4. **Other-Centered Generosity and Curiosity**. Both parties actively seek to surprise and please the other in the love language of their choice - touch, gifts, service, quality time, or praise, ref. *The Five Love Languages* (Chapman, 1995) - as well as to remain forever a stranger in the partnership, operating from a place of curiosity about the other, asking, "Who is my partner? What is her purpose calling her into? What new things can I notice about my partner and engage her in exploring?"

5. **Relationship Stewardship**. Both parties steward the relationship, by creating time for revisiting its purpose and expression, as well as the extent to which the relationship nurtures the life purposes of both parties. They assume full responsibility for their satisfaction in life, in the relationship, for their partner's satisfaction in the relationship and thus from a place of being 100% responsible, they also avoid making themselves, their partner or anyone else wrong.

With purposeful initiation, visioning and communication in place, the couple is empowered to soulfully evolve together, allowing each party a continued expansion in purpose, fulfillment, connection, impact and abundance.

Creating a Family on Purpose

Beyond romance and partnership, purpose also exists at the level of family and is either expressed as a family default purpose (enabling dysfunction, obedience, emulation and social esteem, e.g., "keeping up with the Joneses") or is authentically crafted and expressed. To achieve the latter, family purpose organically moves from the inside out, beginning with the purpose awareness of each parent, their intentionally crafted purposeful partnership, and shared communication protocols.

As common parenting wisdom dictates, children are parented more by what you do more than by what you say. If you love and care for yourself spiritually, physically and emotionally, craft a soulful life and purpose-driven livelihood, and treat others with kindness, you are more than halfway to having a family on purpose. As your child's primary proxy for human adulthood and maturity, and the standard by which the question of the meaning of all of life is viewed by the child, the manner in which you embody your purpose (and explicitly evolve it in their presence) creates the space and ability for them to do the same.

Although being a beacon of purpose, crafting a relationship purpose and shared communication protocols are at the core of a purposeful family, more is needed to achieve purpose at the level of family. The path to creating a family on purpose also requires the following:

1. **Organic priorities.** Give primacy, a slight preference to your own purpose and the purpose of the relationship above that of the purpose of the family or the desires of the children. Your purpose is primary and the strength of your partnership is the foundation of the family. Both are necessary to serve the purpose and well-being of your children.

2. **Soulful Parenting Orientation.** In America, we have two general approaches to parenting: obedience training (a Pavlovian approach that uses carrots and sticks to conform a child's behavior to a parent's will, ethics, peer pressure and idea of perfection) and entitlement training (a reactive approach to obedience training, that abdicates parenting responsibility, one that validates and caters to every want and whim of a child). Both of these leave a child powerless, the former subjugating the child's worth to that of the parent's approval, and the latter robbing the child of personal responsibility, aka "helicopter parenting", wherein the parents take on the impossible task of being responsible for the child always having a positive internal emotional state. There is another way offered by Bill Plotkin, "soul-centric parenting" (Plotkin, pp. 104-105, 2008) – that has as the primary parenting objective, the purpose revelation of the child. So, parents are forever in the inquiry, "Who is my child?" and as a result, they structure the family's rules of conduct, activities and chores based on what purpose seems to be emerging in each child.

3. **Purposeful Contribution.** Beyond priorities and parenting orientation, in order for a child to develop a listening for an expanded self, the child's activities must be reflected and framed within a larger context of contribution and meaning. This means enrolling children in the impact and accomplishment of the larger goal of chores, e.g., the chore of putting toys away is part of the whole family cleaning the house to enjoy it, or raking leaves as part of preparing for a birthday party. Creating a larger structure and narrative around household chores orients a child to the objective-subjective duality, that there is such a thing as meaning, that actions can have a purpose that is greater than the action itself or the near-term sacrifices required. This strengthens the meaning-making muscle, sets a precedent for the child to craft larger meaningful projects and empowering them to explore and play with their own purpose when they are ready.

4. **Acknowledgment.** Regardless of what a child does or how she performs, it is the role of the parent to reflect and mirror the child's experience, actions and impacts. How this is done makes all the difference. Saying "Good job," "Nice work," "Bad boy," or "Bad girl" tends to enforce an obedience orientation, whereas sharing the impact of action (e.g., "That made a big difference in how this room feels to me. How do you feel about that?" or "When I saw you hit your sister, I felt fear and sadness. What

occurred for you?") allows the child to make her own meaning about the outcomes, impacts and merits of her actions. As such, purposeful parenting and acknowledgment is more of a clearing for honest reflection than a standard for approval.

5. **The Languages of Soul.** Soul-centric parents create a rich fertile sandbox for the soulful expression of their children, by encouraging activities that nurture imagination, connection, dreams, fantasies, emotional honesty, touch, play and connection to nature. These are the languages of soul, and parents who encourage soul fluency in the home and beyond will give their children the greatest gift - soulful self-expression - and find their own lives enriched by these creative expressions of soul.

6. **Tribe.** As mentioned before, and as we will soon explore in greater detail, children are instructed by the example adults set, in their self-care, growth, emotional honesty, creativity and purposeful expression. As such, the child's closest friends and family need to be initiated as a tribe, a tribe that has its own purpose and culture and is committed to creating and evolving a shared parenting philosophy. Great care must be brought to initiating and cultivating this immediate circle. More on this below.

As you can likely imagine, "What is good for the goose is good for the gander," so these principles and practices can apply and scale (with tweaking, of course) to larger units of human cooperation: from family to community to company, nation, and species. Now let's take a look at the possibilities for soulful community.

Soulful Community

To imagine the possibility of soulful community, we must first acknowledge that humans are social, that we exist only in community. Throughout our entire 200,000-year history, community has played a vital role in economics, mental health, emotional well-being, self-expression, spiritual growth, self-awareness and education. Over the last 400 years, in the frenzy and fury of industrialization, globalization, scientific achievement and democratic revolution, we have collectively moved away from this fundamental truth of our existence, as we sent our men off to wars, factories and offices, our women first to remote suburbs and then to the same wars, factories and offices, our children to nannies, daycare and school, and our elders to different states, retirement homes and hospice centers.

We have attempted to become individuals in a vacuum. We have tried to function without a vibrant, multi-generational community, driving ourselves into a middle-aged isolation, cannonballing overwork, vice, consumerism and media. Seeing the limitations of this individual orientation, we took to buying back our community in pieces. We can now buy connection to a group in the form of religious ideologies, fandom over sports, filmed dramas, reality TV and social media. We buy our esteem in the form of selfies and luxury brands, and our self-expression in the form of gossip and our opinions on current affairs, celebrities, reality TV and our consumer choices. We have traded actual community for a hodgepodge of half-measures.

Thankfully, we have also begun to question this laborious and indirect arrangement. Over the last 100 years, numerous innovators began experimenting with alternative approaches to stitch us back together. We developed service clubs (Rotary, Lions, etc.), church groups, transformational modalities/communities (Alcoholics Anonymous, large group awareness trainings), economic and social communities (professional organizations, communes, barter networks and college alumni clubs) and intentional communities. But, few if any of these acknowledges, initiates and cultivates the uniqueness of each individual's soul purpose, and thus, without individual soul awareness, the individuals in these communities cannot generate an authentic collective purpose. Since none of these offers a definition of wholeness (soul + ego), nor nurtures soul initiation, they are ultimately unsuccessful in holistically stitching a purposeful human back together with herself, or her tribe. Recently, a pioneer in cultural innovation, Bill Kauth, a co-founder of the ManKind Project, and his wife Zoe Alowan, launched a modern tribal model to express a more purposeful and cohesive culture, without the complications of communal living and economic cooperation in their book, *We Need Each Other* (Kauth, Alowan, 2011).

Bill has learned many lessons in purposeful cultural transformation as co-founder of the ManKind Project (along with Ron Hering and Rich Tosi). MKP shepherded a new purposeful and wildly successful subculture devoted to cultivating and celebrating the authentic masculine. MKP counts numerous cultural pioneers as members, e.g., Terry Patten, Frederic Laloux, Ashanti Branch, Chris Martenson and Charles Eisenstein. Since 1984, the ManKind Project has initiated over 60,000 men around the world to step fully into their wholeness as men, husbands, fathers, community leaders, public servants and purpose-driven entrepreneurs. Through their flagship training, the New Warrior Training Adventure, regular men's group meetings and other advanced MKP trainings in leadership, ritual and process facilitation, men step fully into themselves as emotionally articulate, self-aware, and loving warriors on a mission. Leveraging his experience and success with MKP, Bill and Zoe launched a purposeful community model, "The Tribe".

They discovered the need for "The Tribe" while traveling the country giving talks and workshops on the work of Chris Martenson's *Crash Course*, extolling the dangers of our current global, industrial, environmental extraction, consumerist "purpose-substitute" model. After folks came into a deeper awareness of the crisis humanity is in, they immediately wanted to connect with each other to learn more, support each other in their grief and start crafting more soulful, sustainable and workable solutions for economics and community. As a result of this experience and the collective longing for purposeful culture, Bill and Zoe spent the next seven years researching, designing, developing and testing a model for soulful human culture. In applying their model with their own tribe, Bill and Zoe are pioneering a new way for humans to soulfully connect and express themselves.

They discovered these five, critical success factors of soulful community:

1. **Tribe Purpose.** Members co-create the purpose of the tribe, and determine where it sits on the bonding vs. bridging spectrum. Bonding is an internal purpose to nurture the fullest expression (purpose, connection, creativity, health, fun, right livelihood, etc.) of each member. Bridging is an external purpose wherein a tribe is designed to make an impact in the broader community and/or the human/ecological condition.

2. **Place & Commitment.** Members must be willing to stay put geographically, and publicly express their commitment to the tribe, as well as attend each weekly gathering. This commitment can range from a few years all the way to a lifelong commitment.

3. **Safety & Wholeness.** Members commit to agreed communications protocols that honor the whole person, their emotions, judgments, shadows, purpose, desires and evolution.

4. **Transformation.** Members commit to each other's growth and evolution, holding space and facilitating rites of passage, shadow work/healing through group processes, one-on-one peer mentoring and elder councils.

5. **Evolutionary Transparency.** Members commit to publicly acknowledge the status of all sexual relationships, and give space for honoring the beginning, middle and end of relationships.

The result of this model of purposeful community is loving connection. Bill and Zoe report that their tribe has become a chosen family, one that does not replace their family of origin or other networks and communities, but one where they feel the love and wholeness of a highly functioning family. They smile and hug a lot. They have fun together. They support each other in times of need and transition, as well as in executing numerous community projects.

Collectively, with purpose in their form and function, these tangible units of cooperation make purpose more likely as a default cultural value, and create the fertile ground for purpose to arise in individuals, couples and families.

We have other tools at our disposal to affect a purposeful culture, such as our education system, religious institutions, learning and development organizations (human resources) in companies and social media networks. Why can't awareness of soul/purpose exist everywhere? Clearly there is a hunger for purpose, with 97% of Americans valuing it (Rainey, 2014), and huge opportunity, as only 30% of Americans are purposefully engaged at work (Gallup, 2014).

Why can't religious education take on purpose work (ego deconstruction/

soul discovery) as well? Why can't our elementary schools add soul fluency as an educational outcome? Why can't our high school humanities curriculums nurture the quest for place, soul and calling? The themes are all there. We have the hero's journey told in a thousand ways throughout religion and literature.

If your career and purpose moves you into cultural leadership as a team leader, teacher, clergy member, HR executive or guidance counselor, consider that the purpose movement and the future of the species rests in your hands. Please consider deepening your training with one of the organizations mentioned in "Appendix C: Purpose Transformation Resources".

Now that you have a baseline understanding of what can be possible in our culture, politics and economy if we took on ensouling each corner of life, let us formally and succinctly declare what this Global Purpose Movement is, and what it is that we stand for. Let us plant a flag in our future for what a planet on purpose could be.

CHAPTER 22

The Declaration of Soul

Every generation has its defining works… Every generation expands its definition of equality. Previous generations fought for the vote and civil rights… It's time for our generation to define a new social contract. We should have a society that measures progress… by how many have a role we find meaningful… When more people can turn their dreams into something great, we are all better for it… Every generation expands the circle of people we consider one of us.

-Mark Zuckerberg (Zuckerberg, 2017)

Now that we've explored a path to bring forth a planet on purpose and descend the possibility of purpose into our markets, governments, towns and culture, it is now upon us to create it. Our task is to declare what we stand for and get to work. To do this we need to distill the essence of what humanity on purpose is, so that anyone, anywhere, can hear it. The time is now to let forth our cry for the future.

I offer the Declaration of Soul as a means to trumpet the new guard, to acknowledge that connecting to your soul's purpose is a best practice for life. It is at once personal, honoring each soul's creative potential, and universal, holding purpose as a right and possibility that unifies our species, binding us together as Earth citizens and empowering us to create and implement best practices for human life and ecological biodiversity throughout our home, Planet Earth.

The Declaration of Soul

Preamble

Igniting the soul purpose of each human is the cresting wave of human, terrestrial and Cosmic evolution. This ignition is a rising tide, an amplification of our sciences and faiths, our technologies and arts and our markets and watersheds. This tide now demands that we recognize its sovereignty and start paddling with it and not against it. This tide is our *destiny*, allowing us a deeply personal and spiritual *creativity*, the capacity to use all of our *knowledge* and ways of knowing, reaching ever-greater expressions of *love* and claiming our role as the emerging edge of Cosmic *evolution*.

Destiny. Our true human purpose is to awaken each human to the purpose of his or her soul, to bind humanity together, to illuminate our common origin, to steward the Earth's interdependent ecology, to awaken as the central nervous system of the Cosmos and co-create the future beyond the limits of our imagination.

Creativity. Our true human purpose is to empower every human's soulful creativity in service of the eternal Cosmic principles of unity (goodness), syntropy (beauty) and uncertainty (truth).

Knowledge. Our true human purpose is to know and love every important distinction, narrative, principle, ethos and way of knowing in the Cosmos, to know and honor each soul's purpose and that of every unit of cooperation, to teach not politics or morals, but to explore and awaken the moral sovereignty of each soul.

Love. Our true human purpose recognizes no boundary to our love and compassion, it holds no real North, no South, no East, no West, but knows every human as a human soul, awakening, contributing and celebrating through their soul's purpose.

Evolution. Our true human purpose is that we stand as, of, by and for the Cosmos to create more goodness, truth and beauty; to recognize evolutionary merit wherever found; to have no narrower limits within which to work together, for the elevation of humanity and evolution, than the outlines of the Cosmos.

This Time Is No Different

Periodically, human beings demand radical change, to update the human experience with a new vision or a new best practice for life. These demands are the natural result of the predictable, periodic failures of human systems for meeting core human needs (water, food, safety, shelter, connection, self-expression, and meaning).

Indeed, our history is rich with these demands, and often bloody fights, to increase the workability of human society, to expand individual and collective realization of purpose, prosperity and equality. We have beat this drum furiously during our history, demanding our leaders and institutions adopt best practices (in parentheses below) during these cultural and political revolutions:

- The Enlightenment (cognitive self-determination)
- The Protestant Reformation (decentralizing and personifying spirituality)
- Revolutions for Representative Democracy (political participation)
- The Labor Movement (justice)
- The Suffrage Movement (equality)

- The Civil Rights Movement (equality)
- The Environmental Movement (ecological justice)
- The Sexuality Rights Movement (equality)

In each of these movements, we created art, books, plays and music. We started companies and organizations. We joined in strikes, petitions, marches, and boycotts to demand purposeful reform, in order to implement best practices in human flourishing. Today, as before, we stand for our right to live and soulfully prosper.

We sit not still in a moment in time, but upon the river of evolutionary progress, ferried along by the soulful contribution of ordinary citizens who have risked everything to express their soul's purpose and vision to improve the human condition. The true authors of this Declaration are thus counted in the thousands, if not millions, and rest upon the irreducible voices of people like Harvey Milk, Harriet Tubman, Eugene Debs, Gloria Steinem, Malcolm X, The 13 Grandmothers, Martin Luther King, Jr., Elizabeth Cady Stanton, Cesar Chavez and Angela Davis.

It is now incumbent upon each and every one of us to dip our quills for the next chapter, to seize our soul's power and join together in favor of more purposeful ways of expressing ourselves, serving each other and cooperating. In hearing this call, we each have the power to change the course of human history.

This Time It Is Different

We stand for awakening soul purpose now. We demand that our institutions find purposes and start behaving accordingly, while implementing fair and sustainable practices for human flourishing, ecological resilience and Cosmic evolution. We find ourselves squarely inside a turning point, a moment in time that not only holds the possibility of a better life for all beings, but one that is necessary to ensure any chance of survival for our species. It is time for this movement. The movement of the 21st century is an ignition of soul purpose at every level of human endeavor. It is supported by research from our species' leading institutions, correlating purpose with:

- a vigorous, healthy and long life
- a strong mind
- a healthy heart
- more profitable and rewarding careers
- more fulfilling and dynamic relationships
- a culture of learning and achievement
- a more kind, tolerant and diverse society
- a more sustainable economy.

As such, we demand that every organization on Earth discover and articulate its purpose. We define organizational purpose as an original statement that:

- fosters and deepens self-awareness, self-acceptance and self-love
- is high-definition, originating in the souls of its founders and executives, expressed as a statement of a higher purpose, one that speaks of vision, virtues, core, story, mission, the call, powers, flow, craft and worldview
- propels us collectively into action towards a vision for the world which:
  o is context-aware - based on a philosophically-broad, scientifically-accurate and intellectually-defensible understanding of the state of human, ecological and Cosmic affairs, and
  o creates and sustains a higher level of integrity and a greater collective realization of human potential and ecological resilience than our present state.

Never before in human history has a species-wide purpose awakening been more possible or more needed, as we witness the collapse of our political, economic and ecological systems due to the lack of soulful leadership.

Democracy Collapse

Many of our representative democracies, such as that of the United States, are more rightly viewed as oligarchies of ultra-wealthy and corporate interests, and democracies in name alone.

Ecology Collapse

In failing to find, lead with, and act upon our purpose, our public and private institutions have unwittingly caused the decimation of 58% of the world's wildlife in the last forty years (WWF, 2016), warmed and acidified the oceans and unmistakably diminished our planet's biological diversity and resilience.

Capitalism Collapse

Our current economic system is marked by rampant inflation, unemployment and income inequality. We have documented the often oppressive, racist and sexist effects of unchecked purposeless economic "growth" on the human condition.

Culture Collapse

The majority of us are disconnected from our soul's purpose, jumping from one purposeless job to a purpose substitute to another purposeless job to another purpose substitute. 87% of us are disengaged at work (Gallup, 2014); we are disconnected from our soul's purpose or are afforded no economic opportunity to express it. Our parents are collectively working and commuting 100 hours a week, when 45 hours once sufficed. The result is that our children are more often raised by screens, market morality and peer pressure. We have become a mass culture of media and advertising, serving ends determined by the purpose-ignorant, while paying only lip service to our true human needs for belonging, esteem and self-actualization (purpose).

The result of our democracy, ecology, capitalism and culture, is that as a species we have sacrificed self-awareness; wisdom; creative, joyful and high-impact careers; a sustainable and abundant economy; and a just, tolerant and peaceful society for an unfulfilled consumer utopia. This has created a sharp decrease in the well-being for the many and a sharp increase in financial wealth for the few. Geopolitically, this dynamic is marked by economic, political, cultural and military forces from the industrialized world seizing the resources and oppressing the labor of the unindustrialized world. In the process, we have done more than destroy natural habitats and sustainable economies, but have markedly diminished humanity's great and diverse linguistic, artistic, spiritual and cultural wealth.

The Time is Now

It is clear that, for any of these reasons, we can no longer leave the survival and full realization of human potential to our soul-starved leadership. For all of these reasons, it is time to light the fires. It is time to ignite a soulful revolution. We can no longer afford to ignore the creative and leadership potential of any human soul. The world aches for soul and calls for a massive movement of soulful leadership. We can no longer sit back and wait for someone else to take care of saving the world.

With access to affordable purpose discovery courses and worldview-expanding communications tools like Wikipedia and Twitter, we no longer have an excuse for remaining disconnected from our soul's purpose, for being disempowered or ignorant of our power to influence human affairs and evolutionary emergence. We are powerful creators with the inherent capacity, strength and tools to rapidly make necessary changes that are required for our survival and thriving.

As we do so, it is incumbent upon us to remain aware and inclusive of those who do not share our privileges, whose experience of life is a daily battle against poverty, hunger, violence, and disease – struggles caused and exacerbated by systems and products created by our soul-starved institutions. If we fail to consider, aid and empower them, we will fail to live our individual purpose and to realize the collective expression of soul: fulfilled self-expression, empowerment, economic freedom, and sustainability for all. It is imperative that we stand for and empower each and every one of us to awaken our soul's purpose, engage our craft and make our highest contribution. This is no longer a luxury afforded the favored few. It is now an existential necessity for us all.

The difference between what is possible in life -

1. the individual benefits of modern nutrition, education and healthcare,
2. the individual benefits of purpose awakening (long life, abundant careers and fulfilling relationships), and
3. the collective benefits of purpose awakening (sustainable economy, tolerance, education, creative self-expression, civic engagement, lower healthcare costs, higher participation in democracy) -

and what has been actualized, has never been greater.

Without a true purpose, our institutions, markets and industries do more than just enforce this schism. Collectively, they effectuate a suicidal purpose on behalf of – but without the consent of – the human species. This is what makes this movement different from movements past. We are fighting not merely for a better life, for justice, prosperity, peace, and equality, as we have continually done during the course of our bloody and noble history. We are fighting for the right for every human to exist at all.

We Have the Technology, We Can Rebuild

The last 200 years of scientific advances have illuminated a clear path forward, one marked by purpose-driven city-states and sustainable enterprises, a culture of tolerance, a de-moneyed democracy, and a policy framework that invests in the commons: education (student-driven, liberal arts, system-centric, purpose discovery), conservation, universal healthcare, clean water, sustainable food, renewable energy, mass transit, walkable/bikeable communities, incentives for small businesses, and the exploration of the unknowns (mind, sea and space).

Compassionate Revocation of Purposeless Power

We recognize that all power, rather than being endemic or immutable, is granted. And so, we compassionately revoke the authority of any leader or organization that impedes the adoption of scientifically-vetted best practices for soulful evolution.

We compassionately revoke the sovereignty of government administrations without a higher purpose. We compassionately resist and impede the politics and policies of purposeless leaders. We stand firm for the purposeful evolution of every country, organization, institution and group of people.

Purposeful Cooperation

Collectively, we now choose, for the benefit of all life on this planet, to create and reform institutions that:

- educate and support each and every human to live their soul's purpose in the marketplace, divesting themselves of unaligned workplaces, politicians, investments and consumer experiences, and
- develop, guard, expand, and promote sustainable, just, peaceful and purposeful political and economic systems.

Further, we stand for the purposeful renewal of human political cooperation. This begins with implementing a political economy based on our evolving understanding of the best practices for life on Earth and a rights framework that supports these best practices, such as:

- Biological rights:
  - State-guaranteed free and clean air, water and soil
  - Universal healthcare
- Community and Ecological rights:
  - Sustainable, carbon-neutral and regenerative urban land and resource use policies
  - Conservation and reclamation of poorly used land to meet community and biodiversity goals, e.g., well-designed walkable and bikeable metro areas, biodynamic gardens, wilderness restoration
- Psychological rights:
  - Fully state-funded K-college education in the liberal arts, mindfulness, art, music and purpose-discovery
  - The right to assert domain over one's consciousness through the abolition of advertising for products and services in public spaces and on public airwaves
  - The right to alter and expand one's consciousness through the legalization of plant medicines and other celebratory and regenerative psychoactive substances
- Civil rights and responsibilities:
  - Equal treatment under the law, regardless of race, gender, sexuality, creed, ability, age, culture, religion (in law and practice)
  - Privacy and ownership of identity, likeness and personal information

- o Associate Degree in Purpose-Driven Citizenship, Leadership and Enterprise - a purpose discovery journey that provides each human with a unique sense of place and mission, a unifying experience of service in and for our global community, offering individuals practical, psychological, emotional and entrepreneurial learning opportunities, and serving as a modern-day rite-of-passage, or initiation into a purpose-aware and soulful adulthood and purpose-driven economic and civic participation
- Diplomacy:
  - o Abolition of military action, driven by economic, cultural, religious or racial hegemony
  - o A UN peacekeeping force recruited from purpose-awakened, emotionally mature adults whose life purpose includes resolving conflict and maintaining peaceful resolutions that respect all living beings and the planet
- Electoral and legislative governance:
  - o Implementing the most effective practices for governance, e.g., social democracy
  - o State-sponsored elections and campaign finance, ensuring one person equals one vote
  - o An electoral and legislative system devoid of for-profit lobbying, allowing for greater diversity of values, thoughts and beliefs in government
- Urban planning:
  - o City-state orientation, via 20-200-mile zone of economic and political autonomy, such that all households can support themselves on less than 40 hours of work per week, leaving ample time for parenting, civic participation and leisure.

While standing for and working towards this broader vision, we can act today in our homes, careers and communities. As individuals we start now.

Personal Oath of Purpose

From this moment forward, I_____, take this 10-point personal oath to realize the best possible life for myself and everything I care about. I pledge to:

1. deepen my connection to my soul's purpose via proven purpose discovery technologies (e.g., working with a trained Guide, engaging with purpose

discovery programs, and sacred ceremonies such as vision fasts, plant medicines, and contemplation in nature)

2. create an ensouled, sustainable, creative, and generative career that supports me living my purpose every moment of each day

3. support only purpose-driven enterprises

4. participate in purposeful and efficient economic practices, such as purpose-driven enterprises, demurrage currencies and time banks, to reward and optimize the purpose-driven human contributions offered by our community

5. embrace resource-efficient energy and technologies, such as bicycles, mass-transit, LEDs, solar and wind energy

6. embrace sustainable, net-benefit leisure activities such as hiking, yoga, public art works, film, reading, song, dance, travel, gardening, art or time with friends in nature

7. support soulful, innovative and mindful uses of economic surpluses (e.g., art, culture, sustainable mass transit systems, ecological restoration, space/sea/mind exploration)

8. educate myself in the fields of psychology, history, philosophy, mythology, ecology, economics (suggested scholars in "Appendix C: Purpose Transformation Resources") and engage with others to expand our shared understanding of the state of human and ecological affairs and the nature of Cosmic evolution,

9. develop a daily ritual that roots each day in living soulfully (e.g., yoga, meditation, intentions, prayer, vision board)

10. become a beacon of purpose, standing for the purpose discovery of every human, sharing my soul's purpose with my loved ones, communities and networks of influence, for the mutual benefit of every living being on Planet Earth, the survival of the human species and the continued evolution of the Cosmos.

Together we are one family, one species of, by and for each other, on purpose and in service.

CONCLUSION

We are caught in an inescapable network of mutuality, tied in a
single garment of destiny.

-Martin Luther King Jr.

As we complete this adventure, you and I connect now as Shambhala Leaders of all
that is, was and will be, as Earth stewards and as lovers of an existence to which we
owe everything and on behalf of which we are asked to lead. You and I and our 7.5
billion brothers and sisters are linked arm in arm, touched by the beauty within our
souls. We are now challenged and inspired by the possibility to remake humanity
with an efficacy and purposeful velocity heretofore unseen in our history.

However, this is not a purpose "old boys club." We are not linked arm-in-arm
as the chosen purpose people. Next to you is not only Joanna Macy, but also Kanye
West and Donald Trump. Next to me is not only Bill Plotkin, but also Ann Coulter
and Paris Hilton. Our path is not an escape, not a glorious rise to the afterlife, but
rather a glorious descent into our humanity, into every community and marketplace,
into the listening and values-center of every human on Earth. Our path must make
a difference for everyone we touch.

As Shambhala Leaders, our soul's purpose embraces humanity as it is. We
compassionately explore, understand and love it. While your worldview must be
broad and ever-broadening, taking ever-larger swathes of the Cosmos into your
purview and identity, your mission is acute. You are put here to accomplish a specific
thing, and then another, and another, and so on. Yet, your soul's purpose isn't
something you do *some* of the time. While you will likely work steadfastly upon
your craft and vision, of equal importance is *who you are being*. Who you are being
as you achieve and succeed is what others will remember. They will remember if you
ravaged your body with vice and overwork. They will remember the kindnesses you
extended or withheld. They will remember the way you made them feel.

As Nelson Mandela discovered inside his prison cell on Robben Island, he
could achieve total victory by generating his soul's purpose at the level of being
and fiercely loving his guards, fellow inmates and the suffering he knew they must
be experiencing. He was not doing time, he was leading. He knew there were no
throwaway moments. There are only purpose moments.

As a result of your hard-won efforts, you have won the purpose *discovery* game, and now every subsequent moment is a chance to win the purpose *embodiment* and *radiance* game. Play it all out. Others are watching. You are the standard bearer of the possibility of purpose. Let others step into their greatness through your light, the embodiment of your purpose. Let your light spare no corner of your day, just as Mandela's unremitting light transformed everyone in his proximity. Let your stand boldly radiate, as President Mikhail Gorbachev said to President Ronald Reagan as they ended the Cold War: *"I am here to deprive you of an enemy."*

Of course, this doesn't mean neglecting your own emotional truth, or your need for rest, leisure and repose. Your soul's purpose can be won again and again in the non-doing of meditation or in enjoying each broad vista awarded to you on a hike. Each of these moments is also a victory for the soul. Each moment of your silliness, each time you channel your inner-Robin Williams and play with reality full out, soul wins. Every time you savor the sweetness of life in a loved one's arms, a delicious meal or explore your body or the richness of the world through sex, travel, prayer, language, exercise, humor and art, soul wins.

Yet, as we have explored, there is a broader more active imperative within you that also permeates your experience. As the character Bud Fox in the movie *Wall Street* remarked, "Life comes down to a few moments. This is one of them." What you do now is crucial. Who you are for other people is crucial. You have had an experience, an awakening, placing you in control of your own life, and now, perhaps for the first time, placing full responsibility for the world as it is in your hands. While you are not to blame for man's inhumanity to man in the past, you are responsible for it now and in the future. As a Shambhala Leader, you are fully responsible for the ecological, economic and political predicament in which we find ourselves.

You are a Shambhala Leader of the human species. Now aware of your huge responsibility for all that is, was and will be, and on behalf of the whole Cosmos, I invite you to stand in the middle of it, claim it and lead to make the most of your remaining decades. Let the Cosmos tremble and shake through your courage, leadership and power! And, know that you are not alone, nor can you win alone.

As such, you must be an active, nay evangelical, stand for the soulful awakening of others. You must make others uncomfortable. What they think of you is no longer as important as them having someone in their life that stands for their greatness, the fullness of their soul in the world. If others do not find their purpose and transform their lives and our planet with it, your soul's purpose is incomplete. If others do not awaken, it is not only sad for them, but also sad for us, because without them we will not have the power to remake our planet purposefully and we will not survive the ravages of our soul-starved political economy and culture. A planet on purpose will remain only a dream, and humanity's tenure as Earth steward will end before it reaches its zenith.

As you now know, your soul's purpose not only is the size of the entire Cosmos, but it is actually called forth from the Cosmos. By being 100% responsible for everything, by embracing your Shambhala Leadership inside the grandeur and gravity of your *Cosmosapien* identity, you are also granted an unprecedented level of power, joy, freedom, and fulfillment. And, you cannot have one without the other.

Of course, it is your choice to own this new way of being, this identity, to lead with it and share it with others. It is also your choice to refuse this invitation and shrink from this freedom and responsibility. But, you do not get to choose a smaller identity. Your *Cosmosapien* identity is now a splinter in your mind that you cannot remove. Try as you might to dull or numb this awareness, you will never succeed at extricating yourself from the interconnected web of life and the whole Cosmos that made you. *You* are the whole Cosmos itself, and since you cannot escape from that truth, you might as well buckle up, answer the call of your soul and enjoy the ride.

Every time we move our species forward, it will be because of you. Every time our species takes a step back it will also be because of you. Every time your soul finds a new medium or mode of expression, you will advance the soul of the Cosmos. You are a designer and architect of the future of humanity. Of course, you would not be given this power if you could not handle it, so know that your purpose is all you need to act and lead. It is all you need to create your life, lead your people and responsibly steward the whole of reality.

APPENDIX A

A Note on Use of Spiritual and Psychological Language

I use the term "**soul**" to refer to that part of you that knows your life's purpose (Kelley, 2009). I also use terms like "intuition," "deepest truth," and "highest self" as terms to describe this same knowing. Although your soul is the possessor of your purpose, it is often muted by the mechanics of the ego. When given the opportunity to express itself, your soul is often not very concerned with the happiness and comfort of your ego. Your soul loves risk. It loves pushing you beyond the edge of your comfort zone, empowering you to grow, expand, self-express in new ways and harvest new insights about your path.

Your soul really just wants to explore, express, reveal, deepen, expand and enliven your experience of life. Think of your soul as your most creative, loving and wild friend, with whom you've had the best memories, that part of you that is an unqualified "yes" to anything that is purpose-aligned or expands your experience of life. Soul can even thrust you into danger, onto new frontiers in love, career, travel, personal and spiritual development. It's not bad. It's not good. It's just what soul does.

I use the term "**ego**" to refer to your identity, how you consciously understand yourself. Your ego is that part of you that craves homeostasis, certainty, safety, comfort, the simple pleasures, and is initially a "no" to anything new, different and soul/ purpose-aligned. Your ego is equally as authentic and true as your soul. It is just as integral and "you" as your soul, and when these two are brought into right relationship, when there is a healthy marriage between your ego and your soul, you will know a wholeness, self-love, fulfillment and level of performance heretofore unseen.

I hold that your "ego" and "soul" together represent your whole self. Of course, this does not refer in any way to spiritual experiences or a spiritual identity experienced by those who have become Spiritually Enlightened. That is a whole separate subject, worthy of the thousands of books that have been written on it. This book does not cover any of that ground. This book is about individual and collective purpose awakening, irrespective of spiritual orientation.

Prior to purpose discovery work, you have an ego-centric identity, meaning your desires, fears and biological and psychological history comprises 80-99% of your human identity, driving your decisions and actions. After purpose discovery work, you begin to embrace and embody a soul-centric human identity, where this ratio begins shifting to a more 50/50 balanced relationship. Your soul-initiated ego knows your soul's purpose and acts as its agent. The goal of purpose discovery work is not like that of many spiritual disciplines, focused on the elimination or transcendence of your ego: it is about the creation of a functional, loving marriage between your soul and ego, where your soul reaches fuller expression over time through your ego.

I also use a term I learned from Bill Plotkin, "**soul encounter**", to refer to an event in which your soul makes its way through the defenses of your ego and reveals to you an aspect of your life's purpose. These encounters are moments of clarity wherein the great pattern of your life surfaces, such as during acts of service, insights during contemplative, spiritual, sexual or creative practices, or when awed and surrendered to the beauty of the human spirit, the Earth or Cosmos. On your journey, you will have many soul encounters, the most important of which I define as a "**soul initiation**", wherein your true name and place in the Cosmos is revealed.

I use the term "**adult**" to refer to a biologically-mature (human beings over age 27, the approximate age at which the brain's neocortex reaches maturity), psychologically- whole and purpose-aware human being. An adult is an individual who has had both a soul initiation - through which she is permanently connected to her soul's evolving purpose - AND has done substantial psychological work to be able to understand her own patterns and act with emotional maturity. One grows toward psychological wholeness by identifying and addressing any acute psychological conditions, e.g., depression and anxiety disorders, through working with an elder, a Guide, a therapist or a healer to integrate the multiple parts of their ego structure with their soul's purpose at the center. Thus, an adult is someone who is married in the sense that their ego and soul each have matured through intensive development and have married each other, taken on each other as life partners.

Regarding romance and partnership between two people, I use the term "**authentic partnership**" to signify a relationship between two adults (see above), who choose a romantic partnership not out of need, but because their experience of life together creates a larger expression of each party's individual life purpose, and serves a purpose greater than the two composite purposes, the purpose of the relationship/union itself.

I use the word "**Cosmos**" to describe the largest possible understanding of reality in scientific and objective terms. I use this term instead of "universe" or "nature", because Cosmos means these things (universe and nature) and it also means order, from the Greek "Kosmos". Kosmos as a noun means good order, and as a verb means to equip, deck, prepare or arrange, and thus it has a more active meaning and human implication. Unlike "universe" or "nature", Cosmos includes not only the data and the patterns that we as humans observe in nature and the universe, but also our theories (many of which are quite testable) about why the patterns exist and the actions we take based on those theories. As we humans are also evolutionary artifacts of the Cosmos, so are the patterns we observe, our hypotheses, knowledge, questions and actions. I capitalize Cosmos because I also mean it in a spiritual sense, as I hold the whole Cosmos to be personally sacred. My experience with different spiritual and creative disciplines, with plant medicines, in nature and during sex, have blurred the tidy dichotomy I once held between science and religion. For me, the terms "God" and "Cosmos" are one, containing all major dichotomies: science and art, faith and reason, mystery and certainty. I believe each aspect of these dichotomies is an indispensable and irreducible aspect of existence and each needs to be understood to appreciate the other.

Feel free to interpret "Cosmos" according to your own worldview and spiritual orientation, or even to create a substitute term, e.g., "Source", "Nature" or "Mystery", to point to the all-inclusive reality, the continuously-revealed order, and the unknowns within reality.

Lastly, I capitalize the word "**Guide**" because I hold it to be a sacred function, as it is a service of enormous importance and value to people in search of their true nature, their greatest contribution and fullest expression. Different from upper world spiritual guides like priests, ministers and meditation teachers (who help people transcend and move their identity out of the material and egoic realm and up into a unified nondual realm of Spirit or God), purpose, soul or underworld Guides help people descend into and embody their unique spirit.

The role of a trained purpose, underworld or soul Guide is to help a person descend into soul to illuminate the contours of their unique expression of divinity. Trained Guides help people expand into an identity with the particulars of their lives, the many aspects of their life's purpose, such as their unique vision, virtues, core, story, mission, call, flow, powers, craft and worldview. These are different outcomes than those that generally occur as a result of upper world spiritual practices like praying, reading scripture, chanting or meditating.

Neither the upper nor lower world spiritual path is better than the other. Both the upper and lower spiritual paths are necessary, unique and complement each other well. However, the upper world spiritual path has gotten all the good press over the last thousand years or so. In traditional Christianity, for example, we are taught to transcend the flesh to commune with spirit, to worship a masculine God. Accordingly, the lower world soul path was relegated to the domain of evil or the devil, along with other more feminine, embodied and personal forms of spirituality which might focus on gnosis, nature or sex. (More on this in "Appendix B: The History of Purpose".)

Moreover, trained Guides play a vital role in creating the purposeful cultural, political and economic regeneration of the human species. As we explored in Part Four, this purpose-driven future will be unimaginably bright, and it will need hundreds of thousands of trained Guides to aid in this transition.

APPENDIX B

The History of Purpose

Why are purpose and soul so important to us? Soul and purpose are important, because throughout human history, and across all of our traditions, they are what connect the inner and outer world. They are the sinews, the connective tissue that bind the seen and unseen, that connect the various realms of our experience as individuals, that bind us together as a community, and that source humanity inside of the Cosmos. They give us a materialistic spirituality, an etheric commerce, a sentimental physics, a poetic pragmatism, a sacred run of show. Soul imbues the mundane with the eternal, it gives our lives meaning, individuality and divinity. It gives our leadership velocity, depth, truth and urgency. It instills in us a mystic sensibility and playful poetry as we move through our careers, feeling the grace of an unpredictable and chaotic, but nonetheless syntropic, benevolent and purposeful Cosmos. Soul is our divine tailwind, pushing us through the Cosmos and the Cosmos through us. And yet, this is not our current culture in the West. But it was once so.

As such, I believe it is important to presence the history of soul and purpose, our recent falling out with soul, during the jab, cross and uppercut of Christianity, the Enlightenment and Industrialization, and our rekindled romance with soul over the last 100 years.

The Three Realms of Purpose

According to dozens, if not hundreds, of mystic traditions, e.g., Kabbalah, Tibetan, Sufi, Gnostic, Zuni, Tzutujil, Hopi, Toltec, extending far back into our past, beyond the use of written language, you have three realms of your purpose: the Upper Realm - your transcendent purpose, to become one with existence (which you might call God); the Middle Realm - your human purpose, to become an adult in the world; and the Lower Realm - your soul's purpose, to realize your unique reason for being. Jonathan Gustin, the founder of the Purpose Guides Institute, refers to these realms as "wake up, grow up and show up" - waking up to your largest identity (upper), growing up into a human adult (middle) and showing up with your purpose (lower). Expanding on this three realms model:

1. The Upper Realm is the realm of transcendence, of merging with Universal or Divine consciousness. This is the ascendant spiritual path, where you ascend, move from flesh to spirit, commune with God, the Cosmos, Source, Mystery, etc., experience unitive intimacy and, in certain traditions, possibly become spiritually enlightened (permanently established in this awareness). To achieve fullness of upper realm purpose, you have a number of ego-transcending tools to choose from, tools that bring you up and out of your normal egoic sense of self. Some of these tools include extended time in nature, fasting, prayer, ritual, chanting, meditation, drumming, dance, and psychotropics.

2. The Middle Realm is the realm of your human purpose, of your journey to becoming a mature human adult. As the upper limits of human potential have expanded since the advent of text, agriculture, urban living, industrialization and the field of psychology, we now have a new understanding of what middle realm human adulthood looks like. This is the realm met by the laws of physics, and is expressed in your participation in relationships, politics, society and the economy. In the middle realm your purpose is to grow up, to become a mature adult, defined as reaching fullness in these five ways:

   a. becoming an emotional adult (being able to experience, process and cleanly express emotions; to speak powerfully, distinguishing fact from story, judgment, emotions and requests, using "I statements"); being one who is centered, sourced from purpose and is thus capable of being with anything, as being a clearing for the experience and transformation of others,

   b. being happy, experiencing lots of joy,

   c. becoming economically self-sustaining and gainfully employed in a purpose-driven career, in an economic relationship to the world, similar to what the Buddhists call "right livelihood", whereby the fullest self-expression of your lower-world soul's identity, your powers and craft are exchanged for money, in order that you may provide for yourself and your loved ones,

   d. being one who can freely give and receive love, by disappearing barriers and beliefs in the way, and

   e. being one who cares for their physical form using the available best practices for psychological and physical well-being.

   To more deeply experience your purpose in this realm, you have a number of tools such as therapy, integral somatic practices, a personalized and balanced diet, life coaching, personal development books, retreats and workshops, men's and women's work, mother/father wound healing work.

3. The Lower Realm is the realm of your unique soul purpose, the descendant spiritual path, the path of knowing your niche, your distinct seat assignment on Spaceship Earth. Your soul's purpose is multifaceted and includes your vision, virtues, core, story, mission, call, flow, powers, worldview and craft. Having a high-definition view of your soul's purpose gives you the ability to mature as an adult in the middle realm, to create your unique purpose-driven career and make other purpose-aligned choices. You cannot think your way into your soul's purpose. You cannot figure it out with your mind. You need special tools. The tools of this realm are vision quests, working with a Guide, purpose discovery programs, and medicine ceremonies.

This book is primarily a middle and lower world book, focused on helping you discover a high-definition understanding of your soul's purpose and creating a life and livelihood that expresses it. As such, in this history of purpose, we won't spend any time in the Upper Realm, and will focus on the lower realm, on one's soul's purpose and how it is lived in the middle realm.

History

As we explored in "Chapter 1: Purpose, the New Normal?", purpose is actually an ancient truth, long held sacred by our wisdom traditions and valued by 97% of Americans (Rainey, 2014). In the west, the word "purpose" dates back to the 13th century Anglo-French use of the word, meaning intention, aim, goal or to put forth by design (Etymonline.com, 9/12/2017). The root of intention, "*intente*" – to stretch out – is also from 13th century France. Purpose is, at the core, the bridge from the inside to the outside – from the individual to the world. It is no coincidence that this term originated during the Renaissance, as we leapt out of the Dark Ages and began to reimagine the soul and essence of the human experience, finding a deep sentimentality in religion, love, birth and death.

However, this definition does not address the question of whether or not a life's purpose is born of the soul or whether it grows out of the fears/desires of the ego or the values of society and marketplace. To answer that, we have to dig deeper, go back further and farther East to explore the Sanskrit word "*Dharma*," a Hindu concept which could be said to be ancestral to the concept of purpose.

Dharma is a term in Hindu philosophy and religion, dating back at least to the *Rig Veda* (1400 BCE). It means the order and law of the Cosmos, the way in which the Universe works, all the principles and ideas that describe it and hold it together. To live according to Dharma was to follow Hinduism's spiritual, ethical and caste constructs. This definition is not a personal definition (or purpose). It offers no guidance as to the specific manner in which a person should live, nor what they should do with their powers, craft, flow, virtues, core, etc. Dharma was more a general directive, similar to "doing God's will".

However, the *Rig Veda* did highlight some important distinctions - *vidya, avidya, maya*, and *atman* - that made the concept of Dharma slightly more personal. *Vidya* refers to living in accordance with the *atman* (one's soul or true self), and *avidya* refers to a life obscured from the *atman*, wherein not only does one not know their soul or true self, but they believe it to be something else, e.g., a narrative formed by caste, family, pleasure, egoic desires and fears. In this sense, *avidya* is the embrace of *maya*, the veil of illusion, a belief that the material realm, social opinions and one's station in society are the fundamental truths, and should be the primary bases for decision-making.

With these Hindu distinctions in place, the concept of Dharma became one's unique path to righteousness and purity, the purification of an individual human, the unique way of conforming oneself to this Cosmic order. In this sense, Dharma is more closely related to another Sanskrit word, *upavita*, which means the fine thread or filament that is woven throughout a human life, a unique fate or destiny that, if followed and explicitly cultivated, releases an individual into their soul's fullness, expressing their unique divinity.

> Dharma means the natural law woven within each soul, that which gives each person an inner authenticity as well as natural virtues and noble qualities. Our inner dharma, or way of being, also aims us at particular ways of being in service to the world around us and adding something unique to the greater good of humankind.
>
> -Michael Meade (*Meade*, p. 48, 2016)

In the *Bhagavad Gita* (500-200 BCE), Dharma explicitly descended further into the level of the individual, from a general ethical imperative to conform one's life to the Divine Supreme All, the *Paramatman*, into the Divine personal, one's *jivatman*: the individual soul, true self or unique essence.

> It is better to strive in one's own dharma than to succeed in the dharma of another. Nothing is ever lost in following one's own dharma, but competition in another's dharma breeds fear and insecurity.
>
> -*Bhagavad-Gita*

Roughly around the time of the *Bhagavad Gita*, a series of Hindu commentaries on ethics, responsibility and living one's divinity, the Dharmaśāstras (1250-100 BCE;

the exact date is unknown), were written to explicate a more integrated and soulful path for living in accordance with one's *dharma* (nature) or *upavita* (golden thread woven through life). They described the four main realms of human experience/ desires, or *puruṣārthas*, as:

- Artha (the desire for livelihood/economics/sustenance/food/shelter)
- Dharma (the desire for purpose/reason for being/way to express the Divine)
- Kama (the desire for pleasure)
- Moksha (the desire for Spiritual Enlightenment).

In the West, when biological adulthood sets in, these four realms (Artha, Dharma, Kama, and Moksha) occur as fairly separate, fragmented and even antithetical to each other. We're conscious of experiencing them all, but usually only one at a time. In the United States, we regard them as nearly opposites. Thanks to our Puritan roots, we often hold pleasure and religion as opposites, and work and leisure as opposites. The framework of the *puruṣārthas* weaves these four desires back together into a coherent whole, placing Dharma/soul/purpose at the axle of the wheel around which livelihood, pleasure and spirituality rotate, as well as serve and express each other.

In 600 CE, a new school of thought within the Hindu tradition emerged, Tantra, to further descend spirit into matter, to soulfully bind them, to further personalize dharma and create a more coherent system of thought. Tantra (from the Sanskrit root word "*tan*" – to stretch and expand, to weave, warp, or loom together) allowed the *puruṣārthas* (above) to reach a more full expression.

The Tantrics acknowledged the manifested realm of matter, people, sex, markets, nature, etc., as just as godly as the transcendental states of consciousness available to those who abstained from these realms, namely the yogis and sadhus (the priests, saints, and holy people of the time). What connected this manifested realm to the unmanifested realm of spirit was soul, our Dharma, our *upavita*, our *jivatman*, our purpose, taking authentic, soulful action in light of our desires, fears and social structures. In Tantric terms, Dharma/purpose is the personal path that allows us to heal and soulfully express ourselves, becoming both more ourselves and more godly through serving and creating for others, as well as in the full-throated celebration and enjoyment of creation.

In addition to the *Bhagavad Gita*, another Hindu epic illuminates how to live one's life of purpose by tantrically weaving soul and descending spirit into the world. The *Ramayana* is a story about Rama, who, like Jesus, Buddha and Arjuna (the main character in the *Bhagavad Gita*), wanted to abstain from the realm of leadership, markets, society and caste to live a purely spiritual life. With his brother, Lakshmana, and wife, Sita, Rama endured a 14-year exile from his kingdom, had many adventures and awakenings, and then received the divine command to return and resume his leadership, to live his life's purpose as a benevolent king. The *Ramayana* echoes the lessons of many savior/messiah/hero's journey myths, in which a hero leaves home, finds truth/gold/purpose and then returns to integrate this awareness and give it away through service.

If you were lucky enough to be born near a local shaman or with a tantric philosopher nearby, you likely had a very powerful understanding of the call to live your purpose, your Dharma. However, if you were raised with another tradition or in another culture, the subject of your life's purpose likely never came up in conversation, much less was suggested as an important thing to cultivate. There is a reason for this.

If you grew up in the West, it is likely you grew up Christian or at minimum, you grew up in a culture heavily influenced, institutionalized and governed by Christians. This culture and way of being touts service and obedience, but makes no mention of individual life purpose. There is no passage in the Bible that illuminates anything close to Dharma, or *jivatman* or *upavita*. With the exception of a few vague allusions to soul in *Ecclesiastes* 11:9, *Corinthians* 1, 12:4-11 and the Parable of Talents in *Matthew* 25:23-30, the Bible omits all teachings on your soul's purpose. Instead, the Bible instructs readers to observe the ethics of the Ten Commandments, serve the Church and obey the religious patriarchy.

And, this was not an accident. In the early years of Christianity, there was an ideological war between the Gnostics and the Paulists (the marketers of the early Church) in which the Paulists won. The Gnostics (of which Jesus was a member, if we listen only to the words he said in the Bible) were a Jewish and early Christian sect that had a great deal in common with the Tantrics, in that they believed everything was spiritual, that spirituality was personal, and that we each have unique powers to contribute and express (Miller, 1992, p. 316).

During numerous councils, such as the Council of Nicaea (325 CE), the Roman Catholic/Paulist Church sought to create a cultural and religious order to cohesively govern their expansive empire, and enable political hegemony. To do this, they needed command over the spiritual and religious narrative, to divinely source and legitimize the empire, a need that all empires have. Due to the Roman empire's impressive size and the diversity of its cultures and territories, they needed stronger social glue and a narrow social contract to enable trust, allegiance and expedited commerce.

As such, they streamlined the faith, creating a tidy overlap between the empire and the religion, and in the process removing most of the emergent, creative, nature-immersed, sensual and individual aspects of spiritual life - the Gnostic teachings on soul, personal purpose, mystery, reincarnation, meditation or a relationship to the embodied aspects of a spiritual life (joy, sex, art) and the Divine Feminine. The Paulists were intent on building an organization of people who only sought spiritual refuge in the Church and ethical guidance from the Ten Commandments. To do so, they waged war against other religions, and especially, the Gnostics, polytheists, Pagans and anybody else who wanted a personal experience of God. God was to be experienced only in, by and through the Upper Realm of the God of the Bible, as interpreted by the Church, its cloistered priests and monks and its ethical mandates. God was not to be found in nature, in meditation, in dancing, in personal ceremony or through one's sex life or soul's purpose. These fundamental spiritual practices were soon to be called evil or heretical, and relegated to the domain of witchcraft.

Although the Gnostic tradition continued in the more mystical beliefs of the Desert Fathers and Mothers, Meister Eckhart, Boethius, St Teresa of Ávila, Hildegard of Bingen and others, its influence on the mainstream of Roman Catholicism and the Western World was effectively erased. And, this was the way it was for most of the recent history of the Western World. The Renaissance (14th - 17th centuries) was a revolution in soul, with hundreds of artists reanimating soul, ensouling art, poetry, courtship and culture, without explicitly stating, or possibly even knowing, that this is what they were doing. Around the same time, the 16th-century Protestant Reformation, revolted against Christianity's exclusion of a personal relationship to God. This is also a feature of modern day evangelical and charismatic Christian sects. But, mainstream Christianity continued to eschew meditation, personal ceremony, trance, purpose/soul work or medicine ceremonies as valid paths.

In the early 1900's, Richard Bucke and William James reignited the question of personal spirituality in the West with their landmark works, Bucke's *Cosmic Consciousness* (Bucke, 1901) and James' *Varieties of Religious Experience* (James, 1902), which detailed the experiences of saints and regular people with mystical proclivities who demonstrated a direct connection to God. Throughout the 1900's, interest in personal spirituality (a democratized, personal mystical experience of the Divine) grew, but largely remained on the fringe of Western culture and out of the scope of mainstream Christianity, which still fostered no personal, descendent expression of spirit, or emphasis on soul purpose.

It wasn't until the Nag Hammadi discovery in 1945, when the Gnostic Gospels (Miller, 1992) were reintroduced to religious scholarship and eventually into broader human awareness, that the doors of Christianity blew open. Upon this revelation, we began to discover what was lost in the Paulist expression of the Christian experience - soul.

In recent decades, within the West's newly-minted and more scientific wisdom tradition - psychology - there has been a resurgence of interest in the topic of soul purpose. Modern pioneers in Western psychology (e.g., Carl Jung, Abraham Maslow, Viktor Frankl, James Hillman, Clarissa Pinkola Estés and Bill Plotkin) have begun to reexamine the ancient notions of soul, mystery, myth and purpose. What these leading thinkers have articulated, and what our researchers have begun to measure in the fields of chemistry, biology, psychology, sociology, economics and education (see "The Science of Purpose" chapters in Part One), is that purpose is positively correlated with, and perhaps is a leading indicator of, psychological health, biological integrity, social health and economic flourishing.

This recent purpose re-awakening in the West which began in the 1940's, was accelerated by the foundational work from Viktor Frankl, *Man's Search for Meaning* (1946). Frankl was a famed psychologist and Nazi concentration camp survivor, who observed that the concentration camp prisoners who had a clear reason to live (such as seeing their children again or finishing a book they were writing) had a far greater chance of surviving the brutal conditions in the concentration camp. In response to his observations of those who survived and how they survived, he developed a purpose-focused treatment modality called "logotherapy" – a means of healing in which the patient's life is seen to be about something far greater than pain and pleasure (i.e., a life purpose).

Around the same time, Abraham Maslow offered a similar notion, one he termed *self-actualization* – the process by which you most fully become yourself (1943). He believed self-actualization was the pinnacle of his hierarchy of human needs (provided we are also fed, safe, connected and acknowledged). What Maslow, Frankl, Hillman and Plotkin put forth, and what the Western psychoanalytical tradition is now beginning to discover for itself, is that self-actualization (the realization of soul purpose) is the key to the good life.

As the groundbreaking work of Maslow and Frankl hit the scene, people began to come into the purpose question from the more objective and intellectual door of psychology. Thus, by the mid-20th century, tracks had been laid within both Christianity and psychology to develop a personal narrative of life, a way of interacting with the world, that enabled every human to live a meaningful, actualized and/or spiritual life, to be empowered, creative and fulfilled in living their unique life's purpose in the world.

In 1964, two psychologists, James Crumbaugh and Leonard Maholick, were inspired by *Man's Search for Meaning*, and developed the 20-question Purpose in Life (PIL) test. The PIL test quantifies the extent to which A. one believes that life has a purpose, B. one can uphold a personal value system and C. one has the motivation to achieve future goals and overcome future challenges (Crumbaugh, Maholick, 1963, pp. 43-48). By making purpose measurable, we could now see its co-determinants. Since the 1960's, researchers have been able to link purpose with a long life, a healthy heart, a sound mind, feeling content, love, attraction, higher levels of income and wealth, leadership, attitudes of kindness, generosity, curiosity and tolerance, and a more sustainable, just and abundant economy.

The purpose movement gained a significant advantage in the 1990's with Hal and Sidra Stone's trainings in the Voice-Dialogue method. The Stones' work leveraged the work of Roberto Assagioli, who developed *psychosynthesis* in the early 1900's, as well as Carl Jung's work on archetypes in the 1920's. This early work of intrapsychic parts can also be found in the work of Freud (as *complexes*), in object relations theory (as *internal objects*), in transactional analysis (as *ego states*), and in the Internal Family System Therapy (as *selves*).

The Voice-Dialogue method was designed as a means of healing us of our wounding. However, it did much more than that. It allowed the ego to be more fully understood, dissected and honored, creating greater wholeness and empowerment for people who engaged with these exercises. It also created a greater porousness in the ego structure, allowing soul to be more easily accessed and creatively expressed. Building on the ideas and work of Jung, Assagioli and the Stones, Bill Plotkin's *Soulcraft* (2003) and *Wild Mind* (2013), and Tim Kelley's *True Purpose* (2009), incorporated ego parts work in the soul/purpose discovery process. This process effectively opened the aperture for soul, by clearing out the cobwebs and tangled voices of the unexamined ego, and creating a wider, cleaner channel for the soul to pour forth and continually reveal new aspects of purpose. This resulted in more direct and effective purpose discovery processes which helped people who employed them to develop a cleaner, more integrated, powerful, stable and secure purpose-driven ego structure.

Jonathan Gustin, the founder of the Purpose Guides Institute, began his practice and scholarship in the field of soul in the 1990's. His work is deeply influenced by Tim Kelley and Bill Plotkin, and by the work of other notable soul explorers like James Hillman, Joanna Macy, Thomas Moore, Rod Stryker, Michael Meade, Martín Prechtel, Parker Palmer, Carl Jung, Frederick Buechner, Angeles Arrien, Tom Cheetam, Ibn Arabi, Richard Rohr, Pierre Teilhard de Chardin, Robert Johnson and Stephen Jenkinson. Leveraging the work of these masters, as well as his 20-year background and training in Zen meditation, integral philosophy and psychotherapy, Jonathan began the huge task of creating an integral approach to purpose discovery, digesting and synthesizing the meaningful contributions in the field of soul and purpose literature. In 2015, Jonathan was the first to offer a broad synthetic model of purpose, the Purpose Octagon™, synthesizing dozens of distinctions of a life purpose into four "Being" (Yin) elements of purpose:

1. Vision - for an evolved world
2. Values - the enduring ideals and principles by which you want your life to be known, how you create your life and vision
3. Core Powers - your full-level abilities, your soul-level talents, what you're great at doing
4. Essence - who you are without doing anything;

and four "Doing" (Yang), or "becoming" elements of purpose:

1. Giveaway - your blessing, how you uniquely transform people

2. Task - how you align your values, core powers, essence and giveaway in service of a goal, in fulfillment of your vision
3. Message - the one truth you amplify in all you do
4. Delivery System - how the world economically relates to you in the expression of your purpose, your career, vocation, business model.

The Purpose Tree

To build on Jonathan's work, as well as the work of my other influences, e.g., Tim Kelley, Clarissa Pinkola Estés, Thomas Moore, Joseph Campbell, Bill Plotkin, Mihaly Csikszentmihalyi, and Michael Meade, I created the Purpose Tree. It is designed to spatially relate each aspect of a soul's purpose to the nature and function of the others. I also added a few more elements that I deem to be necessary to a cohesive and dynamic understanding of the personal and world soul - worldview, story, flow and call.

Many purpose models do a great job of illuminating the inner aspects of a life's purpose, but do not address the outer aspects - specifically, one's worldview, the emotional call that ignites the quest for purpose and the desire to make a big impact improving the human and ecological condition. Nor do they root soul in the body (flow), or explicitly place soul inside a personal mythology (story), or give us a visual orientation that demonstrates how the various aspects of our purpose are connected (navigational metaphor). As such, the Purpose Tree includes the call, as well as worldview, flow and one's personal mythology/*upavita*/story in a way that is designed to visually orient, connect and express the various facets of a high-definition life purpose.

Before settling on the Purpose Tree, I searched for just the right navigational metaphor. I spent many months looking and experimenting with models that would dynamically tie together the different aspects of purpose and bring the whole concept of purpose more alive. I explored numerous popular metaphors like the compass, the wheel, the triangle, the solar system, the hero's journey, the birth process and the pyramid, but none resonated more deeply than the metaphor of the tree.

Origins of The Purpose Tree

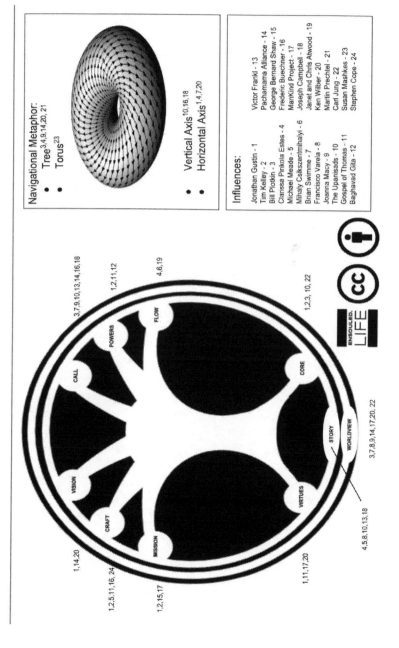

Navigational Metaphor:
- Tree[3,4,9,14,20,21]
- Torus[23]

- Vertical Axis[10,16,18]
- Horizontal Axis[1,4,7,20]

Influences:

Jonathan Gustin - 1
Tim Kelley - 2
Bill Plotkin - 3
Clarissa Pinkola Estes - 4
Michael Meade - 5
Mihaly Csikszentmihalyi - 6
Brian Swimme - 7
Francisco Varela - 8
Joanna Macy - 9
The Upanisads - 10
Gospel of Thomas - 11
Baghavad Gita - 12

Victor Frankl - 13
Pachamama Alliance - 14
George Bernard Shaw - 15
Frederic Buechner - 16
ManKind Project - 17
Joseph Campbell - 18
Janet and Chris Atwood - 19
Ken Wilber - 20
Martin Prechtel - 21
Carl Jung - 22
Susan Mashkes - 23
Stephen Cope - 24

3,7,9,10,13,14,16,18

1,2,11,12

4,6,19

1,14,20

1,2,5,11,16,24

1,2,15,17

CALL POWERS FLOW

VISION

CRAFT

MISSION

STORY WORLDVIEW

VIRTUES

CORE

1,2,3, 10, 22

1,11,17,20

3,7,8,9,14,17,20,22

4,5,8,10,13,18

We've all spent time with or in trees. As children we ran amongst them, sat in the shade beneath them, ate their fruits and nuts, poured their sweet syrup over Sunday morning pancakes, pressed their leaves, climbed them and may have even built houses in them. We rescued cats from them, trimmed them and warmed ourselves on flames of the felled and fallen. As teens many of us danced, drank and had sex among them. In our post-coital glow, we drifted asleep as the wind whistled through their branches and leaves. Trees have been there for us our whole lives, as tactile, generous, majestic witnesses to soul. And they are still here for us in our journey to recapture our own inner wildness and ensoul our lives. As Herman Hesse mused in his poem, *Sometimes,* "My soul turns into a tree... And asks me questions. What should I reply?" (Bly, 1995, p. 86)

With its vital, yet unseen, root system, its impressive appearance, and its seemingly human-like capacity for old age, endurance, mutuality, integrity, generosity and self-expression, I could find nothing more inspiring, cogent, mysterious and yet insanely common than the tree. The tree is a universal archetype used in most, if not all, cultures to symbolize the whole of existence, the duality of opposites, light and dark, seen and unseen. In the West, our Judeo-Christian cultural underpinnings rely heavily on the tree; we see the "Tree of Knowledge" in the Bible's Book of Genesis. Likewise, we see the "Tree of Life" in many mythologies and cultures all over the world: India/Hindu, Iran, Egypt, Mesopotamia/Urartu, Judaism/Kabbalah, Buddhism, Christianity, Islam, Baha'i, Tzutujil, Latter Day Saints, Georgia, Norse mythology, Germanic paganism, Mesoamerica, Sere and Turkey.

> Long ago there was a deep devotion to actual trees, for their ability to die back and return to life, and for all the life-giving things they provided people, such as firewood for warmth and cooking, wands for cradles, staffs for walking, walls for shelter, medicine for fever, and also places to climb to see far and, if necessary, to hide from the enemy. The tree was truly a great wild mother. (Estés, 1992, p. 406)

Mythologically, trees represent the *Axis Mundi,* the world pillar, the center of the world, a symbol that holds up and binds the entire Cosmos. According to many wisdom traditions, the *Axis Mundi* represents the sacred life-giving cord that connects all things, that connects the Heavens, Earth and the Underworld. Trees are a symbol for connecting the manifested (the world, our bodies, lives, markets, relations) with the unmanifested (spirit, soul, God, source, mystery).

> The Tzutujil [people] are a tree... Everybody is metaphorically... a Tree... The tribe is a tree, rooted in the first placenta of creation,

with its trunk coming through the other three layers of heartwood, xylem and bark, into... Earth Fruit. (Prechtel, 1998, p. 104)

Trees are perhaps the most common and vivid expression of the *torus*. A torus is a doughnut-like energy field, form or membrane, wherein the energy or magnetic field flows from below, then up and out, before returning down and inward to the center. As such, the torus is often used to represent the flow of human life force, coming up from below/within and moving up and out into the world, before once again returning to the below/within. Trees draw rare vital nutrients from the soil (soul), take in common nutrients from the air above (spirit) and combine them to develop trunks and branches outward (matter - creative expression, contribution), they offer their bark, leaves and fruit as food and refuge for others.

Once complete with their macro cycle, trees again offer themselves downward to the forest floor for life to again begin. Toroidal energy systems and design patterns are found everywhere, from trees to their fruits (e.g., apples and oranges), to digestive systems, as well as to the matter/energy/magnetic fields of larger cycles and systems like tornados, hurricanes, the Earth's magnetic field, stars, galaxies and possibly black holes (cycling energy/matter between perhaps another point in the Cosmos or in another Cosmos).

As such, it made perfect sense to me to relate the various parts of a soul's purpose in a toroidal configuration, as they are all connected to each other as all points on a torus lies in a singular membrane, feed each other and represent a modicum of direction and causal circularity. From the more static and root level aspects (core and virtues), purpose is sourced from below; dynamically moves upwards, yearning for the sky with the top branches (call and vision); moving out into the world as leaves and fruit (flow, powers, mission and craft), feeding others, transforming (and being transformed by) others before returning, in a downward and inward fashion to the soil; reconciling the transformation with the deepest parts (core and virtues); updating the story and worldview with learning and experience; to finally generating the next active evolutionary upswell. I thank my friend, colleague and editor, Susan Mashkes for helping me see this toroidal pattern and connection.

Moreover, the tree appealed to me, because it seemed so deeply embedded in a greater context, that of the interdependent evolutionary ecology of the forest. With a broad worldview and a connection to a sense of place so deeply missing in our modern lives, in our careers, in the world and in our media, government and corporations, it seemed natural to embed the dynamism of soul within a rich contextual, nature-based narrative, one that allows the soul's purpose of each human, as well as the purposes of our species and planet, to exist and be expressed within the interconnected fabric of the Cosmos.

With an interconnected metaphor like a tree, we can empower and orient ourselves to awaken to our life's purpose wholly embedded in the evolutionary history, culture, marketplace, governance structures and ecology of humanity. With this background in the history of purpose, my hope is that you are now able to ground your personal path to purpose in the knowledge that many humans before you have wrestled with, and come to some conclusion about, how to bridge the worlds of spirit and matter through their soul's purpose.

APPENDIX C

Additional Purpose Transformation Resources

If you completed the Global Purpose Expedition and want to go deeper or engage in a more customized experience, please explore one-on-one and group programs from Ensouled.Life, the Purpose Guides Institute (purposeguides.org), the True Purpose Institute (truepurposeinstitute.com), or the Animas Valley Institute (animas.org).

Guide Training Programs

If you have heard the call to become a Guide please explore these training programs to determine which is right for you now. You are also free to train with more than one school.

- Purpose Guides Institute: Purpose Guide™ Certification program; purposeguides.org
- Animas Valley Institute: Soulcraft Apprenticeship and Initiation Program; animas.org
- True Purpose Institute: True Purpose Coach Certification; truepurposeinstitute.com

If you feel called to deepen your academic understanding of soul and purpose, please explore the best writing on the topic. Although there are hundreds of books written on the subject of soul and purpose, and dozens of books worth reading, I believe these ten stand out as the most foundational:

1. Tim Kelley's *True Purpose* (2009)
2. Bill Plotkin's *Nature and the Human Soul* (2008)
3. Rod Stryker's *The Four Desires* (2011)
4. Michael Meade's *Fate and Destiny* (2010)
5. James Hillman's *The Soul's Code* (1996)
6. Clarissa Pinkola Estés' *Women Who Run With the Wolves* (1992)

7. Stephen Cope's *The Great Work of Your Life* (2012)
8. Thomas Moore's *Care of the Soul* (1994)
9. Viktor Frankl's *Man's Search for Meaning* (1946)
10. Joseph Campbell's *Hero With a Thousand Faces* (1949)

Worldview Expansion Tools

Here are some leading thinkers to explore as you ensoul your life and expand your worldview:

- Psychology: Victor Frankl, Abraham Maslow, Mihaly Csikszentmihalyi, Bill Plotkin, James Hillman, Carl Jung
- History: Yuval Noah Harari, Jared Diamond, Cynthia Stokes-Brown, Howard Zinn, Carl Sagan
- Philosophy: Ken Wilber, Brian Swimme, Michael Murphy
- Mythology: Clarissa Pinkola Estés, Joseph Campbell, Michael Meade, Robert Bly
- Ecology: Joanna Macy, David Abrams, Rachel Carson
- Economics: Amartya Sen, Paul Hawken, Rianne Eisler, Thomas Piketty, Herman Daly, Robert Reich, Joseph Stiglitz, Charles Eisenstein

APPENDIX D

The Buffalo Heart Manifesto

Today I step into my new name, "Buffalo Heart - Who Loves and Wholes the World." Today I surrender the concept, the feeling and the willfulness of "make wrong", the act of persecuting my brothers and sisters for doing their best in a world that rewards suboptimal and suicidal behaviors. I leave behind four preceding and necessary soul images, four successive names that aided my journey over the last decade, Humble Elephant, White Horse, Graceful Whale and Dharma Cylon. Two of these names, Humble Elephant and Graceful Whale, awakened the dormant, receptive feminine in me, while also unwittingly feeding the shadow lover task of pleasing, and the shadow king tasks of spiritual bypass and abdication of purpose. Two of these names, White Horse and Dharma Cylon, awakened a new level of warrior-king energy, devoted to truth, justice and sustainability, while also unwittingly feeding the shadow warrior task of tyranny, of shaming and imposing my will onto others.

Today I step into a new wholeness honoring all the energies, the four cardinal directions (North/South/East/West), Father Sky, and Mother Earth, and I seek respite in the seventh direction, Within, in my own heart, Buffalo Heart. Today I stand as a fierce, whole, loving protector of the Cosmos itself. I stand as a champion and steward for the descendant path of Spirit through integrity, truth and goodness on Earth and the ascension of Soul, seducing mystery and wonder and expressing beauty.

I am Buffalo Heart Who Loves and Wholes the World. I step into Shambhala Leadership, fully embracing humanity's awakening, meeting humanity as it is, wherever it is, embracing the truth and goodness in every level of human development.

I do not stand alone. I stand with my brothers and sisters in integral and transformational communities, like the Global Purpose Movement, Woman Within, the ManKind Project, Burning Man, Esalen, the California Institute for Integral Studies, the Purpose Guides Institute, the True Purpose Institute, the Animas Valley Institute, the Pachamama Alliance, the Sacred Science, the Institute of Noetic Sciences and the Long Now Foundation.

I stand for every human to get what they came here for - safety, sustenance, abundance, connection, creativity, self-love, and self-expression through the awakening and embodiment of purpose in their own lives and livelihood. I stand for purposeful romance, family and community. I stand for an ensouled political economy that rewards the purpose awakening and embodiment of every human, a political economy that expresses and evolves the purpose of the human species and that stewards the purpose of Earth's living ecology.

My stand is for excellence, emergence and integrity at the level of the individual and the collective. Going forward, what you can count on me for is to:

1. Love you as a full and complete human being, embracing all of your powers, your frailties, your humanity and your dark corners.

2. Guide you and stand for your purpose-awakened Shambhala Leadership, as a leader who knows her powers are necessary to the whole of the human species, Earth ecology and Cosmic evolution.

3. Hold you accountable for your actions in a firm but loving way, to surface the impacts of your choices, and invite you to act in a way that serves your purpose, the purpose of humanity and the planet and honors the mysteries within your heart and beyond the night sky.

4. Guide humanity, at its request, to a deeper and fuller collective expression of purpose, to a planetary identity enabled by the aforementioned, in service of a greater splendor, dignity, excitement and hope, a love affair with the soul of humanity and the Earth and the mysteries of the unknown - mind, sea and space exploration.

Of course, I am not waiting like a dutiful pupil to be called upon. I stand now and declare myself a Shambhala Leader who empowers other Shambhala Leaders to make their highest contribution. I will not sit down. I will not be quiet nor will I be deterred by my brothers and sisters who do not welcome my leadership. I will do what I can, with what I have, wherever I am. I am Buffalo Heart Who Loves and Wholes the World.

APPENDIX E

Chicago on Purpose

"I'm buying a gun," I declared to my mother over dinner.

"What?!" She recoiled in horror.

"Lots of guys in our crew have them. Gino has been shot eight times doing this work. I can get a snub nose .38 for $200."

My mom was speechless. Her baby boy who spent his previous summers safely cloistered in the suburbs working at McDonald's, as a caddie and house-painter, was now buying a gun to protect himself. I was 18 years old, and working for the summer doing road construction, as union laborer (Teamsters Local 1001 Cement and Steel Workers) with Palumbo Bros. Construction, an outfit with deep ties to Chicago's mob and Democratic machine / organized crime syndicate. I joined a jack hammer crew, resurfacing Chicago's inner-city streets, and got an enormous education, and an immersion into the realities of hard work and urban blight.

Each morning, I ran my locked fists, swollen shut from the previous day's jack hammer work, under hot water in order to move my fingers and make my coffee. With my coffee in hand, I hopped in the car, left the gilded 'burbs and drove to a much different slice of reality. I rolled up to the job site and immediately started breaking balls with my blue-collar Italian crew. I began developing an understanding of social norms, "cat calling" and Chicago's race dynamics from guys named Ralphy, Tony, Gino and Mario.

Having finished my freshman year on the Dean's List and in a top fraternity at the University of Illinois, "College Boy", as I was affectionately named, got to experience first-hand what a default city purpose really felt like for the people who lived there. Every day I left the white fog, the oak-canopied streets of the suburbs, and watched as they gave way to Chicago's red fog - homelessness, violence, fear, racism, poverty, prostitution, urban blight, gang warfare, and crack cocaine.

When working in the poorest neighborhoods and housing projects (Cabrini Green, Robert Taylor Homes), we'd turn on our machines at 5am and finish our workday by 1pm, before the 100-degree heat and 90% humidity drove people outside to discover eight white guys with pocket money tearing up their neighborhood.

We were constantly hustled and harassed, and like so many guys on the crew, I felt the need to arm myself. I look back on this time with a measure of fond sobriety, as it was the first time I realized how bad life is for many people. It is clear that a city fails when its citizens need to arm themselves. It is clear that a city fails when dark skin and prosperity are mutually exclusive. It is clear that Chicago lacked more than brotherhood, character and bureaucratic effectiveness. It lacked an organic purpose, as no definition of purpose includes such corruption, violence, inequality and suffering. No definition of purpose lays waste to so much human potential. And, without an organic purpose, Chicago has continued to suffer from the red and white fogs edified by its corrupt (and effectively and often overtly racist) Democratic political machine.

Chicago is regarded as one of the most poorly governed and corrupt cities in the world, often called the "corruption capital of America". Chicago's Cook County has had 1,642 corruption convictions since 1976, making it first in the nation. The State of Illinois has had 1,982 corruption convictions since 1976, making it third in the nation after New York and California (Simpson, Gradel, et al, 2015). Four of Illinois last seven governors have gone to prison. Going back to the earliest days of its incorporation in the 1830's, Chicago's network of business interests, organized crime and Democratic politicians colluded to use public funds for private gain, e.g., payoffs, embezzlement, racist zoning, and no-bid city contracts, the effect of which kept power and wealth in the hands of Chicago's white upper and middle class. Chicago's Democratic political machine, optimized by Mayors Richard J. and Richard M. Daley, divided the city along ethnic lines (Irish, Polish, Italian, Mexican, African American), using the tools of urban planning (zoning, housing projects), home lending ("red zones" - not surprisingly a structure to support the "red fog"), resource allocation and police activity.

The resulting dynamic is that Chicago has centralized wealth in the hands of upper- and middle-class whites and shipped its problems away through expressways, ghettos, public housing, smokestacks, sewers and prisons. Yet, as we have explored, we know what is possible when a city-state like Chattanooga, Tennessee, gets real with how bad things are, puts on its big boy pants, defines its purpose and steps into the future like an adult.

With this possibility in mind, let's imagine what Chicago could look like on purpose, and how the entire Midwest actually could benefit from a city-state orientation and a regional economic development overhaul. But first, we must begin with a little history, and develop an understanding of what's really happening now under the default purpose schema in Chicago and the Midwest.

Economic Hypothermia

In the 1980's and 1990's, our family took many road trips through the Midwest and throughout the country. As we crisscrossed Illinois, Iowa, Indiana, Kansas, Missouri, Michigan, Wisconsin, Ohio, and Nebraska, we visited harvest festivals, county fairs and thriving downtowns. In the summer of 2014, I traveled from my home in Berkeley, California, to Chicago by Amtrak; I saw the heart of my country in a far more intimate way than I had in the recent past. Once our train left the Rockies and entered America's bread basket, I was shocked by the extent of economic blight. Sitting in the observation car I saw a hollowed-out country. I lamented how these once vibrant, proud towns were now vacant, their stores boarded up, their vehicles sitting on blocks and their farms derelict.

Where there were once a quaint downtown, a few local factories, fourth-generation farmers and greasy spoons, there were now rampant poverty and unemployment. The heartland was decimated. My country's bones had been picked clean by meth, rust, weeds and Walmart. I felt a deep malaise set in.

How did this happen to my country? Why was the Midwest turning into the Midworst? Why was the once globally relevant, large metropolitan city of Chicago now #6 on Forbes' *list of most miserable cities to live in (Forbes, 2016)? Why is the reality I experienced in my 20's, living in coastal cities like New York City, Los Angeles and San Francisco, so different from that experienced by the rest of the country? Why were coastal cities seemingly moving in the opposite direction of the heartland, seemingly more abundant, prosperous and expensive each year?*

The short answer is that America – and most visibly the Heartland – is dying from its default purpose, and is now immersed in the resulting condition of "economic hypothermia" (Meijer, 2013). Economic hypothermia is a common occurrence when an empire reaches its zenith and stops innovating and producing exports, but continues to centralize wealth in its city-centers (its organs), without nourishing the countryside or investing in human capital (its flesh). Like a hypothermia patient, America's blood (its money and human capital) is rushing to its vital organs. I was part of this brain and capital drain pouring out of the Heartland and into America's coastal cities, as we outsourced manufacturing jobs and centralized profits in corporate coffers.

Because of America's three-decade-long war on the middle class, largely due to the Reagan and Clinton Administrations' war on labor (union-smashing/NAFTA), we realized 6-9% year-over-year inflation and 23% unemployment (shadowstats.com, 2017). Under these pressures, wealth and income silently vanished from America's middle class. Under our current default purpose schema, $2.1 trillion sits in offshore corporate accounts (Worstall, 2015), collecting interest, but not being loaned out for small business, nor being invested in new productive economic infrastructure. As many American corporations like GE, Pfizer, and ExxonMobil started mainlining low corporate tax rates (1980-present), they were incentivized to hold their profits or pay them out as dividends and not to invest their surplus cash flow in new products, facilities, employee training or wages.

The heartland has been pandered to by politicians, but systematically ignored and emaciated by Republican and Democratic policies alike. It is no wonder that politicians like Donald Trump, Bernie Sanders and Elizabeth Warren, have risen to fame on populist rhetoric.

However, it is only a matter of time before even the organs (cities) themselves also begin to collapse. Indeed, it can be argued that this has already happened in Detroit and is happening now in Chicago. When we fail to define our purpose at the level of the nation and the city-state, default purposes begin to operate independently of, and at cross-purposes to, the well-being of the social, cultural, ecological and environmental health of America's rural heartland (the flesh).

As our train chugged along through Colorado, Nebraska, Iowa, and Illinois, I witnessed a countercurrent to my malaise, a renewed love, patriotism and curiosity for my home. I started to think about why Chicago even exists at all. I inquired into Chicago's uniqueness and speculated as to what it could do to reclaim its once national and global relevance.

As a Chicagoan and Midwesterner, I care about my people. The well-being of my family, throughout Illinois, Indiana and Ohio, and of the families of my childhood and college friends in Wisconsin, Iowa, Michigan and Missouri, depend on Chicago not turning into another rust-belt, default-purpose tragedy like Detroit. I see Detroit as the canary in the coal mine. For the last 30 years, Detroit operated from its default purpose (a bloated, inefficient auto industry that preserved wealth and market share at the expense of actually creating better transportation solutions each year, as its Japanese competitors - Honda, Nissan and Toyota - have done). Detroit's default purpose, with the help of its own corrupt politicians, ate away at its foundation like termites until, finally, a strong gust of wind came through in the 2007 financial crisis and it collapsed. Without a well-articulated organic purpose, without a strategic economic advantage and sustainable closed-loop economy, every city and its surrounding area in America will eventually suffer a similar fate. I'm determined that this does not happen to my city, Chicago, the City of Broad Shoulders.

I believe Chicago should re-envision its purpose and begin the transformation required to realize it. This process should begin with a survey of the citizens and industry on the purpose of life, their life's purpose, the purpose of Chicago and what an exciting Chicago future could look like. Obviously, this task is beyond the capabilities of any one person or book, so I merely offer a possible starting point for this city-state reboot, a provisional purpose to carry the discussion forward and inspire each of us to revision our cities.

After a cursory exploration of Chicago's history and its geographic, intellectual, economic and cultural strengths, I believe a starting point for Chicago's purpose could be:

Chicago is the conscious food capital of the world, the leader in designing and delivering sustainable solutions for America's nutritional needs. As the largest city in the American breadbasket,

Chicago innovates sustainable agriculture, nutrition, transportation, and logistics solutions.

Chicago has many of the requisite strengths to accomplish this. It is also important to note that it is not uniquely suited to become a center of excellence in any other industry (as New York and Los Angeles have claimed media, New York has claimed finance, Washington, D.C. has claimed the public sector, Silicon Valley and Seattle have claimed information technology, and San Diego, New Jersey, Boston and North Carolina have claimed healthcare/biotech). Although Chicago is home to a few large insurance companies (Allstate, Blue Cross Blue Shield) and biotech companies (Abbott, Baxter), it is not considered a global center of excellence in these sectors. Let's begin this exploration of how Chicago can embody its purpose with a brief overview of Chicago's strengths and weaknesses.

Strengths

Chicago has abundant fresh water, connection to the Mississippi River and a huge shipping port. It is the weigh station and transfer point for the transcontinental railroad system, the center point of a 500-mile radius of fantastic farmland, and the home of major commodities/options trading exchanges. It is home to first-rate learning institutions (Northwestern University, Notre Dame, the University of Chicago) and is near four globally-recognized engineering programs (Purdue, Wisconsin, Illinois, and Michigan), as well as dozens of small liberal arts colleges. It has a network of industries that support agriculture and transportation – manufacturing, advertising and financial industries – as well as numerous cultural assets, including sketch/improv comedy (Second City), amazing architecture, a major music scene, world class restaurants, great beaches, the Art Institute of Chicago, the Museum of Science and Industry, the Museum of Contemporary Art and, soon, President Obama's Presidential Library and the Star Wars Museum.

Weaknesses

Chicago is blighted with an aging manufacturing and transportation infrastructure, a corrupt Democratic political machine, racial segregation, an aging population, a culture marked by anti-intellectualism and the usual suspects of purpose substitutes: soul-starved religions, consumerism and spectator sports. Chicago is plagued by racially segregated urban neighborhoods (safe, rich, white neighborhoods and poor/dangerous black and Hispanic neighborhoods, as well as wealthy white suburbs 20-40 miles from the center).

The causes of these issues derive as much from the City of Chicago's unconscious adherence to its default purpose and the resulting corruption, and poor urban and economic planning, as they do from the last thirty years of neoliberal federal economic policies (union smashing, financial deregulation and off-shoring of manufacturing jobs). Chicago, like everywhere else in America, is plagued by an evaporating middle class, by 6-9% inflation, by equity returns of 3% a year, wage increases of 1% a year, and rocketing costs of healthcare, energy, housing and transportation. This is where we are. Just as with a human purpose, clues to the purpose of a city can be divined by looking at its past.

A Short History of the Chicago Economy

Upon the completion of the Transcontinental Railroad in 1909, Chicago became the agricultural hub of the United States. The economic surpluses created by the agriculture industry enabled Chicago to develop food manufacturing, meat packing and consumer packaged goods businesses, an advertising industry, a finance/derivatives/commodities network, a residential/commercial construction sector, heavy machinery manufacturing capability (which also supported Detroit's automotive sector), and numerous other supporting service industries.

Over the last four decades and on the back of artificially suppressed/subsidized energy prices, the country became fossil fuel-dependent - for every calorie of food produced, 10 calories of fossil fuel combustion are required (*End of Suburbia*, 2004). The result was the deforestation of the Midwest, the pollution of the Midwestern watershed, the endangerment and elimination of thousands of native species, the depletion of the region's topsoil and water tables, and the creation of an ecological dead zone in the Mississippi delta.

This, naturally, had a detrimental effect on the quality of food, water, air and life, as well as Chicago's position as a food processing and distribution center. Further, as Nixon opened up China in the 1970's and Clinton opened up Central and South America (NAFTA) in the 1990's, the global food industry emerged, creating an expanded market and downward price-pressure for agricultural labor and commodities, forcing family farms out of business. Because of discrepancies in human rights, environmental legislation, fair wage laws and costs of living, it is no longer competitive to pay US labor costs when subsistence wages can be paid to immigrant farm workers in California and farm workers throughout Asia and Central and South America. In this way, Chicago's agribusiness backbone and the Midwest's natural competitive advantage are something with which most Chicagoans and Midwesterners currently have little contact.

Capitalizing on Trends

For many people, there is a growing awareness of how food is made, what is in it and how the people who made it are compensated. As we explored, people now care about the values of companies and the way they do business: 55% of customers will choose a product that has a purpose over one that does not (Nielsen, 2014). Chicago can get ahead of this curve and capitalize on the demand for purpose-driven, sustainable, fair-wage agriculture.

Furthermore, we have to recognize that peak oil is here, meaning each barrel of oil is harder and more expensive to extract. Peak labor is also here, meaning there are few places in the world that companies can run to in order to get cheaper labor. This is not wistful back-to-the-land thinking, however. I'm not advocating we go back to yoking plows to oxen, I'm saying that Chicago can lead the world in the discussion and modelling of how we can do more with less carbon, less exploitation of foreign workers and more utilization of our eager, willing, talented and hard-working American workforce.

There is a huge opportunity for Chicago to not only get ahead of this long-term macroeconomic energy and labor trend, but also to recreate itself, to establish an economic zone of integrity, cleaning up the structural mess, the corrupted market, and the exploited domestic and global workforces created by our current subsidization of fossil fuels. With this sober analysis in mind, let's create a new Chicago!

Chicago's Future as a Leader in Conscious Food

Chicago is uniquely qualified to sustainably innovate the global food business, creating technologies to more powerfully and holistically meet humanity's nutritional needs. As we explored, while Chicago is home to many multinational corporations (e.g., Baxter, McDonald's, Borg-Warner, Waste Management, Abbott Labs, Sears, etc.), and has a large professional services presence, its natural resources and academic/ research/ economic strengths do not qualify it to become a national or global center for excellence in any other industry besides agriculture/nutrition and sustainable energy and food logistics.

I'm not suggesting that Chicago's non-agricultural, transit and logistics businesses move. However, I am suggesting that Chicago act in accordance with one of the only practical ideas of its neoliberal oracle, Milton Friedman, by aligning itself with its strategic competencies, and partnering with other firms and city-states who offer other strategic competencies. To realize this purpose and vision, the following policies should be developed to create long-term wealth for Chicago and to expand the economic potential of the entire Midwest.

Technology

To accelerate this future, Chicago's institutions should secure National Science Foundation (NSF) funding for agricultural, transportation, and logistics innovation. By partnering with venture finance organizations, food companies and research institutions, Chicago could develop new solutions for healthier, more energy/

water-efficient, less expensive, more biodiverse and more local food production and sustainable distribution. The food company and venture finance network could then commercialize these technologies. Chicago could then become a net exporter of innovative food solutions and technologies (e.g., urban farming systems, palletized biodynamic greenhouse plots for rail distribution, live commodity transportation, grey water reclamation, vertical gardens, etc.).

Using Taxes to Regenerate Chicago's Natural Resources

To leverage, preserve and enhance Chicago's natural wealth, Chicago and the Midwest's state governments should put forth a regional food nutrition and security policy (perhaps in conjunction with the guidance of the Food and Drug Administration, Federal Trade Commission, National Science Foundation and Environmental Protection Agency), to gradually shift the state and federal tax structures away from income tax (which penalizes profits, creates downward price pressure on wages and incentivizes ecological destruction) and towards a consumption tax scheme (which penalizes pollution, resource inefficiency and waste, and rewards sustainability, conservation and innovation).

In a sense this would also salvage another contribution of Milton Friedman. Consumption taxes are the only taxes that Friedman believed to be just. By also incorporating social and environmental externalities into the price of resources, Chicago could transform the economy to reduce inefficient energy and water consumption in the production and distribution of agricultural products. Further, by jumpstarting/subsidizing a renewable energy infrastructure (solar and wind), and placing it near points of use/agricultural production, Chicago could enable sustainable/efficient production and distribution of food products.

Transportation and Logistics

Chicago could lead the region's sustainable transportation infrastructure by working with neighboring city-states, food companies, logistics companies and food retailers to create a high-speed, efficient rail transportation system, so that each city-state's unique offerings could be sustainably and rapidly distributed. Another benefit of creating this transportation network is that it would solidify an intellectual capital bridge for engineering, agricultural and logistics innovation via high-speed rail, with Chicago as the main hub, connecting St. Louis, Indianapolis, Iowa City, Minneapolis and Cincinnati, as well as the Midwest's top engineering schools in Madison (University of Wisconsin), Champaign (University of Illinois), Lafayette (Purdue University), and Ann Arbor (University of Michigan).

Real Estate Development

Taking a page from the bold vision and successful urban development of Curitiba, Brazil, Chicago can also become a world leader in high-density urban living, sustainable land use and highly-efficient mass transit. To do so, Chicago would need to partner with the surrounding towns, and create commercial/residential/industrial corridors along Chicago's existing commuter rail lines, such that it becomes prohibitively expensive to develop elsewhere (preventing sprawl and traffic congestion), and provides the incentive to return the middle areas (between the spokes/corridors of industry/commerce/residence) to nature, waterways, recreation areas and sustainable farmland. This effort could be accelerated with tax incentives for removing poorly-utilized buildings, for beginning organic and biodynamic farming and for planting native trees and grasses.

The result will be an organic common-sense economy, one that leverages Chicago's strengths, increases the income and well-being of its citizens (higher wages, less traffic and a cleaner environment), creates novel agribusiness products and services, and positions Chicago as the world leader in this space. This will increase Chicago's ability to withstand environmental extremes, and will nurture local economies. It will also create a short-term boom in real estate and construction. This is both an effort of substantial national benefit (food security and economic growth) as well as a task requiring great vision and political will. I believe the City of Broad Shoulders is fit for the challenge.

Of course, Chicago isn't the only place that can benefit from a vision and purpose. Every city can develop a similar plan, re-organize itself under a unique purpose and create irreplaceable strategic economic advantage in service of the greater good of humanity and the Earth. Doing so will nurture a web of resilient city-state economies capable of meeting the bulk of their dietary and economic needs within a 200-mile radius, reducing the incentives to pollute the environment and exploit workers at home and abroad, and empowering a 21st-century purpose-driven political economy.

APPENDIX F

Starting Point for a Purposeful US Government

As we explored, purpose sources our identity internally, freeing us from religious, partisan, nationalistic, sexual, racial and gender narratives. From this place we can truly look at best practices for what they are, without any of their ideological baggage.

It would take volumes to explore all the best practices, policies and programs needed to effectuate a purpose-driven US government, so I will not even begin that task. However, if we were to do so, we would begin by studying Finland's lead in education, Japan's lead in public transit, Vienna's lead in urban housing, Iceland's lead in renewable energy, Curitiba's (Brazil) lead in sustainable urban planning, Germany's lead in economic equality and labor relations, France's lead in maternity leave, and so on.

There is one decision a country can make right now, however, that has an enormous impact on the speed and efficacy of implementing our species' best practices for governance: determining the form of government needed to maximize the life purpose and well-being of every human, as well as the resilience of our Earth's ecology. Would that be a free-market political economy? Is it communism? Or a monarchy? Or a dictatorship? Or socialism? Contrary to most pre-purpose identities and political dogmas, the question as to which form of government creates the best outcomes for its constituents has already been answered. Having studied this issue and the powerful data on quality of life and ecological health now available, it is my view that:

> *It is overwhelmingly evident that the system of government that effectuates the purpose of humanity as a whole and creates the best outcomes for individuals is a social democracy.*

Social democracies are a Goldilocks solution, neither purely communist or socialist, nor purely capitalist. They are designed to structure the activity of public institutions and private enterprise to optimally serve the needs of the people and the environment. There are still significant social and economic problems in social democracies, but they are less pronounced than those in free market countries. The reason for this is that those who run social democracies do not believe there is an inherent generative morality of markets, and thus, they do not hope that market forces can solve public problems. Rather they employ public institutions to solve public problems and do so with greater effectiveness and a lower cost than the market can provide, e.g., Canada's single-payer health care vs. America's morally-corrupt, bloated, complex, inefficient and expensive free market healthcare system, or private auto ownership vs. mass transit. The data hugely favors this model of governance:

- Nine of the ten happiest countries in the world are social democracies: Switzerland, Denmark, Iceland, Sweden, Norway, Finland, Netherlands, Canada, New Zealand (United Nations World Happiness Report, 2017).
- Nine of the ten countries rated the most favorable in which to do business (despite having higher business taxes), according to *Forbes Magazine* are social democracies: Denmark, New Zealand, Norway, Finland, Ireland, Sweden, Canada, the Netherlands, the United Kingdom (Badenhausen, 2016).
- Eight of the ten countries with the highest GDP per hour worked, a measure that expresses economic productivity during work hours, are social democracies: Norway, Luxembourg, Belgium, the Netherlands, France, Germany, Ireland, Denmark (Conference Board, 2014).

A common response to talks of social democracy is that it cannot happen in a large diverse nation like the United States. Yes, race and religion are common ways to deliver the cultural cohesion required to trust the government to do its job. But this reflects a lack of imagination, and possibly, even hidden currents of racism. Race and religion aren't our only tools now. Once we source identity in soul, once we see and feel the soul purpose of our elected officials, and instill the aforementioned soul-enhancing and life-affirming political, economic and cultural reforms, we could be the first nation to have a cohesive yet ethnically-diverse culture, similar to that reflected in the fan bases of professional sports, e.g., New York Yankees fans from all boroughs, and as is starting to emerge in numerous diverse cities such as Los Angeles, Seattle, Vancouver, Washington, D.C., London, New York, Oakland and Singapore. Once sourced in soul, we can express this communal identity in our political economy, and use the very best practice available to govern ourselves, aka social democracy, and effectuate our human, planetary and Cosmic purpose.

Of course, this isn't a call for all countries to implement social democratic systems; rather, it's a call for the citizens of every country to determine which form of governance they should use to create the best life possible for the greatest number of people. Although the current best practice for governments in the Western World is a social democracy, this form of government might not be best for a new or war-torn country. It is up to each country to decide which form best serves their collective purpose. And, whatever form of government is chosen will also change, as a country and its people newly express their purpose and question, evolve and create the role of government to meet their needs.

It should be noted that in America, in order to have the opportunity to implement any best practices for governance or to change the system of government, we first need a constitutional convention to make structural changes in the electoral mechanism by which we empower leaders to make changes to our government. Our current model is one of democracy in name only. We are a corporate welfare state, an oligarchy effectuated by loose campaign finance and lobbying laws (Gilens, Page, 2015). This corporate welfare state deeply impairs our ability to implement any best practice for governance, such as social democracy.

As such, we now have the twin tasks of getting money out of politics and rapidly upgrading our culture with purpose, beginning with our leadership, such that our politicians can stand in their values and purpose as they fight corruption and implement these best practices. Numerous legislative and campaign finance reform efforts are underway with the goal of creating a government that works, e.g., Brand New Congress, the Incorruptibles, Our Revolution, Harvard Professor Larry Lessig's MayDay PAC, California Democratic Representative Jerry McInerney's constitutional amendment to abolish PACs, and over thirty NGOs dedicated to supporting this mission (full list available at IssueOne.org).

BIBLIOGRAPHY

Abdulrauf, Z. (2017). "50 Companies Supporting Modern American Slavery." [online] *Caged Bird Magazine.* https://www.cagedbirdmagazine.com/single-post/2017/03/28/50-Companies-Supporting-Modern-American-Slavery.

Allison, B. and Harkins, S. (2017). "Fixed Fortunes: Biggest corporate political interests spend billions, get trillions." [online] *Sunlight Foundation.* https://sunlightfoundation.com/2014/11/17/fixed-fortunes-biggest-corporate-political-interests-spend-billions-get-trillions/.

Anderson, R.J., B. Adams, and W.A. Adams. (2015). *Mastering Leadership: An Integrated Framework for Breakthrough Performance and Extraordinary Business Results*: Wiley.

Aspect, A., Grangier, P. and Roger, G. (1982). "Experimental Realization of Einstein-Podolsky-Rosen-Bohm Gedankenexperiment: A New Violation of Bell's Inequalities." *Physical Review Letters*, [online] 49(2), pp.91-94. https://link.aps.org/doi/10.1103/PhysRevLett.49.91.

Assagioli, R. (2000). *Psychosynthesis: a collection of basic writings*: Synthesis Center Inc. (in cooperation with the Berkshire Center for Psychosynthesis).

Awakin.org. http://www.awakin.org. Accessed June 1, 2017.

Badenhausen, K. (2016). "Sweden Heads The Best Countries For Business For 2017." *Forbes*, December 21, 2016. https://www.forbes.com/sites/kurtbadenhausen/2016/12/21/sweden-heads-the-best-countries-for-business-for-2017/#376e19047ecd.

Bassuk, E., DeCandia, C., Beach, C. and Berman, F. (2017). "America's Youngest Outcasts: A Report Card on Child Homelessness." [online] *American Institutes for Research.* http://www.air.org/resource/americas-youngest-outcasts-report-card-child-homelessness.

Baumeister, R. F., & Vohs, K. D. (2016)." Introduction to the special issue: The science of prospection." *Review of General Psychology*, 20(1), 1-2. http://dx.doi.org/10.1037/gpr0000072

Benfit, E. (2017). "I Will Not Be Pinkwashed: Why I Do Not Support Susan G. Komen for the Cure - Butter Believer." [online] *Butter Believer.* http://butterbeliever.com/i-will-not-be-pinkwashed-why-i-do-not-support-susan-g-komen-for-the-cure/ [Accessed 21 Jul. 2017].

Berry, T. (1990). *The Dream of the Earth*: Sierra Club Books.

Błażek, M., and T. Besta. (2012). "Self-Concept Clarity and Religious Orientations: Prediction of Purpose in Life and Self-Esteem." *Journal of Religion and Health* 51 (3):947-960. doi: 10.1007/s10943-010-9407-y.

Bly, R. (1995). *News of the Universe*: University of California Press.

Bohm, D. (1980). *Wholeness and the implicate order*: Routledge & Kegan Paul.

Boyle, P. A., A. S. Buchman, R. S. Wilson, L. Yu, J. A. Schneider, and D. A. Bennett. (2012). "Effect of Purpose in Life on the Relation Between Alzheimer Disease Pathologic Changes on Cognitive Function in Advanced Age." *Archives of General Psychiatry* 69 (5):499-505. doi: 10.1001/archgenpsychiatry.2011.1487.

Brock, D. D. and M. Kim. (2011). *Social Entrepreneurship Education Resource Handbook*. Available at: https://ssrn.com/abstract=1872088 or http://dx.doi.org/10.2139/ssrn.1872088

Bucke, R.M. (1905). *Cosmic Consciousness: A Study in the Evolution of the Human Mind*: Innes & Sons.

Burrow, A. L., M. Stanley, R. Sumner, and P. L. Hill. (2014). "Purpose in Life as a Resource for Increasing Comfort With Ethnic Diversity." *Personality and Social Psychology Bulletin* 40 (11):1507-1516. doi: 10.1177/0146167214549540.

Burson-Marsteller. (2011). "Trust & Purpose Survey 2011." http://www.burson-marsteller.com/what-we-do/our-thinking/trust-purpose-survey-2011/.

Centers for Disease Control (2014). *Up to 40 percent of annual deaths from each of five leading US causes are preventable*. [online] Available at: https://www.cdc.gov/media/releases/2014/p0501-preventable-deaths.html.

Centers for Disease Control. http://www.CDC.gov. Accessed June 29, 2017.

Central Intelligence Agency, United States. Government Publications Office. (2014). *The World Factbook*: Central Intelligence Agency.

Chaisson, E.J. (2010). "Energy Rate Density as a Complexity Metric and Evolutionary Driver." *Complexity*, 16: 27-40. DOI: 10.1002/cplx.20323.

Chapman, G.D. (1995). *The Five Love Languages: How to Express Heartfelt Commitment to Your Mate*: Northfield Pub.

Cittaslow International. http://cittaslow.org. Accessed August 25, 2017.

Clash, J. (2017). "UFO Cover-Ups Must End, Moonwalker Edgar Mitchell Says." [online] *Bloomberg.com*. https://www.bloomberg.com/news/articles/2013-07-16/ufo-cover-ups-must-end-moonwalker-edgar-mitchell-says.

Collins, J., and J.I. Porras. (2011). *Built to Last: Successful Habits of Visionary Companies*: HarperCollins.

Conference Board. *Total Economy Database (TED) - Output, Labor, and Labor Productivity, 1950 – 2013*. (January 2014). https://www.conference-board.org/retrievefile.cfm?filename=Output-Labor-and-Labor-Productivity-1950-2013.xls&type=subsite.

Cooper, H., Blumenthal R., Kean L. (2017). "Glowing Auras and 'Black Money': The Pentagon's Mysterious U.F.O. Program". *New York Times*. December 16, 2017. https://www.nytimes.com/2017/12/16/us/politics/pentagon-program-ufo-harry-reid.html.

Costanza, R., R. de Groot, P. Sutton, S. van der Ploeg, S. J. Anderson, I. Kubiszewski, S. Farber, and R. K. Turner. (2014). "Changes in the global value of ecosystem services." *Global Environmental Change* 26 (Supplement C):152-158. https://doi.org/10.1016/j.gloenvcha.2014.04.002.

Craig, N. and Snook, S. (2014). "From Purpose to Impact." *Harvard Business Review May 2014*.

Cranston, S. and Keller, S. "Increasing the 'Meaning Quotient' of Work." *McKinsey Quarterly*, January 2013.

Crumbaugh, J. and Maholick, L. (1964). "The Case for Frankl's 'Will to Meaning'." *Journal of Existential Psychology* 4:43-48.

Crumbaugh, J. C., and Maholick, L. T. (1964). "An experimental study in existentialism: The psychometric approach to Frankl's concept of noogenic neurosis." *Journal of Clinical Psychology*, 20(20), 200-207.

The Century of Self. [film] Directed by Adam Curtis. (2002). British Broadcasting Company (BBC).

Deloitte. *The Deloitte Core Beliefs and Culture Survey*. (2014). Deloitte, LLC. https://www2.deloitte.com/content/dam/Deloitte/us/Documents/about-deloitte/us-leadership-2014-core-beliefs-culture-survey-040414.pdf.

Deloitte. *Mind the Gaps: The 2015 Deloitte Millennial Survey*. (2015). Deloitte LLC. https://www2.deloitte.com/content/dam/Deloitte/global/Documents/About-Deloitte/gx-wef-2015-millennial-survey-executivesummary.pdf.

Department of Veteran Affairs. http://www.VA.gov. Accessed June 28, 2017.

Diamond, J. (2013). *Collapse: How Societies Choose to Fail or Survive*: Penguin Books Limited.

Dill, K. (2017). "CEOs Earn 331 Times As Much As Average Workers, 774 Times As Much As Minimum Wage Earners." *Forbes*. April 15, 2014. https://www.forbes.com/sites/kathryndill/2014/04/15/report-ceos-earn-331-times-as-much-as-average-workers-774-times-as-much-as-minimum-wage-earners/#30a35ace2520.

Diller, V. (2013). "Under Pressure: Does Stress Accelerate Aging? Fact or Fiction". *Huffpost*. August 14, 2013. http://www.huffingtonpost.com/vivian-diller-phd/the-science-behind-stress_b_1261390.html.

Division of Sleep Medicine, Harvard Medical School. http://healthysleep.med.harvard.edu. Accessed June 27, 2017

Dunbar, R. I. M. (1992). "Neocortex size as a constraint on group size in primates". *Journal of Human Evolution*, 22: 469-493.

Easterlin R. (1974). "Does economic growth improve the human lot? Some empirical evidence." *Nations and Households in Economic Growth. Essays in Honor of Moses Abramovitz.* Eds David P, Reder M. Academic, New York: 98–125.

Easwaran, E. (2010). *The Bhagavad Gita*: Cambridge Scholars Publishing.

Edelman goodpurpose® Study 2012. (2012). Edelman. http://www.edelman.com/insights/intellectual-property/good-purpose/

Edelman Global Trust Barometer. [survey] (2017). Edelman. https://www.edelman.com/trust2017/.

Eileen Fisher. http://www.EileenFisher.com/vision-2020/. Accessed July 5, 2017.

Emerson, R.W. and E.W. Emerson. (1883). *Emerson's Complete Works, Volume XI*: Houghton, Mifflin.

Encore.org. http://encore.org. Accessed June 10, 2014.

End of Suburbia. [film] Directed by Gregory Greene. (2004). The Electric Wallpaper Company.

Estés, C.P. (2008). *Women who Run with the Wolves: Contacting the Power of the Wild Woman*: Rider.

Factiva. [database] (2017). Dow Jones. https://www.dowjones.com/products/factiva/.

Food Inc.. [film] Directed by Robert Kenner. (2009). New York, NY. Magnolia Pictures.

"America's Most Miserable Cities". (2016). Forbes. https://www.forbes.com/pictures/mli45hdlg/americas-most-miserable-cities-2/#2e2f72232ec7.

"Fortune 500 Companies 2017: Who Made The List". (2017). *Fortune.* http://fortune.com/fortune500/.

"The World's Most Admired Companies For 2017". (2017). *Fortune.* http://fortune.com/worlds-most-admired-companies/.

Frankl, V.E. & I. Lasch (translator). (1959). *Man's Search for Meaning*: Beacon Press.

Fredrickson, B. L., K. M. Grewen, K. A. Coffey, S. B. Algoe, A. M. Firestine, J. M. G. Arevalo, J. Ma, and S. W. Cole. 2013. "A functional genomic perspective on human well-being." *Proceedings of the National Academy of Sciences* 110 (33):13684-13689. doi: 10.1073/pnas.1305419110.

Gallup. 2012 Q12® Meta-Analysis Report. (2012). http://www.gallup.com/businessjournal/163130/employee-engagement-drives-growth.aspx.

Gallup. *Gallup-Sharecare Well-Being Index.* [survey] (2013). Well-Beingindex.Com. http://www.well-beingindex.com/.

Gallup. *State of the Global Workplace.* [survey] (2014). Gallup.com. http://www.gallup.com/services/178517/state-global-workplace.aspx

Gardner, H. (2010). *Responsibility at Work: How Leading Professionals Act (or Don't Act) Responsibly*: Wiley.

Gilens, M., & Page, B. I. (2014). Testing theories of American politics: Elites, interest groups, and average citizens. *Perspectives on Politics, 12*(3), 564-581. DOI: 10.1017/S1537592714001595.

Miller, R. J. (1992). *The Complete Gospels:* Polebridge Press

Google Book Search. http://books.google.com/. Accessed June 13, 2017.

Grantham, Jeremy. "The Case for Natural Resource Equities". (2016). GMO.

Greenwashing Index. (2017). Greenwashingindex.Com. http://greenwashingindex. com/green-works-clorox/. Accessed July 12, 2017.

Gurzadyan, V.G., Penrose, R. (2010). "Concentric circles in WMAP data may provide evidence of violent pre-Big-Bang activity." *Arxiv.Org.* https://arxiv.org/ ftp/arxiv/papers/1011/1011.3706.pdf.

Happiness Research Institute. *Job Satisfaction Index.* [survey] (2016) https://docs.wixstatic.com/ugd/928487_d07cbf5521d64ae2bd71371 347361e6a.pdf

Harari, Y.N. (2015). *Sapiens: A Brief History of Humankind*: HarperCollins.

Harvard Business Review / Ernst & Young, *The Business Case for Purpose*, 2015

Heisenberg, W., *Zeitschrift für Physik*, March 1927, Volume 43, Issue 3-4, pp 172-198

Hill, P. L., and N. A. Turiano. (2014). "Purpose in Life as a Predictor of Mortality Across Adulthood." *Psychological Science* 25 (7):1482-1486. doi: 10.1177/0956797614531799.

Hill, P. L., N. A. Turiano, D. K. Mroczek, & A. L. Burrow. (2016). "The value of a purposeful life: Sense of purpose predicts greater income and net worth." *Journal of Research in Personality, 65,* 38-42. DOI: 10.1016/j.jrp.2016.07.003

Hillman, J., and M. Ventura. (1992). *We've had a hundred years of psychotherapy-- and the world's getting worse*: HarperSanFrancisco.

Holahan, C. K., C. J. Holahan, and R. Suzuki. (2008). "Purposiveness, physical activity, and perceived health in cardiac patients." *Disability and Rehabilitation* 30 (23):1772-1778. doi: 10.1080/10428190701661508.

IBM. *Global CEO Study.* [survey] (2012). Available at: http://www.socialvoicebranding. com/product/ibms-global-ceo-study-2012/

"The Inc. 5000 2015, America's Fastest-Growing Companies". (2017). *Inc.Com.* https://www.inc.com/inc5000/list/2015.

Institute for the Analysis of Global Security. http://www.iags.org/costofoil.html. Accessed July 31, 2017.

James, W. (1985). *The Varieties of Religious Experience*: Harvard University Press.

Jaworski, J., and P. Senge. (2011). *Synchronicity: The Inner Path of Leadership*: Berrett-Koehler Publishers.

Jimmy Kimmel Live. "Video: Bill Clinton Guests On Jimmy Kimmel." ABC News, April 3, 2004. http://abc.go.com/shows/jimmy-kimmel-live/news/ news/140403-president-bill-clinton-interview.

Johnson, B. (2017). "Life Design Catalyst Program Overview." School of Health and Human Sciences, University of North Carolina, Greensboro. https:// lifedesigncatalyst.wordpress.com/

Johnston, M. (2017). "'Purposeful Pop': Can Stars Like Katy Perry Create Change Through Music?". *The Guardian*. https://www.theguardian.com/music/2017/feb/14/katy-perry-purposeful-pop-change-through-music.

Jung, C.G. (1969). *Collected Works: pt. 1. The archetypes and the collective unconscious*: Pantheon Books.

Kauth, B. and Z. Alowan. (2011). *We Need Each Other:* Silver Light Publications.

Kim, E. S., Hershner, S.D. & Strecher, V.J. (2015). "Purpose in life and incidence of sleep disturbances." *Journal of Behavioral Medicine* 38: 590. https://doi.org/10.1007/s10865-015-9635-4.

Kim, E. S., V. J. Strecher, and C. D. Ryff. (2014). "Purpose in life and use of preventive health care services." *Proceedings of the National Academy of Sciences* 111 (46):16331-16336. doi: 10.1073/pnas.1414826111.

Komornicki, S. (2010). *2010 Cause Evolution Study.* [online] Cone Communications. http://www.conecomm.com/research-blog/2010-cause-evolution-study [Accessed 1 Oct. 2017].

Kwame A. & Alex Struc. (2016). "Sustainable Investing: PIMCO'S Environmental, Social and Governance (ESG) Initiative". *Pacific Investment Management Company LLC*. https://www.pimco.com/en-us/insights/viewpoints/viewpoints/sustainable-investing-pimcos-environmental-social-and-governance-esg-initiative/.

Leonard, A. (2010). *The Story of Stuff: How Our Obsession with Stuff Is Trashing the Planet, Our Communities, and Our Health-and a Vision for Change*: Free Press.

Lewis, N. A., N. A. Turiano, B. R. Payne, and P. L. Hill. (2017). "Purpose in life and cognitive functioning in adulthood." *Aging, Neuropsychology, and Cognition* 24 (6):662-671. doi: 10.1080/13825585.2016.1251549.

Lifestyles of Health and Sustainability. http://www.lohas.com.

Light, D.W. (2014). "Serious Risks From New Prescription Drugs." *Blogs.Harvard.Edu*. https://blogs.harvard.edu/billofhealth/2014/07/30/serious-risks-from-new-prescription-drugs/#more-11991, 6/30/2014.

LinkedIn/Imperative. "Global Purpose Workforce Index." (2016). *Imperative*. https://cdn.imperative.com/media/public/Global_Purpose_Index_2016.pdf.

Loevinger, J. (1987). *Paradigms of Personality:* WH Freeman & Co.

Hawken, P., A.B. Lovins, and L.H. Lovins. (1999). *Natural Capitalism: The Next Industrial Revolution*: Earthscan.

Mackey, J., R. Sisodia, and B. George. (2014). *Conscious Capitalism, With a New Preface by the Authors: Liberating the Heroic Spirit of Business*: Harvard Business Review Press.

Macy, J. (2007). *World as Lover, World as Self: A Guide to Living Fully in Turbulent Times*: Parralax Press.

Macy, J., and M.Y. Brown. (2014). *Coming Back to Life: The Guide to the Work that Reconnects*: New Society Publishers, Limited.

Mankins, M. C., and Garton, E. (2107). *Time, talent, energy: overcome organizational drag and unleash your teams productive power*. Boston, MA: Harvard Business Review Press.

Martenson, C. (2011). *The Crash Course: The Unsustainable Future Of Our Economy, Energy, And Environment*: Wiley.

Martin, S. (2009). *Cosmic Conversations: Dialogues on the Nature of the Universe and the Search for Reality*: CAREER PR.

Marx, K. (1867). *Das Kapital: Kritik der politischen Ökonomie*: Verlag von Otto Meisner.

Marx, K. (1875). "Critique of the Gotha Program." *Die Neue Zeit*, 18(1).

Maslow, A.H. "A Theory of Human Motivation." *Psychological Review*. (1943). 50: 370-396. http://dx.doi.org/10.1037/h0054346.

McCleod, L. (2012). "Purpose-Driven Selling: It Beats Quota-Driven Every Time." *Forbes*. https://www.forbes.com/sites/forbesleadership forum/2012/11/09/purpose-driven-selling-it-beats-quota-driven-every-time/#64d6cae46047

McDonald's Corporation. http://corporate.mcdonalds.com. Accessed 2013.

McGuire, P. (2013). "Meet Paul Hellyer, the World's Highest Ranking Alien Believer." *Motherboard*. https://motherboard.vice.com/en_us/article/z4mvja/paul-hellyer-the-worlds-highest-ranking-alien-believer.

Meade, M. (2010). *Fate and Destiny: The Two Agreements of the Soul*: Mosaic Multicultural Foundation.

Meade, M. (2016). *The Genius Myth*: Mosaic Multicultural Foundation.

Measure of America of the Social Science Research Council. (2013-2014). http://www.measureofamerica.org/measure_of_america2013-2014/.

Meijer, R.I. (2013). "The Global Economy Suffers From Hypothermia." *The Automatic Earth*. http://dev.theautomaticearth.com/2013/08/the-global-economy-suffers-from-hypothermia/.

Merriam-Webster Dictionary. http://Merriam-Webster.com. Accessed July 21, 2017.

Merritt, A. C., D. A. Effron, and B. Monin. (2010). "Moral Self-Licensing: When Being Good Frees Us to Be Bad." *Social and Personality Psychology Compass*, 4: 344–357. doi:10.1111/j.1751-9004.2010.00263.

MetLife. (2010). "Meaning Really Matters The MetLife Study on How Purpose Is Recession-Proof and Age-Proof." https://www.metlife.com/assets/cao/mmi/publications/studies/2010/mmi-meaning-really-matters.pdf.

"Millennial Impact Report 2014: How Millennials Connect, Give and Get Involved with the Issues That Matter to Them." (2014). *The Case Foundation*. https://casefoundation.org/resource/millennial-impact-report/.

Miller, K. (2017). "The Simple Truth about the Gender Pay Gap." [online] *American Association of University Women*. http://www.aauw.org/research/the-simple-truth-about-the-gender-pay-gap/.

Mitchell, S. (2002). *Bhagavad Gita: A New Translation*: Three Rivers Press.

Moody, R. (2015). *Life After Life: The Bestselling Original Investigation That Revealed "Near-Death Experiences"*: HarperCollins.

Moore, R., and D. Gillette. (2013). *King, Warrior, Magician, Lover: Rediscovering the Archetypes of the Mature Masculine*: HarperCollins.

Moore, T. (1993). *Care of the Soul: A Guide for Cultivating Depth and Sacredness in Everyday Life*: Walker.

Mossbridge, J. A., P. Tressoldi, J. Utts, J. A. Ives, D. Radin, and W. B. Jonas. (2014). "Predicting the unpredictable: critical analysis and practical implications of predictive anticipatory activity." *Frontiers in Human Neuroscience* 8:146. doi: 10.3389/fnhum.2014.00146.

Motesharrei, S., J. Rivas, and E. Kalnay. (2014). "Human and nature dynamics (HANDY): Modeling inequality and use of resources in the collapse or sustainability of societies." *Ecological Economics* 101 (Supplement C):90-102. doi: https://doi.org/10.1016/j.ecolecon.2014.02.014.

Murphy, M. (2011). *Golf in the Kingdom*: Open Road Media.

National Geographic News. (2003). "Big-Fish Stocks Fall 90 Percent Since 1950, Study Says." http://news.nationalgeographic.com/news/2003/05/0515_030515_fishdecline.html.

Nielsen. (2014). "Doing Well by Doing Good." *Nielsen.Com*. http://www.nielsen.com/us/en/insights/reports/2014/doing-well-by-doing-good.html.

O'Connor, C. (2014). "Report: Walmart Workers Cost Taxpayers $6.2 Billion In Public Assistance." *Forbes*. https://www.forbes.com/sites/clareoconnor/2014/04/15/report-walmart-workers-cost-taxpayers-6-2-billion-in-public-assistance/#5433fdfc720b.

Ong, W.J. (1982). *Orality and Literacy: The Technologizing of the Word*: Routledge.

Online Etymology Dictionary. http://www.etymonline.com. Accessed September 12, 2017.

Opensecrets.org Center for Responsive Politics. https://www.opensecrets.org/lobby/indusclient.php?id=h04. Accessed October 13, 2017.

Outside Magazine. (2015). "This is Why Chattanooga is the Best Town Ever." https://www.outsideonline.com/2008956/why-chattanooga-best-town-ever.

Parker, C. (2015). "Sense of Purpose in Young Driven by Action and Passion, Says Stanford Researcher." *Stanford Graduate School of Education*. https://ed.stanford.edu/news/sense-purpose-young-driven-action-and-passion-says-stanford-researcher.

Pazzanese, C. (2016). "The Costs Of Inequality: Increasingly, It'S The Rich And The Rest." *Harvard Gazette*. https://news.harvard.edu/gazette/story/2016/02/the-costs-of-inequality-increasingly-its-the-rich-and-the-rest/.

Phillips, W. M. (1980), "Purpose in life, depression, and locus of control." *Journal of Clinical Psychology*. 36: 661–667. doi:10.1002/1097-4679(198007)36:3<661::AID-JCLP2270360309>3.0.CO;2-G

Piketty, T. 2014. *Capital in the Twenty-First Century*: Harvard University Press.

Plotkin, B. (2010). *Nature and the Human Soul: Cultivating Wholeness and Community in a Fragmented World*: New World Library.

Plotkin, B. (2013). *Wild Mind: A Field Guide to the Human Psyche*: New World Library.

Prechtel, M. (1998). *Secrets of the Talking Jaguar: A Mayan Shaman's Journey to the Heart of the Indigenous Soul*: Jeremy P. Tarcher.

PwC. (2015). *Make it your business: Engaging with the Sustainable Development Goals*. https://www.pwc.com/gx/en/sustainability/SDG/SDG%20Research_FINAL.pdf

QST Magazine. (August, 1995).

Rainey, L. (2014). *The Search for Purpose in Life: An Exploration of Purpose, the Search Process, and Purpose Anxiety*. Master of Applied Psychology, Capstone. University of Pennsylvania. http://repository.upenn.edu/cgi/viewcontent.cgi?article=1061&context=mapp_capstone.

Ray, PhD., P.H. (2010). "The Potential for a New, Emerging Culture in the U.S. Report on the 2008 American Values Survey." *Institute for the Emerging Wisdom Culture, Wisdom University*. http://www.wisdomuniversity.org/CCsReport2008SurveyV3.pdf.

Ray, PhD., P. & S.R. Anderson. *(2000). The Cultural Creatives*. Broadway Books.

Reich, R.B. (2015). *Saving Capitalism: For the Many, Not the Few*: Alfred A. Knopf.

Revill, J. (2017). "Swiss Re shifts $130 Billion Investments to Track Ethical Indices". *Reuters UK*. http://uk.reuters.com/article/us-swissre-ethical-idUKKBN19R22Y.

Riess, A. G. *et al.* (1998). "Observational Evidence from Supernovae for an Accelerating Universe and a Cosmological Constant." *The Astronomical Journal* 116 (3):1009.

Roelfs, David J., Eran Shor, Karina W. Davidson, and Joseph E. Schwartz. (2011). "Losing Life and Livelihood: A Systematic Review and Meta-Analysis of Unemployment and All-Cause Mortality." *Social science & medicine (1982)* 72 (6):840-854. doi: 10.1016/j.socscimed.2011.01.005.

Roger Dodger. [film] Directed by Dylan Kidd. (2002). New York, NY. Holedigger Films.

Rogers, E.M. (1962). *Diffusion of innovations*: Free Press of Glencoe.

Ryff, C. D., Heller, A. S., Schaefer, S. M., van Reekum, C., & Davidson, R. J. (2016). "Purposeful engagement, healthy aging, and the brain." *Current Behavioral Neuroscience Reports*, 3(4), 318-327. DOI:10.1007/s40473-016-0096-z.

Schwartz, R.C. (2001). *Introduction to the Internal Family Systems Model*: Trailheads Publications.

Scoles, S. & S.A. Heatherly. (2011). "The Drake Equation: 50 Years of Giving Direction to the Scientific Search for Life Beyond Earth." *National Radio Astronomy Observatory*. Available at: https://astrosociety.org/edu/publications/tnl/77/77.html.

Seligman, M. & J. Tierney. (2017). "We Aren't Built to Live in Moment." *New York Times*. https://www.nytimes.com/2017/05/19/opinion/sunday/why-the-future-is-always-on-your-mind.html?mcubz=0.

Shadow Government Statistics. http://www.shadowstats.com. Accessed on July 24, 2017.

Shaw, B. (1903). "Epistle Dedicatory to Arthur Bingham Walkley." *Man And Superman*: Cambridge, MA. The University Press.

Shortell, S. (2010). "What's the biggest driver of health care costs? Our personal behaviors." *UC Berkeley blog*. http://blogs.berkeley.edu/2010/10/27/whats-the-biggest-driver-of-health-care-costs-our-personal-behaviors/.

Simpson, D., T.J. Gradel, M. Mouritsen, J. Johnson. (2015). "Chicago: Still the Capital of Corruption, Anti-Corruption Report Number 8." *University of Illinois at Chicago, Department of Political Science*. https://pols.uic.edu/docs/default-source/chicago_politics/anti-corruption_reports/corruption-rpt-8_final-052715.pdf?sfvrsn=0.

Skeele, B. (2011). "Chattanooga Vision 2000 – An Inspiring Story of Citizens Transforming Their World." *Beyond Sustainability*. http://www.beyondsuburbia.com/indicators/jobs/chattanooga-vision-2000-an-inspiring-story-of-citizens-transforming-their-world/.

Sone, T. OTR, BA; N. Nakaya, PhD; K. Ohmori, MD, PhD; T. Shimazu MD, PhD; et al. (2008). "Sense of Life Worth Living (Ikigai) and Mortality in Japan: Ohsaki Study." *Psychosomatic Medicine - Journal of BioBehavioral Medicine*, 70 (6): 708-715.

Smith, A., and C.J. Bullock. (1909). *An Inquiry into the Nature and Causes of the Wealth of Nations*: P. F. Collier & son.

Smith, A., and D. Stewart. (1817). *The Theory of Moral Sentiments: Or, An Essay Towards an Analysis of the Principles*: Wells and Lilly.

Southern Education Foundation. (2015). "Low Income Students Now a Majority in the Nation's Public Schools". http://www.southerneducation.org/getattachment/c2b340ba-c31b-43b8-9d23-333a7f9b090c/A-New-Majority-Low-Income-Students-in-the-South-s.aspx.

Speight, K. (7/31/2016). "12 Big Pharma Stats That Will Blow You Away." Motleyfool.com.

Stiglitz, J.E. (2003). *Globalization and Its Discontents*: W. W. Norton.

Stillman, T. F., N. M. Lambert, F. D. Fincham, and R. F. Baumeister. (2010). "Meaning as Magnetic Force." *Social Psychological and Personality Science* 2 (1):13-20. doi: 10.1177/1948550610378382.

Stone, H., S. Winkelman, and S. Stone. (1989). *Embracing Our Selves: The Voice Dialogue Manual*: Nataraj Publishing.

Swimme, B. (2006). *The New Story*. [video] https://www.youtube.com/watch?v=TRykk_0ovI0.

Swiss Re. (2017). http://www.swissre.com/corporate_responsibility/managing_env_risks.html. Our Sustainability Risk Framework. Accessed 2017.

Tate, K. (2015). "SETI: All About the Search for Extraterrestrial Intelligence." *Space.com*. https://www.space.com/30043-seti-search-for-extraterrestrial-intelligence-infographic.html.

The Telegraph. (2009). "Are UFOs real? Famous people who believed". http://www.telegraph.co.uk/technology/5201410/Are-UFOs-real-Famous-people-who-believed.html.

Telzer, Eva H., Andrew J. Fuligni, Matthew D. Lieberman, and Adriana Galván. (2014). "Neural sensitivity to eudaimonic and hedonic rewards differentially predict adolescent depressive symptoms over time." *Proceedings of the National Academy of Sciences* 111 (18):6600-6605. doi: 10.1073/pnas.1323014111.

Thoreau, H.D. (1910). *Walden*: Thomas Y. Crowell & Company.

Tsipursky, G. (2015). "21 Day Purpose Challenge Web Response Analysis." https://www.slideshare.net/bpeele/the-21day-purpose-challenge-results-82015

Tyson, N.G., M.A. Strauss, and J.R. Gott. (2016). Welcome to the Universe: An Astrophysical Tour: Princeton University Press.

"UNICEF - The Convention On The Rights Of The Child - People And Partners - Dr. Ernest C. Madu." (2017). *UNICEF*. https://www.unicef.org/rightsite/364_617.htm.

United Nations. (2014). "Climate Change 2014: Impacts, Adaptation, and Vulnerability." Intergovernmental Panel on Climate Change. https://www.ipcc.ch/report/ar5/wg2/.

United Nations. (2017). "World Happiness Report." http://worldhappiness.report/.

"Unlocking Millennial Talent 2015: Brand New Insights for Hiring the Fastest Growing Generation in the Workforce." (2015). *Center for Generational Kinetics* and *Barnum Financial Group*. http://3pur2814p18t46fuop22hvvu.wpengine.netdna-cdn.com/wp-content/uploads/2015/06/Unlocking-Millennial-Talent-c-2015-The-Center-for-Generational-Kinetics.pdf.

The Universe. "Beyond the Big Bang." S1E14. Directed by Luke Ellis. Written by Matthew P. Hickey. The History Channel, September 4, 2007. http://www.history.com/shows/the-universe/season-1/episode-14.

U.S. Census Bureau. (2011). "Statistical Abstract of the United States: 2012." https://www.census.gov/library/publications/2011/compendia/statab/131ed.html.

US News and World Report. (2017). https://money.usnews.com/funds/mutual-funds/large-growth/parnassus-endeavor-fund/parwx. Accessed July 7, 2017.

Veblen, T. (1899). *The Theory of the Leisure Class; An Economic Study of Institutions*: Aakar Books.

Whole Foods Market, Inc. http://www.WholeFoodsMarket.com. Accessed July 5, 2017.

Windsor, T. D., R. G. Curtis, & M. A. Luszcz. (2015). "Sense of purpose as a psychological resource for aging well." *Developmental Psychology, 51*(7): 975-986. http://dx.doi.org/10.1037/dev0000023.

World Wildlife Foundation. (2016). "Living Planet Report." Risk and Reslilience in a New Era. WWF International. http://wwf.panda.org/about_our_earth/all_publications/lpr_2016/.

Worstall, T. (2015). "American Corporations Have Vast Untaxed Offshore Profits, So What?" *Forbes.* https://www.forbes.com/sites/timworstall/2015/10/07/american-corporations-have-vast-untaxed-offshore-profits-so/#19b26de26e57.

Yeager, David S., Marlone D. Henderson, Sidney D'Mello, David Paunesku, Gregory M. Walton, Brian J. Spitzer, and Angela Lee Duckworth. (2014). "Boring but Important: A Self-Transcendent Purpose for Learning Fosters Academic Self-Regulation." *Journal of Personality and Social Psychology* 107 (4):559-580. doi: 10.1037/a0037637.

Yong-hee, Hong. (2015). *Values in the Global Age and the Life Spiritualism of Donghak.* Vol. 55.

Zuckerberg, M. (2017). "Commencement Address." Harvard University. https://news.harvard.edu/gazette/story/2017/05/mark-zuckerbergs-speech-as-written-for-harvards-class-of-2017/.

ABOUT THE AUTHOR

Photo by Jared Brick

Brandon is a Certified Purpose Guide™ and the co-author of *Purpose Rising* (2017, with Dustin DiPerna, Ken Wilber, Terry Patten, Bill Plotkin, Tim Kelley, Duane Elgin, Barbara Marx Hubbard and many others). As a veteran teacher of online purpose courses, Brandon has guided thousands of people from over 50 countries to awaken, ignite and embody their life's purpose. His work has been covered by numerous media outlets such as USA Today, Techcrunch, Conscious Company Magazine, The Telegraph, International Business Times and Fox News.

Brandon has worked with professionals and executive teams from Apple, Johnson & Johnson, Illumina, Zeiss, Sapient, Morgan Stanley, Google and the United States Coast Guard, as well as with purpose-driven ventures such as Net Driven, Annmarie Skincare, Sacred Science and Dr. Hops Kombucha, to help them awaken their purpose-driven leadership. He has also guided Catholic Priests, Dalai Lama Fellows, and world-class athletes, scientists, musicians and artists. He has taught and lectured at the University of California, Berkeley, Northern Arizona University, The Institute of Noetic Sciences and the California College of the Arts. He received his MBA from Columbia Business School in New York City and he lives in Berkeley, California.

Made in the USA
San Bernardino, CA
27 March 2018